One Hundred Mile Summers

One Hundred Mile Summers

Hiking the Pacific Crest Trail from Mexico to Canada

Eleanor Guilford

REGENT PRESS
Oakland, CA

copyright © 2005 by Eleanor Guilford

ISBN: 1-58790-114-5

Library of Congress Control Number: 2004118277

Second Printing 2006

design: roz abraham

Manufactured in the U.S.A.

Regent Press
6020 – A Adeline Street
Oakland, California 94608
www.regentpress.net

Dedication

To the memory of
John Muir
And
The organization which he founded
The Sierra Club
And to
My Sierra Club friends who started me and cheered me on
my walk on the Trail.

Table of Contents

PREFACE

On August 27, 1989, I reached the U.S.-Canadian border. It was a great moment—a time for celebration. I had completed the 2638-mile Pacific Crest National Scenic Trail from Mexico to Canada. I was glad that I had someone to share my happy moment. I had envisioned leaning my pack against the Pacific Crest Trail marker and taking a photo. Happily, Donna was there to share in my joyous celebration. Soon, we were joined by another celebrant. Peter from Maine came down the trail shortly after our arrival. He had hiked from the Oregon border. He added to our celebration and to our picture-taking.

At the U.S.-Canadian border, there are two markers: A new, wooden Pacific Crest Trail marker and Monument 78, a 4-2/3-foot-high, bronze replica of the Washington Monument. We lifted the heavy top off Monument 78 to place a note inside, as is the style of placing notes in metal box registers on high mountain peaks. I read a little of the note by Greg, whom we had met at Harts Pass: "Hiking the Pacific Crest Trail presented a microcosm of life—the enjoyable and the difficult experiences were always there and there were always challenges."

I agreed. I wrote on my note that for me it was a great experience. Yes, there were the challenges: where to find water, where to locate a campsite, and how to manage in inclement weather—the heat of the desert and snowstorms (both of which I experienced in May in southern California) as well as the rain in Washington. But beyond the challenges of water and weather there was, for me, the peak experience of being surrounded by glorious scenes of nature.

I often enjoy flashbacks of some of my favorite scenes—viewing the mystical haze covering Anza Borrego Desert Park from the wooded slopes of the Laguna Mountains; gazing up at the luminous silver clouds hovering over the top of Combs Peak; watching a summer rainstorm sweep over Forester Pass and marveling at its fiery power and majestic beauty; discovering the half-hidden miniature mimulus wildflowers lining tiny springs in the High Sierra; spotting Canada geese nesting on a grassy point on Milton Reservoir; sighting, for the first time, the majestic, cone-shaped, snow-covered peak of Mount Shasta; exulting as I gazed at the carpet of multicolored alpine flowers resting on the shoulder of Mount Adams; and seeing the rocky, jagged layers of peaks piercing the sky near the Canadian border. All of these scenes, as well as many others, will remain in my memory forever.

How did it all begin? For me, it began—or at least the seed was planted—before Congress designated the Pacific Crest Trail as a National Scenic Trail in 1968. Two years earlier, in 1966, at a Sierra Club meeting of the Redwood Chapter in Santa Rosa, I overheard a friend say that she had signed up for a seven-day hiking tour led by Joe Wampler on the John Muir Trail, which would start at Tuolumne Meadows and lead south to Red's Meadows. The idea of going along would not leave me. My vacation time was limited, but I could not resist. I signed up for the Wampler tour.

On the Wampler tour, all of our gear was carried by pack horses. A cook was part of the staff, and all meals were provided. We changed campsites every other day. I especially enjoyed the rest days, which I spent exploring the surrounding mountains and meadows. By the end of the tour, I was saying to myself, "I've got to complete the John Muir Trail."

The following year, I signed up again with the Wampler Tours to complete the next section of the trail—south from Red's Meadows. It didn't happen because 1967 was a very heavy snow year. During July, the high passes were closed. I spent a few days on Wampler's substitute outing, at a camp on McGee Creek. Restless from not hiking daily, I returned to Tuolumne Meadows, where my Sierra Club friends had gathered to hike the Yosemite High Camps with Ranger Carl Sharsmith. I joined them. Hiking with ranger-naturalist Sharsmith, I was introduced to flowers, trees, and birds of the High Sierras, and I enjoyed his delightful story telling.

The following summer, in 1968, I joined a National Sierra Club High Trip and hiked in the glorious Evolution Valley section of the John Muir Trail. My desire to complete the trail had grown stronger. I pondered. Could I possibly learn to backpack in order to complete the John Muir Trail? On my return trip from the Evolution Valley, I stopped at Tuolumne Meadows. I went into the Visitors' Center and asked Ranger Sharsmith, "Do you think I could backpack?" He replied, "Try it for a few days."

In July of 1969, after I had participated in a week long University of California outing that featured geology and wildflower identification in the Agnew Meadow area, my Sierra Club friends waved me goodbye. I set out alone on my first backpacking adventure—a six-day tour of the Red's Meadows-Purple Lake area. On my first night of sleeping outside alone, I wondered if I would be afraid. I was not. I loved looking up at the stars. I was hooked on backpacking.

From this small beginning in 1969, I have continued to spend my summer vacations backpacking on wilderness trails. In 1971, I completed the John Muir Trail. Then John Dooley, a Sierra Club friend said, "There is a Tahoe-Yosemite Trail." So, I completed it in 1976 and 1977. By this time, I had read about the Pacific Crest Trail. I purchased the Wilderness Press Guidebook. In 1978, I eagerly started north from the junction of the Tahoe-Yosemite and the Pacific Crest Trail at Middle Velma Lake.

I have spent from ten days to two weeks of my summer vacations on a different section of the trail. I am still not sure when I decided to complete the trail. The idea grew slowly. Each winter, especially when it was dark and rainy, I would read John Muir's books, review backpacking catalogues, and start planning my next summer's trip. I would feel exalted in anticipation of spending my vacation surrounded by the beauty of mountain meadows, singing streams, bright-colored wildflowers, and a roof of cloud-filled sky.

In planning for my backpack trip, an enjoyable winter pastime, I prepare a mileage chart. I line a steno pad page with the following columns: Mileage for the trip; Mileage between points; Water (my #1 priority); Altitude, Campsites; and Names of sites (this will often consist of Lakes, Rivers, Trail junctions, and Road crossings). All of this helpful information is charted from the Trail Guidebook. This mileage chart is carried conveniently— together with pages of the topo map I will be using for the day, clipped from the Guidebook—in my right pants pocket, where it is always available. The chart is well used and becomes frayed and worn-looking by the end of the trip. Sometimes I worry about losing my unsecured portable chart. Once I left a page at a rest stop under a bridge and, miraculously, a camper found it and presented it to me the next day. Actually,

I have backup information in pages of the Guidebook, carried more securely in the map pocket of my backpack.

Before leaving home, I also record a tentative itinerary, listing dates on the trail, names of campsites, and names and addresses of the management jurisdictions I will be passing through. These include district offices of the National Forest Service, National Park Service, and Bureau of Land Management. I leave a copy of this itinerary with a friend and my brother. In wilderness areas, where permits are required, there is space for listing dates of travel and each day's campsite. I once sent an itinerary to a Forest Service Office, which listed two nights in a wilderness area and several days in non-wilderness areas. The office sent it back to me with all the non-wilderness dates crossed out. Thereafter, I did not try sending them itineraries for areas where a permit is not required.

Once on the trail, I do not like to feel bound to a schedule. I rarely look at the itinerary. I like the freedom of moving along with the mood of the day. My tentative mileage plan is usually based on an 11-mile day. This is only an average—I recall walking 15-mile days and 6-mile days. I usually do not decide where I will camp for the evening until late afternoon. Water sources are, however, frequently a deciding factor. I do like to camp near water whenever possible.

Even though I do not like to feel bound to an itinerary, I usually do come out at the planned trailhead on schedule. I am typically a day early, on time, or a day late. A day or two late is built into the schedule, and I tell my friend at home not to expect a call from me or start to worry about me until two days past the planned schedule have elapsed. Fortunately, this has never happened.

Solo backpacking offers advantages in not requiring a lot of space. I often select an impromptu, convenient little hideaway.

This was the case for my first night's camp in the field outside Campo.

The Pacific Crest Trail is often described as traversing five sections: Southern California, Central California, Northern California, Oregon, and Washington. For continuity, I have recorded this story of my trip starting at the Mexican border and ending in Canada. For most sections, I traveled from south to north, the direction narrated in the Pacific Crest Trail Guidebook. My walks on the John Muir Trail and the Tahoe-Yosemite Trail were from north to south, following the directions of their guidebooks.

The Great
**Pacific
Crest Trail**

INTRODUCTION TO
SOUTHERN CALIFORNIA SECTION

Southern California is the longest section of the Trail, covering some 627 miles. Southern California possesses unique characteristics and landscape. The trail leads through an abundance of chaparral, interspersed with mountains and deserts. The ubiquitous chaparral groundcover in this section offers challenges and difficulties to both hikers and trail builders. These tough, dense bushes, which are well adapted to survive in arid lands, can quickly grow over the trail, and their prickly stems and leaves offer strong resistance to hikers attempting to pass through their thickly growing branches. Altitude ranges from 2200 to 9400 feet. Rabbits and rattlesnakes are abundant, and cactus, yucca, and desert poppies dot the landscape.

For the hiker, the Southern California section presents a special challenge. Water is scarce. While a hiker may encounter snowstorms in the mountains into early June, the Guidebook recommends that the desert section be completed before June 1st. In early spring, swollen rivers also pose a danger. For some hikers, the Southern California section becomes a testing ground in deciding whether to continue or to drop out. Trail Registers, located in stores and post offices along the route often contain commentaries from hikers reflecting discouragement with the sometimes-hard-to-find, chaparral-bordered trail. Reportedly, some hikers roadwalk the Southern California section, and others skip this section altogether. Tall, strong, persevering Mike, whom I met in Lassen in 1981, told me that out of 200 hikers who had started at the border that summer, only five reportedly continued on the Trail.

I was both eager to walk the Southern California trail section and, at the same time, felt some trepidation. My main challenges and worries were planning for water stops and planning for rides from the nearest bus stop to the Trail. I looked forward to walking under desert skies and experiencing its special beauty and feeling of space.

My walks in Southern California took place during three summers: 1985, 1987, and 1989. All my Southern California walks were during May.

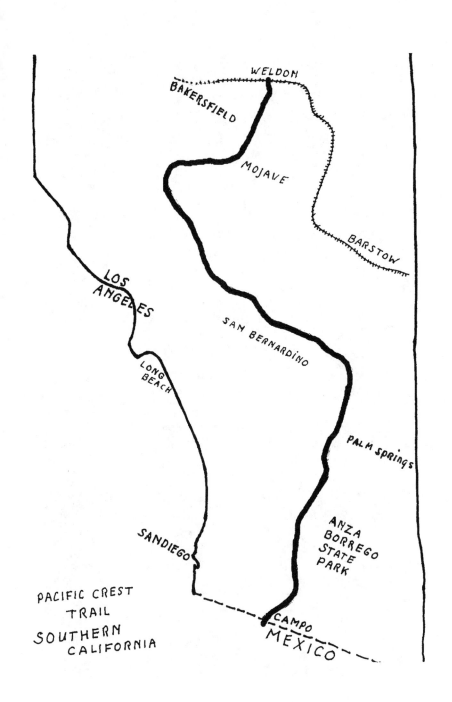

WELDON

BAKERSFIELD

MOJAVE

BARSTOW

LOS
ANGELES

SAN BERNARDINO

LONG
BEACH

PALM SPRINGS

ANZA
BORREGO
STATE
PARK

SANDIEGO

PACIFIC CREST
TRAIL
SOUTHERN
CALIFORNIA

CAMPO
MEXICO

MEXICAN BORDER

Chapter 1
The Mexican Border to Anza Valley
May 1985 • 145 Miles

God never made an ugly landscape. All that the sun shines on is beautiful, so long as it is wild... —John Muir

As is characteristic of the Southern California landscape, much of this section traverses chaparral, mountains, and desert. The beginning section of the trail from the border to the Laguna Mountains crosses through chaparral and traverses through sandy soil. Upon ascending into the Laguna Mountains, the trail passes through pine and oak woodlands. The Laguna Mountains rise around 6000 feet in altitude. The next descent leads across the sandy lowlands of San Felipe Valley and touches the western edge of the Anza-Borrego Desert State Park. Summer temperatures may reach 115°. Approaching Warner Springs, the trail traverses low hills and grassland. North of Warner Springs, the trail climbs up a ridge and circles around Combs Peak before descending again to the sandy, level landscape of Anza Valley. A newer trail now skirts the foothills to the east of Anza Valley.

Although water is not readily available along the trail, for most of the way, fortunately, water can be obtained by making a short detour to developed water sites in nearby campgrounds.

I had been eagerly anticipating my walk through the Southern California section of the trail. This section needed to be postponed until I retired—an event that took place in the summer of 1984. Vacations in the spring were not possible during my working years. Usually my vacation periods were scheduled for July or August. By the time I was ready to head for the Mexican border and hike the southernmost stretch of the trail, I had completed all the trail sections of Central California, Northern California, and Oregon.

I was fortunate to have someone come along to take my picture by the sign marking the Mexican border. The trail starts 1-1/2 miles south of the border town of Campo, which is located 50 miles east of San Diego. I had reached Campo by bus. As I was walking south on the temporary trail—the permanent trail had not been completed on the section—a pickup truck came along, and the driver stopped to ask me for directions to reach the Pacific Crest Trail trailhead at the Mexican border. He introduced himself, and I learned that he was a Forest Service appraiser from Goleta, California, and that he had come to assess and appraise the land for the route of the future permanent trail. Together, we found the trail marker.

In 1985, a white, well-bleached skull nailed to the fence post also marked the trail beginning. After posing for pictures, I followed the custom of stretching my foot under the fence to say that I had touched soil in Mexico, waved goodbye to the Forest Service appraiser, and headed back north.

When I reached Campo, I enjoyed seeing a sign that read, "SENIOR NUTRITION SITE—MEALS FROM 11:00 AM TO 1:00 PM." I felt right at home, as my work before retirement had been establishing Senior Centers and Nutrition Sites in San Francisco.

I soon arrived at the Campo grocery store—a planned stop for filling my water bag. I was met with a surprised response to my request for water from a very cross storekeeper: "You can get your water at the gas station up the road." So, I walked on, puzzling about his negative response. Most requests for water are cheerfully responded to. Many storekeepers respond by being very interested in the trailhiker, which often results in a friendly, animated conversation. I wondered what had happened to this man—why he was so upset and angry. In fact, this puzzling encounter has haunted me on and off to this day.

But, it brought to mind a happier encounter earlier in the day in San Diego, before boarding the bus. I had spent the night at the Armed Services YMCA Hotel, which was listed in my American Youth Hostel Handbook. I was enjoying a tasty breakfast seated at the counter, where an attractive young waitress was swiftly and cheerfully delivering the order. When she came to an older man seated nearby and asked, "What would you like?" he hesitated, said he guessed he'd take some coffee, and then replied in a mellifluous voice, "I really don't want anything; I just want to look at you."

As I walked from the grocery store toward the gas station, I recalled another visit en route from San Francisco to San Diego. I had stopped in Orange County to visit my cousins. On hearing of my proposed walk, one of my cousins was full of anxiety and told me there had been recent shootings at the border. The shootings, reportedly, related to illegal immigrants crossing the border. "It's too dangerous," she said. Consequently, I looked expectantly for migrants hiding by the side of the road or for uniformed border patrols. I saw none.

After arriving at the gas station and measuring out the water I would need until I reached my next water source at Lake Morena, I started to walk north. It was not long before sunset.

As I had not started my first day's walk until mid-afternoon, I had not planned on going very far. It was time for me to find a campsite. I had not reached the permanent trail and, in this section, I was walking on blacktop road. I looked around and saw a large, sheltering tree in a nearby fenced-in field. I sneaked in under the fence, made camp, and spent a peaceful night, albeit lights from occasional passing cars on the road periodically beamed my way. The only evidence of border surveillance I observed was when the sky was bright with a beaming, rotating light focused down from a barren, desert hill.

In the morning, I sneaked out of my hiding place—perhaps I had been camping on private property—and climbed up the hill leading to Lake Morena. The morning sky was beautiful—full of white, puffy cumulus clouds. I looked toward the Mexican border and wondered what it might be like for migrant workers who may have managed to cross the border.

At the Lake Morena store, I stopped for a snack, which I enjoyed munching on by the side of peaceful Lake Morena. I looked forward eagerly to finding the permanent trail for the first time in my journey from the border. After my snack, I searched for the beginning of the trail, described in the guidebook as starting by a fence at the north end of the lake. After a lot of searching, I started out on the only trail that I could find. It was a much used jeep and horse trail. Soon, I met a woman mounted on a horse who, after a brief look at me, exclaimed, "Oh, here's another one of those lost Pacific Crest Trail hikers!" She then gave me directions for where to turn onto a trail leading east.

I searched and pondered. There was such a maze of crisscrossing trails. I took a guess and turned right, leading toward the east, hoping that I was following the trail described by the horse rider. Eventually, I arrived at the highway that led to the bridge crossing Cottonwood Creek. In checking my map and compass,

I knew I needed to reach and cross the bridge, but I shall never know whether or not I had walked on the permanent trail.

After crossing the creek, I started my search for a trail leading east and running parallel to the creek. I did not see any evidence of a trail and decided to inquire. The first person I encountered was a small man crossing the bridge on foot. He smiled, but did not answer. Perhaps he may not have understood English. The next inquiry was addressed to a fisherman. He did not know anything about the trail. He suggested that I inquire at the nearby school. Arriving at the schoolyard, a teacher pointed and gave me directions for finding the trail. I still did not succeed in locating the trail. I knew that I should be walking east. After searching, I found a gravel road leading east, and then turned south on another road, which finally lead me to my next water stop and destination for the evening at Boulder Oaks Resort.

At Boulder Oaks, the resort office was closed, but the water spigot by the gas station was in plain view. After filling my water bottles, much to my delight, I found a real Pacific Crest Trail marker, the first I had encountered since the border. I decided to camp in a little sheltered hollow just off the trail. Soon, the absent resort proprietor returned, and the lights went on in the combined office and living quarters. I had practiced saying, in case I was discovered in my little sleeping-hiding place, that I had intended to ask permission to camp there, but no one was home. No one appeared to discover me. I spent a peaceful night and looked forward to following the real, marked, permanent Pacific Crest Trail the next day.

After my usual breakfast of Mueslix and coffee, I followed the marked trail to Kitchen Creek. As this was a water stop, I decided to eat lunch. I looked around and thought to myself, "This chaparral country will be hot in the noonday sun. Where can I find some shade?" Thereafter, during my journey in Southern

California, I searched and found small, crawl-in, shaded spaces, which provided me with modest relief from the noonday sun.

I arrived at Cibbets Flat campground, my next planned destination for water, around 3 pm and selected a picnic table. Another one of my discoveries that was to serve me well in scarce water areas was to use the campgrounds for supper—the time when I used more water than usual—and then enjoy a pleasant evening hike to a campsite in a secluded area away from the noise of the crowded campground.

While I was waiting by a picnic table at the campground to eat an early 6-o'clock supper, a gentleman appeared and asked, "How long do you plan to be here?" I assured him that I would be leaving soon. He was so pleased that he could occupy my space—apparently the only one left—that he offered me a banana, orange juice, and a sweet roll. I was happy to accept the banana and orange juice, but I declined the sweet roll, as it seemed too rich for my accustomed trail food menu.

While we were waiting, he told me a story, which apparently puzzled and haunted him (and later haunted me), about a sailor who slaughtered a cow in this vicinity and was court-martialed. His commentary was that he had ruined his military career for life. My afterthought was that it is sad that just a very few individuals violate property rights and lessen the chance for property owners to grant trail access to responsible hikers to pass through their land.

After a good supper, supplemented by my camper friend's orange juice and banana, I climbed up a ridge in the cool of the evening and found a cozy, ridge-view campsite beside some desert-blooming poppies and cacti. I had had an easy walk with no need to search for the trail. Now I was enjoying a perfect, star-filled sky. Who could ask for anything more?

The next day's ridge walk to Burnt Rancheria campground

was pleasant and easy. I was excited as I was approaching the Laguna Mountains. As I ascended, I slowly reached wooded areas. First, I saw the small blue oaks in the canyon; then at a higher elevation, I walked through Jeffrey pine groves. Finally, I reached a mixed-conifer forest. The forest cover brought with it lots of sights and sounds of my bird friends—acorn woodpeckers and mountain bluebirds.

My campground stop for water and supper at Burnt Rancheria seemed unusually noisy, with campers' voices amplified by barking dogs. I was eager to wash my dishes and leave this noisy place. As I hurried to the faucet to fill my water bag, a fierce-looking, big-toothed boxer-type dog came barking toward me. He truly looked like he was ready to attack. At last, his owner came and captured him. I was so glad to leave this crowded place and to climb back up to the trail. After a short walk, I found a cozy, level spot to spend the night, with a view of a star-filled sky.

My breakfast was smaller than usual. I had eaten all of my regular, prepackaged cereal and was down to my small reserve package. It was "food drop" day. I was scheduled to pick up a food package at the Mt. Laguna post office.

The guidebook was very helpful in providing a list of post offices along the route where hikers could mail food packages. I would address the package to myself, General Delivery, writing the estimate of my arrival date on the outside label. The term "food drop" came into usage from an earlier custom, when campers hired horses to pack a food cache into a designated campsite and "drop" it off to await the camper's arrival.

Before leaving home, I prepackaged all of my food planned for the trip. I then counted out the packages needed for the number of days between food drops. My Laguna package contained four days of food for the walk from Laguna to Warner Springs.

OVERLOOK— ANZA BORREGO STATE PARK

Nearing the post office, a couple in a jeep inquired, "Where are you hiking?" I replied that I was hiking the Pacific Crest Trail from Mexico to Canada in sections, and that this summer's section was from Campo to Anza. They were impressed. They said that they wanted to try backpacking, and I encouraged them. Soon another, even more eager couple on bikes approached me, wanting to hear more about my hike and proposed that we have coffee together—with breakfast treats on them. The post office sign read: OPEN AT 10:00. I was very eager for breakfast, and they were full of questions, so I followed them down the road to the café that, alas, was closed. So we regretfully bid farewell and I walked back to the post office to wait for my food package. Promptly at 10:00, the post office opened, and I picked up my food package, which had arrived safely. I also signed a Pacific Crest Trail register in the post office.

My next planned water stop was at Laguna Del Prado campground, which I reached around 3 pm, having walked on an easy trail. I was a little disturbed to see a sign stating that the fee for day use at the campground was five dollars. As it is usually the custom for campgrounds on or near the trail to grant free use to Pacific Crest Trail hikers, I was ready to defend this policy to a ranger, but none appeared. After an early supper, I again hiked up to a nearby ridge and found a glorious, quiet, peaceful campsite at the edge of the forest.

My next day's journey through the Laguna Mountains was truly unforgettable! My friends frequently ask me to name my favorite places. My answer is, there are many glorious places of special beauty that, I believe, will stay in my memory forever. These are the places that I enjoy recalling on cold, dark winter evenings. These are the memories that bring me a feeling of uplift and a warm glow. One of these places in Southern California is the Laguna Mountains. The trail through much of the Laguna Mountains is built on a side hill and overlooks the Anza-Borrego Desert State Park—California's largest state park. I feel that this trail experience encompasses the best of two wildernesses—that of the softly shifting colors and vast expanses of the desert and that of the peaceful quiet of the stately wooded forests of the mountains. On this day, the view across Anza-Borrego was covered by a soft haze, not heavy enough to obstruct the view, the present enough to shroud the scene in softness and mystery. To the north, the silhouettes of the steep mountainsides were visible. The mountainsides took on a rosy glow, which added to the beauty. This, for me, was a place of special beauty.

By evening, I found an enchanted forest hideaway not far from the trail for my campsite. This was my first camp since my journey from Campo in which my view of the starlit sky was framed by feathery pine branches.

My next day's journey started along a narrow trail cut into a steep mountain slope. As I rounded a bend, there was rattlesnake who had chosen this sunny trail to warm himself. I stopped and surveyed the situation. The steep side walls climbing both up and down were too hazardous for me to go around the snake, nor did I feel secure in stepping over him. I puzzled what to do. I remember saying to him, "One of us is going to move, and it's not going to be me." Then the thought occurred to me to try rolling a few stones his way. The first stone I rolled toward him brought no response. The second, likewise, brought no response. I decided I was being too gentle. I don't like to disturb nature's creatures. However, I delivered the third stone a little more forcefully and, thankfully, he slithered off down the mountainside, and I went on my way.

As the trail left the forest and desert views and turned toward the west, it descended, often disappearing into thick chaparral. Some of my afternoon's walk was spent by pausing and asking, "Where is the trail?" I needed to search carefully, as in some places the trail was completely covered with bushes. When it was time to make camp, a strong wind was sweeping across the trail. I parked my pack and explored the area, testing the wind direction and velocity with a handkerchief held high. I walked back and forth, testing the wind velocity until I found a little dip between two ridges that afforded some protection from the wind for my shelter that night.

On my journey the next morning, the trail descended to a defunct cement spring, the former Chariot Springs, where two young men had camped. They announced, "There is no water here; the well has gone dry." Fortunately, I had saved some water, as I wasn't counting on water at Chariot Springs. They told me that they were spending the three-day Memorial Day weekend on a walk from Mount Laguna to Banner.

Around ten o'clock, I reached the mining area of Chariot Springs. Again on a temporary trail, I walked by former mining areas where at least one of the mines, the Golden Chariot Mine, appeared to have reopened. There were well-marked, freshly painted buildings and people were moving around the mine areas. Rounding one corner of the road, I heard shots. I moved cautiously. I am really fearful of walking in areas of shooting. I finally located the two shot-makers on the top of the hill and waved frantically to them. They signaled back, stopping their target practice as I walked on.

My next planned water stop was in the town of Banner, a recommended off-trail detour. After replenishing my water supply at a small café, my walk again proceeded on a temporary trail across San Felipe Valley.

In hiking across Southern California, one is frequently aware of being close to military bases. I could look down on some of the bases located in valleys from the mountain ridges. I was often aware of sights and sounds of air maneuvers overhead. Nevertheless, I hadn't expected the close-up view that greeted me at the San Felipe Ranch road crossing. Practically blocking my path was a downed, apparently ailing, green-painted military helicopter. Bending over its engine were four, blue-suited men who had emerged from an Air Force truck. I didn't wait to see if they succeeded in repairing the machine.

About half a mile after passing the downed helicopter, I came within close view of an intriguing Victorian-style ranch house, which occupied a central location in the valley, surrounded by lots of out-buildings and pasture. I wondered about its history. When was it built? Who were its early occupants? I stopped to take a photo.

Back on a road and still on temporary trail, I came to a large cattle guard with a tremendously big NO TRESPASSING sign. Sunset was approaching, and I was starting to think about a campsite. Walking north with thoughts of supper, I was greeted by a still larger NO TRESPASSING sign. What to do? I was ready for supper and camp. I searched around and saw a ravine. I moved cautiously under the fence, tucked my bivouac sack into the ravine, enjoyed supper, and went to bed, hoping that nobody connected to those huge NO TRESPASSING signs would find me.

I did have mixed feelings about sleeping where there were NO TRESPASSING signs. Usually, I avoid such areas. However, at the same time, I must say that I felt a sense of achievement, bordering on smugness, that I had found such a cozy hideaway. It was not until the next morning, after I had safely departed from my cozy campsite and looked back, that I realized that this would have been the wrong place to be if there had been a rainstorm. My hidden ravine could have turned into a swift river.

My next morning's water stop was at a tiny town, which was not exactly a town but a café and house called "Felipe." I turned in. The neon COORS light was on in the café, the door was open, and I went inside eagerly, anticipating a treat of a cup of morning coffee. I walked around inside the store, but no one was in sight. I called, but there was no answer. How mysterious—bordering on spooky! Finally, about to give up, I went out the door to look for a water faucet, when out from the adjoining house appeared a small, smiling, sleepy-looking lady. She apologized and said she did not have any coffee; did I want something else? I suggested milk. I took a swallow from the glass of milk she offered me. It was sour—definitely sour! When I said to her that I thought it was a little sour, she hurried back to her house and found another carton. It was all right. She then started telling me about her 40 years in Felipe. I could have stayed all day. In fact, when I proposed that it was time for me to fill my water bag and be on my way, she said, "Can't you stay overnight? Most of the Pacific Trail hikers stay here overnight." I declined as gently as possible. I suggested that I would like to take her picture. She responded, "Wait a minute—I want to get my hat." She hurried into the house and came out with a brightly-colored hat topped with tall rabbit ears. She posed for the photo and told me that she had worn the hat to the village dance. As I again pleaded with her as gently as possible that it was time for me to fill my water bag and be on my way, she gave me directions for the next several miles' walk. Although I found that her directions were not quite as up-to-date as those in the guidebook, I listened patiently, even though I was feeling somewhat impatient, thanked her, and finally went on my way.

After more road walking, my next lunch and water stop was at Barrel Springs. Here, I found delightfully cold water and a little off-the-road picnic area. I thoroughly enjoyed my stop in this quiet, tree-lined island away from the traffic. After lunch, I eagerly searched for and found the permanent trail. It was so good to be hiking on a walking path again. My afternoon walk between Barrel Springs and Warner Springs traversed undulating hills, passing through fields and meadows interspersed with valleys and creeks lined with small oaks and willows. It was also pasture land, and cows were never far away. I enjoyed seeing cactus in full bloom, with blossoms in several colors—yellow, red, and pink.

Toward evening, I came to San Ysidro Creek, a cool, wooded, shaded area. I selected a tree-lined bedroom. It felt good to be camping away from roads and NO TRESPASSING signs.

In the morning, after a few more undulating hills with some nice views from the hilltops looking out over Warner Valley, I arrived at the Warner Springs Fire Station, my next planned water stop. I had anticipated a quick stop to fill my water bag. When I arrived, however, I encountered a fenced-in, well-manicured grass lawn. Three men in green coveralls were weeding the lawn. I asked, "Where can I get some water?" The man standing nearest me replied, "I'll have to ask the supervisor." and disappeared into the firehouse. Slowly he emerged, saying that the supervisor would like me to come inside. I was escorted into a good-sized kitchen and greeted by, "Would you like some pancakes? I'm making some for the rangers." I declined, feeling that this was more hospitality than I had expected upon seeking to fill my water bag. After watching him flip pancakes for another 15 or 20 minutes, however, I began to wish I had accepted the offer. The supervisor proceeded to give me a long talk, filled with instructions on how to proceed carefully and wisely on the trail. He told me about hikers who had come into the station suffering from heat prostration, and about others who had suffered from dehydration. He was so earnest in his instructions on safety that I tried to respond by politely listening and agreeing with him. I did gently let him know that I had been backpacking on the trail for several years. Finally, as he flipped more pancakes and filled my water bag, he acknowledged that I seemed more experienced than many hikers who passed through the fire station. He let me out the door, wishing me well. As I walked out the gate, I noticed a green van labelled "San Diego Probation Department." This explained the presence of the overalled men who were not inclined to give me permission to obtain water without consulting the supervisor.

In Warner Springs, I stopped at the post office for a food package, which had arrived safely. I sat down in the nearby parking lot to eat my lunch. A horse that was tied to a hitching post kept nudging me. I said to him, "No, I don't have any lunch to spare."

I noticed that there was a mini-bus running between Warner Springs and San Diego. Had I known about this bus in advance, I probably would have used it to end my walk of this section. Warner Springs has become a newly developed retirement community, and the mini-bus is a new addition that was not listed in the guidebook.

I walked west on the highway until I found the trail crossing by a water tank. The fire station supervisor had given me good directions. My next campsite and water stop was on Agua Caliente Creek.

My walk the following day toward the top of Comb's Peak had been described in the guidebook as hot and tedious. My climb was made under cloud cover and was comfortable. I selected a campsite high up on a shoulder of Comb's Peak. What a glorious evening! I was treated to a spectacular light and cloud display. The scene started with a large silver cloud, which lit and reflected the setting sun. First, the sky was bright; then, the silver lining turned to a pinkish-reddish glow. Finally, the sky turned to a deep gray-blue. It was one of those scenes of special beauty that I will always hold onto and bring back into memory. (Have photo.)

My next day's journey to Anza Valley was marked by a long

walk drifting down the other side of the mountain. I paused periodically to gaze northward across the vast expanse of Anza Valley.

Upon reaching the valley floor, I paused by the shoulder of the road for a mid-morning snack. I was feeling good about having reached the desert valley floor while it seemed to me to be still reasonably cool, when an approaching car stopped and a man greeted me with, "Good heavens! What are you doing walking out here in the heat of the day? Don't you want a ride?" "No, thank you." I responded. "I'm walking from Mexico to Canada on the Pacific Crest Trail." "Well," he said, "I'm the editor of *The Anza Gazette*, and I want to interview you. I'll see you later at the Kamp Anza Store." Off he sped.

Trudging on, I arrived at the Village Store and enjoyed the taste of a cold 7-Up, luxuriating in how good a cold drink can feel. I asked the proprietor for directions on how to reach bus transportation for my journey home. He rapidly quoted me mileage in all directions, but let me know there were no nearby bus stops. Feeling refreshed after a cold drink but discouraged by the report that there were no nearby bus stops, I returned to Terwilliger Road and walked on to Kamp Anza. I passed a number of mobile homes and saw a sign attached to a small, square building that looked like a quonset hut: "Carolyn's Beauty Salon." I thought I could surely use a hair wash—but not now.

I was anxious to hurry home to attend the annual Sonoma Group Sierra Club meeting. Originally, I had planned to leave the trail at a trailhead at the mountain resort town of Idyllevield north of Anza, but shortly before leaving home, I realized that I would need to leave the trail earlier to reach home in time to attend the meeting.

At the Kamp Anza store, as scheduled, the editor of *The Anza Gazette* stopped by and completed his interview with me.

He said it would be in the next issue of the paper and that he would send me a copy. However, I did not hear from him, so I shall never know what he wrote.

After the interview, I started my ride search in earnest. The proprietor at Kamp Anza was a most sympathetic listener. He mentioned that he planned to go to Hemet, where there are bus connections, in the morning, and that if I didn't find a ride that evening, I could stay at their campground and ride with him. He pointed out that most of the people who stopped at the Kamp Anza store were coming home from work at Hemet or other nearby towns. After trying unsuccessfully to find a ride, I decided to accept his kind offer. I enjoyed having a sleeping space at the camp, together with the luxurious, refreshing, stimulating treat of a shower.

True to his word, the Kamp Anza proprietor transported me the next morning to Hemet. His first stop was at the busy Automobile Association office. I promptly headed for the information desk. In reply to my questions about buses, a solemn-looking staff person said, "There isn't any bus from here to Los Angeles." I was dumbfounded and struck with disbelief that such a good-sized , bustling town would not have a bus. I was puzzled. What to do next? Thankfully, from this crowded, busy office, with its automated-sounding information clerk, a nearby Hemet citizen rescued me. She told me there was a regular bus that runs from Hemet to the Riverside Transit Mall, where I could board the bus to Los Angeles. She assured me that I could find the bus stop at the plaza in front of Penney's. Thank heavens for an informed, helpful, caring citizen! This most helpful woman gave me a ride to the plaza bus stop. Slowly but surely I was on my way home.

After boarding the connecting bus in Hemet, I arrived at the Riverside Transit Mall, just as a bus to Los Angeles was pulling out. I waited impatiently for the next bus. In the busy, crowded Los Angeles bus terminal, I finally located the ticket window to purchase my ticket to San Francisco. Here, I waited in a long, slow-moving line. When I finally reached the ticket counter, I learned that I had just missed a non-stop bus to San Francisco. I had a three-hour wait for the next bus. Finally, I reached home at 3:00 am. Thankfully, I would be on time to attend the next day's annual meeting.

The next morning, upon checking my answering machine, it seemed to me that I had an extraordinary number of phone calls asking me if I would be at the annual Sierra Club Chapter dinner. I wondered why. After all, I'd rarely missed a meeting, and I had assured my friends that I would return for the event.

Later that evening, I discovered the reason for my friends' solicitude when I was presented with a certificate that read:

SIERRA CLUB
AWARD FOR OUTSTANDING ACHIEVEMENT
ELEANOR GUILFORD

Joined Sierra Club November 1965
Outings Leader 1968-1985
Member of Executive Committee:
Sonoma County Group 1977-1981
Group Secretary 1978-1979
Vice-Chair 1980
Chair 1981
Potluck Chair 1978-1985
Award presented at Sierrafest 1, June 1985

Chapter 2
Anza Valley to Big Bear City
May 1987 • 122 Miles

*When we try to pick out anything by itself, we find it hitched
to everything else in the universe. One fancies a heart like
our own must be beating in every crystal and cell ...*
—John Muir

Shortly after leaving the Anza Valley at Kamp Anza, the
temporary trail climbs up a moderate grade to the Pines and
Palms highway. This well-named thoroughfare is symbolic and
descriptive of this trail section. On its journey north, it traverses
sandy, shoreless desert, passes through shady live oaks, and
climbs up to the shoulder of 10,786-foot Mount San Jacinto
before plunging down approximately 8,000 feet into sandy,
treeless, windswept San Gorgonio Pass at around 1,500 feet.

Moving north from the arid San Gorgonio Pass area, the
trail proceeds up Whitewater River canyon and alongside Mission Creek on its route into the San Bernardino Mountains.
Big Bear Lake and its adjacent Big Bear City lie just three miles
south of the trail.

Planning for my return to the trailhead at Anza was not easy. I had learned from my 1985 hike upon coming out at Anza, that the nearest bus terminal was at Hemet, which was a goodly distance from Anza—approximately 40 miles—too far to hitchhike I decided. During the dark and dreary evenings in the winter months of 1986 when I started dreaming of the trail, I started work on how to unravel the puzzle of how to reach Kamp Anza.

My first plan was to call a Sierra Club friend who had moved to Hemet. There was no answer to my phone call. How disappointing. I called Information and found my friend was no longer listed in the Hemet phone directory. Next, I thought of calling a social-worker friend who lived in Riverside. After pondering this idea, I decided that this did not seem right, as I had not seen him for some time.

The plan that finally felt best to me was to call the Grants— the owners of the Kamp Anza store who had been so friendly and helpful to me on my 1985 trip. I recalled that Mrs. Grant usually drove to Hemet once a week to shop for groceries. I decided to call her. When she answered, I was pleased that she seemed to remember me. She agreed to meet me in Hemet and transport me to Kamp Anza.

I was eager and ready to continue my journey in May of 1986. I had packed and mailed a 23-day cache of food. I was excited. Alas, just two days before my proposed departure, I phoned Mrs. Grant, saying, "I can't come next Tuesday—I broke my arm."

For days and weeks afterwards, friends asked me, "Did you break your arm hiking on the trail?" "No," I replied, "I broke it on the Muni—the San Francisco No. 38 Geary bus." Actually, I had always felt that city streets were much more to be feared than mountain trails. It was hard, however, to convince my urban friends of this idea. So, there was no trail hike for me in 1986. The considerate postmistress in Cabazon returned my food packages, most of which I saved and packed with me in 1987. In May of 1987, I arrived in the shopping mall in Hemet to meet Mrs. Grant. I was apprehensive. How would she recognize me in this crowded mall? At the appointed time, she approached me cheerfully. I was relieved. I asked, "How did you recognize me?" She smiled and said, "No one else here is dressed like you." I realized this was true. There were no other backpackers. The mall was full of smartly dressed, suburban shoppers.

Returning to Kamp Anza in the late afternoon, I decided to spend the night in the friendly, comfortable campground.

The next morning, I eagerly made my early-morning ascent up to the ridge of Look Out Mountain where, at a crossing of the Pines to Palms highway (Highway 74), I would meet the permanent trail. Shortly ahead of me, I saw the silhouette of a backpacker and noticed that he was extending his arm begging for a ride. I wondered where he was headed. I concluded that he must not be a Pacific Crest Trail hiker, as a truly dedicated hiker would not ask for a ride on their walk from Mexico to Canada. Later, I learned that I was wrong. I had a chance to talk to him at the small store at the trailhead where we were both having coffee. I asked him, "Where are you hiking?" He replied that he was hiking on the Pacific Crest Trail. I decided not to question him about hitchhiking. He told me that he was a first-time hiker. He had checked with the Forest Service about the trail and learned that there were no recent reports of floods. He moved on ahead of me and I did not see him again, but I certainly kept wondering, "Did he ride part of the way to Canada?"

It was so good, as always, to come to the end of road walking and to reach the permanent trail. The trail north of the Pines to Palms highway modulated in and out of shallow, sandy canyons, chaparral, and groves of small trees. I was suddenly startled upon reaching a sandy wash and seeing a sign that read: DANGER—PROCEED WITH CARE. I was puzzled over what it meant. What was the danger and, if there was danger, what was one supposed to do? I paused and pondered. My best guess was that these sandy washes could become dangerous, swift-flowing streams following a rainstorm. While I was puzzling over this unexpected sign, I was surprised to see some rain clouds, and soon it started to rain; then I heard thunder and saw lightening. I quickly abandoned my backpack with its aluminum frame and took shelter under small trees. I was taking no chances of exposing myself to a lightening strike. Thankfully, the shower soon ended, I re-shouldered my pack, and enjoyed a pleasant walk to my next watering hole and campsite at Live Oak Spring. The spring was reached by walking a short distance off the Live Oak Trail.

At the spring, I spied a perfect campsite under a huge live oak. As I moved closer, I discovered that there was a camper with a dog who had already claimed the site. I greeted him, saying, "You surely found a nice campsite. Are there any others near here?" He replied gruffly, "There are some sites down the hill." I concluded from his unfriendly manner that he didn't want another camper near him sharing the other side of the huge shade tree. So, I moved downhill and found a flat but unspectacular place lacking the beauty of the big tree. I thought, "Campers are different; some campers share and enjoy friendly company while others are unfriendly and unwelcoming."

After having moved along easily on my first day's walk from Kamp Anza to Live Oak Campground—covering some 15 miles in spite of a morning of uphill walking and of time spent waiting for the lightning storm to end—my next day's journey from Live Oak to the Fobes Ranch area proved to be a slow walk. The trail ascended and descended on rough, rocky terrain. Finding water also took longer than anticipated. The guidebook described a spring one-half mile off the trail on the Fobes Ranch Trail. It seemed like a long walk down a steep trail and a long search before I found water.

By the time I climbed up again, I was ready to stop for the night and made camp on a level platform below the junction of the Fobes Ranch Trail. I thought to myself that, on the trail, no two days are alike. But of course, I reasoned upon further thought, isn't this a part of trail walking as well as part of life?

The following day, after more rocky ascents and descents, I reached the saddle of Apache Springs by mid-morning—my next planned off-trail water site. I was still at the saddle two hours later, trying to find the trail. First, there was the hunt for water at the spring. The tall grass had grown over the water so that it was a time-consuming task to locate the spring. When I finally found the spring, I filled my water bag with fresh water. Then, I climbed back up to the saddle again to a well-traveled trail, which soon seemed to be climbing more to the west than I had anticipated. After checking with my map and compass, I soon discovered I was on the trail to Apache Peak, a well-worn trail used extensively by day hikers. Realizing my mistake, I hurried back down to the saddle and checked again with my map and compass. Where I thought the trail that I wanted should be proceeding to the north, I could see no evidence of a trail. So I spent the next hour in a cross-country search. Finally, upon looking down from a shoulder of Apache Peak, I spotted a faint possible trail below. I scrambled down and finally found real but faint evidence of a trail. I had been hampered in my search because the fast-growing grass had completely hidden the trail. It was not until I proceeded to a sandy area that I could see the faint marks of the trail. Trail walking, I decided, is one continual journey of learning. This day's journey will be added to my store of memories. This was my first experience in grappling with a trail obscured by tall grass.

By evening, I was not only on a good trail, but a trail that afforded exciting views of valleys and canyons to the west. I found a level spot on Tahquitz Ridge for a campsite and enjoyed an evening of glorious views. I felt uplifted at viewing the sharp outlines of Tahquitz and San Jacinto peaks piercing the sky.

In the morning, winding down the pleasant and easy-to-follow trail from Tahquitz Ridge, I passed a good number of day hikers. It was Sunday. I was near Mt. San Jacinto, the mountain just west of Palm Springs. There were many side trails. Suddenly, among the people I passed, a ranger appeared. I remembered that the guidebook had stated that hikers should not only have a National Forest permit (which I had obtained in San Diego), but that one should also obtain a permit for the Mt. San Jacinto State Park. I had completely forgotten about the permit for this short section of the trail. Would the ranger ask me for the State Park permit? Fortunately, the ranger smiled at me, and I proceeded on my way.

Deer Springs was my next planned campsite and watering hole. As I approached the campground, it began to grow chilly. While searching for water and a level spot to make camp, I saw before me a sizeable snow bank; I was at 8000 feet. I hurriedly cooked soup and stew so that I could snuggle into my bedroll to keep warm. Warm and comfortable in my feathered bedroll, I recalled having enjoyed a very pleasant day. I was grateful that I was only camping beside a snowbank, as the Mt. San Jacinto area at 8000 to 9090 feet is known to have snowstorms even into early June.

The following morning was marked by water measuring in anticipation of one of my longest water carries, described in the guidebook as "a punishing 25-mile descent to the next water at Snow Creek."

From Deer Creek Campground, the trail climbed up and down a rocky path, traversing Fuller Ridge. With its steep ups and downs, this part of the trail reminded me of an old-style cross-country trail, in contrast to the newer trails, which generally have 14-degree ascents and descents. I was glad that I had added a walking stick to my equipment, following my experience with a broken arm sustained the year before. Although the trail was slow-going, I found it enjoyable. There were some glorious views looking down at the San Gorgonia Pass and north to the San Bernardino Mountains. Two early-morning runners came along, plotting their courses over rocky obstacles. I thought that they were not only getting a good aerobic exercise, but were becoming skilled in obstacle course running. They assured me that I was not far from the trailhead at the Fuller Ridge Remote Campground. I stopped for an early lunch at the campground, sitting in a pleasant, shaded area under a large pine. This pleasant area, however, was waterless.

Following my lunch and after a short walk, I descended to a dirt road, and I here I began to search for the trail. The guidebook states that the trail is marked by large ducks (three rocks piled on top of each other) and leaves the northwest side of an open area alongside the road. I searched but could find no large ducks. I did finally find a descending trail to the west of the road. I tried this trail, but soon decided that it was not going in the right direction—it was switchbacking south. I grudgingly hiked back to the road again. Next, I tried a faint trail leading northeast. This trail, too, started descending too much to the east, so again I backtracked to the road. On my third try, after much searching, I finally found the trail. I reviewed this latest puzzle. This was different from my experience at Apache

Springs. This hidden trail had not been obscured by tall grass, but was hidden by a high road shoulder.

After a short walk, it was time to make camp. I settled down in a pleasant, level spot amidst some small trees and enjoyed a peaceful night.

My next day was spent slowly winding down the infamous ridge rail to Snow Creek Village and San Gorgonio Pass. The Pass is 7600 feet lower than the Deer Spring Campground. Some of the switchbacks seemed to be winding down so slowly that, at times, they seemed to be going uphill instead of down. To help pass the time, I started counting switchbacks. I counted to 28 before I gave up the count.

The last part of the slow descent was especially tantalizing, as I could see Snow Creek Road. It looked like it was so close that one would reach it in a few minutes, but just as I felt that I was about to reach it, another switchback headed off on another slow, level route.

Finally, I arrived at the road and soon reached the small village of Snow Creek. I was eager to reach the long-anticipated water stop. At the nearest house in Snow Creek, I went to the door to politely request some water. I knocked at the door, but no one answered, although there was a light in the house. I returned to the street and saw a car slowly moving up the road. I waved at the car and smiled, holding out my cup. The car increased speed and rushed by. I was disappointed and angry. I felt that this was not a friendly village. On my next approach, having given up the idea of making a polite request, I found a water spigot at a small house where no one was home. Happily, this pursuit was successful. How good to have fresh water after my long day's descent.

As the wind was sweeping up the canyon creating a bit of a sandstorm, I looked around and found a sheltered place in a nearby sandy ravine. I ate my supper and settled in for the night on a soft, sandy, level bed. The next morning, I was awakened by, "Hey, you over there! This is private property." I arose slowly, poking my head out of my bivouac sack. I attempted to explain my late evening arrival by telling my story of traversing down the long, descending, waterless trail and the need to find shelter. The previously commanding voice of the blue-jeaned interrogator, upon seeing my face, changed quickly to a soft, quiet tone. "Are you all right?" I assured her that I was and asked the directions to White Water. Before departing, she again said softly, "Well, I wanted to be sure that you were all right." Rarely have I heard a voice change so quickly from a strident command to one of gentle concern. As I walked down the road, I kept smiling to myself and thinking, "She probably was expecting to see some young, suspicious-looking intruder and was taken aback upon seeing an older, solo backpacker.

Happy to leave Snow Creek Village and the memories of my difficult search for water followed by "This is private property," I headed north toward White Water on a windswept road, balancing to avoid being toppled by the gusty wind. Before arriving at the junction of heavily traveled San Gorgonio Pass highway—busy Interstate Highway 10, connecting Los Angeles and Palm Springs. I sat down to study the map in order to maneuver through the maze of on-ramps to hopefully locate a pedestrian path to the town of White Water. Soon I heard a voice calling from a car—a car with a bicycle on the roof: "Are you hiking on the Pacific Crest Trail?" "Yes," I replied. "I want to take the right road to reach the White Water post office, where I am going to pick up a food package." The White Water post office has been closed," the driver replied. "Wait here, and I'll be back in twenty minutes to drive you to Cabezon."

My bicycle friend returned promptly as promised and delivered me to the door of the Cabezon post office. He instructed me to tell the postmistress to find a ride for me to return to White Water Canyon. He also pointed to a nearby grocery store, saying this would be a second resource for a ride. Inside the post office, I announced my presence to claim my food package to a smiling postmistress and quickly added that the man who gave me a ride from the White Water junction suggested that I ask if she knew of someone who could give me a ride back to White Water Canyon. This request was answered surprisingly quickly, as a man standing by the counter replied, "I'll take you to White Water." Happily, I claimed my food package and followed him to his car. He, as well as his companion and a young towheaded boy, were relaxed and friendly. Upon arrival at the junction, he offered to drive me further on up the White Water Canyon road. I declined, explaining that I was walking from Mexico to Canada on the Pacific Crest Trail and that the canyon road is part of the temporary trail. I thanked him for the ride, for which I was genuinely grateful. I proceeded down the road, feeling secure with my fresh food supply.

As I was striding along, the memory of the postmistress's bemused smile came flashing back to me. I was puzzled over her smile, and then I thought, "She had plenty of reason to smile." Upon looking at my face in my signal mirror at a rest stop, I discovered that sand had stuck tenaciously to my new "Alligator Total Sun Block" preparation, resulting in blotches of gray-black spots all over my face. I looked a bit like a chimney sweep. In addition, I wasn't sure whether I had turned around in the post office, but I also discovered on the fourth day of my twelve-day hike that the seat of my pants was wearing out. Two 50-cent-sized holes had broken through. No wonder the postmistress had smiled!

It was good to be on the trail again, and I had a new goal to look forward to—to take a half-day's rest to mend my pants. As I walked, I enjoyed recalling the people I had met—some friendly and helpful, others aloof and indifferent—but all of them intriguing and colorful.

The temporary route in 1987 called for walking up the White Water Canyon Road to some cottonwood trees just south of the White Water Trout Farm, where there is a Pacific Coast Trail marker. Then a hiker will experience the adventure of a trail-less walk up along the edge of White Water River for approximately 2-1/2 miles.

I found the sight of this wide riverbed bottom to be awesome. Immense boulders were strewn all over the white, sandy bottom. During the summer months, the river is reduced to a trickle. In contrast, during the winter months following the rainy season, the river is wide, swift, and deep. Looking around at its wide, dry bed, I thought to myself, "My, what a powerful, raging torrent this must be during the spring."

Following the temporary trail became a real challenge. For some distance, I was able to follow some horseshoe imprint marks in the sand, hoping that the horses had been going my way on the Pacific Crest Trail. This was too good to last—the horseshoe rings ended and soon I found myself excitedly and carefully boulder-hopping, asking myself, "Where is the trail?" I proceeded cautiously because I didn't want to miss the narrow canyon turnoff to the north, as I had heard that many hikers had had trouble locating this junction and had spent hours wandering around in the river bottom searching for the trail. Cautiously, I explored briefly one narrow canyon turnoff, but found that it was only a deer track. Looking west and observing the setting sun, I decided that it was time to think about making camp and that it would be better to search for the trail in the morning. I looked around and discovered a delightful little island, complete with a small tree border creating a frame for my bedroom and replete with soft sand for my bed, nearby water, and a view toward the hill-lined ravines. I spent a restful night.

In the morning, I resumed my search for the canyon containing the trail. Happily, near my island bedroom, I spotted a brown plastic Pacific Crest Trail marker. I rejoiced in the find by singing a "hallelujah." I was back on the permanent trail.

The trail heading north winds up and down some gently rolling hills. Approaching noontime, I found a perfect shady lunch stop under a lone cottonwood tree by Mission Creek. This afforded me a good time and place to mend my pants. I was thankful that I was carrying a needle and thread. I pondered over where to secure cloth for the patches. Should I remove a pocket or cut out a patch from elsewhere? My final decision was to cut a little square out of each inside bottom leg. This worked quite well. I completed my patches and moved on for my afternoon walk feeling good about my more secure pant seat and pant legs embellished with little windows.

My afternoon walk led up the delightful gurgling, shaded Mission Creek. The guidebook states that the trail on its ascent toward Forks Springs fords Mission Creek over 20 times. I felt like Alice in Wonderland.

For my afternoon tea break, I spotted a delightful hiding place shaded by tall bushes. While I was chewing on my trail mix, I heard footsteps. I felt it best to announce my whereabouts before scaring the passerby, so I shouted, "Hi!" Nevertheless, I did manage to scare the passing hiker. "Oh, where are you?" responded the startled hiker. Then I met Jim, who was out for a long weekend hike. Jim and I leapfrogged, passing each other for the next two days three or four times. We compared trail notes. He had excellent notes of trail descriptions, which he had charted from the guidebook, including where to find water, altitude, mileage, and where one could leave the trail in the event of an emergency. He proved to be a most helpful and informative trail resource.

By evening, I reached a pleasant tree-covered, level campsite just south of Mission Creek Trail Campground. By early the following morning, I arrived at the campground. The guidebook advised that one should fill one's canteen, as it was 16 miles to the next water. However, somehow or other, I didn't succeed in finding water in the area described and decided to go on to Heart's Bar Creek, where there is a "usually flowing stream" a half mile off the trail.

At Heart's Bar Creek, I enjoyed a scenic off-trail walk, listening and searching for water, but I did not find the "usually flowing stream." What to do? My initial thought was to ration my water and move on ahead. Then, I sat down and "put on my rational thinking cap." I decided that it was not wise to hike on without a better water supply and risk suffering from dehydration. I resolved to return to Mission Creek Trail Camp.

When I reached the road near the camp, a pickup truck came along, and I decided I would ask the driver about water. Fortunately, the driver was a forest ranger. When I told him the story of my search for water, he offered me a gallon of water. I took my needed ration and again headed north on the trail. Feeling secure with plenty of water, I enjoyed a late lunch. I felt good, perhaps a little smug, at having secured my water ration so easily.

By evening, the trail had climbed to a ridgetop that afforded spectacular views looking south toward Mission Creek. Soon, the trail joined the Coon Creek Road. It was time to make camp. I searched for a little hideaway and found a level platform a few yards below the road.

During the night, it became very windy and fog rolled in. It grew cold. The fog swept in waves through the pass below me and reminded me of fogbanks sweeping through the Golden Gate in the San Francisco Bay Area.

In the morning, upon packing my gear, I couldn't believe it—it still seems incredible—but I had lost a sock. I searched and searched but couldn't find it anywhere. Did the wind and fog drafts carry it away?

Nearing the Coon Creek Jump-off Group Camp, I heard voices. As I drew nearer, I saw a group of men working around a cabin. I greeted them, and they explained that they were welding a porch rail. They asked, "Do you know how to weld?" "No," I replied," "I do not." While watching them, I thought that I might ask them for water. Although I estimated that I had enough for the next ten miles, I thought it would be good, as extra insurance, to have a little more. So, I asked them. They happily responded to my request, and I added to my water supply.

Soon I met Jim, my San Diego hiking friend, coming south on his return trip. He seemed relieved to see me and said, "I've been worried about you, and I've brought you some water." I explained my delay in going back for water at Mission Creek Trail Camp. When I told him that I had plenty of water, he proceeded to pour out the water he had been saving for me. Afterward I wished that I had accepted the water. He had been so kind to haul it all the way for me, in addition to his own water. Before we parted, he gave me a good, detailed description of the trail ahead.

I really appreciated Jim's thoughtful concern. At the same time, I sensed that it might be a little hard for a young hiker such as Jim to encounter an older, woman hiking alone. I believe I had aroused a sense of worry in him. He mentioned that the forecast was for cold and stormy weather. Again, he seemed concerned. I tried to reassure him. I told him that I planned to reach Arrastre's Camp that night and that I planned to come out at Big Bear Lake in a few days.

The trail from Coon Creek to the Arrastre Trail Camp was pleasant and easy to follow. Arrastre Trail Camp at Deer Springs, my campsite for the evening, proved to be very pleasant, with piped water, a fire pit, toilets, benches, and a bathtub for the horses to drink. No horses or hikers arrived, and I had the whole camp to myself. Around suppertime, a Boy Scout troop came down the trail, but they did not stop.

This was a day for me to celebrate—it was my birthday—so I got out a candle and placed it on a table stump. I not only enjoyed looking at my warm, lighted candle, but I even bothered to set the self-timer on my camera and took a photo of myself sitting beside my birthday candle. From my bedroom under a big pine tree, I had a glorious sky view framed by the tree.

In the night, a cold, strong wind arose. It was so cold in the morning that when I came out of my warm sleeping bag for breakfast, I quickly returned to my bedroll for breakfast in bed. I also had to anchor everything with weights so nothing would fly away.

After a leisurely breakfast, eaten mostly while still wrapped in my sleeping bag, I packed my gear and started down the trail. I walked quite a way wearing all of my layers, including my vapor-barrier clothing, which ordinarily I wear only at night for added warmth. Actually, this was the only time I could remember during my entire journey that I hiked with my vapor barrier clothing on during a daytime hike.

In about an hour, I met the Boy Scout troop, or rather I came to their camp, and said, "Hello" to one of their leaders who was standing with his bedroll wrapped around him. Pointing toward a group of tents, he said, laughingly, that all of his campers were still in bed. The camp was unusually quiet for a group of Scouts.

As I hiked on, the wind was so fierce at times that I found myself crouching down so as not to be toppled off my feet when gusts of wind buffeted me from west-exposed contours. As the trail turned west, there were views of arid Baldwin Lake. Approaching Highway 18, just north of Big Bear Lake, as I was having a snack amidst some chaparral, I noticed some little white flakes dropping onto the ground. I was puzzled. At first, I thought they were small blossoms flying from the manzanita bushes. Then the little white flakes grew bigger. I looked again. Could it be snow? I could hardly believe it. Soon the white balls grew bigger and heavier. There was no question that this was a honest-to-goodness snowstorm. It was May 25th.

What should I do? Impulsively and on "automatic pilot," I crossed the highway and started to walk toward my next proposed campsite at Doble Trail Camp—about 2-1/2 miles distant. It seemed to me that it was growing colder and stormier. I moved slowly, leaning into the wind and blinking as the snowflakes pelted my face. After walking about 100 yards beyond the highway, I stopped to don my poncho. I had a difficult time getting it over my head and down in the back. Since my last trip, I had acquired a new, taller backpack to accommodate a tent and additional layers of clothing for my August trip in the rainy state of Washington. I struggled, poking at my back with my walking stick, but I did not succeed in pulling my poncho over my backpack. Finally, feeling perplexed and a little worried about getting wet and risking the possibility of hypothermia, I somewhat reluctantly decided to backtrack to the highway and seek a ride to Big Bear City.

Actually, I was planning to come out at Big Bear City, but I had planned originally to come out at a different trailhead—at

Van Dusen Canyon Road—a trailhead listed in the guidebook was eight miles to the west of Highway 18. The Van Dusen Canyon Road had been my going-in trailhead in June 1985 for the next section of the trail.

Just as I arrived at a turnout on Highway 18, a couple walking their dog along the shoulder of the blacktopped highway in the snow offered me a ride to Big Bear City. I climbed into the back of their RV camper. I felt guilty because my muddy boots and wet poncho leaked onto their camper floor. I apologized. They were most understanding. This kindly couple not only took me into Big Bear City, but also waited patiently while I phoned to try to find a camp mentioned in my American Youth Hostel Directory, without success. I then decided to give up on the Youth Hostel idea and aimed for a Motel 6 instead. My friendly RV couple graciously volunteered to take me there, although it was approximately three-quarters of a mile out of their way.

This couple remains in my memory as some of the helpful, friendly people who went out of their way to help me along my journey.

After registering and locating my room at the motel, the first thing I did was to climb out of my wet, dripping rain jacket. Then, I slipped into my goose-down sleeping bag, which I placed on the bed. I soon felt the wonderful warmth and closeness of its soft feathers, which I had enjoyed so frequently during cool evenings on the trail.

As the restaurant was about three-quarters of a mile away and it was still snowing, cold, and growing dark, I opted for another backpacker's supper. I placed my small, fuel-tablet backpacker's stove near the door, which I opened slightly in order to vent the stove. It worked. I enjoyed my soup and stew in the warmth and protection of my Motel 6 room.

During the night, and for many days and nights following the May 25th snowstorm, I have been plagued with this afterthought: Could I have survived safely if I had continued on and spent the night at Doble Trail Camp? The scene that comes to my mind is that I would have searched for a bedroom that was as high and dry as possible. The site would be near a tree from which I could run my clothesline rope and use it to drape my poncho like a tarp. Under the tarp I would have placed my bedroll, covered by my Gortex bivouac sack. Could I have survived without risking hypothermia? I like to think I could have.

The next morning, I grappled with the problem of transportation to Los Angeles. Ironically, I had chosen Big Bear City as the site from which to go into the trail in 1985 because it had bus service. Unfortunately, by 1987, the bus service had been discontinued. I phoned Dial-A-Ride, and a helpful driver agreed to take me, for twenty-five cents, to a place where those seeking a ride customarily stand. (I'm not fond of the word "hitchhiker," although that is the mode of transportation that I did seek when there was no bus directly to the trailhead.) This location was at the south end of the city at a place called Boulder City.

Standing at the shoulder of the road where the Dial-A-Ride driver had deposited me, I extended my arm and smiled at each approaching car. They went speeding by me. I really didn't like this location. It was a place where traffic heading out of town tended to speed up. They were not slowed by stoplights, gas stations, or stores. My usual approach to seeking a ride was to make my request when cars were parked at a store or gas station, where I could be somewhat selective of whom I approached to ask for a ride.

I continued to wave and smile at the speeding cars for what seemed like an eternity—probably 20 to 30 minutes—without

success. I decided to move a few feet down the road, where I
spotted a small store. I turned to shoulder my pack and as I
was about to start walking, a pickup with a couple in the cab
stopped and offered me a ride. They announced that they were
headed to Redlands. I replied that I wanted to reach San Bernardino to catch a bus to Los Angeles. They could take me to
the Redlands-San Bernardino junction. Happily, I climbed into
the bed of the pickup. I soon felt a cold dampness where I was
sitting. The truckbed was still wet from having been blanketed
with snow. I moved around and discovered some protection by
sitting on an overturned dog's dish. The countryside for some
distance was still covered with snow patches. The air was damp
and cold. I crouched down and watched the hillside slide by
as the pickup turned and swayed down the curving mountain
road until it slowed and stopped at a turnoff where the driver
announced, "This is the San Bernardino junction."

I sat up, stretched, gathered my pack, and maneuvered
to climb out of the puddles of the truck bed. I thanked my
thoughtful driver as he turned to go toward Redlands.

Out of the mountains and now in the lowlands, I surveyed
the surroundings. The scene at this junction turnoff made me
even more pessimistic about finding a ride than I had been at
Boulder City. Again, there was little incentive for drivers to
stop or to slow down. I tried different locations. I waved and
smiled at traffic coming from both Big Bear Lake and Redlands. Neither approach was working. A sign indicated that
San Bernardino could be reached in four miles. I decided to
walk to the city outskirts in hopes of finding a store or gas station at the town's edge. I turned to shoulder my pack when,
much to my surprise, a little red sports car pulled up beside me.
Did deciding to change locations produce some kind of magic?
For the second time that day, shouldering my pack and decid-

ing to move to a new location resulted in an offer of a ride. "Where are you headed for," asked a cheerful young man. "San Bernardino," I replied. He readily agreed to transport me to the bus station at San Bernardino. Fitting myself and my pack into the front seat was a bit of a challenge. My pack had to be squeezed under the low-slung, sporty dashboard and balanced between my legs and lap. Jack, the friendly, animated young driver, was full of conversation and enthusiasm. He told me that he was a seminar leader for "Life Springs," a life-enhancement organization located in San Rafael, California. He was full of fascinating stories about Hollywood personages he had met. He was also interested in my hike and asked me lots of questions. Soon, he announced that he could take me all the way to the Los Angeles Amtrak if I didn't mind waiting while he made one brief stop along the way. I responded quickly that I certainly didn't mind. Although I am not usually a devotee of riding in open-roofed sports cars, this was a fun ride. Jack told me that his little Italian sports car was a "Bertone," a limited edition. He scooted in and out of freeway lanes and kept up an interesting conversation all the way. He delivered me right to the door of the Amtrak station in time to board the noon train. This enabled me to reach San Francisco a day earlier than expected and gave me an extra bonus—being able to walk across the Golden Gate Bridge on the day of its 50th birthday, May 27, 1987.

The memory of my ride from the Redlands junction to Los Angeles Amtrak in the little red Bertone will always live in my memory as one of my most interesting, fun-filled, exciting rides during my journey. I knew that when I came out from the trail at Highway 18, rather than at the Van Dusen Canyon trailhead, that I would definitely want to return to complete the eight-mile section between the highway and Van Dusen

Canyon trailhead. Periodically, while walking the trail, I heard accounts of hikers who had skipped or hitchhiked parts of the trail. This was definitely not a part of my trail-walking style. Therefore, while in the vicinity of Big Bear City in 1989, while completing another section of the Trail in Southern California, I returned to Big Bear City and completed the eight-mile section. It was a pleasant and easy walk through pine forest, with some gentle slopes and contours. I enjoyed occasional views looking back toward Highway 18 and the eastern hills, which brought back memories of the May 1987 snowstorm.

Chapter 3
Big Bear City to Cajon Pass
June 1985 • 62 Miles

...The sculpture of the landscape is as striking in its main lines as in its lavish richness of detail... The whole landscape showed design, like man's noblest sculptures. How wonderful the power of its beauty! — *John Muir*

This short section offers a great variety of scenery. Starting at Van Dusen Canyon, the trail wanders through pine forests traversing gentle slopes. For the next 19 miles, the trail hugs high above the banks of Deep Creek, affording spectacular views looking down at the boulder-strewn Deep Creek Gorge. As the creek bed widens and flattens, the trail leads into the arid, treeless landscape of the West Fork of the Mojave River. The walk from the river to large, reservoir-built Silverwood Lake continues on sandy, arid land. From Silverwood Lake, the trail climbs up Cleghorn Ridge and passes through colorful pillar formations before dropping down to Crowder Creek and nearby Cajon Canyon.

It was possible in 1985 to get all the way to Big Bear City on public transportation. I reached San Bernardino by bus and then boarded a small, local van bus to Big Bear City. There were two other passengers riding on the bus, and the trip included hearing intriguing stories about local celebrities. At the local bus terminal, the White Bear City Dial-A-Ride was most generous and helpful in offering me a ride to the base of Van Dusen Canyon. Thankfully, I was on my way.

On my walk to the trailhead in Van Dusen Canyon, I saw a small, bushy-haired animal, which I tentatively identified as a gray fox. I had not sighted a fox before, so I was excited.

As I had arrived at the trailhead rather late in the afternoon, I made camp amongst some small trees not far from the Van Dusen Canyon Road turnoff.

My next day's walk led through some small trees and then climbed up a ridge, opening up an expansive view looking south across Big Bear Lake. By evening, I reached water at Holcomb Creek and found a pleasant campsite under some tall Jeffrey pines. Later, I noticed a tent had been erected a few yards from my campsite. I didn't hear anyone stirring. I wondered.

The next morning after breakfast, a woman accompanied by a good-sized Doberman pinscher emerged from the tent. She came to meet me, and we enjoyed a friendly conversation. I learned that she was from Long Beach. She planned to move on to the West Fork of the Mojave River in a few days, so I agreed to look for her when I reached the Mojave River.

By early afternoon, I arrived at the Deep Creek Road, where I planned to take a detour to pick up a food package at Lake Arrowhead. I decided that it was a good time to look for a ride for the 4-1/2 mile trip to the post office. Although I was assiduous not to accept rides while walking on the Trail—I wanted to walk every step of the way from Mexico to Canada—I was always happy to accept rides to off-trail sites, such as post offices and bus terminals.

I soon met two friendly day hikers, Patricia and Roger. Patricia offered me a ride at 3 pm, when they would be returning to their motel. I was pleased with the offer. However, when Roger returned at the appointed time, he announced that he had found a ride for me. I think that Roger had developed other plans for the afternoon. My new ride offer was from a pleasant young man who deposited me at the post office door a little before five o'clock. At the post office window, the clerk reported that my package had not arrived. What a shock! The thought of food packages not arriving is one that has haunted me periodically, but previously, they had always been waiting for me. I was puzzled. Then, the kindly postmistress suggested, "Could the package have been sent to Lake Arrowhead?" "Yes," I replied. Isn't this Lake Arrowhead?" I learned that the friendly young man had deposited me at the post office at Cedar Glen. Lake Arrowhead was three miles further! It was too late to reach Lake Arrowhead that evening. I would need to stay overnight and go to Lake Arrowhead for my package in the morning.

I searched but could not find a sheltered hideaway for my evening's campsite within a reasonable distance. All the small islands of woods that I explored were surrounded with houses close by on either side. I ended up camping beside a half-built, unoccupied house, hoping that by placing my bedroll in a small ravine, I would be reasonably well hidden. I soon learned, however, that I was not really hidden. A young man walked up and started talking to me. I learned that he hoped to convert me. He was an Evangelist. I listened respectfully to him. I admired his ability to quote Scripture from memory. He was a handsome, redheaded young man. He was well dressed in appropriate summer clothes, had nice manners, and proved to be likeable. He looked like he could have been an All-American baseball or basketball player. I have often thought about him.

To this day, I still wonder if he continued as an Evangelist or whether he moved on to other pursuits.

When it grew dark, I realized that I was even less hidden than I had been in the daylight. People came down a path from nearby houses shining flashlights. I felt conspicuous. To this day, when I see people who are homeless, huddled at the edge of houses and roadways in towns and cities, I remember my experience of being encamped in plain view of people passing by me at Cedar Glen. I recall my bit of experience of what it feels like to be homeless.

At the village coffee shop the next morning, I told a friendly man seated at the counter of my dilemma of the misdirected food package. He responded by offering to give me a ride to Lake Arrowhead. I didn't even have to beg!

At the Lake Arrowhead post office, my package had arrived safely. I rejoiced. I repacked my pack and pondered how to return to the trailhead. The road to Cedar Glen from Lake Arrowhead looked hot, narrow, and full of whizzing cars. The area near the post office was full of fashionable shops and did not look conducive to finding a ride. I decided to walk toward the road leading to Cedar Glen. Just as I turned around to shoulder my pack, the same man who had transported me to the post office earlier reappeared and offered to give me a ride back to Cedar Glen. Again, I was lucky, as he asked me if I would like a ride to Rock Creek—about halfway to my destination. "Yes," I replied. "I would really appreciate the ride." Arriving at Rock Creek, I climbed out and thanked him sincerely. He told me that he had had to hitchhike when he served in the Army in Europe and that he could understand what it was like.

There remained a two-mile walk to return to the trail at Deep Creek Bridge. Soon, a pickup with a homemade-looking brown wooden shingle van approached me. "Are we headed north?"

they asked. I replied, "Yes, you are headed north," and reached into my pocket to show them my map. Just then, their muffler fell off. As they stopped to recapture it, I let them know that I was also going north to reach the trailhead at the Deep Creek Bridge. I said that I would appreciate a ride. They hesitated, then explained that they had a dog in the back of the pickup. They then proposed that they would let the dog decide if I should ride with them. Thereupon, they let the dog out of the back of the pickup. He immediately growled at me. He rejected me. I felt rejected. I walked the rest of the way to the bridge.

When I arrived at Deep Creek, it was midday. I was eager to be on my way, but I realized that I would be facing the mid-afternoon, hot western sun on the trail with no tree cover. My eager impulse stirred me to go on; my cautious reasoning said to wait. So, I waited, washed socks, wrote notes, gathered water, watched the fishermen, and looked at my watch. I had learned to follow a practice, in coping with hot sections of the trail in which there is danger of sunstroke and dehydration, of hiking early in the day; when it grew hot I found shelter and resumed hiking in the late afternoon when the sun sank low enough to create a shade cover and the afternoon breezes began to blow.

When the afternoon wind started to stir, I eagerly started on the Deep Creek Trail. What glorious views! The trail above Deep Creek is cut into a steep sidewall. Deep Creek runs through a narrow canyon. One looks almost straight down at the gentle creek as it weaves its way around granite cliffs and boulders. It was an exhilarating scene—a place of special beauty. It reminded me of a miniature Yellowstone Canyon, but with the light colors of granite, rather than the red rock colors of the Yellowstone country. I thought of John Muir's famous and apt description of the light-colored rocks in the Sierras—"The Range of Light."

DEEP CREEK

Toward evening, the river canyon began to widen. I saw deer paths leading down to the creek bed. I began to feel a strong desire to camp beside the stream. I had read in the guidebook that there was no legal camping between Holcomb Creek and Deep Creek Campground—a 19-mile stretch! I am usually a law-abiding citizen, but there are times when I am ready to deviate. This was one of them. The third deer path down looked hikeable. Down I went and found an idyllic campsite on light-colored sand, complete with a few well-placed rocks that served as convenient tables for my gear. I enjoyed a peaceful night, surrounded by the sights and sounds of beautiful Deep Creek Canyon.

In the morning, after making my steep climb up to the trail, I soon reached Deep Creek Hot Springs. This is a popular hot springs spa, located a few yards off the trail. It is not far from a roadhead at Mojave River Reservoir. It was Saturday and crowded with swimmers. I had no desire to join them. Furthermore, the guidebook stated that the springs were inhabited by a rare microscopic amoeba that had caused serious illness for some swimmers.

I was glad to reach the high bridge over Deep Creek by midday. It was time to seek shelter from the midday desert sun. During my midday sun break, I notice a man moving around at the other end of the bridge. When the evening breeze began to stir, around four o'clock, I came out from under the bridge, we met and had a brief, pleasant conversation. He told me he was from nearby Hesperia. He had been coming here frequently to walk. He said he was moving slowly because he had fallen recently and had cracked two ribs. He seemed ready and glad to share his story with me.

By evening, I reached the Mojave River Fork Reservoir, where I had planned to reach water and camp. By 1985, the campground had virtually disappeared. It was not a very pleasant area. It was full of motorized bikes and dune buggies tearing up and down the sandy mounds by the slow, trickling river. Even though I camped some distance from their playground, it was noisy until late at night.

My next day's walk to Silverwood Lake was, fortunately,

not as hot as the previous day's walk. There was a gentle breeze. Early in the morning, I saw a tent a few yards from the trail, and I was quite sure it belonged to the camper with the Doberman pinscher whom I had met at Holcomb Creek. She was not up, and I decided that it was too early to disturb her. I passed Cedar Springs Dam and soon caught sight of Silverwood Lake. Toward evening, I spotted a little, halfway-hidden trail leading down to a delightful lakeshore camp. I was so pleased with my secluded lakeside campsite that I did not notice the smell of a nearby dead fish until it was time to retire. I decide to try to ignore it. How wonderful to be lulled to sleep by the magical music of the waves lapping.

During the night, I was awakened by a puzzling sound—that of cans rattling. I am always on the lookout for squirrels and small rodents ravaging for food in my pack at night, so I aimed my flashlight on my pack and clapped my hands. There was no evidence of squirrels. In the morning, after climbing up to the ridge where there was a jeep trail, I discovered fresh beer cans. The rattle had not been made by animals, but from late-night human invaders.

Another hot day. It felt hot by 7 am as I climbed up to the trail. I was planning to reach the Cleghorn picnic area on the south shore of large Silverwood Lake for my afternoon siesta and sun break. I reached the breezy Cleghorn picnic area and was pleased to find an unoccupied picnic table, which I happily claimed. I looked forward to enjoying the cool breeze while resting under a nearby shade tree. My pleasure at my seemingly fortunate find was soon diminished somewhat. The beach at the Cleghorn picnic area was one of the dirtiest I've ever seen! Picnic plates and paraphernalia were scattered all over. I thought that the park should sponsor a "beach cleanup day" similar to the one our Sonoma Group Sierra Club sponsors each April at Salmon Creek Beach.

Upon my return home, I wrote a letter to the State Parks Department complaining about the dirty beach. I received a polite reply stating that the park staff was making great efforts to keep the beach clean. It was difficult, however, because the strong, gusty winds tended to deposit all the trash from miles around onto the south shore picnic area. I hope that by now they have found better ways to anchor the picnic garbage.

By late afternoon, as it cooled down, I climbed up to the top of Cleghorn Ridge and found a pleasant campsite on a saddle. It was a clear evening. I enjoyed scenic views looking back over glassy, blue-tinged Silverwood Lake.

On my morning walk from Cleghorn Ridge to Crowder Canyon, I moved ahead on an easy trail. I made good time. I came to some light, sandy-colored pillar-and-post formations, which reminded me of a small-scale Badlands. At lunchtime in the Crowder Canyon, I found a tree by a dry creek bed. What a joy to have a shady spot to eat and rest.

After my noontime siesta, I carefully picked my way through a washed-out trail beside an arroyo. I arrived at Cajon Junction, my trail destination, in the early afternoon.

At a 24-hour coffee shop at Cajon Junction, where I stopped for a cold drink, I was pondering how to locate a ride to the train when, looking around, I saw two highway patrolmen having coffee. I thought, "I'll ask them about a ride." I remembered a trail walker, whom I had met in Southern Oregon, telling me about securing a ride to the trailhead from a helpful highway patrolman. I told them my story. They had no suggestions. They seemed impatient to get on with their coffee and conversations without being interrupted. I was disappointed. Later, when I told a friend about my disappointment, she said that perhaps they didn't respond because it is illegal to hitchhike on freeways. I hadn't thought of that. I then decided to walk across the overpass leading to the other side of the freeway near the Los Angeles on-ramp. I stationed myself near a small grocery store. I approached a young woman who had come out of the store and was about to get into a station wagon. She listened to my story and agreed to take me to a train station near her home in Santa Ana. I was so relieved and pleased. The ride was enhanced by an interesting and stimulating conversation. She was interested in my walk. She had a young child in the car whom I learned was a foster child. She took me all the way to the Santa Ana train depot—a sizeable, attractive station. I was thankful to have a ride all the way to the station, and I thought about how fortunate I was to meet such good people, like her, who bothered to help a stranger.

I boarded the next train to Los Angeles. At the downtown Amtrak station, I was able to secure a reservation for the next morning's Coast Daylight. I arranged to spend the night at the YMCA in Hollywood, which has a section set aside as an American Youth Hostel.

While waiting for the No. 27 city bus in downtown Los Angeles, I had a memorable conversation with a middle-aged-looking Hispanic man. On seeing my pack, he asked me, "Why do you do this? Most people who do this are young." I let him know that I enjoyed walking and backpacking and that I especially enjoyed the beautiful scenery of the mountains. He looked puzzled and replied, "You have to be in good health." I answered, "Yes, I am in good health." As I boarded the bus for the Hollywood "Y," I doubted that I had convinced him about "why I do this."

Chapter 4
Cajon Pass to Mojave
May 1989 • 182 Miles

*All the wide world is beautiful, and it matters but little
where we go... The spot where we chance to be always
seems the best.*
——*John Muir*

The trail in this section traverses the ridge of the San Gabriel
Mountains. Although most of the Pacific Crest Trail, in its winding from Mexico to Canada, heads in a northerly direction, this
section points toward the west, as the San Gabriel Mountains lie
east and west. The westerly direction of the trail continues until
it approaches Lake Hughes, where it heads north again.

Most of the trail in the San Gabriel wilderness passes
through forests. Although within close proximity to large population centers in Los Angeles County, the trail passes through
landscapes that offer the look and feel of wilderness.

I found the walk through the San Gabriels to be most pleasant. I was aware and in awe of the fact that I was such a short
distance from a population center of approximately 12 million
people. As I looked down from openings in forest ridges toward
the west, I recalled visiting my Aunt Ruth in Pasadena and marveled that I was relatively close to her home. I also recalled that
when John Muir had hiked the San Gabriels, he saw bear and
mountain sheep. The bear are gone, but there still are reports of

sightings of mountain sheep on some of the steep trails. I did not see any. I saw very few people on the trail in this section and, except for the frequent crossings of Angeles Highway and talking to the few people in established campgrounds. I felt, on the whole, that I was hiking through wilderness and could understand John Muir's enjoyment of the San Gabriels.

Upon descending from the San Gabriel Mountains, the trail starts its downward journey toward the immense, arid Mojave Desert. In its downward journey, the trail leads across some grassy hill slopes and through some valleys with small trees. At the time of my walk, I passed through the villages of Aqua Dulce, Green Valley, and Lake Hughes and then walked across a section of the Mojave Desert before reaching the town of Mojave.

The original plan, with its objective of leading along the crest of the mountains from Mexico to Canada, called for the trail to pass through the Tehachapi Mountains. The section through the Tehachiapis was the last section of the trail to be completed. Reportedly, the Tehachapi section was delayed pending negotiations with the owners of the large Tejon Ranch to obtain a right-of-way.

It was on June 5, 1993, the day proclaimed as National Trail Day, that the completion ceremony for the Pacific Crest Trail took place. As a member of the Pacific Crest Trail Association, I attended the completion ceremony, which took place in Robin's Nest Park in Soledad Canyon. The keynote speaker was Secretary of the Interior, Bruce Babbit.

To reach the trailhead at Cajon Canyon, I boarded the San Joaquin Amtrak in San Francisco, and when I reached Bakersfield, I transferred to an Amtrak connecting bus to San Bernardino. From San Bernardino, I obtained a ride to the Cajon Pass.

It was a little chilly when I arrived at Cajon Pass the afternoon of May 10. The sand-colored hills were a dull red color, dotted with streaks of shadows reflecting a mixture of patchy clouds and the setting sun. I found the trailhead heading north. After walking a short distance, I felt the chill of the wind and cool air. I decided to make camp. Looking around, I found a small bedroom-sized level spot amongst some small bushes. I was within view of the Mormon Rocks, and recalled the story of the origin of their name—Mormon pioneers who had settled in the San Bernardino Valley had traveled through Cajon Pass.

Earlier in the day, contemplating equipment needs for my walk through the high desert, I had been thinking that my winter ski underwear, so frequently used in the chilly evenings while in the mountains, would be of little use in the high desert. Not so. Here I was in this sandy desert canyon on a cloudy, windy day, getting into my layers of ski underwear and donning my windbreaker. Soon, the sky darkened, and the wind came up. I hurriedly put up my tent and climbed into it. It started to rain. I could hardly believe it. How glad I was to be inside my newly acquired tent that I had purchased for my walk later in the year during August in rainy Washington. It proved, however, to be very useful during May in Southern California.

My next day's destination was the town of Wrightwood. It was a four-mile detour off the trail, but I had heard so much about the generous hospitality of Wrightwood residents toward Pacific Crest Trail hikers that I had decided that I did not want to miss visiting this town.

My route to the west called for crossing the railroad tracks twice. I found the first crossing easily, but the second crossing showed evidence of new railroad construction that had obliterated the trail. Eager to reach Wrightwood, I decided to detour by walking on the railroad service road until I reached Lone Canyon Road. I was aware from glancing at the map that this road generally followed the San Andreas Fault. As I turned onto Lone Canyon Road, I thought, "I'm going to hurry. I am walking along the bottom of the rift of the San Andreas Fault." I soon reached the crossroad leading into Wrightwood and arrived at the center of town in the early afternoon. I sighted a Mobil gas station and announced to the station attendant, "I'm hiking the Pacific Crest Trail, and I'd like to find a place to stay for the night." The response was surprisingly quick and direct. "I'd be glad to have you stay at my house, or, if you would like, you would be welcome to stay at the Methodist Camp, where they have reserved a space for Pacific Crest Trail hikers." I opted to stay at the camp, and the friendly gas station attendant gave me a ride all the way to there.

Arriving at the camp, I was greeted warmly by the director and led to a clean, comfortable cabin. I was then invited to return to the main building for dinner. I joined the staff at the dinner table and enjoyed a delicious supper. One of the staff members had grown up in Petaluma. We reminisced about the Old Mill and the French Cheese Factory. Before I settled into my private cabin for the night, the staff gave me a weather report: A cold front was expected.

The hospitality continued in the morning, when I was served a delicious breakfast. I then had my picture taken for the Pacific Crest Trail register. I noticed that three hikers had recently registered and were a few days ahead of me. I thanked the friendly staff and said goodbye, then walked down to the post office to pick up a food package. I then went to the drug store to buy some postcards, where I found and signed another Pacific Crest Trail register.

After a snack in a nearby café, I walked north to find the Acorn Canyon Trail, a cross-trail to reach the Pacific Crest Trail. Starting my hike up to the ridge, I passed the Rio Stella Camp, where I filled my water bag.

I felt so good at having been treated so generously by the friendly people of Wrightwood. I was glad that I had detoured for this unusual experience. How reassuring to know that there were such people of good will. I vowed that I would send the camp staff a thank-you gift. On my return home, I sent them a box of candy.

It was a steep climb up Acorn Canyon to the Guffy Campground, situated along the ridge at 8200 feet. I moved slowly. I was in a leisurely mood and enjoyed the view looking down at Wrightwood.

When I reached Guffy Campground in the early evening, I soon felt the cold air. I could see patches of snow on a north-facing bank. I hurried to put up my tent. By 6 pm, my thermometer registered 30 degrees! I hurried down the 200 yards of the steep canyon to reach the spring described in the guidebook and filled my water bag for the night. Just as I was ready to retreat into my tent to prepare a simple supper, a woman from the adjacent camp came over to ask, "Can you eat a little chicken?" "That would be very nice," I replied. Soon, a young boy presented me with a paper plate heaped with a chicken breast and home-fried potatoes. It was such a generous helping that I wasn't sure I could eat it all. I ate slowly. Compared to my usual backpack fare, this was more than I was accustomed to eating. However, I didn't want to waste any food, so I ate slowly and finally managed to eat it all. I walked over to thank my benefactors. The couple and their young son were car-camping. As I had discovered, Guffy Campground can be reached by car on a mountain road. The family commented that it was unusually cold for mid-May.

I was glad to crawl into my sleeping bag, wearing all my layers. I soon felt the warmth and softness of being surrounded by the goose-down-feathered bag.

Suddenly, I was jolted out of my sleepy reverie by the roar of cars, followed by a blast of loud voices. At first I was frightened. What could all of this lead to? Then, after listening awhile, I concluded that this was probably a group of young people enjoying a Friday-night getaway. With this assumption, I poked my head down into my bag and was almost able to drown out the noise.

The next morning, I decided to be friendly (and also I was curious), and I walked over to the nearby camp to say hello. One of the young men was stirring a pan over a fire said with astonishment, "I didn't know anyone was here. I hope we didn't disturb you. We would not have made so much noise if we had known anyone was camped here." I smiled and replied that I realized that it was Friday night. They replied that they had come for the weekend. They did indeed appear to be likeable young men. I no longer felt angry and, instead, felt friendly toward them. Later, as I was hiking along the ridge, I thought of how glad I was that I had stopped to get to meet these young campers. How often I had had the experience of feeling angry and hostile on a brief encounter with people and then come to like them after finding them friendly.

My next destination was Grassy Hollow Campground. It was a short walk, only about six miles. However, it was one of the coldest and foggiest days I have ever spent on a trail. I had left camp late, around ten o'clock, as I had waited for the sun to warm the air. It had warmed up from 30 degrees to about 45 degrees. I stopped to take a picture of a fog cloud resting on distant Mt. Baden Powell. A few minutes later, a fog cloud moved in, surrounding me and cutting visibility to a few feet.

I reached Grassy Hollow Campground in the early afternoon. I soon sighted a raised American flag beside a mobile home, the customary sign that the camp was staffed by a camp host. Camp hosts serving in national parks and forests are often retired couples who volunteer during the summer. I approached the camp host and announced, "I am hiking on the Pacific Crest Trail and I would like to camp here for the night." "The campsite fee for one night is $10.00," he replied. "The campsite fee is customarily waived for Pacific Crest Trail walkers," I answered. He looked at me, paused, then suggested, "You could camp in my yard and then I could waive the fee." I happily agreed.

The cold continued. The camp host declared, "This is winter weather!" My thermometer registered 30 degrees. I was so cold that I climbed into my feathered sleeping bag for a before-supper warm-up. When I finally was warm enough to cook my dinner, I followed the camp host's suggestion. I made a pine-needle fire—it smoked, but the warmth felt so good.

Climbing back into my bedroll, I decided to eat often from my cache of foods marked, "Night snacks," to guard against the threat of hypothermia.

In the morning, the friendly camp host and his wife emerged from their camper and offered me coffee. I declined, explaining that I had already eaten my breakfast. Another man, a friend of the camp host who occupied a nearby camper, asked, "Do you mind if I ask you your age?" I replied, "No, many people do ask me. I am 71." He volunteered that he was 75, and the camp hosted added that he was 65. I think that they were proud to be camping at their respective ages. Actually, I thought to myself that they did not look especially young for their ages. I thought they moved rather slowly. Nevertheless, they seemed to feel good about their level of activity for their ages.

SNOW STORM ON MT. BADEN POWELL

Before I departed, the camp host offered me a brochure featuring, "Herbs Which Cure." He added, "You can order these and sell them." I thanked him, waved goodbye, and started north on the trail.

The trail continues along the ridge, passing through pine forests. It was very pleasant and easy walking. It warmed up to around 50 degrees.

When I reached the Mt. Baden Powell trail, I passed a number of day hikers. It was Sunday, Mothers' Day, May 14. One happy group of day hikers on their way down from the mountain announced, "We made it to the top!" Mt. Baden Powell, at 9399 feet, is named after the founder of the Boy Scouts. It is a popular pilgrimage climb for Southern California Scouts.

I made camp in the early evening in a comfortable, level spot near Lemel Springs, at 7700 feet. I was well settled in my tent when I heard the pitter-patter of rain on my tent roof. I could hear thunder in the distance.

Anticipating the 2000-foot climb up Mt. Baden Powell, I started early. I moved slowly up the well-marked trail until, nearing the top, I encountered moderately deep snow banks.

This made it difficult at times to locate the trail, which switch-backed steeply up toward the summit. Gazing down in an attempt to locate where the trail led across a snowbank, I suddenly lost my footing and began to glissade down a steep snow chute. At first, I was frightened. "Now you have blown it." I thought. Then, looking down toward my feet, I spotted a low-growing pine bush that poked its top about two feet above the snow. I steered my feet toward it and came to a stop.

Feeling safe and grateful, I thought, "That was almost fun—like children sliding joyfully down a snowbank." Then, I realized another problem confronted me. I had let go of my walking stick, which had come to rest about 25 feet below me. I was not about to abandon my useful aluminum staff. How was I going to reach it? I surveyed the surrounding terrain. I concluded that the only way to rescue it was to slide down to the next dry spot on the trail. First, I sent my pack down so as not to have it encumber me by pulling me to one side or the other. Then, I steered myself down. Thankfully, I gathered my pole and pack, then laboriously and cautiously started up the trail again. Before I reached the top elevation of the trail, it started snowing, and the fog moved in. I could hardly see. I thought to myself, "I just need to reach the top and then I can start down." I moved slowly with my head bent down, trying to stay on the snow-covered trail. Finally, after what seemed like a long time, I reached the top and started my slow descent. I had not the slightest desire to climb up the spur trail to the summit of Mt. Baden Powell. This was not a day for a "view from the top."

I was so thankful to be starting down. Again, it seemed like an interminably slow walk through the snow and fog. I started counting switchbacks in an effort to pass time. I was aiming for Little Jimmy Campground at 7450 feet. Slowly, the slushy snow turned into rain.

As I approached Little Jimmy, the storm started with increasing vehemence, with blasts of thunder and lightening and heavy pelts of rain. I hurried. The thought occurred to me, "I shouldn't be walking through open spaces wearing my metal-framed backpack in this thunder and lightening storm. I could be a target for lightening strikes." Fortunately, most of the trail led through forest. So, when I came to open spaces, I ran hurriedly to reach the next tree cover. I certainly didn't feel like stopping to wait out this storm. I was eager to reach shelter.

Finally, I reached Little Jimmy Campground at around 4: 30. It was still raining very hard. I hurriedly took shelter in the small vestibule of the restroom. No one was occupying the campground. I decided to wait out the storm under the roof of the vestibule. The hard rain continued to pelt down on the roof and surrounding ground. I was beginning to think it would never stop! I waited and debated: "Should I spend the night here in this cramped, most-unaesthetic quarters, or should I brave the storm to put up my tent?" I measured the vestibule space. It was just six feet by three feet—a little shorter than my nine-foot bivouac sack—and I would be sleeping on a concrete floor! I vacillated and waited. Eventually, feeling a little more rested and regaining some ambition, I ventured out, located a level spot under some tall Jeffrey pines, put up my tent, and crawled in to make my supper and spend the night.

By morning, I was weary of the loud ping, ping, ping of raindrops on the roof of my tent. I was weary of the continuing rain and fog. I even considered going out and leaving the trail for a day or two of rest from the rain. It would be easy to get out from Little Jimmy Campground, as I was very near the Sierra Highway. I could not remember ever considering leaving a planned trip on trail before because of weather. To carry out such a plan, I think I would have felt like a defeatist. I hesitated. I waited a long time before getting out of my feathered bag. Finally, I peeked out and "hallelujah!"—what a wonderful surprise—the sun was out. It was so good to see. Actually, I was still hearing, at a slower interval, the ping, ping on the tent roof because I was camped under a big-branched pine tree that held water in its needles for a long time following a storm. I joyfully started to break camp. I put up my clothesline and dried my damp ground cover and tent so that I was able to pack with dry gear.

What a delightful day! No fog, no rain, no snow. I moved along. It was easy to follow the trail through the San Gabriel Wilderness. The trail continued to follow close to the Angeles Crest Highway, and I made three crossings of the highway during my day's journey. Most of the day, I was walking in a tree-lined area, but around mid-day, the trail broke out into an open area briefly at Kratka Ridge. This is a ski area with signs leading to ski runs. I had a special interest in Kratka Ridge, as a good friend had told me that Kratka was her maiden name. She had tried to trace the origin of the name by writing letters and asking in nearby villages but had not yet found any information on who the ridge had been named after. Was the name's origin part of her roots? I took several photos of Kratka Ridge and ski area signs to show her.

By evening, I made camp beside musical Rock Creek. I felt so good at having experienced such a delightful, sunny day.

After dinner, I watched the sunset light up Eagle Roost—a colorful, sand-colored nearby pedestal.

In the morning as I was packing my gear, two young men appeared. They were the first hikers I had seen in two days. They were hiking the Pacific Crest Trail and hoped to go as far as they could into Oregon or Washington before they had to return to school in September. One of the hikers was from Frankfurt, Germany, and the other was from Virginia. I asked the German hiker, "How did you learn about the trail?" He replied, "I found a trail guide in a mountaineering store in Germany." The two hikers had met near Campo and were hiking together. They told me that they were eager to reach the RV camp in Soledad Canyon where, according to the guidebook, they could have a shower.

I had another good day of pleasant, easy hiking. It was even warm enough to take off my ski underwear—the first time I had had it off since leaving Wrightwood. Again, the trail stayed close to the Angeles Highway and crossed it a couple of times. My camp was near Sulphur Springs Campground, where I found a pleasant camping area near a grassy meadow.

My walk the following day headed north to ascend toward 7124-foot Pacifico Mountain. I had chosen to camp at Mount Pacifico Campground, as it was on a ridge and was described as offering a view looking west toward Pasadena. Arriving in the late afternoon, I detoured off the trail a short distance to fill my water bag at Fountainhead Spring. I then hiked up to the Upper Pacifico Campground and searched for my "view from the top." I walked back and forth, searching and testing for a level spot with the hoped-for view. It was hard to find the place I was looking for. Finally, I set up my tent. The view was disappointing, as the valley below where I had hoped to see the Pasadena area was covered with a cloudy, gray smog.

After I had set up my tent and had my supper, the wind rose and grew steadily stronger. Soon, it was blowing a gale force. My tent was swaying and rattling. It was too noisy to sleep. I was unhappy with my camping spot, but thought that it was impracticable to move. It had grown dark. I crawled into my feather bag and tried to cover my head and ignore the noise. I tried to relax. Another big gust of wind rattled the tent and, around the same time, a car blasting loud music screeched by. That was too much! I decided to move.

First I walked without my tent or equipment to the wind-sheltered side of the ridge. I searched around with my flashlight. My new headlight-flashlight proved to be very helpful. This is a rather flat, round light that fits on a broad elastic band, which fits around one's head and frees both hands to work with gear. Fortunately, a half-moon helped to light the landscape. I found a partly sheltered spot and tested for the wind. It was adequate, but not ideal. It had a slightly downhill slant. I attempted to hurriedly clear the ground of branches and pine cones. I returned, making two trips—one carrying my made-up tent with poles in the sleeves, and a second trip carrying my pack with gear hastily stuffed inside. After placing my tent in the new location, I quickly crawled in and quickly crawled out again. A stick was poking up exactly in the middle of my tent, which would be poking the middle of my back. I got out, tipped my tent, and removed the offending stick. From my new campsite, I suddenly discovered that there was an intriguing view of the lights of east-valley towns, which created a veritable light show. I had missed the hoped-for view to the west of the Pasadena area, but now I was enjoying an exciting, unexpected view.

The following morning, I had a pleasant descent through a forest of small pines and spruce. Some areas showed evidence that they had been scarred by past forest fires.

At Mill Creek picnic area, on the Angeles Forest Highway, I estimated and measured out my water for the next nine miles. While I was occupied with measuring water, an older man approached me and declared, "Walking is good for you." I thought to myself that he looked like he could use some exercise. He was a little pudgy and slow-moving. He continued, "My wife spoils me, but we respect one another." She then emerged out of the restroom and smiled and agreed with him. He went on to tell me that they had been married for 42 years. He had worked for the railroad for 44 years. They were on their way to Palmdale, where they went once a week to eat at a Chinese restaurant.

On my afternoon walk, ascending toward Messenger Flats, I encountered a day hiker coming down toward Mill Creek. He told me that he was walking the Trail by sections, mostly by arranging for day hikes. He had completed most of the sections from Campo to Lake Hughes. He did not think he would ever complete the entire Trail. He needed to hurry, as his wife, who helped him with car shuttles, would soon be looking for him at Mill Creek.

Toward evening, I passed a side road leading to the signed Mt. Gleason Young Adult Conservation Corps Center. I was near enough to hear voices shouting back and forth. Shortly after, I passed a newly erected sign—Camp Buck Trail. I followed the new path leading to a newly constructed but waterless campground. I could pick from many newly cleared campsites. No one else was occupying the camp. I found a level, scenic spot beneath some tall pine trees. At night, I could hear music from the conservation camp.

In the morning, I descended to the Messenger Flats Campground, my next water stop. I was really angry and upset about the condition of the trail. After several days of following a well-marked trail, I reached this section, just east of Messenger Flats, of completely unmaintained trail. I threaded my way down to Messenger Flats on a barely discernible trail that wound down through knee-high chaparral blackened by a 1985 fire. It was hardly a trail at all.

At the Messenger Flats Campground, I measured out my water for the afternoon. A group of talkative, school-aged day campers clustered around the picnic tables.

After leaving Messenger Flats, I soon came to the junction

of the trail to Acton, which, until recently, was the route of the Pacific Crest Trail. From this junction to the North Fork Saddle Ranger Station, again, the trail had not been maintained and was barely discernible. I waded again through bushes knee-high and taller, including high-growing poison oak. I thought to myself, "This trail is not worthy of a National Scenic Trail designation" and vowed to write to the Forest Service complaining about this on my return home.

I assumed that many hikers opted to walk on the road instead of the trail. Perhaps, this is the reason that the trail had been so poorly maintained. When it comes to trail choices, perhaps I'm a bit of a purist. I try to stay on the trail whenever possible.

Arriving at the North Fork Saddle picnic area, eager to fill my water bag, I soon discovered that the water faucets had been turned off. I was angry all over again. What should I do? I looked around and then walked over to the nearby ranger fire station. It presented a "Keep Out" look, with a fence and a big, locked gate. There were several buildings inside. No one was in sight. I looked around and then squeezed through the crossbars of the gate. I spotted a hose near one of the garages. I filled my water bag, then returned to the picnic area where I had left my pack.

The guidebook had indicated that no camping was allowed in the picnic area, so I explored around and found a hideaway to spend the night on a small, sandy, level bench a few feet below the saddle. During the night, I could hear the humming buzz of nearby high-tension power lines.

The trail from North Fork Saddle to Soledad Canyon descends steeply down a sandy ravine. It was a far cry from the usual trail construction standards of the Pacific Crest Trail. The sandy, eroding trail bounced up and down roller-coaster style. The guidebook describes the trail as being hurriedly constructed by the Forest Service with the help of Boy Scouts, poorly constructed, and destined to quickly erode. Near the bottom of the trail, I met a man on a horse. He told me that he was very concerned about the poor maintenance of this section of the trail and said that he was having great difficulty finding out "who was in charge." He added that he had talked to a ranger, suggesting that a sign be posted reading: TRAIL DANGEROUS FOR HORSE TRAVEL. He was disappointed not to have received any response to his suggestion. I agreed with his concerns and added that I thought this was a very poorly planned trail and that as a result, it was becoming badly eroded, making it dangerous. I added that a hiker could easily get caught in a landslide and be plummeted down the steep canyon. I told him that I would write to my Congressperson upon my return home. I was really angry about the lack of maintenance of this section of the trail.

Toward the bottom of the trail, as I was nearing Soledad Canyon, my little toe started to hurt. The steep downhill slope had caused a lot of toe-jamming, which happens when one's toe hits the front of the boot. I stopped to tape it. It was quite painful. This made me more angry about the poorly constructed and maintained trail.

But some good came out of this experience. At home, I wrote a letter to my Congressperson and both my Senators, letting them know about the dangerous condition of the section of the trail from Mt. Gleason to Soledad Canyon. I emphasized that I did not think that this section was worthy of the designation as National Scenic Trail. Senator Cranston replied to my letter and also forwarded my letter to the Angeles Forest district ranger supervisor. The response from the Forest Service superintendent was disappointing. His letter was full of complaints about the lack of funds. I then seized the opportunity to nominate this section of the trail in the Backpackers Magazine contest to name the "ten most neglected trails." It was selected. As a follow-up, a member of the American Hiking Society wrote to me that he would visit and make an evaluation of the trail. I wrote to him about my concerns for this section of the trail and also wrote to members of the Pacific Crest Trail residing in this area. In addition, I revisited the trail two years later. I found considerable improvement in trail maintenance. The trail had been brushed. There was evidence of placement of water bars to prevent erosion. I then talked to the district ranger, who affirmed that the entire section had been reworked, brushed, maintained, and improved. She also reported that a group of horsemen had adopted the trail for maintenance. I was happy to see these improvements and felt that my letters had had some impact. I felt good that I had bothered to make an effort to improve this poorly maintained trail.

Finally, I arrived in Soledad Canyon and stopped first at the Cypress Park Resort, a private membership subscription resort. At the clubhouse, I enjoyed a refreshing root-beer float. It was hot, noisy, and crowded. It was Sunday. I asked for directions and walked to the public RV park called Robin's Nest. I picked out a camping place by a picnic table and then searched for a store described in the Guidebook where I had planned to supplement my food supply. It was closed. What a disappointment! I would have to ration my food until I reached Aqua Dulce, another day-and-a-half walk. As I was sitting by the picnic table, some friendly residents of the RV park came over and asked, "Are you hiking on the Pacific Crest Trail?" "Yes, I replied." They enthusiastically asked me questions about my journey on the trail and invited me to join them for supper. I felt so good. They were friendly and interested in my walk. I suggested that I would like to have breakfast with them (I was running low on cereal). When I let them know that I had planned to buy a few things at the store and was disappointed to find that it had closed, they introduced me to their neighbor who was going to drive to the nearest store, about a mile down the road; she invited me to go along. There, I bought a few things to supplement my supper. I spent the remainder of the daylight hours watching the procession of campers move by my camping space. Suddenly, we were all interrupted by loud screeching sounds of sirens. Emergency vehicles came to a stop near the far end of the campground. A few minutes later, a helicopter roared low and landed. I, together with most of the other campers, followed the happenings by walking nearer to the site, where we could see that a red sports car had missed the turn in the highway and plunged down a steep bank, coming to rest in a swampy area. I didn't wait to see the rescue crew extract the passenger from the sports car. I did not want to watch the disaster—probably not a cheerful sight. I walked back to my camping spot. About 20 minutes later, I could see and hear the helicopter take off.

Back at my campsite, I settled in for the night. Although the campsite was noisy, I had a good rest. The next morning, I joined the friendly residents for a delicious breakfast of flavorful granola and fresh-brewed coffee. I was deeply moved by the generosity and goodness of these people toward me. I especially appreciated their kindness at a time when I was running low on food. They occupied a humble home—a small RV camper—and were so generous to me as a trail traveler. I still remember their generosity to me.

Following my refreshing breakfast with the friendly RV residents, I started north. The trail crosses a culvert under the Southern Pacific Railroad tracks and then climbs up a grassy hill. I soon heard barking sounds, like those emitted from a large animal kennel, only more so. I remember my RV friends telling me that a former animal trainer had established a kennel of lions that had been retired from the movies at Studio City. How strange to be hearing lions on my walk on a California mountain trail.

I was now heading north. Soledad Canyon marked the end of the western traverse along the ridge of the San Gabriel Mountains. By afternoon, I walked on an underpass, which crossed under the noisy, four-lane highway leading from the San Fernando Valley towns to the desert town of Palmdale. I soon arrived at Vasquez Rocks County Park. These rock formations are most picturesque and colorful, dotted with red and pink pedestals, pillars, and posts. I really enjoyed my walk through this area. The Guidebook tells us that these rocks were named after a famed bad man named "Vasquez," who hid out in this rocky area. The Guidebook also tells us that if we lose our path, we should head for the rock that resembles a tilted Matterhorn. I soon lost the path. I spent the remainder of the afternoon occupied in a cross-country hunt for a trail that would lead me through the park. I climbed up and down the red pillars and posts searching for landmarks. I soon became uncertain that I was aiming for the tilted Matterhorn. By the time I reached one tilted-looking Matterhorn, I discovered another and pondered on which was which. It was fun and exhilarating.

By late afternoon, I came to the far side of the park and found a dirt road. It looked like the area belonged to a shooting club. The dirt road soon deposited me on a blacktop road leading into the town of Aqua Dulce.

It was time to look for a camping place. I decided that the best place to camp would be in the vicinity of the north entrance of Vasquez Park. I entered, found the ranger's house, and knocked on the door to ask permission to camp, as the Guidebook had recommended. The only problem was that the ranger was not home. I went to fill my water bag at his hose, but realized that his garden hose might not provide potable water. As I was pondering on what to do next, a car pulled up. The driver was also looking for the ranger. I asked him if he thought the hose water was potable. He replied that he was not sure, and then pulled out a water jug and gave me a generous supply of potable water. I moved a short way of the road and staked out a comfortable camping place. No one else was camped at the park. In the morning, I stopped to say hello to the cheerful ranger. He said he had gone out for dinner when I came into the camp.

I moved up the road a short way to the Aqua Dulce post office, which occupied a section in a food store. When I asked the postal clerk for my food package, she added, "You have some letters." What an unexpected and happy surprise! Not only did I find my food package waiting for me, but I received unexpected birthday cards from my brother and sister.

I moved to a small nearby store and bought cold fruit juice and post cards. I was ready to start walking to Mojave. After writing and mailing postcards, I started on my way. The trail starts by weaving in and out of small roads dotted with ranch houses. I had the impression that the people who live in this area love horses, because horses and stables were very much in evidence. The trail then climbs up the Sierra Pelona Ridge from which I enjoyed a splendid view in all directions. I could look back and see the top of Mt. Baden Powell, of snowstorm memory.

Before reaching Big Oak Springs, my destination for the night, the trail descended down the ridge through a grassy area. The spring itself is surrounded by fairly tall bushes, and the Guidebook warns that one should be careful not to brush against patches of stinging nettles. They can cause an uncomfortable stinging and itching if one brushes against them. My campsite amongst live oaks near the spring was alive with birds.

I enjoyed a beautiful serenade during the evening and again in the early morning.

My next day's walk to San Francisquito Canyon led up and down through low hills. I made a detour in the late afternoon to the village of Green Valley. Approaching with the thought of seeing the village and enjoying some refreshments, I met a young man on a mountain bike. When he learned that I was hiking on the Pacific Crest Trail, he was full of questions and said, "I admire you for your adventure. I would like to do more hiking."

In the village, I went into a café for a sandwich and coffee. It was a busy, noisy place. It was so noisy, with loud music and people talking, that for a moment, I thought of taking my sandwich outside to a picnic table. Then, an unexpected thing happened. The talkative waitress offered me a piece of birthday cake, explaining that they were celebrating one of their customer's birthdays. I smiled and said, "No thank you." The piece of cake looked too big and sweet for me to absorb, but I enjoyed the coincidence. It was my birthday!

I was glad to get back to the trail again. I hiked a little further and found a hideaway up a little-used road near the San Francisquito fire station—my next planned water stop.

In the morning, I arrived at the San Francisquito fire station, which was surrounded by a tall, green fence. I had to search for water, and I finally spotted a man moving around in the fenced yard. I called to him, "Where can I get water?" He replied, "How long will it take?" I said "Just a few minutes. I need to fill my water bag for my hike to Lake Hughes." He pointed to the hose and said, "Hurry, I need to lock the gate in a few minutes." I hurried, filled my bag, and went on my way.

As I walked along the trail leading to Lake Hughes, I debated: Should I take the newly constructed trail that skirts around the edge of Antelope Valley, or should I take the old trail that strikes directly north from Lake Hughes leading straight across Antelope Valley on the western edge of the Mojave Desert. The trails both meet at the Los Angeles aqueduct and pass east toward the town of Mojave. Browsing through the Guidebook, I had been enthralled by a full-page picture of the scene looking across Antelope Valley toward the distant, barren hills. I decided I wanted to take the old route—the route pictured in the photo.

I arrive in the town of Lake Hughes around 3:30 pm and found the small post office, housed in a picturesque old rock house. I collected my food package. Not being sure of a camping place and water on the edge of town, I decided to spend the night in Lake Hughes. I moved across the street to the RV camp and signed up for a camping place, including a shower, for $8.

How good it felt to have a shower, even though the outside shower stall, which looked as though it had seen better days, had a floor that was dotted with moss and algae.

The RV camp was on the shore of small Lake Hughes. A breeze was blowing off the lake. I walked around the campground with my bandana held high, using it like a windsock, and found a spot that seemed least exposed to the wind. Toward dusk, a large woman arrived and announced that her family was coming, adding that they always camped here and had camped in the same place for three years. As she talked on, it became apparent that they had always camped on the spot that I had selected and that she was hoping I would offer to move. I decided to resist her appeal to me to move and to stay put. I reasoned that I had arrived first and didn't want to be exposed to the wind. I responded to her by saying that I would only be camping there for one night. Toward dusk, a pickup drove up and parked near my sleeping bag. Two men got out and started noisily unpacking. I was already resting in my sleeping bag and determined to hold onto my space, when I heard loud hammering about five feet away. The next time I poked my head out of my bivouac sack, I found myself next to a huge tent. One of the men said he was sorry to disturb me and smiled and continued hammering stakes for the big tent. They were a jolly and talkative group. Fortunately, they did not stay up too late.

In the morning, several adults and children kept emerging from their tents. They said to me, "Isn't it cold?" and asked, "Were you cold last night?" I said that I was not really cold because I was wearing several warm layers of clothing.

It was a different experience for me, spending the night in my bivouac sack and having a large multi-generation family move in close to me, pounding tent stakes directly beside me. They were so talkative—bilingual in English and Spanish—and full of the joy of celebrating their traditional holiday weekend. I was glad, however, that I was camping there for only one night.

After leaving the RV camp and leaving behind my camping space, as promised, to the large family celebrating their holiday weekend, I turned north and climbed up to the ridge of the Leibre Mountains. Soon, I had my first view to the north across Antelope Valley and on to the western end of the arid Mojave Desert. I was enthralled. I paused a long time to look. Although it was hazy, I could see faintly in the distance the foothills of the Tehachapi Mountains where I would be heading to reach the Los Angeles Aqueduct. The scene certainly did resemble the photo in the guidebook, which was labeled, "The Long Desert March Through Antelope Valley."

As I walked on, I felt the indefinable attraction of the desert—the feeling of sky and space. I was also intrigued on seeing the shimmering, iridescent airways hovering above the ground. I thought perhaps this was the sort of scene that caused thirsty desert wanderers to visualize a mistaken water hole—a mirage.

The trail descended to the Fairmont Reservoir, a huge body of water storage for some section of the long, thirsty Los Angeles Aqueduct. Reaching a side road, I passed a horse ranch and soon reached straight, level, telephone-lined 170th Street, which would lead north toward my destination in the hazy foothills of the Tehachapi Mountains. Striding across Antelope Valley, I was still intrigued by the desert feeling of space and sky. By late afternoon, I began to realize another characteristic of desert travel—the deceptiveness of the feeling of distance. As I was striding along, the foothills of the mountains seemed relatively close, but by late evening I still had not reached them. I decided that it was time to find a camping place. I hiked off the road a few yards and found a level spot under a Joshua tree. I finished my supper and was viewing the landscape when I noticed a car on the road driving slowly and stopping frequently. I thought to myself, "Although I estimated that I had enough water to last me until I reached the aqueduct, it would be good to have a little more. I'll ask them." So, I approached the car and said, "Water." There was a puzzled response; then I said, "Agua?" The woman I talked to shook her head and said, "No." I started back from the road to my camping place, then heard the car back up to reach me. The woman said, "We have a little water." I ran back, got my water bag, and she and the male driver brought out a jug and filled my bag. My water friends then smiled and explained to me joyfully that they were out having "a little fun" gathering cans. We talked for a few minutes. I learned that they lived near Lake Hughes. I thanked them several times for their generosity. They smiled happily. They also added that I should be able to get some water tomorrow at the sprinklers by the alfalfa fields.

My walk from Antelope Valley to the Los Angeles Aqueduct ended around noon, when I reached the Aqueduct Road. Eager to march on, I hadn't stopped for water at the alfalfa ranch sprinklers. I wanted to be assured that aqueduct-dipping for water still worked. From the Guidebook and from reports of Pacific Trail hikers, I had learned that hikers had adopted a system of lifting the circular iron cover on test holes above the buried aqueduct and dipping a container on a string down to retrieve water. I was prepared. I had my can on a string. Technically, the Guidebook mentioned that this is illegal, but hikers ignore the illegality since it provides much-needed water for many miles of hiking along the aqueduct. When I reached the Cottonwood Ridge water hole, I was greeted by a sign that read: DO NOT DRINK THE AQUEDUCT WATER. This was an unexpected surprise. I had drunk aqueduct water earlier for several days during May while hiking from Mojave to Weldon. As a precaution, I purified the water.

I found some shade under a willow tree by Dry Willow Creek for my lunch stop. The shade was pleasant, but the scene was unpleasant. There was considerable litter in the dry creek bed. I discovered that this was a fairly busy place. It was Memorial Day, and a goodly number of dirt bikers were going up and down the aqueduct road. One of them stopped to talk with me. He told me that he was from Bellevue, Washington. He commented on how different the landscape was here than near his home in Washington. He also commented that we were fortunate to have a cool weekend for the desert.

I stopped early in the evening, around 4:30, as the wind had come up and it was blowing hard enough to make walking difficult. Also, I was tired from my interesting, but long, march across the desert. I found a level place under some Joshua trees just a few yards off the trail. I was tired and lay down on top of my bedroll for a before-supper nap. The nap turned out to be my before-supper nap, my after-dinner nap, and my night's sleep. I discovered that I felt slightly dizzy and nauseated. I wondered about the strange-tasting water my can-gathering friends had given me on 170th street. Whatever caused my upset, I decided to sleep it off. I was fine by morning.

In the mid-morning, as I was walking along the aqueduct road, I heard shooting—to me, a fear-filled sound. As I approached a man standing in the road, I waved. The shooting stopped. When I drew closer to him, he said, "We were having some fun shooting." I smiled and greeted him, saying, "I hope you have a good weekend of camping."

As I continued on, I felt fortunate that I was hiking this shadeless desert section during a relatively cool spell. I had heard tales of hikers who were forced to seek shade during the day because of the scorching desert heat and to hike only during the night.

As I resumed my walk after lunch near an aqueduct water hole, the afternoon westerlies started to blow. They swirled about me with considerable force. I became aware of the need to balance so that I would not be blown off my feet. I walked with my feet spread apart and my hands outstretched. I also learned to be prepared for lulls between heavy, sudden gusts of wind. When I was leaning forward into the wind so that I would not be toppled over backwards and a gust suddenly changed direction, I needed to quickly regain my balance to stay upright. It proved to be a game of balance alert.

I stopped early, after laboring with the wind "balancing act." I found a comfortable campsite amongst some chaparral bushes.

My next day's walk from Water Hole 844 to the town of Mojave—approximately nine miles—was surprisingly fast, perhaps the fastest walk I have ever experienced. As I turned south onto Old Creek Road leading to Mojave, the wind was at my back—I had a tail wind. I really had to walk fast, whether I wanted to or not. As I was pushed along by the tail wind, I still had to be careful to avoid losing my balance. The sudden gusts caused me to lurch from side to side. A car passed me just as I had experienced a sideways lurch. I thought, "What must they think?" They were seeing a hiker lurching like the proverbial drunken sailor.

I was also seeing evidence of the fiercely strong winds, as a field of wind machines generating electricity came into view. Their silver blades were whirling noisily and swiftly. I had expected to arrive at the town of Mojave by mid-afternoon, to spend the night there, and to board the bus the following day. Instead, I arrived at 11:00 am! I had plenty of time to catch the scheduled 1:30 bus.

My first stop in Mojave was at the Pancake House. I ordered a big breakfast, choosing a plate of corned-beef hash and eggs. After ordering, I retreated to the restroom and looked in the mirror—what a horrendous surprise! My face was black! No wonder the waitress had looked at me strangely. When I started my superficial face cleaning, I discovered that the washbasin in the restroom did not have any running water! I attempted to clean my face with some Noxema cleansing cream and Kleenex. That did not do the job. I looked around and decided to lift the toilet tank top to obtain some water. I went to work on my face. Finally, I was able to remove, at least partially, the layers of dirt that had clung to my greasy sunblock-cream-layered skin. To this day, when I hear mention of the town of Mojave, I remember that this was the place where I came out from the trail with a very black face.

In spite of the deficiencies of the small restaurant, especially the rest room, I enjoyed a tasty corned-beef-and-eggs breakfast. I then moved over to the bus stop. The bus was late. When the driver finally arrived, he complained about the heavy holiday traffic. The bus did make the train connection in Bakersfield,

and I climbed happily on board. I felt awkward sitting on the
train crowded with Memorial weekend passengers when I had
not had a chance to shower or to visit a laundromat. Nevertheless, I enjoyed the scenery. I particularly like the section where
the train passes through the Delta, and I could see ducks and
waterfowl from the train window.

It was good to be home a day early. It felt so good to soak in
a hot tub and to peel off several layers of desert dust. Refreshed,
I started thinking of my next trip. It was my summer to complete the Southern California section and then, hopefully, to
touch the border monument in Canada.

Chapter 5
Mojave to Weldon
May 1989 • 67 Miles

...Who could imagine beauty so fine in so savage a place?
Gardens are blooming in all sorts of nooks and hollows...
—John Muir

This short section presents some variety of landscape and interesting contrasts. The first several miles continue along the Los Angeles Aqueduct surrounded by the sandy terrain of high desert. The temporary trail then turns west and heads up Jaw Bone Canyon, which is dotted with colorful red and yellow stratified cliffs and pillars and posts. The canyon leads beside a small creek bordered by willows and cottonwoods and passes a spring-fed pond that has been designated as a bird and wildlife sanctuary. After ascending a ridge, the trail drops down into tree-lined Kelso Valley. I continued on the Kelso Valley Road, the alternate route, to reach Weldon. The newly completed Pacific Crest Trail now passes to the east of Kelso Valley and culminates at Walker Pass on Highway 178 east of Weldon.

The town of Mojave was a trailhead for me. It was the first section that I completed in May, 1989, on my walks in Southern

California. I chose to complete this section early because it contained no high mountains that had the potential of snowstorms into early June. It also had the potential for desert heat. In my planning, I remembered that the Guidebook recommended that hikers complete their desert walks before June 1.

I arrived in the town of Mojave by Amtrak connecting bus from Bakersfield to Mojave on May 2. Although the trail was not far from the town of Mojave—around two-and-a-half miles—reaching it was not an easy or pleasant walk. I started my walk by heading north. Soon, I was buffeted by strong afternoon westerlies. Then, as I reached the north outskirts of Mojave, I came to a busy intersection of Highway 14 leading to the eastern Sierras, then Highway 58, leading between Bakersfield and Barstow. Both seemed to me to be occupied by super-sized trucks. I stopped to study and ponder, "How am I going to get across this frightening, high-speed roadway? Will I ever make it?" At home, friends and family ask, "Aren't you afraid of wild animals?" "No," I answer. But here I am really frightened at crossing a high-speed highway. Finally, there was a lull in the traffic and I hurried across.

After another mile of walking along the shoulder of busy Highway 58, buffeted by the sound of roaring trucks and balancing to stay upright when pitched by gusty winds, I was relieved to finally reach the trail crossing. I turned onto a little-used road that runs alongside the Los Angeles Aqueduct.

I was eager to locate an aqueduct test hole. This was to be my source of water for the next several miles. Would I find it and would my retrieval system—my newly created rope-and-can pulley work? I soon found a test hole, carefully lifted the lid off, and eagerly and fearfully lowered my can attached to a long rope until I felt a tug on the rope. I had reached the swift current of the aqueduct stream. I pulled my can up and was delighted. I felt assured that my water retrieval system really did work.

I felt that I had no more water worries until the trail left the aqueduct. I made camp in a secluded, sandy dip a short distance from the aqueduct road. The wind continued to blow incredibly strongly. I was careful to anchor everything down. I anticipated that it was going to be this way all along the desert walk by the aqueduct. However, I was happy to find that when I awoke around 3 am, the wind had died down. It was calm and quiet in the morning when I made breakfast and broke camp.

My next day's walk continued northeast along the aqueduct road. The ambience of desert views surrounded me. I was viewing a floor of light-colored sand and a roof of pale, green-blue desert sky. The air was relatively calm until around midday, when the afternoon westerlies came to life. By the time I arrived at the small town of Cinco in the late afternoon, the wind was blowing swiftly and noisily again.

The town of Cinco consists of Tokiwa's Restaurant and a gas station. The sign at the restaurant read, "CLOSED ON WEDNESDAY" (it was indeed Wednesday). I searched around the windy landscape and decided to take advantage of the restaurant's closure by eating my dinner at their sheltered picnic table and to use their conveniently located water faucet. I enjoyed my leisurely supper and was relieved not to have to struggle with anchoring everything down while making dinner. For my bedroom site, I explored and found a sandy ditch that I thought would offer a little protection from the gusty winds. However, the wind was still incredibly strong and noisy.

By mid-morning the following day, I reached the small town of Cantil and went into the combination post office and grocery store to call for my food package. The postmaster searched and searched amongst a stack of boxes and then said, "Your package has not arrived. Perhaps it will arrive tomorrow." Thinking back,

I remembered questioning the postal clerk in San Francisco two weeks earlier as to whether I should send my package Fourth Class or First Class. She thought that it was not necessary to send it First Class. I realized that she did not know how small and remote the town of Cantil was and that mail delivery was not swift in this area. What should I do? I pondered and decided I did not feel like waiting for the next day. I was eager to move ahead to Jaw Bone Canyon. I decided to take an inventory of my food supplies and then buy additional food in the store to supplement my existing supplies. I only needed rations for four days. I searched the grocery shelves and bought two granola bars, two small cans of spaghetti, a can of beans and a few nuts and M&Ms to add to my trail mix. As I left to go on my way, I thought, "How lucky I am that at the only post office where my food package failed to arrive, I only needed food for four days."

Shortly after passing the town of Cantil, the trail turns west and leads up Jaw Bone Canyon. By midday, I was feeling the heat. I looked around and took shelter under an aqueduct bridge. Ordinarily, the aqueduct is buried underground, but in Jaw Bone Canyon, where the aqueduct passes a wide, deep wash, the aqueduct is suspended above ground. This overhead structure provided me with a relatively cool place for my afternoon siesta. While waiting hopefully for the cooling afternoon westerlies to blow up the canyon, I reviewed my trail guide and map and plan for my next campsite. I remember that yesterday a friendly aqueduct overseer had stopped his truck and asked, "Are you a Pacific Crest Trail hiker?" "Yes," I replied. "We keep a Pacific Crest Trail register, and hikers are welcome to spend the night in our yard. We have good water and large shade trees. Our house is located three miles west if Cantil, just off the Jaw Bone Canyon Road."

Actually, I hadn't thought too much about his kind offer until now, when it continued to be very warm, and the offer of shade trees and good water became very appealing. I decided to accept his offer. When I left my shaded hideaway to walk the approximately two miles to the caretaker's home, it was very hot. The walk was on blacktop road, and I was traveling west, facing the afternoon sun. It was a relief to reach the shade trees of the caretaker's yard.

I was enjoying the shade and the fresh water when Mrs. Walton (not her real name), the caretaker's wife and her young, school-aged daughter, drove up. "I am walking on the Pacific Crest Trail," I announced. Mrs. Walton was most friendly and hospitable. She invited me into her kitchen, where I signed the Pacific Crest Trail register and drank some luscious ice water. She laughed as she told me that she had just received the results of an employment aptitude test she had completed. She had scored high in three job categories: probation officer, social worker, and lumberjack. She really enjoyed laughing about the third classification—that of lumberjack. She remembered checking something about being able to lift heavy objects and thought this may have led to the lumberjack classification. As I was enjoying the ice water, the phone rang. It was her older married daughter, who was now living in the San Fernando Valley. The daughter's car had stopped, and Mrs. Walton immediately promised to drive over and help her out. As she hurried off, she told me to feel free to use the kitchen, and as a parting gift, offered me some sweet strawberries. They tasted so good.

Outside in the Walton's yard, I picked a comfortable place to lay my bedroll and cooked my supper. I took advantage of the luxury of washing my dishes inside and filled my water bag for an early-morning start. It would be a fairly long walk—approximately eight miles—to my next water stop at Butterbredt Springs.

During the night, resting comfortably on the Walton's soft, grassy lawn, I awoke to find that the Walton's two friendly dogs had plopped themselves down on my sleeping bag and were leaning against me. They had found a soft bed.

In the morning, I started early, and it was pleasantly cool. When I turned off Jaw Bone Canyon Road to reach the temporary trail going up Alphie Canyon, I noticed the Walton's two friendly dogs were romping and circling around me. I was concerned and hoped that they were just out for a short run and would turn away and head for home soon. I tried to ignore them.

When I stopped for a snack, they were not in sight and I rejoiced, thinking, "Now they have started back to their home." My rejoicing was premature; soon they came racing back to my resting place. I was beginning to become concerned. "What should I do to discourage them?" I thought of three possible approaches: first, I could hide in the chaparral. I quickly eliminated this possibility, as I knew they were too smart not to find me. Next, I thought of being firm and throwing rocks at them. I quickly eliminated this possibility. I couldn't bear to do such a thing. I decided that the best approach was to continue to try to ignore them. For the next several miles, I tried not to look at them or talk to them. I tried hard not to respond in any visible way to their amusing antics as they raced after rabbits and other unrecognizable prey and then came trotting back looking like they had achieved some great accomplishment. When we passed by some cattle, I noticed, however, that they were not so brave. They retreated quickly from these bigger animals.

Traveling north up Alphie Canyon, trying to ignore the romping dogs, it was time for me to concentrate on finding the next turn to the left, which would lead up to Butterbredt Canyon. I was being cautious and trying to concentrate on this somewhat obscure-sounding temporary route. I had heard of hikers becoming lost in this area. The Guidebook directions stated: "Continue on Alphie Canyon until you near a hill ahead of a wide diagonal stripe, which is a cantaloupe-colored dike of intrusive rhyolite." Moving ahead slowly, I located what I hoped was the mouth of the canyon and turned to the left. This was an intriguing and colorful area, with its yellow-and-red-striped rock formations. I was not quite sure whether I had located the cantaloupe-colored dike, but the directions seemed right, and I proceeded slowly. I felt more sure of the route when I reached the Guidebook's description of the head-wall of the cross-country section, which "required an easy Class 3 climb." This proved to be easy and fun, and I felt exhilarated and challenged by this cross-country section. Any hopes that the dogs would be discouraged by the climb up the head-walls quickly faded as they happily romped up and down between rock ledges, looking very triumphant with their accomplishments. Gradually ascending, the canyon slowly widened and small willows and cottonwood trees appeared. Shortly afterward, the cross-country section merged into a dirt road. According to the topo map, there had been a number of mines in this canyon. As the road widened and joined another dirt road, I came along-side a man on a motorcycle. "These dogs do not belong to me." I explained. "They have been following me from the aqueduct caretaker's house in Jaw Bone Canyon. I have been trying to ignore them, hoping that they will go home." He looked at them and observed that the brown-and-white dog was panting. He said firmly, "He needs water." This frightened me. I broke my resolve to ignore them, looked directly at them, and said, "We have got to get you to water."

I remembered passing a sag pond earlier near the willows and cottonwoods, so I hurried back to the pond. When we reached the water, Blackie and Whitie (as I started calling them) plunged in, drank water, swam, and splashed happily. I decided to camp nearby.

My supper atmosphere was a little different than usual. Much of my supper was consumed in a standing position. Blackie and Whitie were still intent on rabbit hunting and went dashing off at the slightest sound. When they were gone, I could eat sitting down, but when they returned—their noses aimed at my face and dish—I quickly stood up. I resolved that I was not going to share my carefully measured food supplies with them. I would be careful to see that they got to water, but reasoned that they could survive without food for several days. I still hoped that they would decide to return home.

After watching the sunset from the bank of the pond, I crawled into my sleeping bag. Blackie and Whitie curled up near my bag. I awoke once during the night and they were gone. I rejoiced. I concluded that they had left for home. I laid back and relaxed; then I heard "Woof, woof," and they came racing back after another rabbit hunt.

In the morning while eating my breakfast, mostly standing up, I pondered on what to do. I did not want to hike back to the dogs' owners' home in Jaw Bone Canyon. I studied my map. I knew that I would reach Kelso Valley around midday, and I would be near the junction of Kelso Valley Road and Jaw Bone Canyon Road. From there, it would be an easy run going east on the Jaw Bone Canyon Road to deliver the dogs to their home. This was where I planned to beg a ride for the dogs.

The trail continued to ascend Butterbredt Canyon and soon passed fenced-in Butterbredt Springs, which is set aside as an Audubon wildlife preserve. I stopped for water. A few red-winged blackbirds took to the air as Whitie and Blackie raced to the water, gulping and loping loudly as they drank.

I reached the high point of the canyon before it grew hot and started down the western side. Shortly before reaching the Kelso Valley Road, I passed a new Pacific Crest Trail sign marking the newly completed permanent trail section, which heads north to Walker Pass. I planned to return to walk on this new trail after I had obtained a ride for the dogs.

Just as I reached the road, I saw a pickup approaching. I waved vigorously. I felt hopeful. I told the young man in the pickup the story of the dogs following me and of my seeking a ride home for them. The driver listened and then replied that he was headed the other way—north toward Weldon. It was Saturday. He would be returning on Sunday afternoon and offered to give the dogs a ride then if I wished. How disappointing! I thought to myself that it would be a long wait; I would seek another ride. A few minutes later, a second man in a pickup stopped. He told me that he was on his way to spend the weekend with his parents at their ranch located just off Kelso Valley Road. When I told him the story of the dogs, I asked him if he could phone the dogs' owners upon reaching his parents' ranch. "We don't have a telephone." he replied. He went on to explain that the nearest telephones were in a settlement south of Weldon, approximately 13 miles ahead. He suggested that if I were not able to find a ride for Whitie and Blackie, that I walk to Kelso Road to the settlement. I agreed that this would be a better plan than to take the newly constructed longer trail to Walker Pass. He then volunteered to bring water for the dogs from his parents' ranch. Giving me directions, he said, "I'll meet you at the gate in 20 minutes."

True to his word, Martin was waiting for us when we reached the ranch gate. He handed me a cold Sprite and set down a large dishpan of water for the dogs. They swiftly and noisily attacked the water, "Gulp, gulp, gulp."

I asked Martin about water at the Skylark Ranch Reservoir, which had been mentioned in the Guidebook. He told me that the ranch was no longer managed by a live-in caretaker. It was managed by some distant manager who traveled to the ranch periodically. He thought it would be all right if I used the reservoir and gave me directions to it. I decided it would be a good plan to stop at the reservoir for a siesta to avoid the midday heat. I thanked Martin and moved on toward Skylark Ranch. I thought to myself, "Martin will remain in my memory as one of those helpful persons who aided me on my journey."

The Skylark Reservoir remains in my memory as the most vivid, desert-like oasis and colorful-bird sanctuary that I have ever experienced. Upon arrival, I caught a glimpse of ducks, wading shorebirds, and a multitude of colorful songbirds singing and twittering in the nearby willows. The luckless birds were quickly dispersed, however, as Blackie and Whitie vigorously gave chase. I didn't have time to identify my bird friends. Later, when the dogs were prowling some distance away, I was able to catch a glimpse of some colorful red-and-orange warblers, yellow-gold finches, and bright redwinged blackbirds.

I rested, bird-watched, and ate snacks until the late afternoon, when the sun sank lower in the sky and the afternoon breezes began to stir. The dogs appeared to grow restless. They seemed to have explored all the rabbit holes in the vicinity. Blackie sat down beside me, looked plaintively up at me with his orange-colored eyes, and gave a soft whine. I decided that we were ready to move on.

We walked north on Kelso Valley Road. One car approached. I waved. told them my story and asked for a ride for the dogs. They replied, "We are not going that far. We are going to visit some friends who live nearby."

We made camp a few yards off the road, sheltered by a

group of Joshua trees. I surveyed to find a level spot and laid out my bedroll. Then I turned my attention to my kitchen and to preparing my supper. When I turned around, I saw that Blackie had curled up in the middle of my sleeping bag. He looked content—perhaps a little smug. He also looked photogenic—like the ads in catalogues advertising dog-pillow nests. With his black, shining coat and orange-gold eyes, I thought

BLACKEY & WHITEY ALSO KNOWN AS
TUXEDO & ELWOOD

that he was as photogenic as the dogs in the catalogues. Although he was most appealing, I decided that he should not occupy the middle of my bed. I scolded him. He blinked coyly but did not move. Finally, I took action and pushed him off my bed. He and Whitie curled up nearby. They were relatively quiet during the night. Were they winding down a little?

The next morning we started early. I was eager to reach water and the settlement south of Weldon with the telephone. We soon reached the picturesque town of Sageland, an abandoned Gold Rush ghost town decorated with a couple of weather-beaten buildings. Blackie and Whitie quickly found water in the creek that flowed from Tunnel Springs, which Martin had told us about. It was Sunday, and there were quite a few weekend jeeps and motorcycles passing by. Blackie and Whitie did not seem as aware and fearful of cars as I was, and they continued to romp after rabbits. I was afraid of them being hit by cars. I kept calling to them, urging them to stay at the side of the road. I was beginning to worry about the dogs. Whitie, especially, seemed to be slowing down. He was still chasing rabbits, but not as energetically. I petted him and talked to him, saying, "We are going to get you to town and to your home soon."

Near Sageland, one pickup stopped, perhaps out of curiosity upon seeing a backpacker with two dogs. When I told the driver the story, he turned to his girlfriend and asked, "Shall we take the dogs to Jaw Bone Canyon?" "No." she answered emphatically. He wished me good luck.

Soon, when we reached a rise in the road, I could see the settlement. I felt reassured that we would soon be there. Like most desert views, however, it took longer to reach the houses in the settlement than anticipated.

Finally, we arrived and saw rows of neat-looking houses, surrounded by fences and set back from the road. How was I going to find a telephone? I walked by a few houses until a saw a man stirring near his garage. I waved to him and shouted a loud "Hello." At the same time, his neighbors' dogs started barking ferociously. He came to within talking distance of his fence. I continued to shout, telling him that the dogs had followed me from Jaw Bone Canyon and that I needed to find a telephone to call their owners. "I don't have a telephone." he replied. What a letdown! But then, he looked at us and being responsive to Blackie and Whitie, he let us into his yard. First, he set out a big pan of water and then returned with a bag of dog food, which he poured into another dish. Blackie and Whitie attacked the food vigorously. He seemed interested in the dogs and speculated about their breeds. He was intrigued by Blackie because of his orange-yellow eyes and pointed face. He thought that Whitie, with his gray-and-white fur might be some kind of Shepherd mix.

We thanked our helpful host and moved on to find a telephone. I passed up the home of his neighbor, who had been recommended by our kind host, as his dogs were barking so fiercely. I moved on until I saw a woman in her yard. I shouted to her, telling my story of needing to telephone to reach the dogs' owners. She quickly invited me in, but asked that I leave Blackie and Whitie outside the gate, as she had two small dogs. We found the Waltons' phone number in the directory and proceeded to call them. Nothing happened. She was puzzled. She tried again, with no success. Then she said, "I think my phone is dead. I guess my batteries have worn out. I don't have any battery replacements. She then offered to take me in her pickup to her neighbor-friend. I climbed in. I was, however, beginning to worry about Blackie and Whitie, whom I had left outside the fence. After all, they had come this far with me—I didn't want to lose them now. Besides, we had become close companions.

Thankfully, her neighbor-friend's telephone worked. The Waltons' number clearly rang, but the Waltons were not home. It was 12:50 pm. I remember Mrs. Walton had told me that they were active in their church. It was Sunday. I said that they probably were at church and that I would return around 4 pm. The helpful, kindly resident with the phone suggested that we could rest by the creek across the road while we were waiting. Eager to get outside the fence, I had a fearful moment when Blackie and Whitie were not in sight. After three or four calls, they came racing out from some side road. I was relieved. We made our way through a fence to a very pleasant wooded area beside a shallow, softly singing creek. Even Blackie and Whitie seemed ready to lay down to rest for a while.

Our rest was suddenly interrupted by barking dogs. They soon appeared, racing down a path near us. Then, a man emerged and asked in a stern voice, "What are you doing here? This is private property." As I told him my story, he listened. His tone changed from being stern to becoming sympathetic.

Around 4 pm, we trudged back to the neighbor's house with the telephone. This time the Waltons were home. "I have your dogs," I assured them. "We've been searching for them. Where are you?" I described to them the settlement 11 miles south of Weldon and agreed to wait for them outside a vacant white house at the north end of town. They estimated that they could reach us in about 45 minutes. What a relief! The neighbors and I were all very happy to have finally succeeded in reaching them. This prompted the neighbor with the working telephone to tell me a story about how her older dog had wandered off into the hills and was gone for 20 days. When he was finally found near her home, he was in sorry shape.

We returned to the white vacant house and took up our post on the steps, where we could see cars coming down the road. I coaxed Blackie and Whitie to stay nearby by petting them and telling them, "Your owners are coming for you."

Of course, I was excited in anticipation of their arrival. I kept looking at every passing car. I did not have too long to wait before the Walton's pickup turned into the driveway. Blackie and Whitie made a bounding dash and when the pickup door opened, they joyously leaped in, knocking Mrs. Walton flat onto the seat. Everybody was so happy that the dogs were, at last, reunited with their owners. Joining the excitement were two neighbors' dogs, one black and one tan. They began to bark and race around the truck. Mrs. Walton, being friendly and conciliatory, threw a stick, which the dogs retrieved.

As we reviewed stories of the dogs' walk with me, I learned that Blackie's name was Tuxedo—he had a small streak of white under his chin—that he was 15 months old, and was half Collie and half Weimaraner. This unusual combination accounted for his unique and intriguing looks. His orange-yellow eyes were that of a Weimaraner, and his long, pointed nose was that of a Collie. Whitie's name was Elwood. He was eight months old and was some kind of Shepherd mix.

The Waltons said that, although the dogs had romped in the nearby hills, they had never been away from their home for this long before. When the Waltons discovered that they were missing, they drove along Jaw Bone Canyon Road and up to Walker Pass looking for us. I guessed that we were probably off the road camping or getting water when their pickup had driven by. Finally, the excited dogs were persuaded to settle down in the back of the pickup for their ride home. We happily waved goodbye.

I started down the road for a short evening walk before sunset. I heard a rustle behind me. There, following me, was the new set of dogs—Blackie and Tannie. Blackie had a stick in his mouth. I marched back to their owners' home, which was adjacent to the vacant white house where Blackie and Whitie had waited for the Walton's. I shouted, "I'm going on my way now. Would you please hold onto your dogs?" The dogs' owner appeared, laughing. She knew my story. We had talked to each other earlier. Also, it was her husband who had met us by the creek and questioned me about being on private property. She called the dogs into the fenced yard. Laughing, she commented that her vet had said that young dogs are like "juvenile delinquents." I then turned and moved down the road, this time without any dogs.

I made camp around two miles north of the settlement, just far enough off the road to be hidden by a group of Joshua trees. For my supper dessert, I enjoyed some big, luscious strawberries that Mrs. Walton had brought me.

During my morning's walk to Weldon, I soon passed a very neat house, bordered by an equally neat white picket fence. It was surrounded by a finely manicured lawn containing a little, miniature golf course with a small pool in the middle. After quieting a handsome, prancing Doberman who was barking at me, the owner called out, "Are you the lady who is hiking the Pacific Crest Trail?" "Yes," I replied. "I heard about you and I admire what you are doing." "Thank you," I responded and added, "I certainly admire your nice-looking house and yard."

My next reminder that the inhabitants of the settlement seemed to be well aware of my walk and the story of the dogs occurred when a woman riding a fine-looking motorcycle pulled up beside me. She turned out to be the woman from the house with the dead telephone batteries. She explained that she was on her way to Weldon for shopping. (I assumed that her shopping would include new batteries.) She said that she was glad to hear that the dogs were happily returned to their owners. I learned that she had moved to the settlement from Salinas and added, "I love the desert." I asked her about spring wildflowers, and she said they were unusually beautiful around mid-March and that I should return to view them at that time. I said that I really would like to return to see the spring wildflowers in bloom.

Still another neighbor appeared and stopped her car. She was the woman with the working telephone. She asked, "Would you like a ride to Weldon?" "No," I replied." "I want to walk all the way on the Pacific Crest Trail." She then asked if I had heard the shooting the previous night. I replied that I had not. She said she'd heard shooting and did not know what had happened. She was puzzled and concerned.

As I reached a slight rise in the road, there appeared before me in the distance a glorious and welcome sight—my first view of the Sierra Nevadas. I was elated. The coloring of the southern border of the Sierras was muted and intriguing, with a touch of desert-haze shadows on the mountains. I was still enjoying the characteristics that make the desert attractive— the soft, muted colors, the shimmering hazy air, the long-distance views, and the wide expanse of the sky. I had stored up some good memories of desert views on my walk in Southern California—the Laguna Mountains, the views looking down at Deep Creek, and the long-distance views stretching across Antelope Valley toward the Tehachapi Mountains. Nevertheless, I was eager and excited in viewing one of my favorite trail sections—the Sierra Nevada, described by John Muir as "The Range of Light." I looked forward to hiking the southern section of the Sierras early in July.

I reached Weldon around noon and found Paul's Place, where I would board the Regional Transit bus to Bakersfield at 1:30. As I was enjoying a cold drink, a man appeared and recognized me. He was the owner of the black-and-tan dogs. His comment was: "You were lucky to reach the dogs' owners by telephone. You could have had the dogs for another week!"

INTRODUCTION TO CENTRAL CALIFORNIA SECTION
Weldon to Sierra City
493 miles

The trail on its journey through Central California is unique. It includes the longest section uncrossed by roads—from Walker Pass to Tuolumne Meadows, approximately 290 miles. It ascends the highest pass of the entire trail—Forester Pass—soaring 13,180 feet above sea level. It joins the world-famous and older established John Muir Trail for 177 miles of its journey through the High Sierras. It is overflowing with spectacular mountain scenery—towering light-granite peaks; pristine, sparkling alpine lakes; color-splashed, wildflower-filled meadows; rushing, music-filled streams; and cascading waterfalls. All of these and much more blend together to create a glorious scene to uplift the soul of the fortunate trail hiker.

My experience in hiking this section of the trail holds many special memories—my walk on the John Muir Trail, where I was first introduced to the Pacific Crest Trail and my first experience as a backpacker. In addition, this section is the closest to my home in the San Francisco Bay Area and is the section to which I have returned to most often. All sections of the entire trail hold their own unique natural beauty for me, but when I am pushed to answer, "What is your favorite section of the trail?"—I am inclined to name three or four special places in the High Sierras.

The High Sierras enjoyed special artistic description. John

Muir loved the High Sierras and wrote about them in his many publications, including Mountains of California. Ansel Adams and others have photographed them. During cold, dark winter nights, I lift my spirits by reading and rereading John Muir and revisiting Ansel Adams' photographs.

The Central California section is the only section in which I traveled north to south, rather than south to north, as described in the Pacific Crest Trail Guide. The reason for the reversed direction is that on my first hikes on the John Muir Trail, I followed the Starr's Guide to the John Muir Trail. In hiking the northern sections of the Sierras, I followed the Wilderness Press Guide to the Tahoe-Yosemite Trail. Both of these guides describe the trail from north to south.

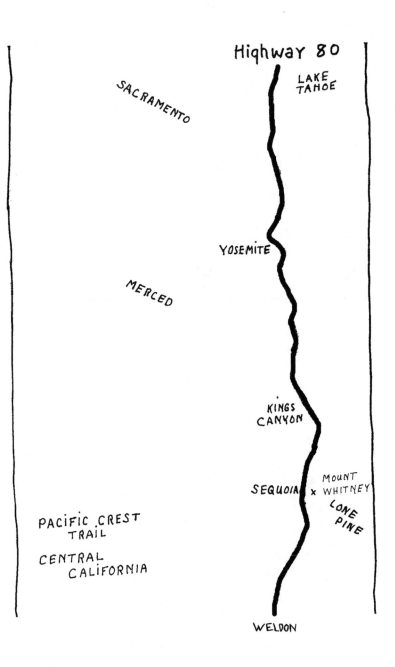

Highway 80

LAKE TAHOE

SACRAMENTO

YOSEMITE

MERCED

KINGS CANYON

SEQUOIA x MOUNT WHITNEY

LONE PINE

PACIFIC CREST TRAIL

CENTRAL CALIFORNIA

WELDON

Chapter 6
Mt. Whitney Trail Junction to Highway 178 near Weldon—July 1989
Lower Kern Trail—July 1973
105 miles

The whole mountain appeared as one glorious manifestation of divine power, enthusiastic and benevolent, glowing like a countenance with ineffable repose and beauty before which we could only gaze in devout and lowly admiration.
—*John Muir*

This southernmost section of the Central California segment of the trail passes through a variety of landscapes. The Whitney area is noted for its high, 13,000 to 14,000-foot peaks. Weldon, at 2,653 feet, is described as high desert.

The trail's descent from the Mt. Whitney area affords views of large, sandy meadows to the west and a view of the drained, salty, dried-up Owens Lake bed to the east. The trail passes through some tall sandstone-colored pinnacles before dropping down to grassy areas along the Kern River, and to large Kennedy Meadows. From Kennedy Meadows to the south, the landscape alternates between wooded areas, chaparral, and grassland.

In walking this section, I remember how good it felt to return to the Sierras after several years' absence. The view of the Owens Valley was puzzling in that it presented such a variety of colored sands—white, yellow, and green. It made me wonder what Owens Lake had looked like before it was drained to provide water for thirsty Southern California.

My Greyhound bus ride to the town of Lone Pine, the gateway to Mt. Whitney, was made more interesting and enjoyable by the presence of a young backpacker from Germany. I had boarded the midnight bus from San Francisco, arriving in Reno at 5:30 am, and then boarded the 6:30 am southbound bus for Lone Pine. Upon boarding the bus, the German asked me where I would be backpacking, and when I told him that I was backpacking on the Pacific Crest Trail and that I would be completing my last California section that summer, he asked if he could sit by me in order to receive advice on trails. I welcomed him. He said that he had tentatively decided on walking the trail from Bishop to Mt. Whitney. I supported his decision and told him that this was one of my favorite sections.

We ended up having an animated conversation about our mutual love for the wilderness. He expressed some very thoughtful ideas about why one chooses to hike alone and about the benefits one reaps from the opportunity to enjoy peace and solitude. We both heartily agreed. He said, "When you are with people, you talk and are distracted from observing the beauty of the wilderness." I agreed and also commented, "I think that you speak English very well." He replied by telling me that he had been fortunate, as a social worker in Germany, to receive an international scholarship that enabled him to work for a social agency in Minneapolis. Now, in addition to his regular work, he takes time out during the summer to lead hiking tours. He had decided to hike from Bishop to Mt. Whitney in order to explore the possibility of leading a tour of this section.

Before he disembarked at Bishop, I described a good deal of the section of trail he would be hiking. He was pleased and excited. I wished him well.

On the next leg of my journey to Lone Pine, two ladies and a gentlemen who had been sitting nearby and overheard our conversation turned to me and said, "Aren't you afraid to hike alone?" I responded that I was not afraid, and that I enjoyed the solitude and beauty of the wilderness. The man then told me that he was a horseman and that he went on a rendezvous with a group of equestrians every year. He liked to be comfortable and so he slept in a van. I couldn't resist asking him, trying to be somewhat tactful, about how he got his exercise. I could see that he was quite overweight. He responded, "I get much more exercise on a horse than you would think." Then he acknowledged that riding does not offer as much exercise as walking.

My first task after alighting from the Greyhound bus in Lone Pine was to find the Forest Service station to secure my wilderness permit. Then I would need to find a ride to the Cottonwood Lakes Trailhead, some 14 miles distant, up a steep, winding road.

I was a bit apprehensive. When I reached the Forest Service permit office, I overheard a couple ahead of me explain to the permit issuer that they were going into the trail at Cottonwood Lakes. I was alerted. As soon as there was a slight break in the conversation, I announced, "I am going into the trail at Cottonwood Lakes. I came to Lone Pine by bus and am hoping to find a ride to the Lakes." The couple was friendly and responded pleasantly that they had room in their car and were more than willing to give me a ride. I secured my wilderness permit with no difficulty. I was not applying to ascend Mt. Whitney, for which quotas had been established because of the high demand.

The friendly couple that offered to give me a ride was very interested in hearing about my Pacific Crest Trail walk. Virginia told me about her experience the previous summer, when she had joined a Sierra Club service trip in the Marble Mountains. She commented, "It was hard work." We enjoyed comparing notes on backpacking and wilderness camping.

Arriving at the Cottonwood Lakes Campground, I measured my water for supper and breakfast and started on my way. I was eager. At the edge of the campground, I met a couple of day hikers coming down the trail. As I stepped aside to let them pass, I announced, "I am headed for the Pacific Crest Trail. I plan to complete my last section of the trail in California. I've walked the rest of the trail, and I plan to go to Washington and walk the last 80 miles in August. Then I will have completed the trail." "Congratulations," they replied. I added, "It's been a great experience." I was really excited.

I moved along the trail until the sun sank low and daylight was fading. I spotted a tree-lined campsite among some large Ponderosa pines. I felt so good. I kept saying to myself over and over, "It is so good to be in the Sierras again."

In the morning, when the trail reached the entrance to the Golden Trout Camp, I turned in. I had planned a leisurely day to allow for altitude adjustment before climbing the 10,073-foot New Army Pass. I was curious about the camp; when I had passed by it on my 1973 walk, a couple from Oceanside, California, was inspecting the camp as a possible Audubon educational center. It had been privately operated and recently given up. The Forest Service was looking for a new lessee. I entered the attractive gateway and soon met some enthusiastic campers. I asked them about Audubon activities, and they told me that Audubon workshops were held. For information about classes, I could write to the Thacher School in Ojai. I was then introduced to the camp naturalist, who lives in Marin County, California. We had a pleasant visit, talking about environmental issues in the San Francisco Bay Area. She told me that she and her husband like to ride their horses in Annadell State Park, near where I live in Santa Rosa, California.

I moved leisurely up the trail to Cottonwood Lakes and, after exploring them in the early afternoon, I found what I thought was the perfect campsite. My level, circle-enclosed camp had side walls of large rocks with an open window that looked out upon the lake and to the distant high cliffs framing the lake.

The next morning, I started off on the trail, which I thought led to Long Lake and the approach to the New Army Pass. After a while, as the trail grew faint, I concluded that I was not on the Long Lake trail. The area around the lakes was crisscrossed by many unofficial fisherman-made trails. Furthermore, my dog-eared 1955 edition of the topo map wasn't exactly up to date. So, back I went to the last major junction, where I found the trail to Long Lake and New Army Pass. As a result, my planned morning ascent of the pass was made in the afternoon. Fortunately, the ascent up New Army Pass was relatively easy. From the top of the pass, at an altitude of 12,300 feet, the views were extraordinary. The view to the east scans three or four ridges and includes views of the White Mountains and the Owens Lake Valley area, with its mysterious whitish, saline-colored, arid desert look. The view to the west leads down to the Kern River trench and to the high Kaweah Peaks. To the north tower the 13,000 to 14,000-foot peaks of the Mt. Whitney complex.

The descent down Rock Creek Canyon was also an easy walk. I was glad to reach water and made camp around 7 pm, near the junction of the Pacific Crest Trail.

I was eager to start my walk south to Chicken Spring Lake and on to Kennedy Meadows and Weldon. During July of

1973, I had walked on some of the present trail from Mt. Whitney junction south to the lower Kern River Ranger Station. The present section of the Pacific Crest Trail to Kennedy Meadows had not been completed. I recalled that on my 1973 walk, I had camped at Crabtree Meadow near the junction of the John Muir Trail, which leads up to the top of Mt. Whitney. I had found a comfortable camp surrounded by tall Jeffrey pines. In the early evening, I had enjoyed bird watching and had spotted pine siskins, robins, juncos, and white-crown sparrows. I had watched the sinking sun light up and reflect a warm red glow on Mt. Whitney and its surrounding peaks. In the morning, however, I awoke to see a very sad sight—perhaps one of the saddest of my walk in the Sierras. Directly above my bed, hanging from a tree limb and swaying in the wind, was a dead hermit thrush. He had apparently been caught on someone's fishhook and was hanging from the nylon fishing line. How sad!

The trail south from Crabtree Meadow to Rock Creek climbs up to an open meadow at Guyot Flat, where I had paused for a refreshing fruit and tea drink and was delighted to be serenaded by a mountain chickadee. During my 1973 walk I had also camped beside pleasant, gurgling Rock Creek.

On the following morning, on my July 1989 walk, I started south on the new Pacific Crest Trail. I soon passed the Siberian Pass Trail and reached a wooded area where I happily found water in a seasonal creek. My lunch stop was at cirque-bound Chicken Spring Lake.

From a viewpoint above Chicken Spring Lake, I enjoyed looking down on Big Whitney Meadow. I found this meadow, together with other large meadows I caught glimpses of from the new trail through windows between the trees, to be intriguing. To me, they have a different look than high-mountain meadows. They seemed to be larger, flatter, sandier, and to possess more

BIG WHITNEY MEADOW IN
SOUTH SIERRA

tall grass cover. Although still high and framed by mountains, the landscape holds a hint of the high desert country to the south. Looking down at Big Whitney Meadow, with its own little wooded island in the center, I was reminded of my meadow walks returning from the Kern River in 1973. I had crossed the nearby Little Whitney Meadow and had hop-skipped over grassy humps, detouring around stolid, staring cows.

My next meadow memory was of elongated, sandy Mulkey Meadow. I had crossed the meadow during my 1973 trip to Cottonwood Lakes. I had camped the night before at nearby Tunnel Guard Station, and my peaceful campsite had been disturbed by the noise of aircraft engines. The next morning, I passed by white tents and white refrigerators and saw a man sitting in a camp chair by one of the white tents. I asked, "What is the name of this camp?" "Tunnel Air Camp," he replied. "I flew in last evening." I was surprised to find an air camp amidst the sandy meadows.

When I had crossed Mulkey Meadow, I was surprised to see two strings of packhorses coming toward me, stirring up a

**PILLARS & POSTS
IN SOUTH SIERRA**

cloud of dust. In the shimmering morning light, I thought of "Lawrence of Arabia." That desert-like image remains with me to this day.

Walking south on the new trail in 1989, I planned to camp at Chicken Spring Lake. I had made good time on this easy trail, so I just kept walking on and reached Poison Meadow.

I found a comfortable and pleasant campsite near Corpsman Creek, with a view toward Mulkey Meadow.

The next morning, after returning to the trail from my comfortable hideaway above Poison Meadow, I was striding along a comfortable, forest-lined trail when I heard voices. As I grew nearer, the voices grew louder. It sounded to me like someone was giving a lecture or teaching a class. Turning around a bend on a side hill, I came upon a group of young men. I found out that this was actually what was happening—a short, stocky man was delivering a lecture to a group of 10 or 12 teenagers. Seeing me, the instructor interrupted his lecture while we compared trail notes. He told me that his group had come into the trail at Kennedy Meadows and were on their way to climb Mt. Whitney. When he learned that I was walking the Pacific Crest Trail in sections, he turned toward me and said softly, "These young men are from Campo." I remembered that there was California Youth Authority facility at Campo. "How good," I thought to myself, "that they are having such an outdoor mountain experience." I hoped that this experience would change and enrich their lives forever.

I was periodically aware that this was a cow-grazing area. On a dip in the trail along the saddle, I found myself climbing down a steep, sandy, cow-trampled area. Soon, I began to question whether it was a trail or a cow path. It did not seem right. It did not seem like a planned mountain trail. I decided to retrace my steps. I climbed back up to the saddle and looking around, I found a faint but planned trail—the Pacific Crest Trail, rather than a cow trail. The trail led mostly through wooded areas with occasional views out across meadows to the west. In this area, the trail still remains high, at around 10,000 feet.

By evening, I arrived at a large, public corral. This camping corral looked relatively new and interesting in style, as it was equipped with its own fenced-in corral for equestrians. I inspected the campsites; no one else was around. In fact, the only hikers I had seen all day were the group of young men from Campo. I picked a level spot in a corner of the corral campground.

On my walk the next day, I climbed up a ridge from which I again enjoyed views of the large meadows of the south Kern River. By evening I found a charming campsite by a spring-fed creek in the vicinity of Death Creek Canyon. I had a little streamside garden of yellow mimulus—one of my favorite flowers. With their bright yellow faces, the tiny mimulus are always a delight to gaze upon.

As the trail continued south on my next day's journey, I began to observe the beginnings of a more high-desert look. The trail led through some red-colored rock pillars and posts. One of these pillar-like pinnacles offered a peephole view looking down to the east at dry Owens Lake—now Owens Valley. The dry, sunlit lakebed from the ridge view presented an interesting range of colors—greenish-yellow and white. It reminded me a little of the gradation of greenish and whitish colors of salt beds. It also reminded me of the story of the bitter water battle between the people of northern and southern California. Owens Lake was drained to ship water through the Los Angeles Aqueduct.

By evening, I reached the trail junction leading to Olancho Pass. There I found a pleasant campsite near a creek that ran through Monache Meadow.

On my morning's walk on a definitely descending trail, I could really sense the landscape changing. I was eager and excited to reach the lower Kern River. I had camped beside the Kern on my 1973 hiking journey. I had also read about the problems and dangers the lower Kern presented to early spring hikers entering the southern Sierras from the south. During spring, runoff waters augmented by melting snow run full and swift.

I recalled that several years ago, I had thought about completing this section during early summer. I am now thankful that I changed my plans. I had studied the Guidebook and pondered how I would cross the swiftly flowing Kern. There was no bridge at that time. The Guidebook presented two different routes where hikers might ford the river—both presented hazards. The Guidebook also advised hikers to use ropes to hold onto in case they were swept off-balance by the swift-flowing currents. I would speculate on which of the two routes I should take. Which route offered the safest crossing? I would also speculate about how much extra rope I would need to pack for this crossing. If I tied the rope to a tree or post before fording the river, how could I retrieve the rope upon reaching the other side? This I could not figure out unless I was lucky enough to have another hiker come along who would be good enough to untie my rope while I reeled it in.

Now the river is bridged and presents an easy crossing. Nevertheless, I shall always wonder if I could have made it safely across with my rope in the days of river fording.

Near my approach to the Kern I met a solo hiker walking north. He greeted me, saying, "You are the first hiker I've met since Kennedy Meadows." "You are the first hiker I've met since Corpsman Creek two-and-a-half days ago," I replied. He was concerned about water, as someone had told him that water was very scarce on the trail north. I assured him that he could find water and reviewed the water stops. He was relieved. He had started at Chimney Rock and was planning to come out at Cottonwood Lakes. He told me that he was walking the trail in sections during his 10-day vacations. We felt commonness in that we both were using vacation time to hike the trail.

By midday, I reached the Kern. I retreated under the new bridge for shade from the noonday sun and to eat lunch and have my midday siesta. Comfortably settled in my shaded hideaway, I soon heard some high-pitched twittering. I looked up and there, clinging to the underpinnings of the bridge, were colonies of swallows. The bridge's underpinnings were plastered with their nests. I amused myself during my lunch and siesta by watching the swallows fly in and out.

Following my pleasant siesta under the bridge, I measured and purified my water and walked down the trail until I reached a junction with an old Indian trail. There I found a comfortable, level campsite. I enjoyed imagining Native Americans treading on this ground. Where were they going, and what was the purpose of their journey?

From my comfortable, warm bed, I enjoyed looking up through a peephole framed by the trees at a beautiful, scarlet sky. What a glorious sight.

The trail the next morning suddenly emerged onto an awful sight—a wilderness holocaust, the Clover Meadow fire. It was depressing to read about this fire in the Guidebook and to find that it was started by a careless hiker! I can accept the devastating look of destroyed trees and blackened earth caused by lightening, but it is hard to accept the devastation of wilderness caused needlessly by a careless camper.

I arrived at the Kennedy Meadow campground around noon. The campground was a planned rest stop for me to wash my clothes and body. I picked a campsite, looking for trees a convenient distance apart to string my clothesline. I had succeeded in hanging up my socks and underwear when it started to rain. What an inconvenient surprise! It rained fairly hard, with intermittent thunder and lightening for about an hour. I decided that this was not the day to dry clothes. I wrung out my wash and placed it in a plastic bag, repacked my bag, donned my poncho, and headed off for the Kennedy Meadow store, which was located about a mile and a half south of the campground. The Kennedy Meadow store was an interesting-looking, rustic, log-style building. It looked like it could have been a movie set for a western. When the store manager found my food package and saw that I was from Santa Rosa, she reminisced. She said that as a child, her family took her to visit her grandmother and aunt who lived in a pioneer house north of Santa Rosa, near Gualala. "Now," she said, smiling, "I'm living in a pioneer house here." As I rearranged my pack with my new food supply on the pioneer store's porch, the owner's young son happily jumped about, asking me questions about my supplies. "What is this?" he asked. I replied, "This is my stove, this is my water sack, this is my bivouac sack to keep my bed dry, and this is my mattress." He seemed a little bewildered.

On the road back to the river to find a campsite, I passed a big red fire truck. The fireman told me that they were extinguishing a lightening-caused fire that had erupted that afternoon. He reassured me that they had the fire under control. Nevertheless, during the night, I smelled smoke. I camped at a grassy spot near the river.

The next planned destination was Woodpecker Meadow. I had debated at some length about whether to take the old temporary route by way of Woodpecker Meadow or the new route to Walker Pass. There were positive and negative arguments for each route. Originally, when I was walking north from Jawbone Canyon in the section of trail south of Weldon, I had planned to hike the newly completed Walker Pass route. My plans were changed when, unexpectedly, the dogs Tuxedo and Elwood decided to accompany me and I needed to take the older Weldon route to reach a phone to reunite them with their owners. Now I favored taking the Woodpecker-Weldon route, which would come out directly in the town of Weldon. In addition, Weldon is conveniently served by a public bus. The Woodpecker Meadow route contains more water than the dry Walker Pass route. The uncertainty and challenge of the Woodpecker Meadow route is that it has a difficult cross-country section south of Kennedy Meadow. I had read about hikers struggling through this section. With some feeling of uncertainty, I had decided to try the Woodpecker Meadow route.

My day's hike started early and easily with a walk along the grassy meadow bordering the west bank of the south fork of the Kern. The difficulty started when the riverbank became steeper and was strewn with moderately large boulders. During the first lap of my journey, I found blue plastic ribbon markers, which I assumed were there to mark the cross-county route. I leaped eagerly from boulder to boulder, and then started hunting for the next ribbon. After about three ribbons, I searched as hard as I could, I looked high and low, but could not locate any more ribbons. The barricade of boulders and bushes became more difficult to penetrate. I was no longer exhilarated by my boulder hopping. I decided to try the low route alongside the river. I climbed down. After advancing a few yards along the river's edge, my path was blocked by tenacious willows with thick branches that extended far out over the water. It was really slow going. Once I lost my sunglasses. I worked hard to retrace my steps, scanning carefully for my glasses. Fortunately, I found them hanging on a bush. I had carried my glasses in my pants pocket when not wearing them and the glass-holder cord had caught on a bush. I rejoiced at finding them.

Growing weary of the difficult barricade of bushes, I paused and contemplated what to do next. I scanned the scene. I looked across the river and could see a trail running parallel to the river. This, I thought, was probably the new trail to Walker Pass. I decided to inspect it. Fording the river during its low, summer flow was not difficult. Secure on the other side, I inspected the sandy, moderately used trail, which was dotted with cow hooves and boot marks. I felt a little uncertain as to whether it was the new trail or just another cow trail. By now, the day was growing late. After my all-day search, I felt that I wanted to be sure of following the right trail. I decided to retrace my steps back to Kennedy Meadow and locate the trail marker for Walker Pass trail.

By the time I reached the trailhead at Kennedy Meadow, it was around 7 pm. I decided to make camp and start fresh in the morning.

I found a level spot near the river and rolled out my bivouac sack and bedroll. I ate a cold supper. I was back where I had started from that morning. I kept puzzling about where the cross-country route to Woodpecker Meadow could have started from.

It was crowded and noisy near the river. I was reminded that it was Saturday evening. Near the bridge there were a number of eager fishermen. I heard one of them exclaim loudly, "I forgot my worm."

In the morning, while I was packing my gear, two young boys drifted by. They asked me where I was hiking. "I'm walking on a section of the Pacific Crest Trail," I replied, adding, "The trail goes from Mexico to Canada along the crest of the mountains. I have been hiking the trail in sections for several summers and plan to finish in Washington—when I reach the Canadian border in August." They looked at me with puzzled expressions and one asked, "Are you doing this for charity?"

I proceeded carefully with my map and compass on my next morning's walk on the new Walker Pass trail. I was curious. Since the map shows the trail going along the east side of the river, where would it lead in respect to yesterday's exploration along the river? I soon found that I had actually stepped onto the new Walker Pass section the day before. The cows had confused me! They had used this section heavily. I was finally on my way.

Shortly after passing the cow hoof-marked section, the trail reached a wide area, the Rockhouse Basin, which is decorated with some large, basalt boulders. Then, the trail leaves the river and climbs east on its route to Chimney Creek Camp. Just as I started to climb up, intending to camp at the next seasonal creek, a young man came hurrying down the trail and asked, "Where is the next water?" I assured him that he would reach water in a few yards. He then asked me, "How many miles is it to Kennedy Meadows?" I hesitated because I had not been concentrating on the mileage. I said that I thought it was probably six or eight miles. He then told me that there was no water for the next 15 miles, where water was available at Chimney Creek. His unexpected announcement led me to promptly turn around and retrace my steps back to the Kern to fill my water bags for the next 15 miles. I had planned on getting water from two seasonal creeks, which were described in the Guidebook. Apparently by mid-July, they had dried up.

Although I was annoyed that this young man was so focused on mileage and made no comments on views from the top of the ridge and interesting natural sights, I had to admit that I was very fortunate that he had come along at this crucial time. Had he not appeared and let me know that the seasonal creeks were dry, I would have had to retrace my steps a much longer trek from the first dry seasonal creek back to the Kern— or worse yet, continued on and risked dehydration.

With full water bags and a heavier load, I climbed up the trail a short way and found a roomy bedroom with a level, sandy floor circled by walls of some large orange-beige-colored rocks. There was a breeze. The night sky was full of stars.

My walk the next day led me up from the Kern River basin some 1400 feet to Long Valley. I climbed up slowly, carrying my heavier-than-usual pack, weighted down with extra water. It was a good trail. It started to grow a little hot in the canyon area. I wished for clouds, and soon my wish was granted, as clouds moved in and an afternoon breeze came up. It became a pleasant day's walk. I made camp early, around 4 pm, in a pleasant, flat, wide spot in Long Valley. The location would leave me with an easy, short morning's walk to Chimney Creek Campground and water.

After dinner, I reached into my pack for my reading envelope—my small library of favorite photocopy readings. I read from Pierre Teilhard de Chardin's Hymn of the Universe and from the Fire Over the Earth chapter. I remembered that it was Sunday, and reading Chardin is one of my ways to celebrate Sunday while I am on the trail. I felt inspired reading, "Lord, that no poison may harm my days, no death destroy me, that in every creature I may discover you."

I also enjoyed an evening of cloud watching. I watched some big clouds travel swiftly across the sky, constantly changing shapes. Later, when the sky darkened, I stargazed. I carry a small star-finder wheel in my pack and during starry nights, I try to identify major constellations. I looked for Ursula Major and Ursula Minor; Draco, the dragon; Bootes, the herdsman; Cyanus, the swan; and Lyra, the lyre. Stargazing is one of my joys while on the trail, and I do miss gazing at the star-bright sky when I return home and sleep inside under a man-made roof. I wonder if people ever place skylights in their bedrooms?

In the morning, on the trail to Chimney Rock, I met three older men headed toward Kennedy Meadows. They told me that there was no water on the newly built trail from Chimney

Rock to Walker Pass and advised me to take the alternate Cane-brake Road Trail.

One of the friendly hikers told me that he had been hiking the trail in sections during his vacations. Now he was retired and he and his friends were planning to walk to Lake Tahoe. We happily compared notes and enthusiastically agreed that hiking by sections was a good way to walk the trail. As we departed, we wished each other good trail travels. How fortunate, I felt, to have had trail advice just when I needed it. This was not a heavily traveled trail section, and the two encounters I had had recently both happened just "at the right time and at the right place."

Arriving at the Canebrake Road at Chimney Creek Mead-ow, I was fortunate again. Although I found trail signs, I did not see a sign leading to the campground—my next important water stop. Just as I was pondering which way to turn to find water, a pickup came along. I waved at the driver, who kindly stopped. When I asked him, "Which way to the campground?" he replied, "I'll take you there." I climbed in for the half-mile ride to the campground and water. At the very pleasant Bureau of Land Management campground—equipped with tables, toilets, and most important, shade trees—I spent my midday siesta.

Exploring near the edge of the campground, I saw some currant bushes. I cautiously tried one and felt assured that it did taste like currants. I thought to myself, "How did the In-dians know which berries were edible and which were poison-ous!" I expect that they learned by trial and error and by stories passed down from generation to generation.

When the late afternoon breezes arose, I started my walk down Canebrake Road. I found a camping place a few yards off the road on a grassy, level spot next to the small, softly gurgling Chimney Creek.

My next day's walk down Canebrake Road to Highway 178 was an easy one. I was drifting easily downhill on gently turning switchbacks. Soon, I came out of the trees and into a clearing with an expansive view looking down toward the valley. In the morning light, the colors were muted. The valley hills were lighted with greens and blues and dotted with cloud shadows. The valley floor colors were generally dark sandy brown, but intercepting the sandy-brown earth colors, in the right center was a bright patch of green—a watered field or pasture. I recalled how excited I was during my walk headed north from Kelso Valley at my first sighting of the southern edge of the Sierra. Now, I was seeing the reverse route. I was looking down from the south of the Sierra to the high desert, that of Kelso valley, which offered a different natural scene of beauty.

Arriving at Highway 178 near Weldon around 11:30, I could feel the midday heat. I noticed that the cars headed west toward Weldon were moving swiftly on a downhill grade. My first anxious thought was that this was going to be a hard place to catch a ride to Weldon, and that waiting in the hot, treeless area might lead to heat stroke. I started to pray, as was my practice on such occasions. Then, within minutes after I had arrived at the junction, I heard a car coming down from Canebrake Road. I waved. The driver stopped and agreed to take me all the way to the main bus stop at Lake Isabella—west of Weldon. I felt so fortunate!

The considerate driver told me that he was building a cabin at Kennedy Meadows, not far from the store. He was working on his cabin on weekends and on his days off. Today, when he started up the Canebrake grade, his radiator started overheating. He decided to turn back. He stopped to fill his radiator with water a couple of times on the way to Lake Isabella.

While waiting for the bus at Lake Isabella, I had time for a snack at the gas station. Looking at me, the attendant said, "You look like a surveyor." I replied, "I'm hiking the Pacific Crest Trail from Mexico to Canada, and I have just 80 miles left to complete in Washington." "Congratulations," he replied.

Waiting for the bus near the combined Senior Center and Community Center, I watched the Senior Center members coming in and out. They seemed so busy and enthusiastic. Two very fat ladies came out for a smoke.

As is often the case on coming out from the wilderness, I was torn: it would be good to return home for clean clothes and after a good soak in the bathtub, but coming out from the wilderness is always a cultural shock. The everyday world is so noisy. I would miss the gentle sounds of the wind rustling through the trees, the singing birds, and the quiet gurgling of creeks. I would also miss my bed under the stars. I'm surprised at how well I sleep confined in my little bag and resting on a thin foam mattress pad. Sometimes I sleep better in my narrow bag, resting on the ground, than I do at home.

Chapter 7
Dusy Creek Trail Junction in Le Conte Canyon to Mt. Whitney Trail Junction, August 1971
Pacific Crest Trail Mileage—65 miles
Total Trail Mileage (including lateral trails to reach the Pacific Crest Trail)—108 miles

When I heard the storm I made haste to join it; for in storms nature has always something extra fine to show us...
—*John Muir*

This section of the trail in the High Sierras, together with the adjoining sections of the John Muir Trail, offers some of the most spectacular mountain scenery of any mountain trail. The John Muir Trail extends from Yosemite Valley to Mt. Whitney. The Pacific Crest Trail follows the John Muir Trail for most of the way. It was also a very exciting year for me. It was my third year of backpacking and my longest walk without any food resupply—13 days. It is a true roadless, wilderness area. It was the summer in which I could climb five high passes, culminating in the 14,494-foot climb up to the summit of Mt. Whitney—the highest peak in the continental United States. It would also be my year to complete the 210-mile John Muir Trail. For me, indeed, it was a mountain-top experience.

On some of my summer trail walks, the lateral trails leading in to reach the Pacific Crest Trail offered very special beauty in themselves. This was especially true in the High Sierras, and especially true of this summer's hike. The Bishop Pass and Dusy Basin trails are overflowing with scenes of special beauty.

The Bishop Pass trailhead is reached by driving 13 miles west on a road from the town of Bishop. The trailhead is located just south of Parcher's Resort and Pack Station and leads into South Lake. Reaching trailhead this year was easy and required no hitchhiking. My good friend, Carol MacMillan, accompanied me to the Sierras, each of us driving her own car. Following some enjoyable exploring in Tuolumne Meadows and the White Mountains, we both drove to Whitney Portal—my coming-out destination—where I left my car. She then drove me back to the trailhead at Bishop Pass. At the trailhead, we were greeted by a group of trail maintenance workers who were hauling out lots of rubbish, including a rusty bedstead! I smiled by the trail sign for a going-in photo and waved goodbye.

As I climbed up the ascending trail with my usual rhythmic, uphill pace, a man, also starting to climb, said to his young son, who was alternately running, panting, and resting, "Look at her—she climbs with a steady pace."

By evening, I found a secluded campsite above Long Lake in a little, hidden den surrounded by whitebark pines and with a floor of soft duff (fallen dried pine needles).

The next morning, I started early for my ascent up steep, rocky, 11,989-foot Bishop Pass. I reached the summit a little before noon. The views from the top were truly spectacular. Looking south, I could see the string of lakes dotting the area around South Lake. To the north, I could look down at U-shaped, grass-covered Dusy Basin. The view to the southeast, looking toward the jagged Palisade Peaks, is particularly spectacular. I remembered fondly climbing up nearby Knapsack Pass during my earlier visit to Dusy Basin on a 1968 Sierra Club outing.

Descending, I spent an enjoyable afternoon siesta on a little platform above Dusy Basin. In the cool of the evening, I moved down the trail and made camp at the overlook of Le Conte Canyon. I wanted to be poised for the long, steep morning's descent down into the canyon.

Le Conte Canyon is named after Joseph Le Conte, an early High Sierra explorer and a Charter Member of the Sierra Club. He was a much-beloved professor of natural sciences at the University of California at Berkeley. In 1870, he led a university excursion party from Oakland to Yosemite Valley, where he met John Muir and enlisted his help to guide the group on to Tuolumne Meadows and Mono Lake. His trip is described in a delightful book, Ramblings—A Journal Through the High Sierra of California, published by the Sierra Club.

On my morning descent down the winding Dusy Creek trail, I stopped often to revel in the views looking toward the Goddard Divide. One of my favorite scenes is a view looking directly across the canyon, where there is a rounded amphitheater with a hanging garden carved into the rock below the peaks. In the morning, it is especially glorious, as it is bathed by the morning light of the rising sun.

I stopped for a rest snack by a willow-lined creek bank. I spotted a tiny hummingbird and watched it hovering over colorful flowers gracefully gathering nectar. What a delight. I was not sure whether or not I was viewing the fairly rare calliope hummingbird, which likes the habitat of the high mountains, or the more common, Anna's hummingbird. I hoped that it was, perhaps, the calliope.

I reached the Muir Trail in the late morning and started my walk south on a level, easy trail through Le Conte Canyon. I soon met a backcountry ranger, Randy Morganson. I told him that I liked some of the notes that he had posted on the trail sign, reminding us to "carry it out" and to "keep the trail clean." He seemed pleased. He asked, "Do you have a wilderness permit?" "Yes, I do," I assured him. I was glad when he didn't ask to see it. It was buried deep in my backpack.

1971 was on of the first years in which trail permits were required. Before permits were required, the crowds on some of the popular sections of the trail were growing large, and there was concern regarding the impact of the crowds on the trail and its surrounding environment. In my first few years on the trail, before the permit system had been established, I would often pass large groups, such as 40-60 members of a Scout troop tramping along the trail. It is good, I believe, that the Park Service and Forest Service saw the need to issue permits, as in recent years when I hike in the High Sierras, I no longer encounter the large groups. Usually groups of Scouts are limited to around eight per group.

In the evening, I found a pleasant, secluded campsite at the edge of Grouse Meadow. I found a few tasty wild huckleberries. I enjoyed views of the Citadel, a tall, rounded, granite knob looming up to the south. From my bed at my campsite near Grouse Meadow, I awoke to see a doe and two fawns standing quietly about 40 feet from me. I thought they were looking at me as if to say, "What's this?" They stood still for several seconds. Finally, one of the fawns started moving slowly toward the stream, and then the doe and other fawn followed.

My morning walk was an easy one along a level stretch through a forested corridor dotted with aspens whose rustling leaves turned in the breeze. I spent my afternoon siesta at pleasant Deer Meadow. In the early afternoon, I started the climb up to the Palisade Basin. With the hot western sun reflecting off the rocks on this steep climb, I began to realize that my plan for the day had not taken into account sufficiently the difficult 2000-foot ascent. I had learned early on to plan my ascent of major passes for early in the day when the air was still cool and

I felt fresh and strong. I had not as yet discovered that there are some difficult and rugged ascents that do not bear the label of a "pass." The Palisade staircase was one of them.

I learned later that the ascent up Palisade Creek is known as the "Golden Staircase." It was built on the cliffs of the gorge of Palisade Creek and because of the difficulty of carving the trail into the gorge, it was the last section of the Muir Trail to be constructed. As I plodded slowly upward, I stopped periodically to drink in the view and to look at wildflowers. One delightful find was discovering some delicate, nodding rein orchids tucked in by a small dripping spring.

I finally arrived at 10,650-foot Upper Palisade Lake and made camp around 7:30 pm. I decided to have a cold supper, not for lack of wood but because of the shortage of daylight and because I was weary. I did, however, have a pleasant, small, after-dinner fire. Upper Palisade Lake offered an alpine lake scene. Although my camp on the east side of the lake was dotted with low-growing, windswept pines, the opposite side was completely bare of vegetation and was bounded by a steep slope of light-covered talus rocks.

I arose early the next morning in anticipation of the ascent up 12,000-foot Mather Pass. The pass is named after Steven Mather, the first director of the National Park Service. The climb was not especially difficult. I reached the top a little before noon, in time to enjoy an early lunch "at the top." Whenever possible, I like to pause and eat at the top of a pass. It's a time to drink in the view. It's a time to celebrate. I especially liked the view to the south, looking back toward Palisade Basin. I could see its small, deep-blue lakes surrounded by light-gray granite—John Muir's "Range of Light."

On my descent, I spotted a cluster of mountain primroses growing in the shade of a rock. Lower down in a grassy area,

I saw some pink-purple-colored shooting stars. I had not expected to see as many flowers in late August. I was delighted.

Arriving at the Upper Basin of King's Canyon, I made camp early upon first sighting a cluster of trees. It was my afternoon of planned leisure, with time to wash socks. Although I did not think that the campsite I chose had been used before, I discovered a rock at the border of my campsite that, strangely and mysteriously, was painted with a silver cross. I wondered how long it had been there.

My walk the following day was pleasant and easy. When I arrived at the South Fork of the King's River, which is crossed by a ford, I decided to keep my boots on. In earlier years, when I hiked with the Sierra Club, there was much discussion on how to ford a stream. First, hikers were advised to search for a shallow area—usually a wide place where the river spreads out rather than running deeply and swiftly as in narrow passageways. Many hikers chose to take off their boots and carry them to the other side. I can well remember hearing loud exclamations when a hiker's foot hit a sharp rock.

Another technique advised was for the hiker to remove his or her boots, but leave on a pair of heavy socks to cushion the impact of the rocks. When I started backpacking alone, I decided to keep my boots on. I feel more comfortable and safer with my boots on. Upon reaching the other side of the stream, I empty my boots, wipe out the inside, and put on dry socks. The dry socks absorb moisture from the wet boots, and soon they are both dry and comfortable.

I stopped for a snack by a spring near the trail junction to Bench Lake. Soon, four hikers arrived and stopped. One of them looked at me and said, "I remember you from last summer." I was puzzled and surprised. "I remember that you were enrolled in class at the Gerontology Center of the University of Southern

California," he explained. "What a good memory you have," I replied. He told me that they had been hiking in the mountains for nearly one month. Dr. James Binen, a faculty member whom I remembered, had been with them for one week.

By evening, I arrived at Lake Marjorie. It was windy. I found a campsite partially sheltered from the wind by waist-high rocks. After dinner, I enjoyed watching the setting sun light up the steep granite walls on the eastern side of the lake.

During the night, I discovered my rock-walled bedroom was a little short and that it was also hard. It was not very comfortable.

In the morning, I was again up early to ascend the next pass—Pinchot Pass. I had no trouble getting up. I had no desire to sleep any longer in my short, rocky bedsite.

On my way from Lake Marjorie to the trail, I spotted a cluster of lovely pink phlox. What were they? I wondered. Bending down and examining them more closely, I concluded that they were mountain phlox. These were the first I had seen, and I was delighted.

The climb up to 12,000-foot Pinchot Pass was not difficult. On the top, I enjoyed a splendid view looking to the south toward Woods Creek, which was embellished by some tall, dark peaks.

The climb down was a little steep, and the trail was covered with some rough, jagged talus. I moved slowly. I found a campsite on one of the Twin Lakes. From my bedsite, I enjoyed glorious views looking across the lake, where granite peaks rose up from the lake basin.

In the morning, from my scenic campsite at Twin Lakes, I returned to the Muir Trail. I was eagerly anticipating my arrival at the beautiful Rae Lakes. I had seen many attractive photographs of them. After a week of beautiful weather, a dark, threatening cloud appeared in the sky, and I began to wish that I hadn't washed three pairs of socks yesterday. The socks were hanging, attached by large safety pins, from my backpack to dry. A few drops of rain fell but, fortunately, it did not last long.

The trail descends down to Woods Creek—8500 feet. Arriving at the Woods Creek crossing, I found a beautiful rest spot to eat my lunch, surrounded by rushing, gurgling water and beautiful, colored rocks. At the junction near the crossing of Woods Creek, a group of Boy Scouts came down the trail headed for Rae Lakes. They had come in on the much-traveled trail from Paradise Valley and Cedar Grove, which can be reached by car on roads leading from Fresno. This easy-access trail contributes to the large crowds of hikers who are attracted to the Rae Lakes. In more recent years, camping at Rae Lakes has been restricted in order to restore vegetation.

In the afternoon, as I approached the first of the two Rae Lakes, I heard the considerable noise of camper voices. Not wishing to join the crowd, I retreated and found a secluded campsite near the lake's outlet. I felt so good on being close to the lake but away from the noisy crowd. One of my delights in the evening was watching a water ouzel bobbing and feeding in the stream. The water ouzel was one of John Muir's favorite birds, and he would tell of looking for one by each waterfall. This remarkable, black, medium-sized bird, now classified as a water dipper, is able to actually walk on the bottom of streams, searching for aquatic insects.

On my next day's hike around the Rae Lakes, I could appreciate the attraction of this beautiful area. The small lakes are deep blue, with grassy shorelines, sandy beaches, and small bays and inlets. They are surrounded by some most-interesting rock formations. I kept looking at, and taking pictures of, the magnetic Fin Dome, a large, tall, granite-colored dome that rises abruptly from the lake shore. At the lower lake, I also marveled at the Painted Lady, another steep, jagged, granite peak, colored with a touch of red.

As I circled around the lower lake, I came to the summer ranger's station and was delighted to meet Ranger Mary Evans. She was the first backcountry woman ranger I had met. Happily, women rangers are now numerous. However, before 1971, they were uncommon. To me, she was a pioneer.

I enjoyed the glorious views as I walked slowly around the picturesque Rae Lakes. Added to the spectacular scene, the trail crosses over a narrow isthmus between the two lakes before moving south to climb 11,900-foot Glen Pass.

Glen Pass proved to be one of the most difficult passes to climb, not because of its height—there are certainly higher passes in the Sierras—but because the trail bed was covered with large, loose, crumbly rocks. Often, as I placed my foot ahead, it would slide back. It was slow going.

Finally reaching the narrow, rocky top, I enjoyed a glorious, expansive view looking in both directions. The scene was especially spectacular looking south toward Bubbs Creek and the rugged peaks of the King's Canyon-Kern River Valley divide.

On the top, I met another Boy Scout troop. Their leader volunteered to take my picture and then asked me questions about my hiking alone. He seemed puzzled. I don't think he understood the idea of the freedom and solitude of hiking alone.

Shortly after, I started my descent. I met a large man with a tremendously large pack sprawled out, resting at the side of the trail. He looked exhausted. I commented, "It looks like you are carrying a heavy load." He replied, "I'm going to be in for four days!" I didn't have the heart to tell him that with my relatively smaller pack, I had been in nine days and had four more days to go. He had come in to the trail from the east, over Kersarge

CHARLOTTE CREEK CANYON

Pass, which leads to the Onion Valley roadhead from the town of Independence on Highway 395. This route also provides a fairly near access to the Rae Lakes.

I loved the hike down from the pass, which provided glorious views looking toward Kersarge pinnacles and later looking up broad, glacier-carved Charlotte Canyon. Again, there were some threatening rain clouds and a few drops fell. Looking up, the sky was spectacular, sprinkled with fast-moving storm clouds. I turned off the trail onto the Kersarge Pass trail for a short distance and found a secluded campsite along the outlet of Bullfrog Lake—a lake of special beauty. I was camped a short distance from a small waterfall and enjoyed the stream music all during the night. Bullfrog Lake had been closed for camping to allow the fragile shoreline to recover. After supper, I walked to drink in the beauty of the scene.

My next day's walk south along the side of gurgling Bubbs Creek was an easy one. I passed the Bubbs Creek trail going west, which provides still another route out to Paradise Valley and Cedar Grove. At large Bidette Meadow, I met some trail workers who were camped near the meadow. I learned from one of them that they were doing some restoration work on the Forester Pass Trail.

At noon, when I stopped for lunch near an enticing waterfall on Bubbs Creek, it started to rain, and then to hail. Then, during my after-lunch siesta, it was alternately rainy and sunny. How changeable high-mountain weather can be! My afternoon walk was most eventful and unforgettable. As I was moving up the trail, planning to find a camp so that I would have a short approach for the next day's climb up 13,180-foot Forester Pass—the highest pass on the Pacific Crest Trail—I met an older hiker coming down the trail. He strongly advised me to camp below Center Peak in a cluster of small whitebark pines. I turned off-trail, as he had advised, and found an attractive campsite with a tree-sheltered bedroom and a spectacular view looking out toward towering Mount Stanford, which bordered the west gate of Forester Pass.

Mysteriously, while I was clearing some small branches for my bedsite, I found under a small rock a pencil-written verse. I

wondered who had penned it. Was it my hiker-adviser, whom
I had just passed?

I'm climbing up the trail,
I'm walking past the creeks,
I'm tripping over stones,
And I won't be home for weeks.

It's a hot and dusty trail,
The trees are in my way,
And all I have to do,
Is sit and work and play.

I'm going up the hill,
I'm tired all day long,
I'm wobbling to and fro,
As I sing this little song.

Just as I had completed setting up my tube tent, sheltered
under the low-branched whitebark pines, a threatening storm
broke loose. The sky grew darker, and then the full fiery force
of the storm descended—thunder, lightening, wind, and rain.
For the next 45 minutes, I watched it all from my whitebark
pine shelter. Thunder echoed and rumbled; lightening flashed
and zigzagged along the rocky ridge; and—most spectacular
of all—storm clouds raced, tumbled, and swirled above and
through the pass. I was watching an incredible lightening show.
Quick changes took place as white, puffy clouds swept into
dark clouds, only to be followed by another set of white clouds.
It was as if the white clouds and the dark clouds were fighting
for possession of the ridge. Gradually, the white clouds became
more numerous and patches of blue sky peeked through above

Mount Stanford and Junction Peak. Slowly, the thunder grew faint, the lightening subsided, the wind died down, and the rain stopped. The wilderness was quiet again.

As I recalled the spectacular power and beauty of the storm on Forester Pass, I wondered if John Muir had experienced such a storm. I know that he would have loved this one.

The night was calm, and I was dry and comfortable. It was cold, however, so I slept with all my layers on, including my windbreaker.

The following morning was calm and sunny. I started early for my ascent up Forester Pass. It proved to be a surprisingly easy walk up the north side to the summit on a trail that was smooth and well maintained.

Nearing the summit, I saw two young men wearing some unusual packs with platforms above their heads. When I asked the young men if I could take their picture and told them that I was interested in their packs, they replied that their Scoutmaster, who was ahead climbing up to the pass, had made them. Happily, when I reached the top of the pass, I caught up with the Scoutmaster, who was leading a mule with a birdcage perched on top. What a delightful and interesting hike leader. He told me that he was from Strathmore, near Tulare, which is a little south of Fresno. "Every summer I lead Scouts into the mountains. I also raise homing pigeons. I send the pigeons home along the route with a message telling the Scouts' parents that their youngsters are safe and healthy." He went on to tell me that he had originally made the overhead-backpack frames to carry the birdcages. He also found that they provided a sunshade. I noticed that he, himself, was somewhat balding. I wondered if protection of his own head had led him to create the platform sun cover.

He talked on, expressing his concern that the birds had been blown around in their cages by the previous night's storm. He said that even though he had tried to protect them by covering their cages, the heavy winds had jostled the birds from side to side. He was afraid that their wings might be broken. I looked over at a cage atop a nearby pack animal and caught a glimpse of a quiet white dove huddled in a corner. The Scout leader hoped that they were recovering and that they would be all right.

What an interesting and creative leader, I thought. I encouraged him to think about patenting his innovative backpack. I told him that I admired his fine work in introducing young people to the mountains. I wished him well as I moved along my way.

The view from the top of high Forester Pass was exciting. The storm had cleared the air. I was fortunate to see clearly 14,496-foot Mt. Whitney, the highest mountain in the continental United States, on a clear, sunny day. Surrounding Mt. Whitney was its 14,000-foot neighbors—Mts. Williamson, Tyndall, Barnard, Russell, Le Conte, and Langley. While I was gazing and marveling at these 14,000-foot giants, I began to notice a change in the landscape. I felt the difference. There were fewer trees. Sprinkled below these giants were some flat, sloping, light-sand-colored plateaus. Although these were the highest mountains I was to encounter on the entire trail, there was, nevertheless, a hint of the high desert. I was looking down along the Kern plateau, the headwaters of the Kern River. I became so intrigued with this difference in the landscape that I decided I wanted to see more of this area. This feeling led me to plan a loop trip during the summer of 1973 along the lower Kern.

Although the trail down to the south is steep and winding, I did not find it difficult. The trail, it seemed to me, was well planned and maintained. The steep descent is maneuvered by well-placed switchbacks. All the way down, I enjoyed the tremendous panorama of views of the Kern plateau and the surrounding 14,000-foot giants. I also enjoyed spotting some brightly colored wildflowers—penstemon and rock fringe were clustered among the rocks. After the trail reached level land, I found a campsite alongside Tyndall Creek among some small trees. Camped a few yards away was a young man who came to my camp and asked if I could give him some toilet paper. I declined, saying that I hardly had enough for the rest of my trip. Afterwards, when I had gotten to know him better, I wished that I had spared him some paper. I would be seeing him often in the next two days, as we periodically passed each other on the trail. I came to know him as "Blue Stocking Cap."

We talked about our experiences during the storm. He told me that he had been camped at the top of Forester Pass when the storm struck. He rushed down the trail, admitting that he was scared and said that he was ready to give up any pretense of being brave to reach a safer site.

Arriving early the next morning at Big Horn Plateau, I began to hear some low barking sounds. As the sounds grew louder, I realized that I was hearing coyotes. Soon, the nearby pack was singing as in a chorus and made music as if they were singing in harmony—in different pitches with blending notes. In between the chorus harmony, there was intermittent barking. The chorus lasted quite a while. I had never heard anything like it before. It added a mystical feeling to the already intriguing high-country plateau. From this sand-colored, gently sloping plateau, there are many fine views offering a sweeping panorama of the high mountains and valley floors. The walk was an easy one. I was drifting downhill toward Crabtree Meadow.

At the Wallace Creek Junction, I met Blue Stocking Cap coming down the trail. He had gotten lost and gone up the Wallace Creek Trail to Wallace Lake. He was annoyed that he had lost so much time. I thought that he looked somewhat forlorn. One of his packs—he was carrying a small daypack in addition to his backpack—had a broken strap, and he was carrying the pack awkwardly at his side.

By early afternoon, I had reached 10,500-foot Crabtree Meadow. The meadow is notable as the western approach to Mt. Whitney. It has a large campground with a ranger. Although Mt. Whitney is not officially on the Pacific Crest Trail—it is the southern entrance to the John Muir Trail—many Pacific Crest Trail hikers take time out to climb the highest peak in the continental United States.

I was excited. I planned to search the campground to see if, per chance, my good friend, Koreen Osbun, who was hiking with Joe Wampler Tours, might be camped there. Searching around, I saw a group of tents. I was looking for a familiar green dome tent. I asked some of the campers, "Is this the Wampler Tour group?" "Yes, it is." they affirmed. "I'm looking for my friend, Koreen Osbun." In response to my inquiry, Koreen appeared, poking her head out of the entrance of a green domed tent. What a happy surprise! We had talked about our hiking plans before leaving home, but were unsure that we would both arrive at Crabtree Meadow at the same time. Joe Wampler had led groups on the Muir Trail for a number of years. The hikers walk and animals carry their gear. The Wampler Tour was my introduction to the Muir Trail in 1966, before I started backpacking.

Koreen and I had a happy time exchanging stories of our experiences. She had seen a long-tailed weasel. I told her about being serenaded by coyotes. Joe Wampler appeared and invited me to stay for dinner. I declined. By now, I was attached to my solo backpacking experience and to finding my one-person bedroom campsite and eating my freeze-dried stew around my small fire. I wasn't ready to change the mood and feeling of solitude. I said goodbye and moved up the trail. I wanted to be in a good position for my climb up Mt. Whitney the next day. I walked until dusk and then found a small off-trail campsite. As I was preparing my supper, I heard footsteps and then, "Can I camp near you?" It was Blue Stocking Cap. "Of course, you are welcome," I replied. We were both excited in anticipation of the climb to the top of Mt. Whitney.

The next morning, I arose early. My Blue Stocking Cap friend was rattling around packing his gear. While I was waiting for my coffee water to boil, he walked by my campsite on his journey up the trail, saying that he was too cold to fix breakfast. In my early years of backpacking, including my backpack trip in 1971, I was still using a wood fire for both my breakfast and dinner. The style at the time was to carry a billy can, i.e., a coffee can that one placed on the fire to heat water. How different our style of camping is now, in which some type of stove is required in order to eliminate the large number of fire rings and blackened stones in the wilderness.

For me, the climb up to Mt. Whitney was not difficult. I just kept walking up with my usual slow, steady pace. I reached trailcrest, which is the junction leading to the Whitney summit. Near the junction, I was delighted to spot two very special flowers, which I had hoped very much to find—the lovely alpine gold, a member of the sunflower family, and the deep-blue sky pilot, which is in the phlox family. They grow only at high altitudes.

I parked my pack at the junction, along with other packs, as was the custom for the mile-and-a-half climb up the spur trail to the summit.

I was so excited arriving at the top. Looking around, I found that it was quite crowded, with lots of hikers. It was Sunday. Most of them had hiked up from the eastern side of the mountains, from Whitney Portal, or had camped at some of the popular lakes, such as Mirror Lake on the eastern trail. Among the crowd, I was soon greeted by Blue Stocking Cap. He happily announced, "I am going to spend the night at the top of Mt. Whitney in the rock shelter. There are around 20 other campers who plan to sleep there." He seemed very happy. Although I could well understand his enthusiasm, I had no desire to spend the night in the crowded, cold, rock hut. He quickly volunteered to take photos of me. I posed, smiling, perched by the rock hut.

The view from the top was truly glorious beyond description. I was looking at so many mountain peaks, I did not try to count them or to identify them. There was also a magnificent view looking down toward the east at sandy-colored Owens Valley. I felt to so fortunate to have climbed to the top on such a beautiful day. Reportedly, the previous day the mountain was shrouded in fog, was about 22 degrees, and a light snow fell.

When I felt fulfilled after drinking in the views from the highest mountain peak I had ever climbed, I started down around 2:30. Actually, I was a little late at starting my descent. Most of the crowd, having come up the east side from Mirror Lake, had already started down. To me, it didn't matter. It was good that I had the trail pretty much to myself. I was euphoric. I had been to the summit and had completed the John Muir Trail. I felt a "backpacker's high." I seemed to sail down over the rocky, steep trail. I had to remind myself periodically to be careful—not to stumble and fall on my coming-out journey. I kept going on past the crowded campsites, such as Mirror Lake, where there appeared to be wall-to-wall campers. Again, I was very fortunate to encounter an older gentleman who advised me to camp at Outpost Camp, a meadow below Mirror Lake. I just made it into the camp by dark. I went to bed after hurriedly eating a dry supper. I was still feeling elated. I had been to the top and had hiked about 14 miles on my coming-out journey.

From Outpost Camp to Whitney Portal, it was an easy

morning's downhill walk. I arrived at Whitney Portal around 10 am. I asked a man standing near the trail sign to take a "coming-out" picture of me at the Whitney Portal sign.

There were lots of excited Boy Scouts who were greeting their proud parents at Whitney Portal. I stopped in the gift shop to write some postcards, and then got in my car, which had been parked at Whitney Portal when Carol had shuttled me to the Bishop Pass Trailhead at Lone Pine. I stopped at the camera shop and viewed inspiring photos of Mt. Whitney and the Alabama hills, which rise in the foreground of the Sierra on the eastern slopes. I told the camera shop photographer about my storm experience near Forester Pass. He pulled out some of his most spectacular storm-cloud photographs.

I happily headed for a hot springs located between Lone Pine and Bishop. At the Lone Pine junction, two of the young hikers I had met at the top of Mt. Whitney had their arms stretched out looking for a ride. I picked them up, and we enjoyed comparing stories of our experiences. Like Blue Stocking Cap, they had camped at the top of Forester Pass on the night of the big storm. They were frightened and worried about the danger of lightening strikes. And, like Blue Stocking Cap, they had hurried down the steep trail at dusk.

I let my young hiking friends out at the road to the hot springs. When I returned to the highway, after a most refreshing soak followed by a hot dog, they were still there. Of course, I picked them up again. They complained that hitchhiking on this busy highway was very slow. I gave them a ride to Bridgeport, where they could catch a Greyhound bus home. I drove on to the Carson Pass highway and spent a pleasant night camped at Grover Hot Springs State Park. I was feeling elated. I had reached the summit of Mt. Whitney and had completed the John Muir Trail.

Chapter 8
Piute Pass Trail Junction to Dusy Creek Trail Junction
July 1968—Sierra Club High Trip
August 1991—Solo Backpack
John Muir and Pacific Crest Trails—24 miles
Total miles from the North Lake roadhead
to the South Lake roadhead—55 miles

Another glorious Sierra day in which one seems to be dissolved and absorbed and sent pulsing onward we know not where. Life seems neither long nor short, and we take no more heed to save time or make haste than do the trees and stars. This is true freedom, a good practical sort of immortality...   —*John Muir*

On my second year of hiking on the John Muir Trail, which was for the most part subsumed into the Pacific Crest Trail in 1968, I and my Sierra Club friends Evelyn Dodge, Koreen Osbun, Madeline Coles, and Marguerite Ross signed up for a national Sierra Club High Trip. There were 98 hikers, 13 staff members, plus a crew that was in charge of the pack animals. They moved our gear from campsite to campsite every other day.

What a crowd! The historical roots of this national outing were interesting, in that the idea of introducing members to the wilderness was inaugurated by John Muir and his friends. The purpose of organizing trips into the high Sierra was to convince members to support wilderness preservation—to explore, enjoy, and preserve the forest, waters, wildlife, and wilderness became the goal of the Sierra Club. Looking back from the vantage point of 25 years, it seems incredible that anyone would think of having such a large crowd trampling through fragile meadows, clearing spaces for tents and bedrolls (almost everyone used a tent) and scooping out fire rings. How our attitudes on preservation of wilderness have changed! It was the last year of the Sierra Club-sponsored High Trips with unlimited numbers of campers. Shortly thereafter, the National Park Service and the Forest Service started the wilderness permit system. A few years later, hikers were required to carry stoves and to build fires only in established campsites. "PACK IT OUT" signs are now posted on trailhead signposts, together with other regulations directed toward preserving the wilderness. I no longer have to, as in my early years on the trail, step aside to let a large contingent of Boy Scouts pass. In recent years, groups have been limited to eight or ten. During my 1991 backpack walk in the Evolution Valley, traffic was definitely limited, and the few groups I passed usually consisted of two or three people. What a change from my 1968 hiking-trip experience.

The Evolution Valley certainly offers one of the most magnificent landscapes in the Sierra wilderness. It offers such a variety of scenes—views from high mountain passes looking down into gorges, passing through large grassy meadows, walking through forests and along alpine lakes. The lake views include the glorious Evolution Lake, which is surrounded by views of the Evolution-named peaks. An early mountaineer explorer decided to name the peaks after the evolutionists, so we view Darwin, Fiske, Wallace, Haeckel, and Spencer. When I reached the Muir Pass, I especially appreciated these names. I felt that in this area, there was a sense of the earth still evolving.

For our first day's outing, our group met in the evening at the North Lake campground, which is reached by car by driving west from the town of Bishop. The next day, we were awakened from our sleep by a 5 am rising bell. I struggled to pack my duffel bag in the dark. It was my first trip with a newly acquired Eddie Bauer down sleeping bag, and I did not know how to get it into its small stuff sack. I struggled with rolling it into a tight circle; it did not begin to fit into the bag. Luckily, my friend Madeline came to my rescue. I learned from her to fill the bottom of the stuff sack first and then go round and round until it all disappears into the small sack. Having completed this process hundreds of times by now, I still marvel at how a good-sized bedroll can be reduced to fit into the tiny stuff bag. This marvel can be attributed to the amazing flexibility of natural-product goose down.

In the still dim light, we delivered our duffel bags to the pack-animal crew, snatched a hurried breakfast, and started our climb up to 11,400-foot Piute Pass, a climb of around 2,000 feet. We arrived at the pass in the late morning and had lunch near the top. We enjoyed the view looking down to the west at light-colored rocks above tree-lined slopes and beyond to the lower-altitude forest, where we would find our camp. We arrived at our campsite at the edge of large Hutchinson Meadow around 3 pm. It had become cloudy, and a few drops of rain began to fall.

As one hiker among a group of 98, it was truly a mad scramble to find a campsite. I, not being among the first to arrive at the meadow, located a site on a grassy slope above and some distance from the main commissary. I needed trees to string my rope to suspend my plastic tube tent, which I was using during my early hiking years. It was literally a tube nine-feet long, held in place by a rope at the top and by the weight of my bedroll and belongings at the bottom. It was open at both ends for ventilation. Ordinarily, unless rain was threatening, I did not string my tent up, but slept on top of it, using it for a ground cloth. This afternoon I put it up, as rain was threatening.

Soon it was raining steadily. Three of us camped on the upper slope attempted to make a rainy-day fire, using somewhat dry tree branches broken from nearby trees. It was a slow and uncertain process, but we finally succeeded. The warm fire felt so good. Noticing that our fire was blackening a sheltering overhang rock caused me to have a tinge of doubt. Looking back now after years of becoming more aware of wilderness preservation, the idea of smudge on a rock bothers me much more than it did then.

At suppertime, I came to realize it was not good to expect to eat right away. With 98 campers, the line-up at the serving table was long. Another long line occurred later when it was dish-washing time.

It rained quite steadily during the night. I learned to adjust my tent ends with clothespins so that the water did not flow in. Once during the night, when I was snuggled firmly into my sleeping bag in my see-through nylon plastic tube, looking out into the dusky mist, I suddenly saw a brazen pack animal trotting rapidly toward my tent. I was frightened. At the last minute, he reared up and turned to the side.

In the morning, when I walked down the slope to my friends' tents, I heard Marguerite exclaim, "My tent has been flooded. My things are wet." Marguerite and other campers had pitched their tents in a low, flat area, where water stood in puddles. Marguerite and nearby campers were busy trying to dry out their tent floors and then digging trenches around their tents to divert water. I learned a lesson from their experience—look for a campsite with good drainage.

This was a layover day. I pondered about what to do. Some of our group was standing around drinking coffee in the commissary, which was covered by a large canvas tarp. Others remained in their tents. I would find it confining to stay inside a tube tent during daylight hours. I wanted to explore. Could I manage to stay reasonably dry? It was not raining hard, but there appeared to be a light, misty rain. I started down the trail. Soon, I came to a trail junction sign that read "Pine Creek Trail." I turned onto the trail and reached a delightful meadow. I had arrived at colorful, rock-walled French Canyon. I took time out to enjoy eating an orange by pleasant Pine Creek. Here, I met two backpackers who announced, "We are on our way out. We have been hiking for nine days and most of the time it has been raining: we are weary of the rain." I wondered what was ahead for us. Ordinarily, summer rains in the Sierra do not last long. This appeared to be an exception.

My walk back to camp in the light, misty rain was pleasant. I managed to stay reasonably dry. I decided that I was more comfortable and content walking in the rain than standing around in camp.

After supper, the group in the upper campsite again gathered around our rock-sided campfire.

In the morning, I learned that two of my Sonoma Group friends were leaving. Catherine, after two nights at 9500-foot elevation, had developed chest pains. The trip doctor—doctors were recruited to accompany High Trips—had examined her and ordered her to return to a lower elevation. Marguerite decided to accompany her. She kept telling us, "I don't like rainy-day camping." The staff arranged with the packer for Catherine and Marguerite to ride out on horses with pack animals carrying their duffel bags.

I was glad to hear upon my return that Catherine had recovered quickly upon returning to a lower elevation.

It continued to rain off and on during the day, and I explored the trails around Hutchinson Meadow. I was beginning

RANGER STATION NEAR MCCLURE MEADOW

to get used to the rain and wet feet, but at the same time I was hoping for sunshine. The next morning, I awoke to see the sun. I rejoiced. It was a moving day—a day when we were scheduled to move to the next camp. I packed my damp gear and added it to the pile of duffel bags to be transported by the pack animals. After breakfast, my friends and I started our day's walk striding down the Piute Pass Trail. Around noon, we reached the junction of the John Muir Trail—a happy event. We enjoyed a beautiful lunch spot near the junction where the Piute Creek flows into the South Fork of the San Joaquin River. I enjoyed the sights and sounds of the swiftly flowing stream, racing over the rocky streambed.

After lunch, we followed the John Muir Trail as it lead south along the side of the South Fork until we reached the Goddard Canyon Trail. We then crossed the river on a bridge and climbed up a steep, rocky gorge. Upon reaching Evolution Creek, we were confronted and challenged by the need to ford this rocky, cold stream. This caused lots of excitement and exclamations amongst the hikers as their feet hit the rocky stream bottom. "Ouch. H---!" exclaimed one of our group. This exclamation, coming from a usually mild-mannered friend, surprised and amused the rest of us. It also created lots of opportunities for picture-taking. I discovered one of the more-experienced hikers had splashed through the stream with her boots on. What a sensible idea. That would become my style in the future.

We arrived at our campsite in beautiful Evolution Meadow rather late in the day. We had hiked 14 miles.

The next day was a layover day. I walked up to the next meadow—McClure Meadow. Of the three great meadows in the Evolution Valley—Evolution, Colby, and McClure—McClure is the largest. I believe that McClure Meadow is one of the most beautiful meadows in the Sierras. From the upper end, the viewer is treated to a rich and varied panorama. Evolution Creek meanders through the middle of the scene, surrounded by grassland and then finally framed by the ascending light-granite peaks. Both years that I have exulted in meadow views, I've been treated to a ceiling of bright-blue sky dotted with large, puffy, gently moving white cumulous clouds. I spent much of the afternoon drinking in this glorious view.

The backcountry ranger stationed at McClure Meadow came to our evening campfire program. We learned that he spends the summer patrolling the area and observing wildlife and environmental changes. His food and supplies are flown in by helicopter. On my return to the Evolution Valley in 1991, the trail had been rerouted from the meadow to the tree border in order to preserve the fragile meadow grasses. Arriving at the ranger station, I intended to tell the ranger that I appreciated the improvement in the trail route, that I was glad that I had not seen nearly as many campers as I had during my 1968 trip, and that I had seen less litter. The ranger was not home, however, so

my message of appreciation would have to wait until I came out
and passed another ranger station outside the valley.

The following day, we moved a short distance—five
miles—up the canyon and then climbed up above Evolution
Lake to Darwin Bench. Here on this high shelf, we enjoyed
splendid views of the tall granite peaks. Above Darwin Bench
and timberline are several small, granite-bound lakes. I had
time to take a short hike up to one of these alpine lakes. There,
I was delighted to find one of my favorite flowers—tiny, bright-
yellow mimulus.

On our layover day, I hiked with my friends Madeline and
Koreen down to Evolution Lake. We decided to try our luck

MCCLURE MEADOW

fishing. I put together the small telescoping pole and line that
I had brought along, and Madeline tied a line and hook to her
bamboo walking stick. Soon, she caught a small trout. We were
amazed and delighted. She had found her line and hook in a
survival kit, which, theoretically, a hiker is supposed to use in
case of an emergency. We were amazed that it had worked—

Huckleberry-Finn style. A little later, I managed to catch another small trout. Returning to our campground, we had our own small fire (pre-environmental awareness days) and cooked our little fish strung on willow sticks. They were so good! The following day was a moving day. We descended to Evolution Lake, and after a last look at this beautiful gem with its surrounding peaks, we started our climb up to 11,955-foot Muir Pass. En route, we passed clear, sparkling Sapphire Lake. I don't remember seeing another lake in which the water was so clear. From the shoreline, I could see large rocks resting on the lake bottom. We then hiked around the side of large Wanda Lake, named after one of John Muir's daughters.

The climb up to Muir Pass presented a different look and feel from the other passes I had climbed. Above timberline, the rocky trail was strewn with rocks of different shapes and colors. It had a primordial feeling—of a part of the earth that seemed unmade. I remember saying to Madeline, "This feels like the underworld." Geologist Jeff Shaffer describes this section as "land scarred as when the ice left it about 10,000 years ago, and the aspect all around is one of newborn nakedness." I wondered if this ancient look may have influenced the early mountaineers who bestowed the name of "Evolution Valley" to the area.

We arrived on top of the pass for lunch, where we enjoyed inspecting the picturesque Rock Hut—the Muir hut with its impelling dedication plaque that reads:

To John Muir
Lover of the Range of Light.
This shelter was erected in 1931.
Sierra Club and U.S. Forest Service

Evelyn, having knowledge of the hut's tradition, carried a few small sticks of firewood and placed them in the hut. It was a tradition to keep the hut supplied with wood and a few provisions to provide emergency shelter to hikers caught in a storm.

After drinking in the view from the top, we started our descent down the rocky trail and soon reached Helen Lake, named after John Muir's other daughter. The above-timberline trail continues to be surrounded by rocky crags, and I still felt the primordial ambience of the area. Slowly descending, we finally reached small trees and then arrived at a forested campsite at upper LeConte Canyon.

I searched and searched for a suitable campsite and finally ended up in a small space near the pack animals. It seemed to me that there wasn't really space for 98 campers, even though some of them had climbed up and placed their bedrolls on rocky platforms above the grassland.

At breakfast the next morning, the leader announced, "We need three volunteers to go ahead to the next campsite for 'bear duty.' The commissary supplies will arrive a day early, and they need to be guarded from hungry bears." I volunteered, along with three other campers. I was eager to walk along the trail without being in a crowd and to seek out a roomier campsite. It was a good walk. The trail first descends through the LeConte Canyon, with its forested valleys and high granite sidewalls, passing Big Pete Meadow and then Little Pete Meadow. At the Bishop Pass trail junction, I turned off the John Muir Trail to climb up beside Dusy Creek to our next campsite in the broad valley of Dusy Basin. This was my first view of this beautiful scene. Gazing across the canyon from the Dusy Creek Trail, a hiker is treated to glorious views. I looked forward to these views during my two subsequent walks in 1971 and 1991. In addition, I felt a wonderful sense of freedom walking along the trail by myself.

In the evening after the commissary arrived, I and my

volunteer companions, enjoyed being able to choose our own supper menu. We had a small campfire. I picked a bedsite near enough to hear and, hopefully, to scare away any potential marauding animals. The next day, I had time to explore and select a campsite before the large group arrived. I found what I believed was the perfect site—on a high platform in view of two tiny twin waterfalls. I was delighted. There was room enough for all my friends. Evelyn, Madeline, and Koreen were very pleased upon their arrival in the afternoon when I showed them this very special campsite. I also walked down to explore the nearby Dusy lakes and talked to a couple that was camped by the upper lake. They were interested in hearing about our group. They had arranged to have their provisions brought in by pack animals and were planning to stay for four days.

The following day was a layover day. I decided to climb up Knapsack Pass, which bordered Dusy Basin on the east. The view from the top, I believe, is one of the most beautiful of all the Sierra Pass views. Looking to the east, one can see the Palisade peaks and basins, dotted with snow patches and glaciers. To the south, one looks down toward the Dusy lakes and the granite peaks and amphitheaters rising up from the LeConte Valley. I was fortunate to be viewing this spectacular scene on a clear, sunny day.

On my trip back to camp, I passed by the deserted campsite of the couple I had talked to the previous day that had come in with pack animals. They were gone and had left a very messy campsite. There were cans and boxes stuffed into the fire ring. This bothered me very much. Thinking back, I can say that some things have improved greatly since the National Park Service and the Forest Service have advocated for a "Pack It Out" policy. I have not seen this kind of mess in recent years.

The next morning we packed up, said our farewells to our

hiker friends, and climbed up over rocky Bishop Pass and down the other side to our trailhead at South Lake. A car shuttle had been arranged to reach our cars parked at North Lake.

I departed from the Sierra Club's High Trip with a store of rich memories of the beautiful Evolution Valley—a very special place.

I returned to the Evolution Valley on a backpacking trip in 1991. How different was my mountaineering experience. During the 1968 walk, I had not as yet learned to backpack. By 1991, I had completed the 2638-mile Pacific Crest Trail from Mexico to Canada. Reminiscing, I asked myself, "Did I have any idea in 1968 of backpacking from Mexico to Canada?" I think not. I only remember having a growing desire to complete the 200-mile John Muir Trail. Actually, looking back, I do not think that I even knew about the Pacific Crest Trail in the summer of 1968. My first knowledge of the trail came to me upon seeing a newspaper report of Eric Ryback's trail walk in 1970. I bought the book The High Adventure of Eric Ryback, published by Chronicle Books. I read it eagerly. What a disappointment to read later in the first publication of The Wilderness Press Guide to the Pacific Crest Trail that there was evidence that he had not walked the complete way.

By the time I knew about the Trail and was ready to walk on it, I realize that the seed had been planted during the early walks when I was introduced to and inspired by the beauty of the mountain wilderness.

After reaching the Canadian border in August of 1998, my friends asked, "Where are you going to hike now?" I replied, "I want to make a return visit to some of my favorite places." The Evolution Valley was one of them. Although 23 years had passed and my mountaineering experience had greatly expanded, the landscape had changed little. The Evolution Valley has

MUIR HUT

remained a very special place—a place of extraordinary beauty.

On the summit of 11,400-foot Piute Pass in late August of 1991, I was greeted with snow flurries. Hutchinson Meadow was tranquil—there were no campers. My campsite at McClure Meadow again presented me with a magnificent view—a wide expanse of valley framed by trees and granite peaks and crowned with a ceiling of deep-blue sky dotted by puffy white cumulus clouds. The views surrounding Evolution Lake challenged me to look upward to identify the Evolutionists—Darwin, Fiske, Wallace, Haeckel, and Spencer. Climbing up to the Muir Pass, the stark, rocky, sandy surroundings still presented me with the same primordial feeling as on my previous walk. I was pleased to see the John Muir Hut looking strong and sturdy, still guarding the Pass. I camped at Little Pete Meadow and was treated to a full moon reflecting brightly on a nearby granite cliff. At the Dusy Basin, I searched for the twin waterfalls. I could not find them. Had they dried up by late August? I settled for a campsite looking toward the granite cliffs and peaks rising above the LeConte Canyon. I climbed out over Bishop Pass, my third Bishop Pass trip, holding onto a treasure trove of memories.

Chapter 9
Purple Lake to Piute Pass Trail Junction
August 1970
John Muir Trail—38 miles
To and from roadhead to reach the Muir Trail—
19 miles

…Small lakes abound in all sorts of situations,—on ridges, along mountain sides, and in piles of moraine boulders, most of them mere pools…How pure their waters are, clear as crystal in polished stone basins. —John Muir

This short stretch along a middle section of the John Muir Trail encompasses another landscape of extraordinary mountain scenery. For a hiker, there are many ups and downs as the trail climbs up passes and descends to valleys. The trail edges around numerous alpine lakes and follows beside cool, rippling streams. Granite peaks and cliffs are frequently within view. A hiker is forever surrounded by glorious wilderness scenes.

This was my second year of backpacking. This was the first and only year in which I approached the trail from the western side of the Sierras. This was my first experience and, indeed, a learning experience in hitchhiking from the road to the trailhead. I approached this trip with mixed feelings. I was excited and eager. At the same time, I felt some uneasiness. I was still a learner.

Approaching the middle Sierras from the western side of the mountains, I drove east from the vicinity of Fresno, passing the busy boating and fishing reservoir lakes of Shaver and Huntington, which are all a part of the hydroelectric system of Southern California Edison. I then drove to Florence Lake. My plan was to come out at Florence Lake and go in at Thomas Edison Lake, which is approximately twelve road miles north of Florence Lake. I wanted to leave my car at the coming-out trailhead. I felt that I would feel so much better coming out to the certainty of my car, so I would plan to find a ride from Florence Lake to Thomas Edison Lake at the beginning of my journey.

Arriving at Florence Lake, I searched for a parking place. There were not many. In addition to being a trailhead for hikers, Florence Lake attracted fishermen. I ended up maneuvering into a small place on top of a broad slab of rock. I then found a small store, which seemed to me about the size of a bus shelter. I went in an asked the store attendant, "How can I find a ride to Lake Thomas Edison?" "Well, you will have to hitchhike," he replied. "There is no shuttle service." I walked back up the road for a short distance. Then, I selected my "beg-for-a-ride place" about half a block from the end of the road. After leaving my pack slightly out of sight against a rock, I started my ride-seeking. As a car approached, I extended my hand out from the elbow. Three cars passed. They paid no attention to me. I put my hand out a little further. Two more cars passed and ignored me. I was beginning to feel a little desperate, and so when the next car approached, I put my hand out all the way and stared directly at the driver. It worked. Two fishermen stopped and gave me a ride in their pickup for five miles to the "Y" junction, where they let me off. They were returning to Fresno, and I needed to take the other road to Lake Thomas Edison. I was thankful for the ride and decided that I could walk the remaining seven miles. I turned around to shoulder my pack just as a man and his son stopped and gave me a ride all the way to the Lake Thomas Edison store. I felt so lucky. After visiting the store for a snack of crackers and cheese and filling my water bottle, I started on the trail. I walked around the north side of the large Thomas Edison Lake—a reservoir lake. By evening, I found a campsite near the lake's outlet. I felt so elated at having accomplished what I thought would be the hardest part of my journey—hitchhiking to the trailhead.

The next morning, I started up the trail. My plan was to approach the Muir Trail by way of the Goodale Pass Trail. I was following a trail line on my 1953 topo map of the Mt. Abbot Quad. I found a trail that would turn left, leading away from the lakeshore. Soon, I noticed that I was walking on a fairly newly constructed jeep road. I was puzzled. I was walking on the north side of Cold Creek, and my map indicated that the trail followed the south side of the creek. At midday, I grew more concerned when the trail veered to the northwest. I kept checking my compass, expecting the northwesterly direction to be temporary. Then I came to a sign that read "Devil's Bathtub." This was definitely the wrong trail. I started back. By late afternoon, I came to a trail junction with another jeep road leading to the east. This seemed to be the right direction to take me to Goodale Pass. I walked a ways on the jeep trail and came to a mosquito swamp. I felt uncertain. I turned back. It was getting dark. I decided to camp by a small stream near the junction of the two jeep trails.

Soon I noticed that two hikers had come up the trail and were camping near me. I went over to their camp and told them of my plans to reach the Goodale Pass by way of Graveyard Meadow and said that I was confused by this new jeep trail. They replied that they were also headed for Graveyard Meadow and that they thought this new jeep trail would reach the meadow. They planned to travel on it the next day. Not completely reassured, I went to bed.

During the night, I kept thinking about the confusing jeep trail and weighed plans for the next day. I made a decision. Although I acknowledged that it was highly probable that the jeep trail leading to the east would connect with the Goodale Trail, I decided to return to the junction I had left in the morning, where there was a sign that read "Muir Trail." I wanted the security of a sure route.

In the morning, I arose early and was on the trail at 7:30 am. I made very good time. I was eager and was headed downhill. I arrived at the junction at 10 am. The sign read "Muir Trail-Quail Meadow—4 miles." I was disappointed, as I did not want to reach the Muir Trail by way of Quail Meadow— the meadow trail would mean a lot more mileage for me. I resigned myself, however, to going to Quail Meadow. I wanted the certainty of reaching the trail.

Feeling a little discouraged as I strolled along the trail, soon I came to a new sign that read "Graveyard Meadow-Goodale Pass." Hallelujah! I felt so good as I turned onto the Goodale Pass Trail. Now I really knew where I was and that I was on the right trail.

By noon, I reached Lower Graveyard Meadow for lunch and siesta. I was enjoying shade under a pine tree when a ranger walked by and stopped to talk to me. He assured me that I would be walking on a good trail all the way over Goodale Pass. He was impressed that I was hiking alone. I was not sure that he really approved of the idea. Actually, I didn't see other solo women hikers during the '70s, and it was only during the last years of my walk that I saw other women hiking alone.

Walking at a leisurely pace, I reached upper Graveyard Meadow by evening. Like many high-alpine meadows, it offered a pleasant scene. For a hiker, the meadows usually offer water and a level spot for camping. Meadows also offer a feeling of space after walking through heavily wooded areas. They offer a variety of colors with the usually green, waving grasses, often dotted with wildflowers. Birds also flock to meadows. Meadows are like little oases.

While I was selecting my campsite, I spotted another party of campers. As I approached their camp, I saw that it was the same couple that had been camped near me the previous evening. They had reached the meadow by way of the jeep trail. I then realized that I had walked some additional miles by backtracking to the Muir Trail sign, but I didn't mind; I'd had a good walk. They invited me to their campfire, so after supper I joined them. They told me that they had a ranch near Madera and that they liked to come to the mountains often during the summer. As we talked about Yosemite trails, they asked me if I had ever met Ranger Bill Nealey. I replied, "Yes, I met Bill Nealey on a hike that he led to the Yosemite High Camps in 1962. I shared with them Bill's disdain for steel bridges. When we came to a steel bridge near Lake Tenaya, Bill expressed his dislike by persuading us to ford the stream rather than walk across the new steel bridge. "Wilderness bridges should be of wood," declared Bill Nealey.

They told me that Bill Nealey's children were staying at their ranch that summer while Bill and his new bride were traveling in Copenhagen. He had lost his first wife shortly after the 1961 High Camp trip and also tragically lost one of his six children. It was an interesting coincidence to hear about Ranger Nealey while camped at Graveyard Meadow.

In the "cool of the morning," I climbed to the top of 11,000-foot Goodale Pass. It was not a difficult climb. It was a rocky trail, however, and I did pass a couple coming down from the pass that complained that they thought that it was difficult.

From the top, I enjoyed views looking back at the elongated, green Graveyard Meadow. Then, looking to the north, I had a glimpse of my familiar and favorite peaks—Banner and Ritter. I was delighted. They had become like old friends to me.

On my walk down the north side of the pass, I met a large group of hikers. I learned from their leader that it was a group of 60 hikers on a Sierra Club outing. They were followed by a long pack train. They had been camped at Wilbur May Lake. As I was stationed at my post above the trail waiting for all 60 to march by, I was greeted by questions and comments. The most frequent comment was "Aren't you afraid to be hiking alone? What would you do if something happened to you?" One lady commented that she would like to go backpacking with about four people with a pace similar to hers. Another woman admired my homemade pants and asked where I had bought them. She seemed surprised and impressed when I replied that I had made them. Another woman, who learned that I was from Santa Rosa, knew a fellow Sonoma County Sierra Club member, Charlotte Stephens. One man commented that I was "a brave woman." Finally, a man toward the end of the line expressed a favorite thought and one that I shall always remember. He said, "It is good to have solitude sometimes."

Further down the trail I met a tall man riding a horse. I was surprised and delighted to be introduced to Mr. Bob Cutter, a man who had made a great contribution to the comfort of hikers. Mr. Cutter, of Cutter Laboratories in the Bay Area, was the developer of Cutter's Mosquito Repellent. I asked him how he had put together this helpful formula. He told me that he and his colleagues had tested various lotions for a number of years and had tried them in heavily mosquito-laden areas in Alaska and on Hudson Bay. One of the first they tried worked well, but turned their faces black. Finally, after many trials, they developed the present formula. I assured him that my friends and I had found the lotion to be very effective. I thanked him and added that I knew that many hikers appreciated the lotion, which enabled them to hike more comfortably. Actually, today it is easy to find many formulations of DEET to protect against insects; however, to my knowledge, Cutter's was the first effective one to be developed and was quite new during my early years of backpacking.

At a junction, near the Lake of the Lone Indian, I turned onto a heavily used trail. As it veered to the left, I soon realized that I was on the trail that led to Wilbur May Lake. I retraced my steps and returned to the Goodale Pass Trail. It was barely discernible in comparison to the Wilbur Lake Trail. The horde of 60 Sierra Club hikers had trampled out a very wide swath of trail as they descended from Wilbur May Lake.

My siesta was spent beside the beautiful Lake of the Lone Indian. I marveled at the glorious scene. I was enjoying the shade of a large Jeffrey pine while gazing across the deep-blue mountain lake, edged at the far side by a light-colored granite cliff. In the midst of this calm, peaceful setting, trout sporadically surfaced, leaving a little circle of waves.

Shortly after my siesta, I reached the John Muir Trail and turned north. I found a little hideaway for my campsite—a small shelf above the trail near Helen Lake. Helen Lake is now listed as Squaw Lake on newer maps.

Upon awakening in the morning, I was eager to carry out my plan. I would day-hike north to Purple Lake, which I had reached from the north on my 1969 walk, and then turn around and retrace my steps to my campsite near Helen Lake. On the following day, I would proceed on my walk south toward Piute Creek, which I had reached from the south on my 1968 walk. I would be filling in an unhiked section of the trail sandwiched between my two previous hikes.

I stuffed my bedroll so that it would be smaller and less conspicuous, then pushed my pack under a bush and stowed my keys, lunch, money, and water bottle into my windbreaker pocket. Moving cautiously down to the trail from my hideaway, I took a last glance upward and felt satisfied that my pack was sufficiently hidden from sight.

For years, it had been generally assumed that packs left at camps while hikers were exploring the nearby country were safe. On my 1969 hike, however, near Agnew Meadow just north of Purple Lake, there was a report of stolen packs, and the rangers advised us to be careful. How discouraging to hear this report. To me, such a practice did not blend in with the spirit of the wilderness.

When I reached the junction of the trail to Cascade Valley, I studied my map and decided to take the lower trail—the Cascade Valley Trail—and then I would return on the John Muir Trail. In this way, I would be making a little loop and would be enjoying the variety of two different trail scenes. The Cascade Valley Trail did, indeed, leap down into a valley, and I was soon enjoying a spectacular scene as I looked up at the light-colored granite canyon sidewalls.

Arriving at the Fish Creek-Purple Lake Trail junction, I was viewing a familiar scene—the trail that I had hiked on during my first year's backpack in 1969. I paused and looked at the surrounding meadow fondly. I turned slowly and started climbing up the two-and-one-half-mile trail leading to Purple Lake, all the time remembering familiar scenes. Arriving at the lake, I recalled that it seemed to me to be well named. Again, it reflected the dark-blue color that I had remembered during my last visit. I found a comfortable viewpoint and enjoyed lunch while looking out across the deep-blue lake. Once again on the John Muir Trail walking south, I soon reached Virginia Lake. I enjoyed the view of the small, pleasant lake, but did not feel that it was quite as colorful as Purple Lake. As I began to descend shortly after passing Virginia Lake, I came across a most-unusual view—the view looking down at Tully Hole. I could see a narrow, grassy meadow and through it snaked, making several distinct curves, a narrow stream. It was quite an amazing sight. I had heard from rangers and naturalists how grassy meadows are continually competing for space with streams. The grassland is continually spreading and taking up more space and, at the same time, the stream is continually running through the grassy meadow, tearing up the grassy soil. Looking down at Tully Hole, I was seeing this competition taking place. I was also intrigued by its combination of space, color, and design. I reached for my camera and took several photos.

Shortly after passing Tully Hole, I came to the junction of where the Muir Trail meets the Cascade Valley Trail, which I had hiked on in the morning. As I climbed up toward the Goodale Pass junction, another tremendous view came into sight—the view looking down into the Cascade Valley, and to the east, the view looking toward the Sierra Crest.

Shortly afterward, I returned to my hideout. I was pleased to find my pack and all my possessions safely in place. I also felt pleased that my plan of day hiking without the weight of my pack had worked out so well.

My next benchmark the following day was to climb the 10,900-foot Silver Pass. I reached the summit around ten in the morning. Again, I enjoyed spectacular views from the top. To the north, I could see the Cascade Valley and beyond it I could see the silhouette of my perennial favorites—Banner Peak and Mt. Ritter. To the south, there was a fine view of Mt. Gabb.

I decided to make camp early. Although there had been very few people walking the trail during the last two days, I anticipated that there might be a crowd ahead, camping in Quail Valley with its proximity to Lake Thomas Edison. I found a pleasant, tree-lined campsite at Pocket Meadow. I spent a luxurious afternoon bathing, reading, and absorbing the good feeling of the peaceful surroundings of the river and woods.

It was Sunday, and I had time to read from Pierre Teihard de Chardin's "Hymn of the Universe." Although I didn't carry complete books with me when backpacking, I packed small photocopies of favorite readings.

The following day, I had an easy walk, coasting down to 7,800-foot Quail Meadow. During the descent, I enjoyed some fine views, looking toward Mono Creek. Arriving at Quail Meadow, I encountered heavy traffic. First, I stepped aside to make room for a noisy, enthusiastic Boy Scout troop. Shortly afterward, a Presbyterian Church group from Santa Cruz appeared. As I approached the ascent to Bear Ridge, a helpful couple advised me to carry a good supply of water. This proved to be useful

MARIE LAKE

advice, as there was no water for approximately six miles.

The climb up to Bear Ridge was pleasant and not too difficult treading on a well-graded, well-planned, and well-maintained trail. At the top, I was treated to spectacular views looking toward the famed Seven Gables and Mt. Hilgard. I searched and found a campsite near trickling Bear Creek. It was pure delight. I was next to a rock-walled pool and in view of a small, picturesque waterfall. I had water music all during the night.

The trail on my next morning's walk continued south along the side of trickling Bear Creek. I decided not to hurry. I was ahead of my planned schedule. I did not want to come out early. I wanted to enjoy all of my allotted time in the beautiful wilderness of the John Muir Trail. Furthermore, I loved the sights and sounds of Bear Creek.

My lunch stop was at grass-covered Rosemarie Meadow. In the afternoon, as the trail climbed up toward 10,600-foot Selden Pass, I sought out a campsite. To my delight, I found a dream of a campsite on a little peninsula between upper and lower Marie Lake. What a glorious panorama. There were so many silvery granite peaks rising up from the border of the lake I could not begin to count them. A large rock protruded from the water near my campsite so that I had water music as the gentle waves lapped against the rocks. After sunset, a three-quarter moon arose, extending this extraordinary scene of natural beauty far into the night.

My morning scene was one of equal delight. From the warmth and comfort of my bedsite, I watched the peaks come alive with the light from the rising sun. First, the highest peaks came alive with light; then, slowly, the next lower level received the sun's morning rays. Slowly, the golden glow inched down the peaks to reach the lakeshore. I finally arose to make breakfast. What a beautiful morning!

This scene of morning light on Marie Lake has remained with me to this day. Early in my mountain hiking experience, I stumbled on the practice of visualizing the campsites of my summers' walks. I practice to bring the scenes back during winter nights and whenever I wish to enjoy scenes of natural beauty. In addition to bringing back visual pictures of my campsites, when I want to bring back memories of special beauty, scenes will spontaneously return to me and I will bask in the enjoyment of their beauty all over again.

In recent years, I have discovered that there are books and workshops on visual imagery with the objective of promoting relaxation and reducing stress. I had no knowledge of this practice in my early hiking days when I stumbled onto the practice of visualizing my favorite campsite and scenes of special beauty. To me, it was and remains a means of pure enjoyment.

The next day's climb up to 10,872-foot Selden Pass was an easy one. Views from the top looking north again included Marie Lake, Bear Valley, Mt. Hilgard, and a multitude of unnamed peaks. To the south, I could see small, heart-shaped Heart Lake.

As I was descending from the Pass, a good-sized crowd was climbing up from the south. The first group I encountered was a Girl Scout troop. Then, a still-larger group followed. While waiting for them to file past me, I thought I heard a familiar voice. I was puzzled—then I decided to explore the source of the familiar sound. "Where are you from?" I inquired. "San Mateo," was the answer. "I think I know you." Whereupon, I took off my glasses and confirmed that it really was Father Bill Barker, whom I had worked with at Catholic Charities. What a surprise! We had fun comparing notes about our hiking experiences. He was walking with a group from the Trinity Episcopal Church in San Mateo. As one of his fellow hikers said, "What a small world!"

I drifted down easily to Salley Keyes Lake, arriving around 11 am. Again, I decided to make camp early. I did not want to come out at Florence Lake until Friday. I planned to spend the afternoon bathing, washing socks, and most of all, drinking in the view. For most of the afternoon, it was quiet and peaceful and I enjoyed the not-everyday treat of afternoon tea. Unfortunately, the afternoon peace and quiet was broken around suppertime when two large, noisy groups arrived—including more Boy Scouts. Surprisingly, one of the groups even engaged in shooting firecrackers! How unwelcome a sound in the pristine wilderness. This proved to be one of my noisiest campsites. How much better it is on the Sierra trails now that wilderness permits are required and large groups are no longer allowed.

Returning to the Muir Trail junction the next morning, I encountered a man and a woman on horseback. The woman recognized me, saying, "Hello, I remember you from Florence Lake when you were trying to find a ride to Lake Thomas Edison." Indeed, I did remember that she had emerged from a nearby camper next to where I was struggling with my first hitchhiking experience and offered me a welcome cold drink.

She told me of a difficult happening that she and her companion had experienced while riding over from Florence Lake on the upper Blaney Meadow Trail. When they came to a rocky section, her horse fell! Luckily, she survived with only a minor leg bruise. What a frightening experience, I thought to myself. I'd rather walk.

My walk south to Piute Creek was mostly downhill, but it was not a swift and easy walk. I moved slowly. I do believe that sand and rock makes for one of the hardest and most treacherous descents, as the sand on top of rock can act as a slide, creating a great opportunity for falling. I was cautious. Approaching Piute Creek for a late lunch, I had visions of seeking out a peaceful lunch spot beside a river, much as I had enjoyed on my 1968 Sierra Club hike. It was not to be. The bridge and bridge approach had been preempted by two nude bathers—one sun bathing and the other splashing. It was not a quiet, peaceful place. I decided to move on, but before turning north, I stopped to drink in the view. I had remembered and enjoyed the majestic dome-like rock rising up from the river's edge. As I gazed at the dark, granite dome, it still seemed majestic and awesome.

I had reached my John Muir Trail junction destination for this year at Piute Creek, where I had hiked with the Sierra Club in 1968. I turned north and found a quiet lunch spot. Soon after lunch, I reached the junction with the Florence Lake Trail, where I turned off to reach my trailhead at Florence Lake.

As my trail map did not cover much of the Florence Lake Trail, I wondered and worried if I would find water for my evening campsite or if I would have to make a 'dry' camp. I was so relieved when I learned that the trail was following close to the San Joaquin River. For my evening camp, I not only had water, but I had a place of special beauty. My bedroom rested on a small level spot on soft duff, which had fallen from a nearby large Jeffrey Pine. I was high enough from the river to stay dry and yet near enough to see and hear the water music. To my delight, soon after I went to bed, a nearly full moon arose, and its light reflected on the river. There were special lighting effects as the moon highlighted the ripples on the water. How glorious!

My last day's hike was an easy one. It was mostly downhill. The trail passes by the entrance to the privately owned 7-D Ranch (in newer books it is called the Muir Ranch). I was fortunate, as I arrived at the east shore of Florence Lake just as the small ferryboat that plies between the roadhead, where my car was parked, and the east end of the lake near the Muir Ranch, had arrived. I climbed in the boat and enjoyed a pleasant ride to the other end of the lake. When I arrived at the Florence Lake roadhead, I met a couple that was looking for a ride back to their car, which was parked near Lake Thomas Edison. I smiled and assured them that I was most happy to give them a ride. I knew what it was like to beg for a ride. We enjoyed comparing notes on our hikes. They had hiked from Lake Thomas Edison to Florence Lake, climbing over Bear Ridge.

My next destination was to nearby Mono Hot Springs Resort. How good it felt to soak in the mineral water in an old-fashioned, big bathtub. To this day, when I come out from a backpack hike, I remember how good it felt to end a hike at a hot springs. I wish that every trail ended at a nearby hot springs.

Chapter 10
Reds Meadow to Purple Lake
August 1969
John Muir Trail—14 miles
Round-trip—29 miles

Then it seemed to me the Sierra should be called, not the Nevada, or Snowy Range, but the Range of Light.
—*John Muir*

This short section starts near the Reds Meadow Resort and climbs up to Crater Meadow, passing by the Red Cones displaying evidence of past volcanic activity. After passing Duck Creek—the outlet to Duck Lake—I left the Muir Trail to descend to the Cascade Valley, which borders Fish Creek. Before reaching Reds Meadow on the return trip, I was treated to a view of one of the most beautiful waterfalls outside of Yosemite Valley—Rainbow Falls.

This was a momentous year, a decisive year, for me—my first year of backpacking. The hike was only for a short distance but, for me, it was a big beginning for my future journey. Perhaps had it not been a successful walk, I might never have completed my journey, 20 years later, on the Pacific Crest Trail. Fortunately, I felt good about my walk and returned ready for more.

The decision to learn to backpack was arrived at after being introduced to the Muir Trail by Joe Wampler in 1966. I came away from the walk with the Wampler Tours determined to complete the trail.

The following summer, in 1967, I eagerly signed up with the Wampler Tours, planning to complete a section of the trail south from Reds Meadow. I was excited in anticipation of the walk, when I heard from Joe Wampler that the tour could not proceed. Because of a very heavy snowfall, he could not obtain a permit to enter the High Sierra with pack animals. Although I accepted Joe Wampler's substitute offering—a Beauty Camp on McGee Creek on the east side of the Sierra north of Bishop, I found camping in one place disappointing and left the group early. Fortunately, I was able to join my Sonoma hiking friends for a walk with veteran Tuolumne ranger, Carl Sharsmith, on a most enjoyable walk, visiting the Yosemite High Camps—Tuolumne, Vogelsang, Sunrise, and Merced. The High Camps walk completes a section of the John Muir Trail between the Yosemite Valley and Tuolumne Meadows. It also offers glorious views of the Yosemite National Park backcountry. The walk was greatly enhanced by the gentle humor of Ranger Sharsmith, by his knowledge of natural history, and especially by his delight in finding alpine wildflowers. For me, he enriched all of my future walks with his contagious love for flowers and mountains. I have walked and talked with Carl Sharsmith for many years following the High Camp trip. He has become, for me, a living inspiration.

In 1968, I completed the Evolution Valley section of the John Muir Trail via a Sierra Club High Trip. Emerging through these group tour experiences, I continued to feel determined to complete the Muir Trail. I was also beginning to have a desire for a more simple style of wilderness hiking. I was beginning to feel that I no longer wanted to be part of a group where there was so much talk about, "What's on the menu for dinner," and, "Don't you think the breakfast pancakes were overcooked?" With this growing desire to seek a different style of hiking, I approached Ranger Sharsmith and said, "Do you think that I could learn to backpack?" He replied, "Try backpacking for a short walk." So, in August of 1969, I was ready to try a short, six-day trial walk.

During the winter and spring of 1969, my backpacking preparation included reading the Sierra Club publication, "Going Light with Backpack or Burro." It was published in 1951, and I had purchased the 1966 edition. In the intervening years, I have browsed through this little book countless times and cherish it for its simplicity.

Equipment and styles in backpacking have changed considerably since 1951. Presently, hikers can attend workshops and read any number of recently published books to prepare for backpacking. As part of my preparations, I made numerous visits to small backpacking equipment stores in San Francisco before I chose my pack, a Camptrails Horizon pack, weighing 24 ounces, together with a medium-sized Summit pack frame weighing 25 ounces. The frame was made from superlite magnesium. I still have this pack and use it today. It worked satisfactorily for me and I have become attached to it. I have, however, changed hip belts three times, as the original pack did not have a padded belt, only a broad, stout, cloth-woven belt. It seems strange and laughable now, looking back over these 25 years, to have the doubts I had upon changing hip belts; would a padded hip belt really give sufficient support?

My down sleeping bag had been purchased upon the recommendation of a friend by catalogue from Eddie Bauer for my 1968 Sierra Club trip. My Abercrombie & Fitch boots, however, have been greatly improved. For rain protection, I chose a poncho and a plastic tube tent for rainy nights. My food consisted of some freeze-dried dinner packages, together with cereal, nuts, and dried fruit. My menu has changed and improved a great deal through the years by way of trial and error. During my first few years of backpacking, I didn't own

a stove. I depended on a small, twig campfire for cooking. I
heated water in a billy can—a topless coffee can—a practice
I had learned on my 1968 Sierra High Trip outing. With my
new equipment and knowledge gleaned from Going Light
with Backpack or Burro, I was ready for my trial run.

In 1969, prior to my first backpack experience, my friend
Evelyn and I had participated in a University of California,
Berkeley-sponsored field trip studying biology and geology of
the nearby Sierra mountain region. We had gathered together
at Agnew Meadow and walked to Lake Ediza. A biologist and
geologist were our teachers. I chose as my course elective study
to write about the gray-crowned rosy finch. This is a most interesting bird. It nests on high, rocky cliffs at around 11,000
feet. Upon my return home, I completed more research on this
intriguing bird and wrote a paper about it.

Upon our return to Agnew Meadow at the end of our U.C.
course, I said goodbye to my teachers and fellow students.
Some of my classmates expressed concerns about my plan
to backpack alone. "Wasn't it dangerous to hike alone?" they
asked. My good friend Evelyn extended her warm best wishes
for the success of my journey. Did she seem a little worried? I
thought I detected a hint of anxiety as we parted.

I drove to nearby Reds Meadow and parked my car at the
trailhead. My first destination was the ranger station. I had
resolved to check with the ranger about trail conditions before
starting out. It had been a heavy snow year, and I had heard
reports about bridge washouts. I went to the ranger station and
found no one home. Little did I know at that time in my backpacking career that backcountry rangers spend most of their

time out in the forest checking trail conditions.

I kept checking and watching for the ranger's return. It did not happen. I looked around, seeking other sources of trail information. I spotted and walked to the nearby pack station. In answer to my inquiry about the John Muir Trail, a wrangler mumbled and said he had heard reports of a big washout at the Fish Creek crossing. This report added to my uncertainty. It was now early afternoon and I was growing impatient. I was torn between being cautious and my desire to start hiking. For my first backpack experience, I had chosen a loop trail that I had read about in Starr's Guide to the John Muir Trail. The trail would lead south to Fish Creek and return by way of the Muir Trail. Not wanting to delay my start any longer, I made a decision. I would start walking south on the John Muir Trail and, if the Fish Creek Bridge was out and the river crossing appeared to be dangerous, I would turn around and return the same way I had come.

My next doubt arose when I proceeded to lift my pack from my car trunk. It seemed so heavy! At home, it had weighed 24 pounds. Now it seemed heavier than it had in the protective corner of my kitchen.

Finally, starting from Reds Meadow, I climbed up a ridge that afforded glorious views looking back at Banner Peak and Mount Ritter—perennial favorites. The trail then passed the Red Cones—red volcanic posts standing near the trail, which gave evidence of past volcanic activity.

By evening I had reached Upper Crater Meadow, where I found a pleasing spot. Situated among some small trees a few yards off the trail, it was supplied with plenty of wood and water. No one was camped nearby. I had met only one other hiking group, a father and son who had also started at Reds Meadow headed for the Fish Creek Trail.

I was pleased with my campsite. I cooked my supper of freeze-dried chicken stew, prepared my sleeping place, and waited for dark. I remember thinking, "I thought I would be frightened sleeping out alone, but I am not." I felt good. Now when people ask me, "Aren't you afraid to camp out alone?" I reply, "On my first night I thought I would be afraid sleeping out alone, but I was not. I have enjoyed sleeping out alone in the wilderness ever since."

The following day, my walk continuing south was full of more glorious sights. Awestruck, I stopped at a viewpoint overlooking the Fish Creek Valley, with its granite cliffs and exclaimed aloud, "Oh, how beautiful!" Then, turning around, I saw a couple of hikers approaching. I was a little embarrassed to have been caught talking to myself. Now, looking back after years of backpacking, I think nothing of muttering my thoughts out loud whenever and wherever I feel the urge.

On my second day's walk, there was no water between Deer Creek and Duck Creek, a walk of approximately six miles. I grew thirsty and tired. I did not carry an auxiliary water pack on my first trip. I was still learning.

Although I passed very few hikers—none going north and just two groups going south—I was glad to meet a young, strong hiker at the ford over Duck Creek. He kindly offered to help me across by supporting me while I made big steps from one stone to the other. Had he not appeared, I probably would have waded across and arrived at the other side with wet boots.

By evening I found what I thought was the perfect campsite—a small, level spot slightly above and overlooking the outlet of Duck Lake. My bedsite was on a little platform amidst some trees, which provided a bed of soft, dry duff. My kitchen looked out toward a lovely waterfall. I could listen to the waterfall music all through the night. It became, for me, one of those idyllic sights that I like to bring back into my memory all through the years.

In the morning, I had a short walk south to Purple Lake, where I was to turn off the John Muir Trail to head for Fish Creek Valley. Purple Lake is, I believe, appropriately named, as it has a dark, rosy-purple glow. I enjoyed gazing at it as I ate my mid-morning snack of milk and honey. I then found the trail leading down to the valley—a steep descent switchbacking down along the rocky canyon wall with intermittent views to the western mountain peaks and to Fish Creek.

When I arrived at the grassy Fish Creek Meadow, there were mosquitoes and a troop of Boy Scouts. I was glad to leave them and turn northwest onto the Fish Creek Trail. I was headed for the uncertainty of a high-water ford at Second Crossing. Soon, I met the man with his son whom I had talked to when we were both departing from Reds Meadow. They were on their way to Purple Lake. I was eager to hear about the river crossing. They told me that the water was swift and high when they waded across at Second Crossing. I was worried. Should I turn back? Not until I had seen and studied the scene, I decided. Later in the afternoon, I met a ranger who was working with a small crew of trail workers who were sawing trees that had fallen across the trail. There appeared to have been a small avalanche at this location in which the snow had swept the trees downward across the path. The ranger said, in response to my inquiry about Second Crossing, that there was a log across the creek a little upstream from the usual trail crossing. I felt hopeful. I made camp on a level clearing near the approach to Second Crossing. I wanted to tackle the decision and challenge of the river crossing on a new day in the calm of the morning.

I arose early in the morning. I ate a cold breakfast and drank cold tea instead of hot tea. I was eager to be on my way. Soon, I arrived at the wide, swiftly moving river. I kept moving north beyond the ford, feeling both hope and fear. There it was—I found the log crossing. It was broad and sturdy looking. I decided that I would practice. I would try going across the log without my pack. It was easy. Then, unbuckling my hip belt—a recommended practice for crossing streams that enables a hiker to slip out of the pack if necessary in case of a fall that might result in being submerged in water. I started across. Again, it was surprisingly easy. Safely on the opposite bank, I rejoiced that I had made the worrisome crossing. When I was ready to move on, I found that the log's base was surrounded by a thick tangle of elderberry bushes. How could I wade through these? Taking off my pack, I explored. I found a red bandanna, indicating that some other hiker had had trouble penetrating the dense undergrowth. I still have the bandanna as a reminder of Second Crossing. I decided after my exploration that it hardly seemed possible to bushwhack through the dense undergrowth. I came up with another plan. I would climb up and slide myself and pack over two huge, approximately five-foot-high, boulders. By inching along carefully, I succeeded in climbing over and around the boulders. Finally, I arrived at the trail crossing. I felt so good at having succeeded in making this difficult crossing safely. I felt a little regret, however, at having scratched my shiny new pack frame as I slid it along the rock. Oh well, now it was broken in.

Climbing up the trail toward Fish Creek Hot Springs, I met a couple that greeted me, saying, "We remember seeing you at Goddard Canyon last year. You were trying to identify a hummingbird." What a surprise! They told me that they were spending a whole month in the mountains that summer. Their daughter and a friend were with them and their daughter had quit her job in order to have the time to hike in the mountains. They exclaimed, "We love camping in the Sierras."

When I arrived at the hot springs, it was occupied. Someone's bandanna was decorating the entrance as a sign of occupancy. I waited my turn and then was soon enjoying the luxurious soaking offered by the rock-walled, open, natural hot springs. I felt so relaxed. Although I followed the bath with a siesta, I still did not feel much like hiking for the rest of the afternoon. I thought I learned a lesson for the future. Try to plan for the hot bath at the end of the day.

Iva Bell Hot Springs, near Fish Creek

My campsite near Island Crossing was a rather ordinary one. Although I hunted around, I couldn't find an attractive place. I was learning that not every hiking day would end at an idyllic spot such as the campsite by the waterfall at Duck Creek. I reminded myself not to cook such a big meal. I had cooked too big a kettle of stew the night before and, not wanting to waste it, ate it up and felt uncomfortably full all during the night. Another lesson to learn.

My next morning's challenge was my final log crossing at

Island Crossing. The log was broad and strong, but some of its branches were still attached and were sticking up where I wanted to walk. I had to weave myself around these branches and at the same time, be careful not to lose my balance. It was a little scary. I rejoiced when I reached the other side. Now, with my feet planted safely on terra firma, I felt free to look at the nearby remains of the fallen bridge. What a sight! This good-sized steel-supported bridge had completely caved in in the middle. How heavy the weight of the snow must have been!

While climbing up the trail on the other side of the creek, I met a trail crew. They announced that they had killed a rattle-snake near the next higher switchback. They warned me to step carefully and be on the lookout for snakes. This was a surprise, as usually rattlesnakes are not found at such high altitudes—rarely over 7,000 feet—and this trail was at approximately 6,400 feet.

My midday walk beside Crater Creek was pleasant. Soon, I arrived at a beautiful sight—Rainbow Falls. It was spectacular! The middle fork of the San Joaquin River plunges over a cliff and at its base is a misty, sunlit pool that usually produces a col-orful rainbow. I was fortunate. The rainbow was in full view.

After pausing to drink in the beauty of the falls, I moved along the trail leading to the Devil's Postpile National Monu-ment. Here, I gazed at the black basalt, vertical posts. A most interesting and different sight. The Devil's Postpile was formed when the andesile lava flow cooled and cracked into some hex-agonal posts.

I arrived at Reds Meadow at around 3:30 pm. I was ahead of schedule. I had planned and had food for a six-day walk and had returned in four-and-a-half days. I felt good. I had survived and enjoyed my first backpacking trip. I followed the custom introduced to me by my friend Madeline of celebrating by having a beer and a sandwich at the Reds Meadows store.

I happily recalled Carl Sharsmith's recommendation when I asked him if he thought I should try backpacking and he had replied, "Try a short trip." I had tried my short trip; I had made it, and I was ready for more the next years.

En route home, I stopped at Mineral Hot Springs, located southeast of the town of Bishop. This was a strange and different hot springs. The hot water rises up through the stony bottom of a cold, flowing stream. Bathers wade into the cold stream and try to find the hot water. I waded out slowly and reached the hot part of the river. Soon, I was too hot and moved hurriedly back to the cold stream to cool off. I experienced a mix of the cold and hot just by moving around a few inches. It was interesting and strange. I did not find it as satisfying, however, as the hot springs flowing into a bathtub, as at Fish Creek, where one can soak and relax.

Returning to nearby Mammoth Lakes, I reserved a vacant space at crowded Shady Rest Campground. I then headed for the Mammoth Lake Café and ordered a full-course meal—salad, entrée, and dessert. Never again! I learned from this experience that I could not comfortably eat a full meal after coming out from a backpacking trip. I think that my stomach shrinks after several days on backpack fare. Thereafter, I chose frequent, small meals for my "back to civilization" menu.

Squeezed into my tiny camp space, surrounded by monster RVs, I experienced "coming-out blues." I missed the solitude and magic of the wilderness.

Chapter 11
Tuolumne Meadows to Reds Meadow
1966 • 36 miles

Oh, these vast, calm, measureless mountain days, inciting at once to work and rest! Days in whose light everything seems equally divine, opening a thousand windows to show us God. Nevermore, however weary, should one faint by the way who gains the blessings of one mountain day; whatever his fate, long life, short life, stormy or calm, he is rich forever.
                                                    — John Muir

This was my first walk on a section of the John Muir Trail. It would, in a few years, become a part of the Pacific Crest Trail. The John Muir Trail starts at Yosemite Valley, leads to Tuolumne Meadows, and traverses the High Sierras, ending at the top of 14,494-foot Mt. Whitney. Most of the Muir Trail was subsumed into the Pacific Crest Trail.

This was a short walk, but for me, a giant step—catapulting me into mountain hiking for years to come. This was my momentous beginning.

My eventful beginning started at a Sonoma County Sierra Club potluck, when I heard a fellow member say, "I am going to walk on the John Muir Trail with the Wampler Tours in July." I tried to put aside this trail-walking idea. I had so many other things to do—a new job, a new house, limited vacation time—but I could not turn off the idea. I gave in and signed up with Wampler Tours for a week's walk, from Tuolumne Meadows to Reds Meadow. By the end of the walk, I was hooked. The idea of completing the John Muir Trail was born.

My beginning rendezvous with the Wampler Trail Tours was not altogether smooth and orderly. The group was scheduled to meet at Delaney Creek, at the north end of Tuolumne Meadows, on Saturday, July 16. I would be a day late, as I planned to take my nephew, Bill, to Lee Vinning, on the eastern side of the Sierra, where he would be boarding a Greyhound bus to return home.

I returned to Tuolumne Meadows the following afternoon and located the encampment at Delaney Creek. I surprised my Sierra Club friends, Evelyn, Kareen, Madeline, and Marguerite, as I hadn't told them I had signed up. This was an expression, I believe, of my uncertainty about joining the group. But nevertheless, I was excited.

My first night of camping with the Wampler Tours at Delaney Creek was a cold one. I had purchased a surplus Army sleeping bag stuffed with duck down. At that time, I had no knowledge of the difference between duck feathers and lofted goose down. This was one of my first equipment lessons. For the following night, Joe Wampler loaned me a horse blanket. It helped. The scent of horses wafted up to me at night for the rest of the trip.

The next morning, the day we were scheduled to start our walk, I went to the parking lot to arrange for a car shuttle, and there I saw my car tilting to one side. I had a flat tire. So, my first day's walk started late and I walked alone. I had been supplied with travel directions.

The trail led south through pleasant meadows and forests, and it hugged closely to the bank of the Lyell Fork of the Tuolumne River. I passed a young hiker sitting by the side of the stream with pencil and notebook in hand. Was he meditating or was he writing poetry, I wondered. What a beautiful setting, with periodic glimpses toward Mt. Lyell. The first eight miles of the walk mostly on level ground was easy. On the last mile, the trail began a fairly steep ascent. I arrived at base camp panting slightly and a little tired, just before the sky was beginning to darken and just in time for supper.

The following day was a layover day. The practice on the Wampler Tours, and of many tours using pack animals to carry gear, was to move camp every other day. Tour members were free to spend the day as they wished. I followed a suggestion I had heard from one of the tour members—exploring an informal trail winding beside nearby McClure Creek. I followed the faint trail up to an opening onto a high meadow dotted with colorful wildflowers. Returning to camp, I felt good at having explored and found such a beautiful mountain scene.

The next morning, we arose early in anticipation of our ascent up and over 11,100-foot Donohue Pass. It was a steady, moderately steep climb. Near the top, I had my first look at pink snowcups. Evelyn, who knew about this phenomenon from earlier mountain walks, explained to me that the summer sun penetrating the high-mountain crests melted the snow into irregular dents, and pink algae attached itself to these snow mounds, creating pink snow. How interesting to look at these strange configurations.

Descending from Donohue Pass, the trail drifts down, following a southeasterly course to Island Pass. Here, we had our first glimpse of the towering Ritter Range. Soon afterward, we arrived at the eastern edge of rock-dotted Thousand Island Lake. It was here that I first became fondly attached to the views of Banner Peak and Mt. Ritter. I have looked for them on all my subsequent trips in this area and have often caught a glimpse of them from Highway 395, which travels along the foothills of the eastern Sierras. To me, Banner Peak and close-by Mt. Ritter are special and spectacular. They both rise up steeply from the valley floor of the middle fork of the San Joaquin River. From the vantage point of looking across Thousand Island Lake, Banner is more prominent than Ritter. For most of the trail views, they appear to blend together as two towering peaks. What makes these peaks special for me? I think it is their aloneness in towering high above the surrounding mountains and their steep, jagged, knife-like tops, which pierce the sky and, at the same time, hold snow glaciers in their folds. I have often been pushed to name my favorite places along the trail. Of course, there are too many sights of special beauty to single out any one place, but certainly, Banner and Ritter are high on my list.

Still another fond memory of Banner and Ritter for me is John Muir's story of his challenging climb to the top of Mt. Ritter, as narrated in "Mountains of the Sierras." Casually, he bids goodbye to a group of artists camped in the valley and sets out to scale Mt. Ritter. He winds his way through numerous canyons, often having to backtrack, but persistently exploring and slowly moving forward. Climbing, he finds himself on a rock ledge from which he can't seem to move either up or down. For a brief moment, he is marooned, and then he senses a "new spirit" and climbs up to the top, as if being lifted by some unforeseen force. He reaches the top, glories in the views, and then manages to return to his base camp in the dark. The next day, he returns to the artists' camp.

Near the outlet of Thousand Island Lake, the John Muir Trail and the Pacific Crest Trail separate, with the John Muir Trail traveling on the west side of the river and the Pacific Crest Trail traveling on the east side of the river. They both come together near Reds Meadow.

I have traveled on both these trails and am equally fond of both. The older John Muir Trail skirts Garnet Lake and Shadow Lake and affords off-trail walks to beautiful Lake Ediza and the high, snowy Iceberg Lakes.

The San Joaquin Trail, traveling on the east side of the river, affords glorious views looking toward Shadow Creek and Banner and Ritter.

In 1966, before there was a declared Pacific Crest Trail, the Wampler Tours used the San Joaquin Trail. During my 1990 backpack walk, I also followed this trail, which had by then been designated as the Pacific Crest Trail.

By evening, we reached our base camp, which was a little off the trail on a level, grassy area bordering the middle fork of the San Joaquin River.

The following day was a free day. I chose to walk alongside the river and sought out some quiet pools, where I hoped trout might be hiding. I had brought along a folding rod and a lightweight reel. I caught two. I brought them back to the camp and they were cooked so that my friends could each have a little bite.

The walk along the San Joaquin the next day to Reds Meadow was full of glorious views. Tall, purple lupines and red Indian paintbrush colored the trail edges, growing especially high near ravines, which contained small running streams. Banner and Ritter were in view across the river canyon for most of the day, bathed with constantly changing colors cast by the shifting sun. One of the most special views to me was looking toward Shadow

Lake, where Shadow Creek falls down the steep canyon walls, plunging toward the San Joaquin riverbed.

By mid-afternoon, we reached our cars, which had been shuttled to Reds Meadow. It was with mixed feelings that I left the trail. I knew that I wanted to see more. I resolved to return the next year.

Tuolumne Meadows to Reds Meadow
July 1990 • 36 miles

This was a walk full of memories. I kept saying, "I remember this scene," and "Where did we leave the trail to find our campsite?" Actually, sometimes I could remember familiar sights and sometimes I could not. Then I would remind myself, "That trip took place 24 years ago!"

I arrived at Tuolumne Meadows mid-day, having taken the Yosemite bus from the Valley to Tuolumne Meadows. I was excited. I stopped for a snack at the Tuolumne Lodge store, and then I stepped outside and walked a few yards to have a nostalgic look at the Miller Cascade, an inviting series of waterfalls just south of the Lodge. I was ready. I located the John Muir Trail sign and started on my journey.

Walking beside the tranquil-flowing Lyell Fork of the Tuolumne, I remembered that on my first walk in 1966, I had passed a young man sitting by the stream writing on a small easel. Was he writing poetry? He looked content and inspired.

By evening, when it was time to seek a campsite, the trail was still following beside the Lyell Fork. I walked off-trail for a short distance and selected a level spot for my bedroom with a nearby open space for my kitchen. I cooked my vegetable stew and made ready for the night. I propped my pack by a nearby tree and sprinkled mothballs around its base. I was in bear country.

During the night I awoke upon hearing a loud, explosive noise. Was it a rock in the river that had become dislodged and was crashing about in the water? Was it a bear looking for a meal? I shall never know. I flashed my light on my pack and, thankfully, it had not been disturbed.

On my morning walk, as I approached a regularly used campsite, a ranger walked toward me. "Have you had any bear problems?" he asked. "No, I have not." I replied. "Did you bag your food up on a tree?" he continued. "No, I am not able to throw my rope up over the tree." I explained. He looked puzzled. Then I commented, "I do not carry any smelly food and I do not camp in heavily used campsites." "I see," he responded, nodding his head. He seemed satisfied.

Soon after walking a few yards, I met a couple who were unhappy and upset. They told me that they had spent the night at a regularly used campsite and had been visited by a bear. The bear had rummaged through their supplies, bit into their food, and made a general mess. They were discouraged and decided that they were going to return to Tuolumne Meadows. I was thankful that I had not camped at a regularly used campsite.

On the trail to Donahue Pass, I searched and searched for the turnoff that led to our campsite during the 1966 Wampler Tour. I could not find it. Had the trail been abandoned or closed in an effort to restore overused sites to their natural wilderness state? Large pack parties are no longer permitted by the National Park and Forest Services. I reluctantly gave up trying to find the sight and moved on to climb Donahue Pass.

By mid-day, I was climbing up Donahue Pass. I smiled as I

recalled encountering snow cups on my first walk. On this trip, they were no longer any snow cups. The snow had all melted. I did pass an energetic-looking trail crew. I said to them, "I appreciate the good work that you are doing." They smiled in return and seemed pleased.

By evening, I was walking down the south slope of Donahue Pass when it started to rain. I stopped, put up my tent, and made camp. But soon, the light rain stopped and I enjoyed a beautiful view looking down toward a grassy meadow.

In the morning, I awoke to such a glorious view from my campsite below Donahue Pass. I was treated to an early-morning light show from my tent door as I watched the sun light up the mountain peaks one by one until finally, they were all lighted and the sun peaked up from behind the taller peaks. I was looking toward the east.

Moving along the trail, I soon emerged out into an open space, and there appeared before me in the distance my familiar friends, Banner and Ritter. I was overjoyed to see them again.

By mid-day, I was viewing majestic Banner and Ritter from across picturesque Thousand Island Lake. I stopped for lunch and a siesta so that I could spend more time gazing at this spectacular sight.

During my afternoon walk, first along the lakeshore view and then from the trail moving southeast toward the San Joaquin River Valley, I looked in awe at the changing shapes of Banner and Ritter as I viewed them from slightly different angles. They appeared to me as always to be compelling and majestic.

I spent the night at Badger Lake—a small, tree-lined lake bordering the Middle Fork of the San Joaquin River.

At Badger Lake in the morning, I had a brief conversation with a camper who announced that he had caught 96 trout. He was very pleased with his catch. Still, he wanted to break his record and catch 100 in one day. He used a non-barbed hook and threw all of his catch back.

I was soon walking on the trail that hugs the slope above the Middle Fork of the San Joaquin. Such spectacular views opened up for me. Banner and Ritter were brightly lit in the morning light. Looking across the river toward the west, I could see the narrow but spectacular long, descending waterfall of Shadow Creek as it made its way from its source of high, rocky-alpine Shadow Lake.

The trail led across numerous small, trickling streams whose banks were covered with wildflowers. I remembered seeing some of these familiar flowers during the 1966 walk. Again, I delighted in spotting lupine, larkspur, Indian paintbrush, and tiny mimulus—one of my favorites.

By evening, I reached Agnew Meadows Campground. It seemed crowded and noisy. I walked on to Upper Soda Springs Campground and, after filling my water bag, I retreated across the river to an informal campsite overlooking the San Joaquin.

In the morning, I was eager to reach Reds Meadow. I hurried along, but the walk was longer than anticipated. I was going out to the town of Mammoth Lakes to pick up a food package for my return trip. I arrived at the Reds Meadow store and café around noon. Inside the store, memories of my 1966 walk flashed back to me. I remember that this was the coming-out sight on the 1966 walk, and some of my friends celebrated by ordering a beer. At that time, we thought that we had walked a long way! Now, to me—having completed the walk from Mexico to Canada—it seemed like a relatively short walk.

I was lucky in finding rides to the Mammoth Lakes Post Office and back to Reds Meadow. On my return trip, I was offered a ride by a delightful couple that served as hosts at the Forest Service campground.

After repacking my pack and filling my water bag. I retreated to a quiet hideaway across the river.

For my return trip to Yosemite Valley, I had found an intriguing and exciting route by studying Starr's Guide to the John Muir Trail and the High Sierra Region. My route, west from Reds Meadow led to Granite Creek; then I climbed up Isberg Pass from which the views offered me one of the most exciting experiences of all mountain pass scenes. I could see in all directions. The pass marks a ridge that separates the San Joaquin watershed flowing to the east and the Merced River watershed flowing to the west. Looking toward the northeast, the Ritter Range came into view. Looking to the west, I could see the Clark Range. This was, for me, a real mountain-top experience.

On my descent from the pass, I camped by a small streamlet. There was no sign of the Merced River as yet. Continuing my descent to the west, numerous small streamlets joined to form the beginnings of the mighty Merced River. I felt the excitement that I imagined early explorers felt as they traveled beside rivers to discover new lands.

When I reached the Merced Campground, I felt at home. I was traveling on familiar trails. I knew these trails from trips to the Yosemite High Camps. Soon, I was reviewing the familiar sights of Nevada Falls.

Chapter 12
Kennedy Meadows Near Sonora Pass
to Tuolumne Meadows
1977 • 74 miles

Every day opens and closes like a flower, noiseless, effortless.
Divine peace glows on all the majestic landscape, like the
silent enthusiastic joy that sometimes transfigures a noble
human face.
— *John Muir*

There was a pause between my completion of the John
Muir Trail in 1971 and my next walk to the north. In 1973,
I completed a backpack circle walk on the Lower Kern and in
1975 a loop walk from Yosemite Valley to the Ten Lakes Basin
and return. Then, at a Sierra Club potluck, a hiker friend told
me there was a Tahoe-Yosemite Trail. I was intrigued. I bought
the guidebook, The Tahoe-Yosemite Trail, published by Wilderness Press. Studying the guide became my winter diversion.
I completed my plans and spent my summer vacations of 1976
and 1977 walking on the Tahoe-Yosemite Trail.

Much of the Tahoe-Yosemite Trail was subsumed into the
Pacific Crest Trail. It was used as the temporary trail in the early
years. Gradually, new trail sections have been completed. A new
section leads the hiker to the east of the older trail, which passed
through the Kennedy Meadows Resort and reaches the Sonoma
Pass. The new trail section follows more closely the crest of the
mountains. I walked on this newer section recently and enjoyed

its spectacular views. To me, both the new section with its higher elevation and the older section with its grassy meadows have their own attractions. I have enjoyed both of them.

In walking from Kennedy Meadows near Sonora Pass to Tuolumne Meadows, I noticed a gradual change in the look and feel of the mountain landscape. The trail gradually moves from surroundings of red and yellow volcanic rock colors to the lighter granite color upon approaching Tuolumne Meadows. The trail passes some peaceful, attractive lakes, three of which I enjoyed camping beside—Tilden, Smedberg, and Benson. These appealing lakes are tree-bordered and are below timberline. The southern section of the trail from Dorothy Lake lies within Yosemite National Park. My last day's walk was beside the splashing, waterfall-dotted Tuolumne River.

To reach trailhead at Kennedy Meadows, ten miles west of Sonora Pass, I boarded a Greyhound Bus in San Francisco for the resort town of Pinecrest. This was the bus' final destination. For the last 30 miles, I needed to beg for a ride. Disembarking from the bus in the early afternoon, I found myself on a road bordered by small stores and very busy with traffic. I thought, "This crowded shopping area doesn't look like a promising place for a ride." Slowly, I realized that I was not on the Sonora Pass road, but on a "Y" turnoff into Pinecrest. I walked out toward the junction and was glad to see a forest ranger station—a welcome sight. Inside, a friendly ranger affirmed that I needed to move across the junction to reach the Sonora Pass highway.

I found what I thought would be a favorable place on the Sonora Pass road. Raising my arm and smiling, I was fortunate, as very soon the driver of a camper pulled over. I had a moment to notice that the license plate on the Commando camper read, "God is our Commander." A warm, friendly young couple offered me a ride to Cold Creek, where they would be turning off to reach a campsite. I was delighted to have my ride and to put off worrying about the next leg of my journey—approximately 14 miles—until later. They were a most enjoyable couple to talk to, as they were full of enthusiasm about camping. Thanking them, I climbed out and took up my post at the Cold Creek junction. I again raised my hand and smiled. I didn't have to wait long when another friendly couple in a camper stopped and offered to take me to Kennedy Meadows. They were a delightful couple from Palo Alto. The man was a retired Stanford professor, and they were traveling to the eastern side of the Sierra.

Alighting from the camper around 6:15 p.m., I walked in one mile to the Kennedy Meadows Resort. The Resort is an old, well-established recreational center with cabins, a lodge, a café, a small store, and a much-used pack station. With its old-style frame buildings with their peaked roofs, the main hub of the resort could, I thought, look like a scene in a western movie. I looked around, found a water spigot, and measured out my water quota for my evening meal and breakfast. I moved on a short way and found a delightful campsite near a small creek and just far enough off the trail to be hidden from the main trail traffic.

On my first day's walk, leading south, I soon passed elongated, grassy, Kennedy Meadows. At a crossing of the Middle Fork of the Stanislaus River, I followed a broad, well-trampled horse trail. I was greeted by a large sign: HORSE FORD—WARNING—SWIFT WATER. I realized that I had followed the horse trail rather than the hikers' trail. I backtracked a few yards to a junction, turned onto the hikers' trail, and crossed over the creek safely on a bridge. It is a fairly common practice on rivers deep and swift enough to be bridged to have the two crossings—one for hikers and one for horses.

The trail after crossing the river ascends and offers many views of the nearby large Relief Reservoir. By evening, I reached a delightful campsite beside a small spring on a shelf below Reliet Peak. In the dusk after supper, I enjoyed a spectacular view looking toward the east. In the foreground above the spring rose a gray, granite wall. In the background and looming above the granite wall towered red and gray pinnacles silhouetted against the skyline. Looking at one of the pinnacles, I imagined that I could see in its jagged outline the face of a cat. I wondered what might lie in the space between the granite wall and the more-distant red and gray pinnacles. Perhaps there was another meadow lying in this space. It would be fun to explore this area and see what it held; I thought, however that I had better keep moving along the trail on my journey to Tuolumne Meadows.

About 10 p.m., my peace and solitude were disrupted by two men who came up the trail beaming flashlights, shouting loudly, and blowing a whistle. Apparently, they were looking for their friends who had already gone ahead and found a campsite. I hoped they wouldn't stop too near me. Thankfully, they passed by and I enjoyed my tranquil campsite, complete with a view of a starlit sky.

In the morning, I ascended the 9680-foot Brown Bear Pass—an easy climb. Looking around, I became aware that I was viewing a different landscape than that of the light-colored granite of the High Sierra. I was gazing at red and brown rock formations displaying evidence of its volcanic origins.

Upon descending the Brown Bear Pass, I was viewing a sweeping panorama of meadows and lakes of the Emigrant Meadow Basin. This scene, for me, brought forth images of pioneer wagon trains encamped by the lake. Periodically, when the trail passes historic sights, I ask myself, "What was life like for these courageous adventurers?" Perhaps there is a common kinship of adventure between today's wilderness backpackers and the pioneer emigrants who braved crossing the wilderness to seek a new land for their homes.

I ate my lunch and had my siesta on a grassy point on the shore of large Emigrant Meadow Lake. I amused myself by trying to see if I could catch some fish. I had no luck.

The trail leading southeast passes still another attractive meadow—Grizzly Meadow, where I stopped for my afternoon snack and reveled in the beauty of a magnificent carpet of colorful wildflowers. From Grizzly Meadow, the trail ascends to 9800-foot Bond Pass. On the route to the Pass, the trail joins a jeep road and passes by quarries and a rock house. I poked my head into a window of the rock house and could see a wooden table and bench. It appeared that the mine may have been worked fairly recently. Approaching Bond Pass, I saw a man on a horse who was leading another packhorse coming toward me. When we met, he stopped and was eager to talk. He told me that he was retired, that he lived in the foothills near the Calaveras Big Trees, and that he liked to ride his horse into the mountains. He complained that when he was camped on the shores of Emigrant Meadow Lake, a ranger had come by and told him that he should move his campsite back from the lake. The ranger said that under the present regulations, no camping is allowed within a hundred feet of lakes or streams. He seemed indignant. He said that he had always camped where he wanted. I listened. As a conservationist, I am committed to the idea of preserving streams and lakeshores. However, listening to him, I knew that the freedom of camping where he wished had always been important to him and that he was not ready for change.

As I was ready to start on my way, he offered me advice on the trail. He recommended that I look for a campsite with water on the other side of the pass near the outlet to Dorothy Lake. When I finally was able to say goodbye to the talkative gentleman with the horses, I climbed up to the top of Bond Pass. There, I was greeted by a welcome sign: YOSEMITE NATIONAL PARK BOUNDARY—DOGS, GUNS, AND HUNTING PROHIBITED.

After I had descended a short way, I followed my horse friend's directions and turned off at the Dorothy Lake trail junction. I found a delightful, quiet campsite beside the outlet of Dorothy Lake. I appreciated his helpful advice.

My morning's walk led through broad, grassy Jack Main Canyon. Most of the trail bordered shallow, slow-moving Falls Creek. The creek was dotted with many quiet pools, which kept tempting me to try my luck at fishing. I could visualize trout hiding under the shaded overhangs of the grassy banks. Twice, I stopped to drop my line in the water. No luck. I could see the trout darting in and out and around the shaded pools. Perhaps they weren't hungry. Perhaps I was using the wrong bait.

At lunchtime, after I had been sitting for some time scanning the creek bed, I saw a deer resting quietly near the opposite bank. He blended so well into the landscape, I hadn't even noticed him. He didn't stir. I guessed that he, too, was having his midday siesta. Finally, when I got up to leave and walked a little closer to his resting place, he slowly stood up and sauntered off.

By mid-afternoon, the inviting stream beckoned me again, and I stopped for a refreshing wading bath, i.e., standing in the water and rinsing off with my campers' washcloth. More often than not when hiking in the high mountains, my bathing did not consist of floating or emerging in high lakes and streams, which are often icy-cold and sometimes rocky and swiftly flowing. Instead, I opt for washcloth baths, which are less risky and more comfortable.

Toward evening, I climbed out of the canyon to find a campsite on scenic, grassy, tree-lined Tilden Lake. While cooking supper, three deer kept creeping closer and closer to my dining area. The bolder of the three came within five feet of my dinner kettle. I kept shooing him away. He was pesky. I also found him sniffing my laundry—socks that were drying on a nearby rock. This was my first encounter with "camp deer." I concluded that previous campers had unwisely thrown food treats to the deer. This is unfortunate, as wildlife becomes accustomed and dependent on people food, which is not as natural and healthy for them as forest food.

That night, I decided to sleep inside my plastic tube tent, as there was a sprinkle of light, misty drizzle. On and off during the night, I heard the stomping of the three aggressive deer. I was glad I was inside my tent, as I could imaging that they would be sniffing and nuzzling in my face if I had slept outside.

Early the next morning, a hiker came by my campsite and stopped to chat. He told me that he was hiking on the Pacific Crest Trail. He had started at the Mexican border with two companions and after two days, they had given up and left him. He decided to go on alone and planned to go as far as he could before he was stopped by cold, snowy weather.

The Tahoe-Yosemite Trail leads southeast along the Tilden Creek Canyon—an easy, level walk. The Pacific Crest Trail, in contrast, continues south down Jack Main Trail to the Wilmer Lake Trail. Both trails join a little before reaching Stubblefield Canyon. The Tilden Lake Trail is an alternate that many hikers take to reach and enjoy the campsites on the scenic Tilden Lake.

By afternoon, I was climbing up steep, rocky Macob Ridge and then down the other side on an equally steep, rocky, difficult, slow-going trail. I had reached the area described in the guidebook as "The Washboard." For the next several miles, the trail moves up and down through southwest-running canyons, from which creeks flow into the wide, swiftly moving Tuolumne River.

Plodding ahead on this up-and-down trail was slow going. There were compensations, however, in climbing these washboards in that there were glorious views from the ridgetops, including scenes of tall, light-gray granite Piute Peak. By late afternoon, I arrived at Stubblefield Canyon, where I found water and campsites. I had only gone five miles from Tilden Lake. I debated and decided not to tackle the next up-and-down washboard leading to Kerrick Canyon until the next day. I was learning that lines on the map could be deceptive in terms of mileage. A line on the map cannot show the true distance on uphills and downhills. A map line does not show a hiker how much longer it will take to climb up and down than it takes to walk on a level, easy, smooth trail.

I soon discovered that bushy Stubblefield Canyon attracted mosquitoes. I searched. Looking up, I spotted a small flat-topped rocky pedestal. I wondered if I would be able to climb up to the top. I circled around to the back side of the pedestal and happily discovered a way to reach the top. I was delighted. I liked my out-of-sight, private hideaway very much. I felt a big smug when I heard later-arriving campers stopping for the night in the lower bushy mosquito area.

The memory of my delightful pedestal-top campsite has returned to me frequently. It became one of my favorite campsite memories. Thinking back about its attraction, I think that in addition to its privacy, it provided me with a feeling of being on a mountaintop. For me mountaintops provide their own special magical feeling.

My walk the next day from Stubblefield Canyon south was a hard, long one, as the trail climbs up and down two steep, rocky washboards. The first ascent climbed up to a ridge separating Stubblefield Canyon from Kerrick Canyon. I started early, but finished late. There is a short respite after reaching Kerrick Canyon before the trail makes the next ascent up 9150-foot Seavey Pass. After plodding up and down the steep, rock ascents and descents, I looked forward to camping at Benson Lake, described in the guidebook as a "not to be missed side trail." Benson Lake is about half a mile off-trail.

I arrived at the lake at about 6:30. I heartily agreed with the guidebook's recommendations. Benson Lake is surely one of the most beautiful mountain lakes in the Sierra. On three sides, granite walls rise up from the lakeshore. On the fourth side, the east side, there is a broad, light-colored sandy beach. This indeed is an unusual and welcome find among mountain lakes. Presupposing that the beach campsites at this popular lake would be occupied, I explored a little south of the picture-postcard beach and found another elevated pedestal for my campsite. I was delighted. I felt so good in having my own little hideaway. I relished spending the evening drinking in the glorious view of the quiet lake and its surrounding cliffs from my peaceful pedestal.

In the morning, I enjoyed a leisurely breakfast while I watched the morning light move across enchanting Benson Lake. I decided that this would be a leisurely day. I planned to ascend and descend the next ridge and then make camp before tackling another up-and-down washboard. The trail leading up was sprinkled with rocks. I felt good in not having to hurry. Toward the top, from the shoulder of Volunteer Peak, there was a sweeping panoramic view highlighting surrounding peaks and valleys. The trail then winds down a steep canyon and reaches 9000-foot Smedberg Lake. I arrived there at around 2:30. I felt a wonderful sense of freedom in knowing that didn't have to hurry, that I could pause to drink in the scenery whenever I felt like it.

Smedberg Lake is yet another beautiful lake in the north Yosemite backcountry. It is surrounded by light granite walls and dotted with small granite islands. The lake and its surrounding landscapes expressed to me the feeling of the High Sierras—its neighbor to the south.

It was good to have a free, unhurried afternoon. Frequently I've met hikers who talked of planning a layover day—to rest and clean up. Actually, I don't remember taking a full layover day during my walks, but I have fond memories of some pleasant half-day rest stops.

I spent the afternoon washing socks, bathing, and I even had time to do a little mending of pant seams, which were beginning to peek through. Some creatures—squirrels and rodents attempted to steal my cereal and gnawed a little hole in my pack. Fortunately, they stopped before they reached my double-bagged plastic food bags. A backpacker passed my tent walking north toward Lake Tahoe and proudly announced that he was completing the trail from Mt. Whitney to Tahoe. When I replied, gently telling him that when I reached Tuolumne Meadows, I would have completed the trail from Whitney to Tahoe, he seemed surprised.

Later, a northbound Pacific Crest hiker arrived and asked me if I had any spare matches. "I'm down to my last three," he reported. I told him that I would take a count of my match supply. Later, when I looked for him at a nearby campsite to offer him a few spare matches, he had already succeeded in borrowing some. I met so many interesting people on the trail.

The trail from Smedberg Lake to my next destination in Matterhorn Canyon first ascends to 10,139-foot Benson Pass, where I paused to enjoy views of magnificent North Yosemite peaks before circling down around large granite blocks to reach Matterhorn Canyon. I arrived there around 3 p.m., having enjoyed another day of leisurely hiking. I had ample time to enjoy the look and feel of the long, broad Matterhorn Canyon and to search out a campsite. Matterhorn Canyon has a feel and is suggestive of a "little Yosemite." Of course, nothing can truly resemble or rival Yosemite Valley. It is, however, a beautiful canyon with high granite sidewalls and a grassy floor. Although I had ample time to choose a campsite, I couldn't find my "wished-for" sleeping space—there were no tree-lined bedrooms or hidden pedestals. I reluctantly settled for a place that had been previously used, as evidenced by a campfire ring full of wood ash. The compensation, however, was a glorious view looking up and down the canyon.

Awakening in the early morning, I heard the singing and barking of coyotes. Then, to my delight, I peered out of my bedroll to see two coyotes trotting by, passing within 15 feet of my sleeping bag. What a beautiful sight to have a close-up view of these graceful animals.

In the morning, I climbed out of Matterhorn Canyon slowly, looking back to see the views of this Yosemite-like valley from different heights and different angles. I remember the scene fondly. I would have one more day of up-and-down washboards before reaching Tuolumne Meadows. My first climb led to 9490-foot Miller Lake. The following downhill led to Spiller Creek, followed by a steeper downhill leading to 8600-foot Virginia Canyon. I remember Virginia Canyon for its pleasant, refreshing waterfall. The last trail ascent climbed up out of Virginia Canyon to a ridge near the junction of the McCabe Lake Trail. From this ridge, the trail drifts gently down through scenic Cold Canyon. My plan was to stop shortly before reaching the Glen Aulin High Sierra Camp, as I knew from past hiking experiences that the

camp's garbage cans attract marauding bear. Therefore, I stopped
a little early and found a campsite beside a broad meadow with a
shallow creek running through it.

After dinner, I enjoyed the view look east toward Mt. Conness, with the setting sun illuminating its light granite peaks. I
watched its light color change and fade until it grew dark. I had
another treat when I awoke in the night and peeked out from
my sleeping bag to see the silhouette of Mt. Conness looking
silvery-white in the moonlight.

I had a late start on my last day's hike out to Tuolumne
Meadows. I had been so attracted by my bedroom view of Mt.
Conness from the meadow that I had placed my bedroll in the
low, grassy area. I awoke to a meadow-dampened bedroll. Not
wanting to pack my damp sleeping bag, I brushed the dampness off and waited for the warm morning sun to complete the
drying of my sleeping-bag cover.

I arrived at Glen Aulin Camp, where I passed some guests
who were sitting in front of their tents. A few yards further, I
reached a welcome and glorious sight—the Tuolumne River
Canyon. The river flows west from its headwaters in the High
Sierras on its journey to Hetch Hetchy Canyon. Here the water is impounded behind Hetch Hetchy Dam, which stores
water for release to San Francisco and surrounding suburbs.
The building of the dam in the once-spectacular canyon was a
painful loss to John Muir, who fought to preserve the canyon.

The trail follows the river closely from Glen Aulin Camp
to Tuolumne Meadows, a distance of around seven miles. I was
soon gazing fondly at the white, splashing waters of Tuolumne
Falls. They seemed to me more spectacular than when I had
last walked this trail. Perhaps it seemed different because on
my other three trips I had been walking with a group. Walking with a group sometimes creates distractions. Walking with

TUOLUMNE MEADOWS

a group sometimes requires a hurried pace. Walking with a group sometimes means that I don't have time to absorb deeply the sights and sounds of the beauty of my surroundings.

I recalled that on one of my earlier trips, I had made a special trip north to walk up-river to view the intriguing Water-wheel Falls—approximately three-and-a-half miles northwest of Glen Aulin. At these falls, the white water in high-water season hits a rock and shoots upward in an arc, making a very spectacular sight.

Midway through my walk to Tuolumne Meadows, I began seeing more day hikers. Scanning the view toward the river, I suddenly saw an unattended, burning campfire. I was angry. Upon closer inspection, I saw that the fire had crept out of the fire ring and was smoldering amongst some nearby duff. I went to work. I hauled three buckets of water from the river before I succeeded in putting the fire out. I vowed that I would report this incident to the first ranger I met.

Soon, I crossed Delaney Creek, a familiar place where I had met the Joe Wampler tour group on my first walk on the John Muir Trail in 1966. Soon, the fond views of broad Tuolumne Meadow, framed by familiar Cathedral and Unicorn peaks, came into view. To the left, I could see Lembert Dome, which I had climbed on my first trip to Tuolumne Meadows.

Upon arriving at the Tuolumne Meadows ranger station, I told the nearest ranger about finding and putting out the unattended fire. I was disappointed. He was not nearly as upset by this incident as I thought he should have been. Had he become overwhelmed by the large number of complaints and the variety of behaviors on the part of the crowds that passed through Tuolumne Meadows?

It was an unusually hot day. It was crowded along the highway and near the store and café. I wondered and worried if I would have a hard time finding a ride. I ate a snack in the café and then selected a place near the bridge where the traffic slowed down. I took out my "TO BUS" sign. There were other hikers holding up signs near me. In about 20 minutes, a man driving a camper pulled up and motioned to me. I ran forward, passing several sign-holders. When I said that I was looking for a ride to catch the bus at Lee Vining, he offered me a ride. After I climbed in, he said he was glad to give me a ride, but he had pulled forward because he didn't want to pick up the other ride-seekers, whom he thought were "hippies." He told me that he was on his way to Nevada and implied that he was going to visit a casino.

I arrived in Lee Vining at 5:45 in plenty of time to board the 7 p.m. bus. Unfortunately, however, the bus was three hours late. I was joined in my long wait sitting by curb by another "coming-out" backpacker. He commented, "I wish I was still in the mountains." I agreed. I recalled the beauty of looking at Mt. Conness from Cold Spring Meadow. I also recalled the beautiful lake scenes—Benson, Smedberg, and Tilden—and the lovely falls in Virginia Canyon.

There was one compensation in coming out. I was looking forward to a real hot-water soak in my bathtub at home.

Chapter 13
Lake Fontanillis Near Lake Tahoe to Sonora Pass
July 1976 • 89 miles

Walk away quietly in any direction and taste the freedom of the mountaineer. Camp out among the grass and gentians of glacier meadows, in craggy garden nooks…—John Muir

Nineteen seventy-six marked the first of my two years of walking on the 180-mile Tahoe-Yosemite Trail. The 1976 walk led from Meeks Bay on the North Shore of Lake Tahoe near the town of Tahoma to Sonora Pass. I followed the Wilderness Press' 1970 edition of *The Tahoe-Yosemite Trail* and found it to be a helpful trail guide.

Much of the older Tahoe-Yosemite Trail has been subsumed into the newer Pacific Crest Trail. The Tahoe-Yosemite trail served as the temporary trail until new sections of the Pacific Crest Trail were constructed. The present trail remains basically the same from the ridge above Lake Tahoe near the Velma Lakes to Frog Lake, located a little south of Carson Pass. There are some minor changes around the Echo Pass area. South of Frog Lake, the newer Pacific Crest Trail ascends higher along the crest of the mountains. I have traveled some of the new trail and found it interesting. I especially like some of the views from the high passes and peaks around Carson Pass and Ebbetts Pass. To me, both trails hold much of interest and beauty. The older Tahoe-Yosemite Trail passes intriguing pioneer village sights. As a less-developed and less-well-maintained trail, it presented to me, as a hiker, challenges to finding and following some barely discernible trail sections. It is also dotted with short sections of cross-country travel. The newer Pacific Crest Trail climbs higher and, therefore, fulfills the original goal of the Pacific Crest Trail as a scenic trail—following along the crest of the mountains.

The Tahoe-Yosemite Trail continues to lead through some light granite landscape so distinctive of the Sierra. It still holds the beauty of the light-rocked mountains and granite-rimmed lakes, but at a slightly lower altitude than the High Sierras.

My approach to the trailhead at Meeks Bay was an easy one. In 1976, there was a Greyhound Bus leaving San Francisco that traveled up the north shore of Lake Tahoe to Tahoe City. I was able to ride all the way to Meeks Bay on the bus without worrying about begging for a ride—I could leave the problem of begging for a ride until I came out.

Disembarking at Meeks Bay Resort, I had time to phone my mother and to eat a sandwich at the resort café. I then started hiking up the trail around 6 p.m. When the trail reached Meeks Creek around dusk, I found a pleasant, unoccupied campsite. I had just enough daylight left to prepare an evening snack. I felt so good about being in the wilderness again. As I was organizing my gear for the night, I suddenly realized that I couldn't find my faithful Sierra Club cup. I was alarmed! Had I lost it? I did have another plastic cup that I used for soup, but there was nothing like the wide-brimmed metal Sierra Club cup that hangs on my belt. With it, I could scoop water from a very shallow stream and also hold it between rock crevices to catch small, delicious drips from an overhead spring. I started my search. In the dim light, I retraced my steps to the stream where I had gathered water. There, sitting alongside the bank, was my faithful cup. I was so happy to retrieve it and to know that it was safe.

The next morning after spending a peaceful night beside quiet-flowing Meeks Creek, I started my climb up to the ridge. The trail alternates between forest and open, rocky switchbacks in its climb up toward the crest. The trail also passes a group of lakes. First, I passed small Lake Genevieve, and then I came to larger Crag Lake. Next, appearing on the right side, was tiny Shhadow Lake, followed by the bigger Stony Ridge Lake. From the lake's end, there is a fairly steep climb up to reach the beautiful Rubicon Lake, where I had planned to camp. This would place me in a good position to climb 8500-foot Phipps Pass in the cool, fresh morning air. As I arrived at Lake Rubicon around noon, I had plenty of time to select a campsite. I chose one on a little rock ledge above the lake, which offered me a secluded place with a view. This proved to be a good site, as during the late afternoon and evening, groups of campers, including a Boy Scout troop, arrived and the lakeshore grew noisier.

In the cool, fresh air of the morning, I climbed Phipps Pass. From the top, I enjoyed some splendid views looking down at small mountain lakes that were nestled between rocks and forests. From Phipps Pass, the trail switchbacks down toward the west and soon meets the present Pacific Crest Trail a little north of Middle Velma Lake. The Tahoe-Yosemite Trail and the newer Pacific Crest Trail follow the same route from the Velma Lakes south to Echo Lake Resort. To the south, the trail soon skirts the west side of little Velma Lake, and then Upper Velma Lake comes into sight Again, I chose to stop early so that I could climb 9380-foot Dicks Pass in the cool of the morning. I chose a camp at the small Lake Fontanillis, which lies a few yards west of the trail. This jewel of a lake is certainly one of the prettiest lakes I have ever seen. The steep, light granite side walls drop steeply toward the water's edge. In between the rocks, there are spaces dotted with small pines. I found a perfect hideaway bedroom. My small space was surrounded by a low-growing whitebark pine. I could crawl out of my tree-lined bedroom to a close-by, small, sandy-floored kitchen. After dinner, I climbed up the small rock ridge a few yards from my campsite, and from there I had a sweeping view of Lake Tahoe. I spent an inspired evening—first watching the sunset to the west, then watching the changing evening light move across the lake. Finally, I could look up at a bright, starlit sky. Such a glorious evening to behold.

When I awoke in the early light of the morning, I climbed up to the rock ridge viewpoint and caught a glimpse of the glorious colors of sunrise over Lake Tahoe. I watched as the first light changed into a deeper pink color, into a rose color, and then the full, round, bright eastern sun broke through, lighting the blue waters of Lake Tahoe. It was a great way to start a new day.

After breaking camp, I climbed up the steep trail to 9380-foot Dicks Pass. Near the top, there were more views to enjoy of Tahoe and looking down at tiny, deep-blue Lake Fontanillis of happy memories.

The saddle near the pass still retained a snow bank. From the pass, my walk for the rest of the day was mostly downhill. The trail passed more lakes—first Lake Gilmore and then the small, grass-lined Susie Lake. When I approached Susie Lake, I passed a group of hikers who stopped to talk. They were on a three-day excursion and had come up to the ridge trail from large, popular Fallen Leaf Lake, not far from Tahoe. They asked me where I was going, and when I told them that I was on my way to Sonora Pass, they were impressed. The said that they did not think they would be able to hike that far.

Passing more hikers than usual, I remembered that I was now hiking in the Desolation Wilderness, which is known as one of the most popular and well-used hiking areas in the state. I would continue to be walking in the Desolation Wilderness until I reached Echo Pass.

By late afternoon, I reached large, rocky Lake Aloha. I had tentatively planned to camp on the lake, but I was discouraged. It was windy, and there was no tree cover. The trail followed by the rocky, windy lakeshore for almost a mile. I continued to search for a possible campsite but did not see any that I felt was right. I decided to move on and to take a chance that I would find a more desirable place before sunset. The next side trail led down to a low-lying lake—Lake of the Woods. The sun was creeping down toward the horizon. Would I find a campsite if I hiked down this trail? I turned onto the trail and started down. Soon, the trail became very steep and, glancing down, the lake seemed far away. I hesitated. I concluded that it would also be a slow climb up in the morning. It didn't feel right. I stopped and studied the map and decided to continue on to the Lake Lucille trail. At the trail to Lake Lucille, I turned in and soon arrived at the pleasant, small tree-lined lake. With dusk fast approaching, I hurriedly found a small campsite. There was one other tent nearby, and I had a brief conversations with its occupants. They told me they liked Lake Lucille and planned to stay for two days. The hoped to do some fishing. I felt good at having found Lake Lucille and rejoiced that I had not remained at windy, rocky Lake Aloha.

Back on the trail in the morning, above peaceful Lake Lucille, it was a moderately easy three-mile walk down to Camp Harvey West on Upper Echo Lake. At the junction, there is a dock for the water taxi. Another passenger was already waiting and had phoned for the boat when I arrived. The guidebook

recommended using the water taxi, which plies the water between Camp Harvey West and the Echo Lake Resort, approximately three mile's distance. The trail was described as steep
and rocky. Soon, the water taxi arrived and I enjoyed a scenic
ride through Upper Echo Lake and then into larger, Lower
Echo Lake. These lakes are controlled by a dam owned by
PG&E, and much-coveted permits are granted to build summer cabins along the lakeshore. I enjoyed viewing the many-
colored summer cabins, complete with their boat docks.

In recent years, I have revisited the Echo Lakes and walked
on the three-mile trail between Camp Harvey West and the
Echo Lake Resort—the trail I had omitted on my 1976 walk
when I had taken the water taxi. By walking this short section, I felt a sense of completion. On my 1976 walk, I had no
thought of walking from Mexico to Canada. That came later.

Arriving at the Echo Lake Resort, I noticed that there were
a goodly number of boats anchored at the docks. I learned that
most of the summer cabins could only be reached by boat.

Out of curiosity, I peeked inside the resort store. It was
busy. It offered an assortment of candy bars, drinks, and groceries as well as a large supply of fishing gear.

After filling my water bottle, I started on my way. To reach
the Echo Summit on the old trail, the hiker is directed to follow small roads that wander around summer residences. My
first benchmark was the highway maintenance station on the
Echo Summit highway. Arriving there, I surveyed the scene. I
dreaded crossing busy Highway 50, with its speeding cars and
trucks. I paused by the highway and looking around, I saw a
break in the traffic. I hurried across. I was thankful to arrive
safely on the other side. The trail using a small road passes the
entrance to the Berkeley Municipal Camp. From the distance, I
thought that I saw a Berkeley friend. I wasn't close enough to be

sure and, in addition, I was so eager to reach the junction where the trail leaves the road that I wasn't keen on stopping to greet anybody. Finally, after weaving through the maze of roads, I reached the trail. At last, I had the walkway to enjoy by myself. My next benchmark was Benwood Meadow. What a pleasant surprise I had upon reaching the meadow. Here, I gazed upon a spectacular display of wildflowers. I paused for a good while to enjoy and identify familiar flowers. I found aster, mimulus, penstemon, columbine, larkspur, and one of my very favorites—the bright, yellow-orange alpine lily. What a treat. I later told one of my flower-loving friends about Benwood. She made a point of visiting the meadow and was also delighted to find its many wildflowers. After feasting on the beauty of the wildflower garden at Benwood Meadow, I walked on and when I reached a small creek beside a small meadow, I made camp.

The next morning on my journey south, I reached Bryan Meadow. This very large meadow was pleasant but not as spectacular as the smaller Benwood Meadow. Soon, the trail traversed along a slope in the Upper Truckee River Basin and, there again, were spectacular displays of wildflowers. Small streams periodically drained downward across the slopes, and beside the trickling waters, I found tall aster, columbine, and penstemon.

By evening, I arrived at small, picturesque, granite-walled Showers Lake. I found a campsite with a view looking across the lake. After supper, I enjoyed watching the light fade and the lengthening shadows creep across the rippling water. During the night, a brisk wind arose and I had to zip up my sleeping bag to stay warm.

The next morning, I arose early. I was excited. I had arranged, tentatively, to meet my friend, Ruth, at Lake Winnemucca. It was approximately seven miles away. Ruth was vacationing at a resort at Silver Lake near Carson Pass. At home, we had agreed on a possible date for a chance meeting, but I had insisted that my arrival dates when I was backpacking were only very approximate. Happily, I was on target as I hurried along. I reached Carson Pass earlier than I thought possible. Then, I continued to stride on swiftly, even on an uphill grade. I reached the lake in the early afternoon. I searched excitedly and, there in the distance, two figures rested by the lakeshore. Approaching, I could see that it was my friend, Ruth and her friend, LaVerne. How happy and excited we were to see each other. Back home, we have delighted in telling our friends and showing photographs of our rendezvous at Lake Winnemucca.

Ruth, who is one of my Native Plant Society friends and is exceedingly knowledgeable about plants and flowers, suggested that we might search for a somewhat-rare primrose. I was eager. We climbed slowly up a steep, rocky bank bordering the lake's south shore. Soon, Ruth found the primrose, called "rock fringe," and we all rejoiced as we looked at the tiny red-purple flowers half hidden among the rocks. What a happy find. On the way down, we also spotted some tiny blue-purple gentians. By late afternoon we parted, as it was time for my friends to return to their cabin for supper. I had planned originally to camp at Lake Winnemuccca. I searched but didn't find a campsite that I liked along the rocky lakeshore. It was windy. There was still daylight, so I decided to hike on.

The trail leading south skirts around Round Top Lake, which is bordered by a dark red, rounded mountain called Round Top. Then the trail zigzags down steeply to the secluded Fourth of July Lake. I found a sheltered, room-sized campsite beside this beautiful little tree-lined lake, which the guidebook described as "the jewel" of the Mokelumne Wilderness.

From the Fourth of July Lake, the next morning I found

the trail leading down to Summit Creek. Here, the trail turns south for a long walk along the floor of Summit Canyon. Soon, I came to a sign announcing, "Site of Lower Summit City." Here was another landmark commemorating early pioneers. Again, I wondered, "What was life like for them? Did they stay here during the winter and, if so, how did they manage the deep snowdrifts?" Continuing to descend on the floor of the canyon, I looked up and saw rising above me sleek, sheer, light granite walls dotted with spots of green. Looking closer through my binoculars, I could see that small bushes had managed to emerge from what looked like solid, perpendicular rocks. I marveled at how they had managed to survive. What an amazing feat of nature.

After walking down the canyon for about two hours, the trail came to an end. The guidebook states that the Forest Service has plans to build a new trail in this area but, for the present, hikers need to follow ducks (stones piled on top of each other as markers) and plastic flags to reach the next trail near the Mokelumne River crossing. Going ahead cautiously, not wanting to lose the trail, I could sometimes see signs of bent grass, indicating that other hikers had trod the way before me. With my eyes cast downward to stay on course, I saw a tiny white patch near my feet. I reached down and found a small handwritten note. It said, "I saw a snake ahead—warning!" I was duly warned. I kept looking, but I could not find the snake.

After a while, the trail turned away from Summit Creek and climbed up to a ledge above the river. It was on this ledge that I unexpectedly came to a little cliff—a little drop of about 10 to 15 feet down a cliff wall. I wondered, "Is this really the trail route?" I took off my pack and looked around to see if perhaps there was another side route leading down. I found none. I looked down again and decided that this little cliff was too steep for me to slide down with my pack on. I pondered and then decided on a plan. I got out my rope and tied it to my pack. Slowly I lowered my pack down to the cliff bottom. With my pack setting upright against the rock wall at the cliff bottom, I then carefully slid down feet-first and succeeded in landing with my feet on top of my pack. From my pack down to the ground was an easy step. I rejoiced in my safe landing and felt good about my accomplishment. Following the informal trail markers, I continued south, hoping to reach Camp Irene on the Mokelumne River by sundown. I wanted to camp there so that I would be in a good place for the next day's 3600-foot climb up out of the Mokelumne River canyon to Lake Alpine near the Ebbetts Pass. It was slow going, however, on this temporary trail, finding and following the plastic markers. Toward dusk, I reached a maintained trail with a sign announcing, "Cedar Camp Trail and Alpine Lodge—8 miles." I rejoiced. I was reasonably sure that I had reached the right trail.

Soon I met a hiker and asked, "Is this the Irene trail to Camp Irene?" "Yes." he replied, "You will reach it soon." I felt reassured that after sloshing through the tall grass and sliding down the cliff on this cross-country section, I had come out at the right place. I reached the Mokelumne River crossing just before dark and found a campsite. This had been an interesting and challenging walk, I thought as I recalled the snake warning sign and sliding down the little cliff.

In the morning, I arose early in anticipation of the 3600-foot climb. As I started my walk up, I turned around and looked down at the river canyon. I found it intriguing. It looked wild and rugged. I wondered what kind of hiking trails lay within this wild, rugged-appearing Mokelumne Wilderness.

I arrived at the top much earlier than I had anticipated. It had been a fairly easy climb. What a good feeling it is to expect a hard climb and find that it was not so hard as expected. This is better than sometimes happens—to expect an easy walk and encounter a difficult one. I recalled my unexpected climb up the Golden Staircase to the Palisades Basin in the High Sierra, which had caught me unprepared. One's mind and heart and anticipation can make such a difference to the enjoyment of a walk.

At the top, walking along little-used roads, I soon reached summer cabins and then arrived at Highway 4—the Ebbetts Pass highway near Lake Alpine. I crossed the highway and headed for the Silver Creek Forest Campground where I had planned to spend the night. Arriving at the campground, it looked crowded and noisy. I felt like moving on. I leaned my pack against the fence to study my map and guidebook. The next water would be Duck Lake, but the guidebook cautioned, "Campers should purify the water at Duck Lake, as cows graze near its shores." Debating what to do, I looked up and met a backpacker coming from the south, I asked him about Duck Lake and said that I was not sure that I should camp there, as I did not have any water-purifying tablets. He responded by reaching into his pack and pulling out a small bottle of iodine tablets. He explained, "I've been hiking in the rain for two days and I'm tired of it—I'm going out. You can have these." I thanked him profusely. How lucky I was. This gift of iodine tablets was my first experience with using purifying tablets. Thereafter, they have been added to my equipment list, and I have been carrying them ever since.

I was delighted with peaceful Duck Lake. I was all alone and found a campsite under a tree with a view toward the lake. Since it was a shallow lake, I decided to fill my water bag by wading out from the shore, with the idea of reaching cleaner, less-disturbed water. The sandy bottom felt good on my feet. I kept saying to myself, "Don't lose your balance." I was fully dressed, with pant legs rolled up and didn't want to come out with wet hiking clothes.

At suppertime, I had my first experience with iodine-flavored water. It wasn't too bad, but it was not as pleasant and flavorful as mountain spring water.

In the morning, after studying the map, I decided to take a short cut to return to the trail. I had reached my tree-shaded campsite by making a semi-circle around the end of the lake. It seemed logical to head straight southeast to intercept the trail. By not walking the semi-circle around the lake, I should save about a mile. On the first part of my short cut, there was a definite trail. Soon, it faded out and my way was blocked by tight-branched bushes. I looked around and found a dry, sandy wash and was able to follow it by ducking under low-growing branches. It became more and more difficult, however, to make my way through the dense thickets. Then, I discovered that the sandy wash was veering away from my planned compass angle. Reluctantly, I decided that I had better give up this cross-country hiking plan. I had better "play it safe." I started back. The return walk did not prove to be as easy as I had thought. I tried at first to follow my footmarks in the sandy wash, but soon I lost the markings. I had expected to arrive at the lake trail in a short time, but I was moving slowly and not seeing any sign of the lake. What should I do next? I studied my compass angle again. I should see the lake soon, I thought. Searching around, I spied a small, raised rock butte. Now I had a plan. I took off my pack and climbed up to the top of the butte. "Hallelujah!" I exclaimed thankfully. From the butte's top, I could see the lake. Admittedly, it was farther away than I expected after wandering along the sandy wash. Climbing down, I headed straight for the lake. Soon, I was safely back at the lakeshore. I felt relieved. I was, however, somewhat humiliated that I had not been successful on my short cross-country adventure. I then followed the long semi-circle-route—the sure route around the lake to reach the trail.

Friends and acquaintances often ask me, "Were you ever lost?" I always say that I was never really lost but, of course, I got off-trail sometimes when there were unmarked junctions. Of all my off-trail walks, this was the one, I must admit, on which I came the nearest to being lost.

After reaching the trail, the walk south for the remainder of the day was a pleasant and easy one. The trail led through forests with gentle ups and downs. Stopping at a high point that afternoon, I looked to the south and saw silhouetted against the late afternoon sky an interesting and different shape. I was gazing at a distinctive formation of dark-red cones jutting sharply upward. I learned from the guidebook that these were the Dardanelles. They were named after the famous Dardanelles, which guard the straits of the Aegean Sea between Europe and Asia. In later years on trips to Sonora Pass, I would anticipate and search for these dark-red volcanic cones and exclaim, "I see the Dardanelles."

By late evening, I reached Gabbot Meadow, where I made camp beside the clear, slowly flowing Highland Creek. As I was preparing m supper, I heard a familiar sound. I stopped and reached for my binoculars. Yes, it was a favorite bird friend—a spotted sandpiper. He was busily feeding at the edge of the water.

My next morning's walk was also pleasant and a moderately easy one. After a gentle ascent, the trail descended steeply to Wood's Gulch. There I met with a small stream, which the trail crossed by a ford. Fortunately, it was a gentle stream, which I easily splashed through. Toward late afternoon, I reached a blacktop road—the Clark Fork Spur. This dead-end road veers off the Sonora Pass highway near the small resort village of Dardanelle and ends at Iceberg Meadow. Along this route are a number of campgrounds. After turning east onto this road, by late afternoon, I found a "walk-in backpacker's campsite" at Sand Flat Campground. I felt reasonably comfortable. I was not surrounded by the crowds and noise of wall-to-wall RVs.

In the evening I joined the ranger-led evening campfire program. To my surprise, the ranger presented a movie on hypothermia. This movie had a lasting impact on me. Although I had read often in backpacking and winter camping literature about the dangers of becoming cold and wet, losing body heat, and becoming disoriented, this movie made hypothermia more real to me. It was a cold and damp evening, with a light drizzle that created an atmosphere that caused me to become more alert to the danger of hypothermia. From that time on, I became more cautious.

In the morning I had a short walk to the road's end at Iceberg Meadow. There, I was greeted by a gigantic, towering, upright rock. It was what geologists call an "erratic"—a rock from some faraway place, which had been lifted by an ancient glacier and left resting by itself in a different environment. There, setting at the base of the erratic rock, was an artist with her easel. Obviously, she had been inspired by the shape and setting of this upright granite boulder. It was indeed well named, as it could well resemble the shape of an "iceberg."

I was glad to leave the blacktop and turn south onto the trail leading into the forest. From here to the Clark Fork Meadow, some seven miles distant, the trail climbs up and stays close to the gurgling waters of the Clark Fork stream of the Stanislaus River. I liked this river canyon trail. To me, it had a wild and unspoiled feeling. Its side banks were dotted with straggly bushes and small grassy meadows interspersed with pines.

In about an hour, the trail reached the Boulder Creek ford and a trail junction. Two hikers whom I saw eating lunch near the junction announced that they were going to climb up to Boulder Lake on the Boulder Creek Trail—a popular day-hikers' destination. The Tahoe-Yosemite Trail, which I was following, proceeded straight ahead to the south, staying close to the stream.

I started my search for the next benchmark. The guidebook indicated that there would be a boulder ford of the river near a stock-drift fence. Climbing up rather steeply, I came to a cattle fence and what appeared to be a ford. I surveyed the stream. This looked like a really difficult ford. A big, steep, slanting rock sat in the middle of the stream, and it would take a big leap for me to reach this rock. If I were able to make the big leap, it would be difficult to find footing and to balance on the rock because of its steep slant. I studied my plan of attack. I found a stick for support, then I pushed hard, taking my longest step. I succeeded in reaching the rock and held on tightly to its top. From there, I took a second leap and landed on the far shore. I was relieved to be safely on the other side.

I found the trail on the other side and followed it as it climbed upward. I noticed that the trail had been used by cows. I was following their hoof-marks. I kept hoping to see the meadow soon, but the trail stayed in the woods. Finally, I came to a clearing with an overlook. Approaching a cliff's edge, I looked down and saw, below me, a large, grassy meadow. Then I knew that I had taken the wrong trail. How disappointing! I had crossed the river on the difficult ford too soon. Now I knew the location of the meadow. I started my walk back.

I did not look forward to the river ford with its leap to the slanting rock but, thankfully, I made it again. As the day was growing late, I realized that I would not reach Clark Fork Meadow in daylight. I looked around and found a very pleasant campsite beside the river.

In the morning, I had a slow, somewhat difficult climb. The trail leads up a steep, rocky bank and weaves in and around some large granite boulders. Around noon, I reached the meadow in time for lunch. What a beautiful sight. I was gazing at a large, grassy meadow. The grassland is ringed at its edges by small willow and alder trees. These are then framed in the next-distant layer by sandy, reddish-brown mountain slopes. Included in the view are the high-pointed cones of Sonora and Stanislaus Peaks.

After enjoying lunch and gazing out over the peaceful meadow, I started my search to locate what was described in the guidebook as an informal ducked trail that would lead up and out of the meadow by way of St. Mary's Pass and down the other side to the Sonora Pass road. The guidebook directions seemed a little complicated: "At the head of the meadow, we cross a little tributary not shown on the map and turn directly uphill beside this brook." I started up the meadow, searching for this little tributary. I passed one tributary and explored it briefly; I decided it didn't fit the guidebook's description. Coming up to the second tributary, it looked to me as if it would lead up to the ridge. I started my ascent. After a while, I could see the top of the ridge, and I visualized that St. Mary's Pass was somewhere near the ridge top. The climb grew steeper. I felt that I was slowly inching my way to the top. Like most mountaintops, the top seems to move a little further away as the hiker approaches upward. I named it "the vanishing mountain top." I had found that ridge tops could be deceptive when viewed from below. Little by little, however, I drew nearer. My climb to the top was interrupted for a pause when, on a slightly level, moist, sandy platform, I found one of the most charming miniature flower gardens I have ever seen. There were tiny, deep-purple lupines and asters, so tiny that I had to examine them closely to make sure that they were real. They were so delicate, and yet so bright in color. I believe that I shall always remember these dainty, precious flowers. Finally, reaching the very top of the ridge, I eagerly peered down the other side. I saw a very distinct horse trail leading down. I felt reassured. I started my walk down. It was an easy hike, gliding and sliding down the steep, rocky path. Upon reaching the valley, I realized it was growing dark. I decided to look for a campsite. I found a little trickling stream and started my search. The wind had come up and was blowing up the valley in strong gusts. I selected a low place under some whitebark pines and strung up my tube tend for wind protection. I ate a cold supper, as it was too windy to safely light a fire. Snuggled into my bedroll, I was still visualizing the exquisite, miniature wildflower garden.

In the morning, I took out my map and compass and lined up my map, looking for landmarks. Where was I? I discovered that I had camped at the north end of Wolf Creek Lake. I had missed St. Mary's Pass. I had come down from the ridge east of the pass. I hadn't found the right "little tributary." Having missed St. Mary's Pass, it was time to puzzle over and figure out a way out to reach the Sonora Pass road.

From Wolf Creek Lake, the map showed a road leading from the upper end of the lake out to the highway. This road, rather than climbing directly over the ridge and descending to Sonora Pass, a relatively short distance, circles on a long loop around the ridge. I was not tempted, however, to try the cross-country climb over this rocky ridge. I was ready for the easy but long, sure way out.

I packed up and started on my way, seeking to find the roadhead. As I approached Wolf Creek Lake at the upper end, I saw trail equipment—shovels, picks, and a pulaski—lying beside a section of newly made trail. The trail-makers were nowhere in sight, however; they were not working that day. This, I surmised, was to become a new section of the Pacific Crest Trail. How interesting. I walked a short distance on the new trail section before it ended. Years later, I returned to walk on this new section of the Pacific Crest Trail.

I soon reached the gravel road and started my long (about nine miles) but easy walk out to the highway. Apparently, the road is little used, as no cars passed. Arriving at the roadhead, where there was a pullout for cars to park, I did not have to wait long before a pleasant young couple in a pickup offered me a ride all the way to Bridgeport where there is a bus stop. I was fortunate to arrive in Bridgeport just a little before the northbound bus arrived. I soon boarded the bus for Reno and then transferred to a San Francisco-bound bus and home.

This beautiful and intriguing Sonora Pass area was certainly one of the highlights of my entire journey. I have returned to the area on four separate trips. I have now been in and out of the Clark Fork Meadow from the St. Mary's Pass area on four different routes. Each time, I have searched for the elusive route, marked by "ducks," which starts up "by the little tributary." I have found and followed two different routes marked with ducks up to the ridge leading to St. Mary's Pass. I have concluded that there are many ways to hike in and out of the Clark Fork Meadow—all of them seem to me to be relatively obscure. On one of my last trips, as I climbed around not far from the St. Mary's Pass, I found another miniature rock garden. This alone was worth the journey.

Chapter 14
Lake Fontanillis Near Lake Tahoe to Sierra City
August 1978 • 82 miles

From form to form, beauty to beauty, ever changing, never resting, all are speeding on with love's enthusiasm, singing with the stars the eternal song of creation. — *John Muir*

This was another peak year for me—my first acknowledged year on the Pacific Crest Trail. My first mountaintop journey was completing the John Muir Trail in 1971. My second journey was completing the Tahoe-Yosemite Trail, which I accomplished in 1976 and 1977. By now, a ten-day summer vacation backpacking had become something that I eagerly anticipated. I dreamed of and planned my summer trip throughout the spring and winter. I had by now become aware of the Pacific Crest Trail. I had purchased Volume I of California, the Pacific Crest Trail—A Guidebook published by Wilderness Press. After studying the guidebook, I was eager to start north on the trail.

In 1978, I still did not have a definite plan of completing the Pacific Crest Trail. A dim idea was stirring that I might wish to complete the California section of the trail. For the most part, however, I was just going out for a trail walk for the pure joy of being surrounded by mountains, meadows, streams, and forests.

From the Lake Tahoe area to the north, my summer journeys were in sequence, completing a nine- or ten-day walk each summer (except for 1986 when I missed my trail walk after fracturing my arm on a San Francisco Muni bus). By traveling from south to north, I was able to follow the trail descriptions in the guidebook.

Hiking in this section, I was still traveling through the glorious Sierras. Although the altitude was somewhat lower than that of previous walks in the High Sierras, the land of 12,000-foot peaks, I was still enjoying scenes of beautiful mountains, meadows, lakes, and forests.

Reaching the trail for this year's journey near Middle Velma Lake was relatively easy. Basically, I knew the route to the trailhead, as it was the same route that I had followed to reach the Tahoe-Yosemite Trail in 1976. After studying the map, I decided on a slight variation from my 1976 route to reach the trail. Instead of going in at Meeks Bay, I decided to disembark from the Greyhound bus at beautiful Emerald Bay on Lake Tahoe's west shore and climb up by way of the Eagle Creek Trail. I was eager for the variety offered by exploring a new route.

My first night's camp was at Eagle Lake. I found a ledge above the lake for my bedroom, complete with an adjoining kitchen. I was so excited to be walking and camping in the wilderness again. I felt so uplifted upon hearing the music of the wind stirring through the trees, the rushing water of the nearby stream, and the chirping of mountain birds. I also became aware of the mountain fragrance and the glorious scent of pure, fresh air. The total ambience of the wilderness was so satisfying. I kept recalling and repeating John Muir's apt prose, "Climb the mountains and get their good tidings. Nature's peace will flow into you as sunshine flows into trees. The winds will blow their own freshness into you, and the storms their energy, while cares will drop off like autumn leaves."

The following day, I climbed up to join the trail at 8310-foot Fontanillis Lake. The memory of my 1976 tree-lined campsite near this charming rock-bound lake prompted me to return. I arrived in the early afternoon and found my small, tree-line bedroom. I looked forward to spending another peaceful evening absorbed in drinking in the beauty of my surroundings. Soon, however, my peaceful reverie was rudely interrupted. I heard disturbing noises. I saw that two young men, one wearing white pants, had arrived and were chopping on a tree below me. As I looked down to observe their activity, I found that they were also piling up rocks to construct some kind of rock wall. I was upset. I walked down and said to them, "Do you know that cutting trees and moving rocks is not permitted in a national wilderness? The lake is in the Desolation National Wilderness." One of them replied, looking puzzled, "But we are only going to stay here for two days." I was so disappointed and angry. My words had no impact on them. They went back to their chopping. I wished so much that a ranger would have appeared at that moment. Unfortunately, rangers in the wilderness have a lot of territory to cover and the chances of them catching two young people in the act of chopping a tree is not good. I still feel badly when I think that these two young people had so little sense of preservation of the wilderness. I take comfort, however, in knowing that in recent years, more young people have participated through their schools in environmental workshops such as those offered by the Yosemite Institute. I do believe that there is much less destruction of trees and moving of rocks today than in earlier years and that there is much more appreciation of the preservation of wilderness.

My next day's journey heading north offered attractive

views as I walked by the Velma lakes. Twice I stopped to enjoy views of deep-blue Tahoe, seen through peepholes through breaks in the forest. I also enjoyed a spectacular view looking west toward Black Rock Reservoir. By noon, I reached Phipps Creek, where I had originally planned to camp. It was much too early to stop for the night. I ate my lunch by the creek and soon found that I was surrounded by swarms of mosquitoes. What an uncomfortable campsite this would have been! I was thankful to walk on, and by evening arrived at General Creek. There I found a comfortable, small, open space, which, happily, was free of mosquitoes. The water source was not ideal. The stream contained a stagnant pool, so I used my iodine water-purifying tablets. I enjoyed my dinner of chicken stew and settled in for a peaceful night.

Shortly after leaving my campsite at General Creek the following day, the trail left Desolation Wilderness and entered the El Dorado National Forest. Shortly thereafter, the trail merged into a jeep road and for the rest of the day, I was walking on a temporary trail, most of which was a jeep trail. When the trail reached low-lying, shallow Miller Lake, I noticed that it was packed full of yellow water lilies. I paused to gaze at them. I am very fond of water lilies. I do not think that I have ever seen so many lilies crowded into one little pond. It was awesome.

By noon, I reached forested Bear Lake. I found a pleasant overlook at the edge of Bear Lake and stopped for lunch and a siesta. I enjoyed watching two fishermen with their dog get into a boat and row out to the middle of the lake. They appeared to hauling in quite a few fish, and each time their lines came in, the dog got excited and barked. He must have been trained to accompany them on their fishing trips as, although he barked and wagged his tail, he did not move from the front seat of the boat.

Just as I was thinking that I had been so lucky in not encountering any motor traffic on the jeep road, I heard a roar—two motorbikes were approaching. I ducked into the forest to avoid their sight and sound. By afternoon, now hiking on a wider road, a large group of about six motorbikes came noisily up the road. The riders wore brightly colored outfits, which looked to me like racing uniforms. I said to myself, "I will be so glad to get back on hiking trails—I don't like road walking." By evening, I reached Barker Creek, which offered water and campsites. I picked out a level site and then, to my surprise and displeasure, I saw through the trees a parked recreational motor vehicle. I moved. I wanted a peaceful place, alone and surrounded by wilderness. I walked down the creek's edge until I was safely away from the RV and made my camp for the night.

I started out early the next morning. I was eager to hurry on, as I knew I would soon reach a forest trail and be through with road walking—for a while at least. Climbing up a moderately steep hill, I came to a small, bright-red lumber company office with a sign that read, "Welcome to PCT Hikers." I went inside. No one was there, but I found that they had a Pacific Crest Trail register. I wrote: "I'm hiking the Pacific Crest Trail to Sierra City and I will be glad when I reach the completed trail again. I don't like road-walking."

By late afternoon, I turned off the road onto a trail into the forest. It felt so good to be in the woods again. I picked out a scenic spot to have my mid-morning snack. I was comfortably seated when I heard a roar. I ducked out of sight as 13 brightly suited motorbike riders came trooping by. How disappointing! I had reached a forest trail but was not yet on the motor-restricted trail.

After the noisy bikers seemed to be out of my range, I hiked on. The trail led down a steep incline into a scenic, wooded canyon. Soon, I reached the trail crossing of Powder-horn Creek at Diamond Crossing. I filled my water bottle and was looking forward to a peaceful lunch by the trickling creek when I was again interrupted by the sound of loud motors. Again, I retreated to a hiding place behind a big tree. How frustrating! The motorcycles stopped by the creek. I had hoped and assumed that they would move on. I could hear them talking about where they thought they could catch some fish. Suddenly, one of them said, "There is a backpacker by that tree." He had discovered my hiding place. He approached me and asked, "Where are you hiking? I replied, "I am hiking on the Pacific Crest Trail and am headed for Sierra City." He listened and seemed interested. Soon I was surrounded by six men, all of them looking at me and all of them expressing interest in my hike. I found them to be quite human and somewhat likeable. In fact, I rather enjoyed talking to them. As they wished me well and I moved on down the trail, I kept saying to myself, "Some bikers are human and fairly nice people and they seem to have some appreciation of the out-of-doors." Nevertheless, when I finally arrived at the sign "Granite Chief Motor Vehicle Closure Area," I rejoiced.

By evening, I found a pleasant campsite by Five Lakes Creek.

In the morning, I started early in anticipation of the climb up to the 8550-foot Granite Chief saddle. Before the trail makes a major ascent to the saddle, it leads past Whiskey Creek Camp. When I arrived at the camp, I searched for the trail marker. Looking around, I saw a man and woman with a young child standing in the doorway of the cabin. I noticed that they were airing their bedroll on a post. I also noticed a sign pointing to the "toilet." I was puzzled. I could not see any other trail sign. I decided to hike ahead on a well-used trail, assuming it must be the main trail route. After walking awhile, the trail direction did not seem right to me. I was heading east, and I should be going north. I was puzzled. I remembered that some trails are in one direction for a short distance and then circle back, but this still did not seem right. I decided to return to Whiskey Creek. Just as I arrived at the camp, the woman came out of the cabin and lifted the bedroll from the post. Then I saw it—a good clear sign marked "Granite Chief" pointing north. This was my first experience and, hopefully, my last in missing a trail junction because a bedroll was being aired on a signpost.

Feeling secure that I was now on the right trail, I moved north. The trail started to make a moderate climb through a brushy area dotted with mule ears. Soon I emerged out into the open and saw the approach to rock-covered Granite Chief. At the time of my walk, the permanent trail had not been completed in this section. The guidebook advises hikers to head for the low point of the saddle. I glued my eyes to the saddle, searching for the easiest route. I was determined not to lose the direction.

On my approach to Granite Chief, I encountered some day hikers who had walked over from Squaw Valley. Granite Chief lay just a little west of Squaw Peak. One of the neatly dressed women looked at me and said, "You look like you've been in for a long time." Although I felt like saying that I had only been in for four days of an eleven-day planned hike, I smiled and said, "I'm backpacking a section of the Pacific Crest Trail. I started near Lake Tahoe and plan to walk to Sierra City." She commented, "That must be a long hike." It was not until the middle of the following day that I discovered a sizeable rip in the seat of my pants! Perhaps that is why she looked at me, smiling strangely, when she commented that I must have been in for a long time.

Arriving at the top of the Granite Chief saddle, I was treated to a glorious view. Looking east, I could see the deep-blue waters of Lake Tahoe framed in the far distance by the towering peaks of Mount Rose. To the south, I could see the winding, tree-covered valley through which flows the swift-moving Truckee River.

My next destination was the North Fork of the American River. The guidebook indicated that hikers would find campsites soon after reaching the river.

Just as I arrived at the North Fork with eager anticipation of making camp—it was growing late—I was greeted by a large sign: "Private Property—No Trespassing—Patrolled." What to do? I did not want to go further. I wanted to rest for the night. I thought for a moment and decided on a plan.

I walked back just far enough so that I could no longer see the sign. I looked around and spotted a small rock shelf near a spring. I climbed up onto the little shelf, which was hidden among a cluster of willow bushes. It was just barely big enough to accommodate my bed. I felt good, perhaps a little smug, at finding this hidden place, even though I could not say with certainty whether or not I was camped on private property.

I spent a noisy night in my hideaway on the rocky shelf, which I had been so pleased to find. Some animal was thrashing around in the willow bushes all night. I could not see its size or shape. I shall always wonder what it was. Was it a deer, which were relatively common, or was it one of the nocturnal browsers, such as a raccoon or a skunk?

Knowing that I would be road walking, I changed from my long hiking pants, my usual hiking outfit, into my homemade denim cutoffs. It was then that I discovered the sizeable rip along the seam of my pants. What a surprise! Although I travel light, I always do carry a needle and thread. Several times it has been useful. I decided that I would mend my pants when I had the time in the next day or two.

By late morning, I came to the small summer-home community of Old Soda Springs. What an interesting and different-looking village. In the center was a small lake, and children were swimming and boating. The homes were attractively and solidly built. They had built-in front porches and the wood trim around the windows was painted in contrasting colors. They looked to me, from the style, as though they may have been built around the 1920s.

Since the community was at the end of a gravel road, there was no noisy traffic, and people were wandering along the road. I passed a woman near the little lake and asked her, "Are there active soda springs here?" She replied, "Yes, these are mineral soda springs. My children drink the water and they are healthy." Soon another resident, wearing a Pebble Beach golf hat and riding a red jeep came along and asked, "Where are you going?" I replied, "I am walking on the Pacific Crest Trail to Sierra City." He seemed satisfied. I did wonder if he were on "patrol," as the "No Trespassing, Private Property, Patrolled" signs continued to be very numerous.

A little further on, I passed another summer-home community with an entrance over the roadway and a large sign announcing "The Cedars." One of the cottages had a sign reading "Church Office." I wondered if a church group owned this community. No one was around to ask. Both of these communities were located in a beautiful area. To the west, I could see far up into the rock-walled valley of the North Fork of the American River. To the south, when there was a window between the trees, I looked back at the tall, rocky outlines of Squaw Peak and Granite Chief.

The guidebook cautioned that there would be no legal

camping for 16 miles, until I reached the new Soda Springs Village on old Highway 40. I was worried. That was too far for me to walk by evening. Would I be able to find a hideaway? I started my search. When I reached the crossing of Onion Creek, I saw a legal-looking Forest Service sign that read "Onion Creek Campground." What a welcome relief! I made camp early and had ample time to wash socks and relax.

I started early the next morning in anticipation of a dusty, hot road walk to Soda Springs. The road was busy with noisy lumber trucks. The truck noise had started at 4:30 a.m.! When I saw one truck driver peer out his window at me, I waved. One man in a passenger car stopped and offered me a ride, saying, "Are you one of those die-hards—walking on a hot, dusty road?" I thanked him and replied, "I'm walking on the Pacific Crest Trail from Mexico to Canada."

After climbing up on the hot, dusty, noisy road, the terrain leveled off, and I came to the shallow Ice Lakes, which are now called Serene Lakes on most maps. Around the lakeshores were a number of ski chalets. They appeared to be deserted now. Soon, I reached large, shallow, Lake Van Norden, where I found a pleasant lunch spot with a view of the lake. This was my first visit to the Soda Springs area in the summer. I had been coming to the Sierra Club's nearby Clair Tapaan Lodge at Norden for winter skiing for the past 25 years. How different the lake looked in the summer. In the winter, it is a snow-covered frozen lake with cross-country ski trails circling the shoreline. Now, it was mostly a meadow, with just a few puddles near the west end where the dam is located. As I walked along the north shore of the lake before climbing up the ridge at Norden, I was surprised to find a horse stable with corrals toward the center of the meadow where I skied in the winter.

I was reaching the Norden post office. I was delighted and

relieved to find that my food package had arrived safely. I spent a leisurely hour repacking my pack, writing postcards, and treating myself to iced tea and yogurt. This small former post office and store has now become a bed-and-breakfast inn.

I walked the short distance to Clair Tapaan Lodge and went into the dining room to fill my water bag. A neatly dressed man in white pants asked me about my walk. He had a worried look and asked, "Do you think that it is safe to hike alone?" I replied, "Perhaps there are some risks, but I enjoy the solitude and I enjoy being alone when I am surrounded by the beauties of nature." When I started to leave, the sky had darkened and rain was threatening. He asked, "Why don't you spend the night at the lodge?" I let him know that I was prepared for rain and said my good-byes. He still looked puzzled and, perhaps, a little worried.

Going out the back door of the lodge, I was eager to see what the ski trail looked like during the summer. How different it looked! I found myself pushing through waist-high bushes. I had no idea when I had been gliding through the snow path in the winter that bushes would be growing underneath in the summer.

Soon after I left the lodge, it started to sprinkle, and then came thunder and lightening. I had planned to climb Boreal Ridge before making camp. I changed my plan. It would not be good to be on a barren ridge during a lightening storm. I began thinking that perhaps I should have followed the man's advice and stayed at the lodge, but I quickly discarded that idea. I did not want to break the spell of being surrounded by nature until I was ready to come out. I took shelter under a tree by nearby shallow Lake Lynton. After a while, the thunder and lightening let up, as so often they do in the Sierras—the familiar short afternoon showers. I made camp at the edge of the trees and enjoyed the view looking up toward Signal Hill, with its flashing beacon. This sight brought back memories of the Clair Tapaan Lodge's old rope ski tow—the longest in the Donner Pass area. The old ski tow pushed up toward the top of Signal Hill. The old ski tow is long gone, replaced by newer and safer chair lifts.

More recently, I have returned and hiked a portion of the new Pacific Crest Trail in the Donner Pass area near Norden. The section south of the old Highway 40 at Donner Pass affords glorious views from the Mt. Judah and Donner Peak area. The section north between Donner Pass and Highway 80 offers glorious views looking east down at Donner Lake and toward Mt. Rose. It also includes views of colorful rock formations as the trail weaves in and out around cliffs and dikes, moving north toward the Boreal Ski Resort and Highway 80. This new section of the trail, I believe, well deserves the description of "Crest Trail."

My next day's walk from Lake Lytton north to the Peter Grubb Hut and Paradise Valley was overflowing with beautiful views.

First, I explored and found a passage for my cross-country ascent up Boreal Ridge. I found a little ravine, which was good for zigzagging up to the top, I stepped carefully to balance and not lose my footing while maneuvering between loose rocks and protruding bushes. Climbing up constantly brought forth reminiscences of winter cross-country adventures up this same ridge. I recalled how, full of curiosity and anticipation—could I make it to the top?—I had slowly and laboriously climbed by selecting diagonal stripes alternating, when reaching a steep angle, with herringbone steps until finally and triumphantly I reached the top. At the summit, I was skiing with downhill skiers who had arrived by sliding off a ski lift launched below in Boreal Valley. They chose the easy way to the top. On my winter trip, the view was spectacular. The scene was full of snow-topped peaks. Now, on my summer cross-country hike, I paused at the top. The view was pleasant but, to me, not as spectacular as the winter's white-peak scene. Now the scene was predominately a pleasant green.

Except for a little brush and small rocks, the descent was fairly easy. I came out near a little pond and needed to spend some time figuring out a route around the pond without having to wade. I ended up sloshing through a damp meadow. Near the Boreal Ridge Ski Resort Lodge, I discovered a faucet of good, fresh water. I measured out my needed water, then walked under busy noisy Interstate 80 by way of an underpass and started my climb up to Castle Pass. I was on a familiar route, but I had never before hiked the trail in the summer. For me, it had been a ski trail. From the pass, I drifted down toward Round Valley. I was excited. What would Peter Grubb Hut look like in August? Peter Grubb Hut is one of four back-country huts built by Sierra Club members for winter camping. Striding down the ridge, I recalled a winter experience of approaching the hut during a white-out. Nearing the hut, we could hear the voices of our friends who had arrived earlier, but we could not see them. We moved ahead slowly until finally we caught sight of our friends and the hut. Now, in August, I could see the whole valley clearly. When the hut came into view, how different it looked. It appeared to be so much taller. The winter groundcover of 5 to 14 feet of snow had made such a difference. Also, in summer the trees looked so much taller, and I was looking at a whole different set of colors carpeting the ground. There were fields of corn lilies and partially dried grasses intermingled with a light-green carpeting in damp areas near springs and meadows.

I was able to enter the hut through the lower door, whereas during winter, I have always had to enter through the top door, one story above the lower door, and then climb down on a ladder to the kitchen. I climbed outside again and, after exploring the hut, gazed at one of the most amusing sights—that of the outhouse. It looks so very tall now in the summer. It affords an easy entrance into it through the lower door, whereas in winter, I would climb in through an upper door.

I selected a view site to eat my lunch, looking out over Round Valley toward Castle Peak and enjoyed gazing at its familiar volcanic-colored turrets outlined against the blue sky.

Climbing out of peaceful and nostalgic Round Valley, the trail ascends up to a ridge offering still another splendid view looking west toward the Black Buttes and Emigrant Gap and to the south, toward the North Fork of the American River's deeply cut Royal Gorge.

From the top of the ridge, my view was somewhat obscured by a gray haze—or was it smoke? It looked especially dark toward the north. Was it a forest fire? I speculated that is was and hoped that I was not going to be walking into it.

The next descent wound down to beautiful, green Paradise Valley. Paradise Valley is also known for its mosquitoes. I decided to move on. I climbed up again over still another ridge, and then down to White Rock Creek, where I found a pleasant campsite for the night—relatively free of mosquitoes.

From White Rock Creek the next morning, the temporary trail returned to roads. First, there were little-used spur roads, and then came wider roads with car traffic. I wondered where they all were going. As I approached Meadow Lake on a still-wider road, I encountered heavy RV traffic. I noticed as one wide RV passed me it bore a big sign proclaiming "Fremont Pathfinder." I assumed that the Fremont Pathfinders were meeting and celebrating at Meadow Lake—a popular lake, I learned, for fishing and boating.

The noise and dust after a day of scenic views and solitude were an unpleasant let-down for me. As a distraction, I pulled out my Sierra Club songbook and sang and hummed familiar tunes: "Home on the Range," "You Are My Sunshine," "It's a Long Way to Tipperary," and "Amazing Grace." It helped to make the unpleasant road walk section pass more rapidly.

Arriving at the shore of large Meadow Lake, I stopped to read the historical marker: "Summit City, gold rush town, existed in 1862 and had a population of between 2000 and 5000 people. It was abandoned because it proved too expensive to haul out the ore." How disappointing Summit City must have proved for hopeful miners holding onto dreams of riches.

As the road skirted the north shore of the lake and I was out of reach of the celebrating Pathfinders, I found a quiet, secluded spot for my afternoon snack, and I enjoyed a footbath as I waded out into the lake.

Back on the road, which was now quiet and free of traffic, I climbed up a ridge and then drifted down to attractive Toll House Lake. Here I found a peaceful campsite with a view of the small rockbound lake. After supper, I enjoyed gazing out across the peaceful waters of the small rock-bound, tree-framed lake.

Walking north from Toll House Lake the next day, I came to big, busy Jackson Meadow Reservoir. The lightly traveled road I had been walking on joined with other roads, and soon I was catapulted into a wide road with noisy traffic. A few yards further on, I met some big construction trucks and huge tractors with rollers. Next, I came to yellow and red flashing lights. A sign read, "Road construction." I waded through the noise and confusion and, arriving at the north end of the lake, I searched for and found a quiet lakeside lunch spot. No one was nearby. I enjoyed my peaceful retreat as I listened to the noise of the waves lapping against the rocky shore.

By evening, I reached Milton Reservoir and started my search for a campsite. There were very few choices. The shoreline was marshy and bordered by tall grasses and rushes. After surveying the landscape, I chose a small, dusty mound where I unrolled my bivouac sack. There was much evidence of heavy use by car campers. Although this site was dusty and small, it did offer a view looking out at the water. There, gazing out over shallow Milton Reservoir, I was treated to a glorious scene. Gliding the length of the lake on gentle up-drafts and maneuvering most gracefully was a beautiful bird. Sighting it with small binoculars, I was not positively sure, but I judged it to be a Forster's tern. Upon reaching a small, grassy, rounded point adjacent to the lake's inlet, the graceful bird dropped down, making a smooth landing on the grassy shore. Soon, my bird friend flew back over the lake and made a return trip gliding and landing again. As I watched, the graceful tern repeated this pattern four times before disappearing. I thought of the story of "Jonathan Livingston Seagull"—the story related by Richard Bach. As in the Jonathan Livingston Seagull story, this bird epitomized to me the glorious feeling of freedom. Following the tern's flight with my glasses, I discovered still another splendid sight. Huddled near the grassy point where the tern had landed were three Canada geese. These were the first Canada geese I had seen throughout my hike. I watched them and admired the way their feathers blended in with the grass. They were perfectly camouflaged. I was so pleased with this scene of quiet beauty that I remember it well to this day. It was very special.

My walk the next morning on my coming-out day was an easy one of approximately eight miles. The trail contoured around Hilda Peak and passed by the Hilda Mine where, unlike many former mining sites, two mining buildings still stood. I poked my head inside one of them. I wondered what life had been like for these miners. Did some of them make fortunes? Did some of them suffer disillusionment and give up?

Approaching Wild Plum Campground at the edge of my coming-out trailhead, I was greeted with a surprise. Tacked on the campground gate was a picnic plate reading, "Welcome, Eleanor." My good friends, Carol and Marge, had arranged to meet me in Sierra City. Their welcoming sign made me feel more ready to come out of the wilderness and to join them. I soon found my friends at Harrington's Resort in Sierra City. We were excited and eager to exchange news. They had encountered the fire fighters who had been camped by the side of the road just west of Sierra City. They were anxious to know if I had been near the fire. I told them that I had seen smoke from the ridge above the Peter Grubb Hut but, fortunately, I had missed the major area of the fire. They had had an exciting time watching the fire fighters assemble their gear. By now, the fire was out and the fire fighters were packing up and departing.

We enjoyed a pleasant evening at Harrington's. In the morning on our ride home from Sierra City, we viewed the lofty peak of the Sierra Buttes. I hoped to climb to the top of the Buttes on my next year's hike.

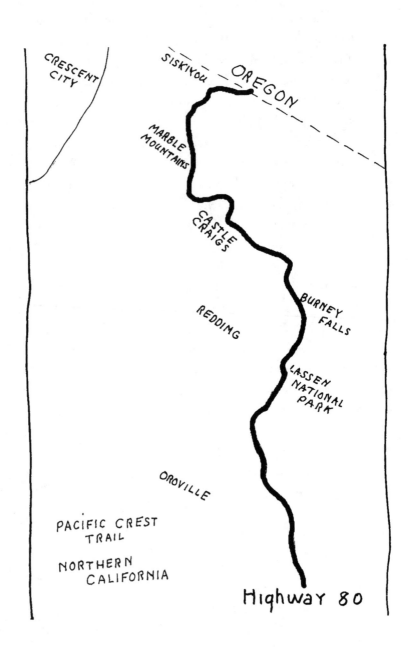

INTRODUCTION TO NORTHERN CALIFORNIA
From Highway 80 near the Donner Pass to the Oregon border
546 Miles

For the hiker travelling through Northern California, the high, granitic peaks of the High Sierra—John Muir's "Range of Light" gives way to the reddish-brown colors of volcanic peaks and ridges. Most prominent of the high volcanoes are the snow-dusted peaks of Mount Lassen and Mount Shasta.

For the hiker, however, the up-and-down climbs of the high mountain passes of the Sierra are replaced by the up-and-down climbs through the river canyons. First are the crossings of the Feather River and its branches, followed by the crossing of the Sacramento and Klamath Rivers.

Special sights of interest and beauty include the Castle Crags, just beyond the Sacramento River—marked by their high, jagged peaks—and the white-hued rocks of the Marble Mountains, just south of the Klamath River.

The approach to Oregon is marked by the crossing of the mighty, swift-flowing Klamath River and entering the forested, gentle ups and downs of the Siskiyou Mountains.

For me, hiking through Northern California during the late 70s and early 80s meant travelling mostly on uncompleted trails. I walked on temporary trails, which included old logging roads and sections of cross-country hiking that presented me with an exciting and challenging adventure.

Chapter 15
Sierra City to Little Grass Valley Road
near La Porte
July 1979 • 52 miles

*How many hearts with warm red blood in them are beating
under cover of the woods, and how many teeth and eyes are
shining! A multitude of animal people, intimately related to
us, but of whose lives we know almost nothing, are as busy
about their own affairs as we are about ours. — John Muir*

As I traveled north from the High Sierras toward the
Feather River, I felt the gradual change in the landscape. I was
slowly drifting downhill from the higher altitudes of 10,000
to 12,000 feet of the High Sierras to lower altitudes of 5,000
to 8,000 feet. Volcanic reddish rocks interspersed with granite
became a common sight. I would soon arrive at the north tip
of the Sierras—the Feather River town of Belden.

The route was dotted with small lakes, especially in the area
just north of Sierra City, called the Lake Basin area. These were
quiet, tree-lined lakes, in contrast to the rock-bound Alpine
lakes of the High Sierras. The Pacific Crest Trail route in this
area in 1979 was primarily routed on temporary trails. Closed
logging roads were frequently used. Occasionally, there were
sections of newly built trails and trails in the process of being
constructed. I found the walk pleasant, but not as spectacular
as the High Sierras.

Getting to the trailhead was a pleasant adventure, as my good friends, Carol and Marge, drove me all the way to Sierra City. We had lunch together at the Wild Plum Campground. I posed for pictures wearing my new boots, and I waved goodbye. As I started up the road in a light rain to meet the trail near Lower Sardine Lake, a backpacker approached me. Eager to learn more about the trail route, I asked, "Have you been walking on the Pacific Crest Trail?" He replied, "I have been walking south from Belden." He then gave me some startling news: "The bridge at Hartman Bar has washed out. I took a long detour by road walking all of the way from Bucks Lake to Quincy, and then returned to the trail near the Little Grass Valley Reservoir." This was startling news. It gave me something to ponder over for the next several days.

I was quite sure that I did not want to walk the long distance to Quincy on a busy highway. Could I find another way to cross the Feather River near Hartman's Bar? I hoped so.

Two years later, I discovered the identity of this hiker. He was Karl Ellingson. I answered a small ad in the Backpackers Magazine to order a book entitled "2500-Mile Walk—An Old-timer on the Pacific Crest Trail" by Karl Ellingson. When I received the book, I recognized that it was he from the picture on the cover. He had a special identity as he had only one arm. Upon receiving the book, I eagerly turned to the page describing his arrival in Sierra City. It affirmed that he had arrived on July 21, 1979.

Upon receiving the interesting book describing his trail journey, I wrote him a note, telling him that I was delighted to know that he was the backpacker I met at Sierra City.

By evening I arrived at the Sardine Lake Resort. I looked

around, as Carol and Marge had said they might meet me at the resort's dining room for dinner. When I did not see them, and when I found out that dinner was $9.75, I was rather glad they had not arrived. Today, this sounds like a bargain dinner, but for me in 1979, it was expensive.

I walked on and stopped for water and ate a light supper at the Sardine Lake Campground. After supper, I walked on a little farther and found a small, level spot on a ledge overlooking the lake. I enjoyed watching the western sun sink behind the Sierra Buttes.

My morning's walk leading west traversed above the shores of Lower and Upper Sardine Lakes, offering pleasant views across the blue-green water. Small boats moving out from the resort dotted the lakes. I climbed up the trail to the small, tree-lined Tamarack Lakes. Arriving in mid-morning, I selected a secluded place to park my pack against a tree. I planned to spend the rest of the day detouring south to climb to the top of the Sierra Buttes forest fire lookout. The trail winding up to the lookout was invigorating and challenging. The first section wound up a steep, narrow rocky path, and then I came to the really steep part—176 steps up on a perpendicular steel ladder. Reaching the top, there was plenty of room to straighten one's legs in the glass-enclosed forest ranger's station. What a tremendous view! It was well worth the climb. The friendly ranger reported that on an exceptionally clear day, one could see the Golden Gate Bridge, and to the north on moderately clear days, one could see Mt. Lassen and Mt. Shasta. My day's view was not that clear, but the near view was still magnificent. I could clearly see large Jackson Meadow Lake, where I had eaten lunch the year before, and the nearby Sardine Lakes, rimmed by dark-reddish rocks. All in all, I had a good "top of the world" feeling.

On the return trip, after climbing down from the lookout, I passed a family of hikers who greeted me with a customary "Hello," but we didn't stop to talk. Back home a few weeks later, an office colleague amazed me by asking, "Did I see you hiking on the trail to the Sierra Buttes forest station?" "Yes," I replied. What a surprise! We were both delighted to discover our common fondness for wilderness hiking. We have been comparing our hiking and backpacking experiences ever since.

During the night, there was a warm, gentle rain. I felt so pleased with my newly purchased Gore-Tex bivouac sack. It worked. It kept me dry in the rain. I was also pleased with my new home-sewn, lightweight sleeping bag, which I had made from a sleeping bag kit. It had taken a lot of time stitching back and forth to attach all of the many baffles that keep the down in place. Finally, there was the task of stuffing the packets of down into each section before sewing the section shut. I was apprehensive that I might miss a section. When it was finally finished, I crawled into it for a test fitting. It felt fine and I was pleased.

I had decided after my previous summer's hike to switch to a lighter-weight bag, as I was feeling too warm as the trail descended from the High Sierra to lower altitudes. My home-made bag proved to be a good choice. I am still using it. It has become the favorite of my four sleeping bags.

I drifted off to sleep felling so very good. It was such a glorious feeling to be in the mountains again.

From the Tamarack Lakes, the trail—now a closed jeep road—headed north. The trail passed close to a number of lakes—Packer, Grass, Deer, and Summit. Water was plentiful, as the trail crossed creeks and creeklets. Near Packer Lake, sitting amongst the willows, I spotted a bird, which I had seldom seen before—a Lewis' woodpecker. That is what I find so intriguing and delightful about bird watching—the surprise sighting of a new bird.

I made camp at quiet, peaceful Snake Lake. No one else was camped there. I was delighted to find a small, sandy beach and took advantage of this treat by wading out and swimming and splashing about while enjoying views of the lake and the sky.

While swimming, I thought of how I would navigate myself and my gear across the river at Hartman's Bar where, reportedly, the bridge had washed out. I thought of a plan. I would tie my backpack and gear, a few at a time, onto my blown-up air mattress and swim across the river, towing my air raft. I planned on three or four trips. First, I would separate the things that needed to stay dry and enclose them in my two large, plastic garbage bags. This group would include my down sleeping bag, a bag full of dry clothing, my food, and my fuel tablets and matches. My pack and cooking utensils could tolerate a little water. I could, I thought, swim on my side holding the air mattress on my hip, much like I had learned and practiced doing in my Red Cross lifesaving course. The idea was intriguing, and I thought about my plan often during the next several days' walk.

After supper, I gazed out over the lake and saw the silhouette of a duck floating by. It was too dark to make a positive identification of the bird, but I thought that it was about the size and shape of a female mallard. It added to the beauty of the peaceful lake scene.

Upon studying my topo map in the morning, I decided to take the alternate route leading from Snake Lake to the junction with the trail to the Four Hills Mine. The choice was that of choosing between two sides of a rectangle. I chose the southwest side out of curiosity. Soon, I was greeted by a chorus of high, happy voices. As the trail, again on a jeep road, drew nearer to the next lake, I saw a sign proclaiming "Hawley Lake Summer Camp."

Soon after arriving at the junction and rejoining the temporary trail, I came to Four Hills Mine, an abandoned gold mine. Curiosity led me to climb around in its tailings. I picked up and examined some pretty green-and-white stones. They had no hint of gold specks.

I continued following the trail as it led north over some rolling hills. In the afternoon, I arrived at the crossing of the Johnsonville-Gibsonville Road, which leads to the Plumas-Eureka State Park. I remembered that my friend Carol had told me that this was a very fine ski area in the winter.

At the trailhead near the road crossing, there was an excellent, newly constructed section map of the Pacific Crest Trail. It was one of the finest trail maps I had seen—large and clear, with trail sites noted in color. I studied it for quite a while.

By evening, I had reached McRae Meadow, which offered water and campsites. Looking over the small meadow while selecting my campsite, I discovered a couple of hikers. I said, "Hello" to them, and when I let them know that I was hiking a section of the Pacific Crest Trail, they replied that they were also hiking on the trail. They were traveling south from Grass Valley Reservoir to Sierra City. They were the first Pacific Crest Trail hikers I had met since talking to Karl Ellingson near Sierra City.

From my campsite at McRae Meadow the next morning, I followed the trail as it climbed up McRae Ridge and then turned west, descending the ridge. I found an enjoyable lunch spot on the west branch of Nelson Creek. The creek was flowing briskly and loudly as the swift-flowing water crashed over the rocks.

I soon arrived at a new trail sign at a junction, directing hikers to turn. I turned onto the newly constructed trail. After walking awhile on the new trail, a startling thought crossed my mind: will this trail lead me to Lake Delahunty, where I had mailed a food package to the Baptist Camp? I was perplexed. I stopped and got out my map. After studying my map and trail guide, I reluctantly realized that I was considerably north of the road leading to the camp. I found that I was near Hopkins Creek. What to do? I decided that I would have to retrace my steps to retrieve my food package at Lake Delahunty. By now, it was too late. It was almost dark and time to make camp. I decided to stay near the creek to be sure of a good water supply. I made camp hurriedly on an unaesthetic widening at the side of the trail. It proved to be not only devoid of scenery, but also my bed was rocky and somewhat uncomfortable.

In the morning, I started my tedious walk back. Now on a gravel road, a pickup truck came rattling and bouncing toward me. I waved. Two older men obligingly stopped. I asked them for directions to Lake Delahunty. They cheerfully gave me clear directions. I felt relieved in knowing that I was headed in the right direction. Further down the road and around the bend, I met a white-and-brown spaniel-like dog that barked ferociously at me. Soon, a man appeared from the side driveway and hushed his dog. When I reached him and told him the story of my detour, he listened sympathetically and responded by telling me about a shortcut I could take. He explained that I could turn to the right in half a mile and follow an abandoned logging road.

He became friendly and talkative as he told me his troubles. His eyesight was failing and his doctor told him that he had cataracts and recommended he undergo surgery. Looking very troubled, he said that he was not sure that he wanted to have surgery. At the same time, he was worried that he was losing his eyesight. I listened, nodding my head, and replied that I hoped that whatever treatment he chose would help him. Departing,

I thought, "What interesting people I have met while walking on the trail."

The shortcut he directed me to proved to be a very pleasant and easy-to-follow road through the woods. I felt sure that I saved time by following his directions.

The guidebook had advised that "…the Baptist camp at Lake Delahunty may hold a food package for hikers if you contact them in advance." During my spring trip planning, I had obtained the name of the camp director from the Forest Service. I had called him and he willingly gave me permission to send a food package. I greatly appreciated his helpfulness and responded by sending him a donation.

Arriving at the camp, I went to the dining room, where a few people were sitting. I gave my name to a young man, who never introduced himself, and said that I was calling for my food package. "We do not accept Pacific Crest Trail hikers' packages." he responded angrily. "You should not have sent it." I was startled. I explained that I had phoned the director, Mr. Herbert, and he had given me permission to send the package. "Mr. Herbert is not a director. He should not have given you permission." he replied sternly. He was so unpleasant. He finally went to the corner of the dining room and returned with my package. I retreated to the porch, where I had parked my pack and commenced to repack. He stood over me all the time that I was packing. Repacking entailed lifting my clothes off the top, followed by my cooking kettle and stove, in order to get down to my food bag, which rests on the bottom part of my bag. Then I placed the new food supply in the food bag and replaced the other items. This procedure, involving exposing dirty socks and underwear, seemed to me somewhat personal. All during this time, the cross young man, for reasons known only to him, continued to stand guard over me until I had completely repacked my bag. On leaving, I consciously made an effort to thank him. He did not change—he stood erect, looking cross and stern. I went on my way feeling bewildered and rejected. I felt so puzzled by this unhappy encountered. It seemed to me especially puzzling to not be welcomed in a religious camp. I thought of the age-old tradition from stories in the Bible, in Canterbury Tales, and in more recent times, of the tradition carried out at the Zen Center in the Marin headlands north of San Francisco, of offering hospitality to travelers. I puzzled and wondered what had happened to produce such an unhappy young man. To this day, I still feel badly when I recall this hostile reception. I also hoped that there were friendlier and more pleasant people amongst the camp staff. While walking out the driveway, I stopped to view a small cemetery enclosed in a picket fence near the camp's entrance. A woman smiled at me when I said "Hello" to her. I hoped and assumed that she was part of the camp's staff. Her manner was pleasant in my brief encounter with her, in contrast to the angry young man.

From Lake Delahunty, the temporary trail leads onto the Quincy-La Porte Road to reach the bridge crossing the South Fork of the Feather River. I was planning to camp near a spring alongside the riverbank that was described in the guidebook.

I climbed uphill slowly. I was tired. I still felt sad and rejected from my puzzling camp encounter. When I arrived at the spring, I found some noisy people huddled around two pickup campers. I said to myself, "I can't sleep here in this noisy place." I filed my water bag from a pond near the spring and moved up to the next campsite, just a few feet before the river crossing. After settling in for the night, two young boys from the camper group came to see me, and we had a pleasant conversation. The older boy said that his father was a "feller"—he gathered logs—and he needed to get the logs out in another ten days. I said that I thought his father needed to be very good to be a "feller." "Yes," he replied as he smiled. We both enjoyed our friendly conversation before the boys returned to their camper. I looked forward to the next day when I would leave the road and be hiking on the trail again.

After crossing the South Fork of the Feather River the next morning, I happily left the road and turned west onto a no-car trail. The trail paralleled the north side of large Little Grass Valley Reservoir. I could hear the distant sounds—the putt-putt of fishermen's motorboats.

It was an easy trail, but I moved slowly. I had acquired a sore toe. I tried hard to pad and protect it. I stopped about every 15 minutes, experimenting with different remedies. I tried to create a little island around the sore place—it was my right little toe, a hard place to pad. I tried moleskin, foam, and tape. Through all of my trials, the pain remained. I even tried to walk using different gaits, shifting the weight to the inside of the foot. Still, I felt the pain.

In the afternoon upon ascending a little hill, I arrived at an interesting rock formation—a tall, reddish pillar that is named Chimney Rock on the map.

By evening, campsite time, I arrived at a picturesque wooded area by Black Rock Creek. I found a small, circular clearing for my campsite. I even had a sitting log by my kitchen fireplace. After dark, in lieu of a fire, I lit my candle and enjoyed watching its flickering flame. I really appreciated this campsite because it had been several days since I had had a picturesque bedroom—since Snake Lake.

Limping along with my sore toe the following morning, I came to a crossing of a wide logging road. I sat down by the shoulder, making another attempt to pad my toe. A pickup truck came rattling up the road and stopped. When the friendly pickup driver heard my sore toe story, he reached into his supply box and returned saying, "Here is a bottle of tincture of benzidine. It has helped my dog's feet." I gratefully smeared the brown liquid on my little toe. My toe was all brown and sticky, but it smelled pleasantly. In fact, I smelled the tincture of benzidine for several days. The friendly pickup driver expressed his concern. He gave me his card, which indicated that he was a logging company official, and said, "Send me a card telling me that you arrived home safely." (Indeed, I did send him a card.)

At around noon, it suddenly hit me with great force that I must give up. The toe pain was too great to continue! I hobbled slowly to the next crossroad. Upon reaching the road, I sat down on the ditch to wait for a ride. It was not too long before a pickup with two men came along. I waved at them. They stopped. They were friendly and quickly agreed to give me a ride to La Porte, the nearest town. They had come from Oroville by way of Feather Falls, not too far to the west from this junction road. Arriving in La Porte, I thanked them and stepped out. The decision to come out, although reluctantly made, now seemed right.

I looked around the town of La Porte. It was my first visit to this small hillside town. It was crowded with fishermen and campers stopping for groceries and gas. It was Saturday. I was annoyed at a man who got out of his pickup to go into the store and left his engine running. With my commitment to save energy and use public transportation as much as possible, this really made me angry.

I purchased a carton of milk and plotted my plans. I could seek a ride in either direction—either west to Marysville or east to Quincy. I could not seem to locate my "To Bus" sign that I always carry with me, so I got out my pen and paper and made a new sign. I had just barely taken my post and raised my sign when a couple in a van stopped and cheerfully offered me a ride to Quincy.

I learned that my friendly transportation helpers were teachers from Southern California and that he was employed for the summer by the National Forest Service to make a tree census. The were enjoying Quincy and the surrounding country.

Approaching Quincy, where the road crosses the Middle Fork of the Feather River on a high bridge, they pointed out to me that there was an informal squatters' camp perched on a sandy beach by the riverbank. They said that these were summer gold panners and that there was a rumor in town that one of the panners had struck a lucky wash and had come up with a sizeable gold nugget. Reportedly, the lucky panner had been collecting his unemployment benefits while camped by the river.

Our first stop in Quincy was at the bus depot. I learned that I was too late for that day's bus. There was only one bus a day and it had left in the morning. The generous, hospitable couple offered me space in their home for the night. At first, I protested, but soon acquiesced. Their housing for the summer was at the University of California Extension campus not too far from the bus depot. I spent a delightful evening as we shared information about wildflowers and birds in the surrounding forest area. A student friend joined us for supper. He had been enthusiastically drying foods in a newly purchased food dryer. He offered us dried tomatoes and tasty but tiny crayfish claws.

In the morning, I boarded the bus for Marysville and then transferred to the Greyhound bus to San Francisco. At home the next morning, I visited the podiatry clinic and learned that I had an infected toe. It was slow in healing. Reluctantly, I realized that I would not be continuing my trip until the following summer. The challenge of crossing the river at Hartman Bar would have to wait until then.

Chapter 16
Little Grass Valley Road Near La Porte to Highway 36 Near St. Bernard
July 1980 • 107 miles

This is one of the still, hushed, ripe days when we fancy we might hear the beating of Nature's heart.
—*John Muir*

The landscape changes that I had seen and felt in my last summer's walk became more pronounced. I would be walking at lower elevations—between 4000 and 6000 feet. I would be walking through more forests. The lakes I would be passing would have grassy shores and be tree-bordered. At Belden, approximately midway through my journey, I would be leaving the approximately 400-mile-long Sierra Nevada mountain range. I would be leaving the light-granite peaks and rockbound Alpine Lake and moving on toward the volcanoes of the Cascade Range.

My walk was highlighted by ascents and descents in and out of the deep Feather River canyons. I was to discover that hiking through the ups and downs of these steep canyon walls was to become a challenge. I would need to check my water supply more frequently, as the trail no longer passed the many mountain springs and creeks that had been so abundant in the High Sierras. I was being introduced to and coming to know a whole different country with a different flavor and its own special landmarks.

Reaching the trail of my last year's coming-out location near the town of La Porte and the Little Grass Valley road was not an easy feat. I called Caltrans and learned that there was a local bus from Marysville to the town of Challenge. I then called the forest ranger station for Challenge. They could not offer any suggestions on transportation to my destination. Challenge is approximately 20 miles from my coming-out trailhead. I hoped for success in finding a ride.

I reached Marysville by Greyhound and spent a pleasant two hours in the public library before boarding the afternoon bus to Challenge. As a supporter and user of public transportation, I was glad to see a nearly full bus, including wheelchair passengers.

At Challenge, the last bus stop, a friendly, cheerful young woman introduced herself and her baby, White Star. She offered me a ride to the town of Strawberry—almost 10 miles beyond Challenge. I held bouncy, good-natured White Star on my lap in the cab of the pickup while Donna told me most enthusiastically that her husband was working an abandoned gold mine. It was a tunnel mine that had been closed for years. He and his family were hopeful that it would be a very profitable adventure. She was so enthusiastic and hopeful that I was carried away with hoping for them and have wondered for years afterwards whether their venture had been successful.

We reached Strawberry at around 7 p.m. I still had about 12 miles to go—too far to walk. I extended my arm as cars whizzed past but was not having much success finding a ride. It was almost dark, and I was beginning to think I might need to spend the night camped by the side of the road when a rattling pickup with two young men stopped. "We can give you a ride if you don't mind our smoking pot," they called out. I replied that I didn't mind, and I climbed in. If anyone were to ask me today, or when I ask myself, I cannot believe that I so readily accepted a ride with pot smokers. What a difference the pressure of the moment can make! The pickup driver explained that they were going to work near Quincy and they started working at 5:00 a.m. at a logging operation. They gave directions to helicopters to lift logs, which they hook up to a tow chain and then "run for their lives." I could appreciate the hazards of their work and could partly understand the pressure that contributed to their smoking pot.

They left me at the entrance to Little Grass Valley Reservoir Campground. I crept into the park, feeling my way cautiously in the dark, and found a small campsite by the creek. I made my bed as quietly as possible, trying not to excite a nearby barking dog.

My next day's walk led along the border of Little Grass Valley Reservoir. As a reservoir, I found it to be quite attractive, with trees growing close to the shore. Late in the afternoon, I arrived at Little Grass Valley Road, my coming-out trailhead of last year. While I was studying my map to find my next benchmark, a helpful logger came along and gave me directions to a beautiful campsite with cold spring water and a grassy flat. Arriving at the flat, I indeed found a delightful scene, with bright spring grass surrounding the cold-water spring. The spring attracted a multitude of songbirds. What a cheerful place to spend the night.

The following day was a road-walking day, with lots of junctions and lots of warnings in the guidebook—"Don't take this road." To further complicate the directions, some of the signs had disappeared. When I came to a sign-less V-shaped junction of two roads—both of which headed west—I was very puzzled and hesitant to move on. How confusing. I sat down and waited. Fortunately, I did not have long to wait before a Forest Service worker came putting by on a motorbike. I hailed him and asked, "Which road leads to Hartman Bar?" "The road to the right." he replied. Then I asked, "Has the bridge across the river at Hartman Bar been repaired?" "Yes," he assured me. I was basically relieved but, at the same time, I felt somewhat cheated at not having the opportunity to carry out my plan to float my equipment across the river on my air mattress. I shall always wonder if I could have made it across successfully.

I arrived at the south trailhead leading to the Hartman Bar—about four-and-a-half miles south of the Middle Fork of the Feather River—around 5:30 p.m. The south trailhead sits high on a ridge. A nearby piped-cold-water spring provided a comfortable campsite. I had the campsite to myself; there were no other campers. After I settled in my bed for the evening, the peace and quiet of the night was interrupted by the loud noise of some animal chewing on wood. The sound was coming from high in a tree. Who was this loudly chewing animal? I wondered. It was a sound that I had not encountered before. I was puzzled. The chewing noise seemed to grow louder. My curiosity grew also. I got out my flashlight and focused the beam up high toward the noise. At first, I could not find anything, but finally, after much searching, I was able to make out the silhouette of a huge porcupine. This was the loudest animal noise I had experienced at any of my campsites.

On my morning walk south from the Hartman Bar trailhead, the trail zigzagged down steeply 2500 feet from the ridge to the Middle Fork of the Feather River. I arrived at the Hartman Bar around noon. Looking around, I soon decided to spend the rest of the day at this beautiful poolside retreat—one of the most beautiful river pool sites on the trail. The campground rests on a little platform close to the water. The still, quiet pool itself is bordered by steep, gray-granite walls. Hanging above the pool is a slender, delicate-looking suspension footbridge. The scene reminded me of photographs of Himalayan footbridges. I had my own vision of a Shangri-La-like scene.

Not only did this pool present a beautiful scene, it also offered a warm-water swimming hole. Not a courageous cold-water swimmer, I truly enjoyed this pool. I enjoyed its warm, still water so much that I went for a dip twice—once before lunch and once before dinner. While I was swimming, two bold, gray squirrels foraged in my backpack. The first time they managed to pull out the bag of mothballs that I carry to discourage animals from approaching my pack! The gray squirrels were not discouraged.

Although I was alone at the campsite, I could see that it had undergone heavy use by the disturbance to the sand and bushes. Obviously, the squirrels had learned how to acquire a free lunch.

In the morning, I climbed up to the bridge approach to start my trek north. From the middle of the bridge, I stopped to take a last, nostalgic look at this picturesque scene. The bar was shrouded in a gray haze, as the morning sun was just barely breaking through to reach into this steep, rock-lined canyon.

The climb up the 3500-foot north bank of Middle Fork was long, hot, and tedious. I found myself perspiring. I took several rest breaks before the trail leveled off at around 5500 feet. I reached the top at around 2:30 p.m. I passed two interesting landmarks: first, I came to an abandoned hut surrounded by overgrown, brightly blooming sweet peas and sweet William. They seemed to be thriving in their abandoned environment. I then came to a huge, tall tree with a Forest Service marker proclaiming, "Champion Tree—Largest ponderosa pine in USA— height 223 feet; diameter 7 feet 7 inches, circumference 23 feet

11 inches." I spent some time walking around the tree, gazing up at its heavy branches and its hard-to-see top. I thought that it was good that a relatively common pine tree was singled out to have a marker. Usually, it seemed to me, rare and unusual trees are chosen for markers, albeit, few people walk this trail to view this large ponderosa pine.

By evening, I found a quiet, level site by a stream in the forest and made camp. I had not passed any hikers for the last two days.

The following morning, I soon found myself walking through the forest saying, "Decal—where is the next decal?" I was looking for the "Blue Diamond" attached to trees marking the temporary Trail. The previous day's trail, which had been used as the California Riding and Hiking Trail, had disappeared. It had been replaced by a cross-country stretch marked by the blue diamonds. It was not hard walking, as the forest floor was relatively free of undergrowth. I would simply sight a blue decal, walk toward it, then walk slowly until I sighted the next blue decal. It was rather fun and stimulating, but it was slow going. By mid-morning, I came to a road junction. I searched, but I could not find a decal. I was perplexed. Which way should I go? I stopped and took a compass reading. With some uncertainty, I chose to follow the road leading north-west. After a while, I saw a pickup moving slowly toward me. I waved vigorously. The pickup, with two men sitting in the cab, stopped. "Which way do I walk to reach Bucks Lake?" I asked. "Just follow this road," they replied. I was reassured.

The guidebook had listed the Bucks Lake route as a recommended alternate. I chose this route, as I had never been to Bucks Lake before and was curious to see it.

I arrived at the Haskin's Valley store close to the shore of Bucks Lake at lunchtime. I bought some milk and peanuts to supplement my lunch. They tasted so good.

After a while, I felt that the Bucks Lake resort area was too crowded and noisy. There were car people, boat people, horse people, and RV people moving in and out of the busy little store. I was ready to move on. I walked along the lakeshore and found a quiet little beach. I tested the water and decided that it was warm enough for an afternoon dip.

I searched and found a somewhat secluded place to park my pack and clothing. Slowly, I waded out into the sandy-bottomed, shallow lake. Gradually adjusting to the cool water, I ducked down and had a most enjoyable little swim.

Back on shore, I was delighted to look up and see a flock of about 50 Canada geese come in for a landing on the lake. What a beautiful sight!

After my refreshing dip, I walked on to White Horse Creek Campground, about a mile east of the lake and a recommended camping spot before the next ascent. After picking a campsite, I strung up my clothesline and washed my socks and hung them to dry. Soon, I grew restless and uncomfortable. I was hemmed in by RVs and noisy car campers. What a contrast to my days alone at quiet, picturesque Hartman Bar and the secluded forest campsites. I looked around. Could I find a quiet site? I explored and discovered that I could easily cross the nearby creek. I moved myself to a woodsy, non-developed campsite not too far away, but far enough to be relatively quiet and peaceful. I felt more at ease, even though I could still hear some of the noisy campers and their radios, but much less loudly.

This was not the first time and would not be the last in which I had fled from a noisy, crowded campground. I was not in tune for that style of camping. My desire to feel surrounded by the tranquility of the wilderness prompted me to move.

Soon after leaving the campground in the morning, I

reached the junction where the trail meets a newly constructed section of the Pacific Crest Trail. How good it was to be walking on trail again—no more road walking, at least for a while. The trail leading north climbed up to Bucks Summit, from which I enjoyed a sweeping view looking east toward Meadow Valley and large, shimmering Silver Lake. The trail then ascended to one side of Spanish Peak and Mt. Pleasant and continued to offer attractive views of the valley. As I was sauntering slowly along the trail, I heard approaching footsteps. Soon, a tall, blonde, husky-looking man caught up with me. He introduced himself: "I'm Mike." It was a delight to meet him, as he was the first Pacific Crest Trail hiker I had met on this section of the trail. He was ready to share some of his experiences with me, which made it most interesting. He had started at the Mexican border on May 29. He estimated that of about 100 hikers who had started at the border in the spring, only eight of them were still hiking the trail. The majority of them had dropped out. He had reached the Sierras in July and had several days of walking through snow. In the snow-covered areas, he tried to start early, when the snow pack was still frozen and covered with a crust so as to stay on top of the snow and avoid sinking down deep with every step. Nevertheless, he reported that it was very slow going. He felt lucky if he managed to make ten miles in a day. He thought that one of the highlights of his trip was meeting some very helpful, welcoming people in the town of Wrightwood who had opened their homes to him, as they had to other Pacific Crest Trail hikers. One man offered to call his father to let him know that he had arrived in Wrightwood and would not even accept reimbursement for the phone call.

Mike hoped to reach Canada by early October, before the heavy snowfall in the Cascades. Because of the closure of the trail in southern Washington due to the eruption of Mt. St. Helens, he planned to walk along the eastern slope of the mountains in Washington. He estimated that this would be the time of apple harvest and was looking forward to eating lots of fresh apples.

Mike walked with me for a long time—it seemed to me about two hours. I knew that with his long stride and husky frame, he could have walked much faster than walking at my pace. I was puzzled. Then I thought, "He is ready to talk to someone."

After Mike finally bid me goodbye, he said, "I will probably see you in Belden." He added that he planned to take a couple of layover days there and fill up on "junk food."

I turned off the trail for a short distance to camp at nearby Three Lakes. Rain was threatening, so I strung up my tent rope and put my poncho up lean-to style, using it as a tarp for rain protection. After I felt prepared for a rainy night, it only rained a few drops. I enjoyed a quiet evening by the first of the Three Lakes. No one else was camped there.

From Three Lakes the next morning, I climbed up to the trail and soon started on a steep, difficult, six-mile, 3000-foot descent down to the North Fork of the Feather River and to the town of Belden. Downhill walking tends to be hard on the toes—pushing the toes toward the tip of the boot and causing toe-jamming. Therefore, I had started out with three pairs of socks for extra padding. Soon, my feet were uncomfortable and began to sting. Crammed into my boots, they didn't have enough room. I stopped and took off one pair of socks and my feet felt better. I continued my long downhill descent. I was discovering that the steep ups and downs of the Feather River canyon and its branches could be almost as challenging as the ups and downs of the High Sierra passes.

I finally reached the valley, crossed the railroad tracks, and then crossed the bridge over the wide-flowing North Fork of the Feather River. I headed for the post office in hopes of claiming my food package. Inside, was relieved—it had arrive safely. Carrying my package outside, intending to carry it to the nearby campground, I heard a cheery, "Hi." It was Mike. Smiling broadly, he announced that he had found a trail friend who had caught up with him and that they were planning to hitch a ride to Quincy and to eat a lot of good food. He looked clean-scrubbed and happy.

At a vacant campground table, I repacked my food and washed my socks. I had intended to spend the night at the campground. By mid-afternoon, it had become hot in this narrow, still valley. I returned to the store for refreshments. I searched the shelves and ended up with milk and applesauce. Inside, I observed a colorful scene at the bar. A smiling young woman was serving up glasses of beer to a group of men who fully occupied the bar stools. They were colorfully dressed in western-style attire. One of the men, bedecked in a dark felt hat, wore a celluloid collar. I hadn't seen one for years. I wondered if he and some of his barstool friends had come to Belden to try their luck as miners during the depression years and had stayed on.

Returning to my campground site, it seemed to be growing hotter. I was restless. I studied the route ahead and decided to move up the trail to the next water site. I waited until the bright, setting sun sank behind the western hills and then started my evening walk.

When I reached water at the Ben Lomod trail junction on Chips Creek, I hurriedly made camp and cooked my supper in the diminishing daylight. I had just finished my camp housekeeping chores by dark and had lighted my candle. I was almost ready to climb into my sleeping sack when I saw a flashlight beaming off and on. It was coming toward me. I was startled. I had not expected anyone to appear on the trail at this time of the evening. I had hurriedly made my camp on a small, level place quite near the trail. I felt awkward, as I had been unexpectedly discovered camping so near the trail. Soon, the possessor of the flashlight caught a glimpse of my camp. Approaching, he uttered, "Hello," and said, "I did not expect to find a camper here." Perhaps he was a startled as I had been upon seeing someone, perhaps more so. He explained that he had driven into Belden late in the evening and had decided to start up the trail. He was on his way to his mining claim by the creek. He had been exploring the creek for several weeks, mining for gold. He sat down and talked for quite a while. He told me that he and his sons had purchased a new-style vacuum dredge and they dive under water to search for underwater veins in the rock of the creek bed. He was quite hopeful that they would find gold.

He was also interested and asked me questions about my walk. He seemed quite impressed that I was backpacking on the Pacific Crest Trail. Arising to depart, he wished me well and walked on, carrying his equipment box and flashlight.

My next day's climb was gentle and pleasant. The climb up from the North Fork of the Feather River was not nearly as steep and slow going as the climb up from the Middle Fork had been. The trail for most of the day stayed close to gently flowing Chips Creek. I had had no water problem as yet, even though I was saying goodbye to the granitic Sierras and entering the volcanic, red-rocked country. In volcanic country, I knew that I could anticipate some future stretches of long walks between water, as in many of the volcanic areas, the water remains down below in its underground channels.

Two hikers came down the trail, heading south. "We are picking up a food package in Belden," they announced. "Will we reach there soon?" I assured them that they would be walking on a gentle trail and should have no trouble reaching the post office by early afternoon. They told me that the were from Crete, Nebraska, and had come into the trail in Oregon. They hoped to hike for three or four weeks.

By mid-afternoon—upon entering a pleasant, forested, level flat—I met up with a very intriguing and different sight, the Williams Cabin. There was a sign above the door that read "Welcome." I stepped inside and there was another sign stating, "You are welcome to use the cabin and use things, but just leave it clean and if you use wood, replace it."

Stepping inside, I found a well-furnished hut complete with two beds, kerosene lanterns, and dishes. It was quite well furnished. As a city dweller imbued with guarding and padlocking all possessions, I was overwhelmed with admiration for the Williams' welcome and "open door" policy.

I was moved to write in the Williams' logbook, "I admire your kindness in opening your cabin to hikers. I believe that you have expressed the true meaning of love of neighbor."

By evening, I found a delightful campsite just beyond Myrtle Flat on a little creeklet, which tumbled down little cascades making water music all night.

The following morning, I labored up the steep, hot climb leading up and out of the head walls of Chips Creek. I began to feel hot and started to perspire. I slowed my pace. I was glad, finally, to reach good water, where I stopped for lunch. I wondered how this spring flowing with such good water acquired its name of Poison Spring. The guidebook gave no hint.

My walk in the afternoon, happily, was much easier as the ascent leveled off. By evening, I reached delicious cold water at Cold Springs and made camp nearby on the edge of a grassy meadow.

In the morning, I realized that I was now more fully into volcanic country and I would need to carry water. I measured out enough water from tasty Cold Springs to carry for 13 miles. The trail north included some fine views. Boosting up my heavier-than-usual pack, I started my walk to the north. By midday, I came to some interesting and intriguing red volcanic pillars and posts. Looking ahead, I was excited to see, framed in a doorway space between two pillars, the outline of Mount Lassen Peak. I could see that it was decorated with a patch of white—a snowbank or glacier. Lassen, the southernmost, most conspicuous of the volcanic cones, would be my introduction to many volcanoes that would follow in northern California, Oregon, and southern Washington.

By evening, I reached water and a campsite near upper Carter Meadow. After dark, as I was enjoying my after-dinner reverie, I heard faintly the sound of music. It seemed nearby. I listened. The music was soft, but pleasant. It sounded like a flute. Who could be playing a flute on this wilderness trail? I wondered.

In the morning, when I reached nearby Carter Meadow Junction, there was my sociable hiking friend, Mike. He smiled and asked, "Did you hear my flute?" I replied, "Yes, I enjoyed your melodies very much." He proudly showed me his shiny, silver flute. He continued to tell me about his reunion with two trail friends in Belden. Then he commented on our meeting again. "We are like the tortoise and the hare," referring to my slow, steady pace and his faster strides with stops. This was my third encounter with Mike.

The following morning was my "coming-out day." I arose early, packed up quickly, and moved on eagerly in anticipation of my coming-out. I soon discovered that a new section of trail had been built since my 1977 edition of the guidebook. I turned onto it and was delighted to find it freshly built and easy to follow. The new trail contoured gently around some ridges and afforded several clear, sweeping views to the northeast of large, blue, Lake Almanor, which lies close to the town of Chester. The trail then winds down to Soldier Meadow. After crossing a hodgepodge of logging roads, I came to a meadow sign reading, "You are crossing private property. Please stay on the trail." I obediently obeyed the sign, while glancing from side to side to observe some small patches of color revealing tiny meadow wildflowers.

By mid-afternoon, I came to a wide, well-graded road. I assumed it was Highway 36, the east-west highway leading to the town of Chester and my planned coming-out trailhead. I stopped a few yards short of the roadway and changed my shirt and cleaned my face a little in an effort to look halfway presentable before taking up my post by the side of the road with my "To Bus" sign. I waited. Just as I was beginning to think that there was no traffic on this road, a green Scout jeep came along. I waved and the slow-moving jeep stopped. I told my story, saying that I was looking for a ride to reach the nearest bus. The man in the jeep replied: "I never accept hitchhikers." I smiled and was halfway ready to accept his statement when he offered, "I can take you to the bus station in Chico." I replied, "That would be just fine." I climbed in.

This considerate gentleman told me that he had been botanizing at Soldier's Field. We had an interesting conversation about identifying wildflowers. Approaching Chico, I was reminded that George, a next-door neighbor when I was growing up in Minnesota, had moved to Chico. I asked the gentleman if he knew George, and he replied that he had been in a bird-watching group with Barbara, George's wife.

For a gentleman who stated that he never accepted hitch-hikers, I found him to be very considerate and concerned. When we reached Chico, he accompanied me into the bus station to make sure that there was a bus going south to San

Francisco before he bid me farewell. Fortunately, a bus was scheduled to arrive in 45 minutes.

In the depot, while waiting for the bus, I tried to call George, but there was no answer. At home I wrote to him, and he replied, "Goodness, I haven't heard from you for around 40 years." We had a good time in our letters updating news of our respective families.

I reached home easily, riding on the Greyhound bus. I enjoyed reliving memories of traversing the ups and downs of the Feather River gorges and my encounters with friendly, long-legged Mike.

Chapter 17
From Highway 36,
Near St. Bernard to the Town of Burney,
Near Burney Falls
August 1980 • 90 miles

One is constantly reminded of the infinite lavishness and fertility of Nature—inexhaustible abundance amid what seems enormous waste. and yet when we look into any of her operations that lie within reach of our minds, we learn that no particle of her material is wasted or worn out. It is eternally flowing from use to use, beauty to yet higher beauty... — *John Muir*

The trail in this section presented a definitely volcanic environment. Mount Lassen, the southernmost volcano in the Cascade Range, was a highlight of this walk. Beyond Mount Lassen, the trail follows the edge of the Hat Creek River, a popular fishing area, and results in a trail section of rather level walking. Early during this walk, I descended and ascended on a gentle climb, down to and out of the North Fork of the Feather River and said goodbye to its many river crossings.

Just ten days after my coming out at Highway 36—in August of 1980—I returned for a second trail walk during the same summer. I was eager to complete more of the Northern California trail section and was able, fortunately, to arrange for office coverage.

I was happy when my good friend Carol again offered to drive me all the way to the trailhead. Our first stop was at the restaurant in the small town of St. Bernard, where we planned to meet our friend Marge from Sacramento. We hoped that Marge had arrived, and we all rejoiced at meeting together again. Carol and Marge planned to spend a few days at Drakesbad Guest Ranch, a small resort tucked away at the south edge of Lassen National Park. I agreed to look for them when I passed through the park in two days. I was eager to start my journey.

Finding the trailhead was not as easy as I had anticipated. I thought that I had memorized the exact trail crossing just east of St. Bernard and could lead Carol and Marge right to the spot. I searched and searched as we drove slowly, but could not find a trace of the trail crossing. I was puzzled. I got out my map and compass to review the crossing location. It was then that I discovered that I had actually come out onto a private logging road, which runs parallel to and just a few yards south of Highway 36. No wonder I had had such a long wait for a ride on my coming-out journey until my considerate botanizing rescuer—who had announced, "I never pick up hitchhikers"—had come along and had kindly taken me all the way to Chico.

Finally locating the trail crossing on the private road at about 2:30 p.m., I happily waved goodbye to my friends and started on my way. I planned to reach Stover Camp for my first night's camp where, according to the guidebook, I would reach cold, spring water. In this often dry, volcanic country, I am careful to plan my walks with water stops in mind.

After a pleasant, easy, three-mile walk, I arrived at Stover

Camp at around 4:30 p.m. I felt good. I kept saying to myself, "It's so good to be back on the trail again."

I had a leisurely time choosing my campsite. I found my bedroom in a cluster of trees with an adjoining kitchen within easy reach of a pleasant, small, gurgling stream. I had assumed as I poked my way around my little campsite that I was alone, when suddenly—out from a nearby cluster of bushes, a young hiker appeared. He enthusiastically introduced himself: "I am Larry from Monterey Park. I am a Pacific Crest Trail hiker. I started at the Mexican border on May 29ᵗʰ." I congratulated him. I told him that I was hiking the trail in sections.

After supper, Larry reappeared and asked, "May I join your campfire?" I replied, "Yes, I would be glad to have you join me." In the dark around the campfire, he readily told me about his trip. He had had a slow, difficult time plodding through the snow in the Sierras. Now he was trying to make up time by walking 20 miles a day. Eagerly, he went on to tell me of his ideas about backpacking equipment and then about backpacking food. He recounted how he had shopped for a lightweight backpack and for lightweight shoes. His idea was to carry as little weight as possible. I heartily agreed with him on this point and shared with him some of my ideas on lightweight backpacking equipment.

He then went on to tell me that he was eating and cooking natural foods. Whenever he had a chance to restock his supply when near stores, he would buy some fresh fruits and vegetables. He also relied heavily on rice. He was carrying a small plastic carton of fresh eggs. I thought to myself that this was really dedication. Although I also like natural food, I could not image juggling a pack of fresh eggs in my backpack. Is not freeze-dried food natural? I wondered. It is real food that is dried and then rehydrated.

After he had decided that it was time to return to his camp and I had wished him a good night, I soon heard him exclaim, "The deer have upset my camp. They have chewed on everything." I went over to his campsite and listened to his sad story as he hunted around to recapture his equipment. He said that they had nuzzled and chewed around the zipper of his sleeping bag. He was fearful that it would not work. He had found his T-shirt hanging on a bush near the stream and covered with saliva. Some of the other things in his pack had been pulled out and strewn around. However, much of his food was still intact, packed safely in the lower level of his pack. He indeed sounded very upset. I listened and said, "I'm sorry. I hope you'll be able to recover most of your equipment."

In thinking back, I recalled that I had had an uneasy feeling when he joined my campfire. I wondered if he had secured his equipment—especially in view of his cache of natural foods. I wondered if this was his first experience with "camp deer"—deer that have become accustomed to raiding campsites for food. Hopefully he had learned an important lesson.

The next morning when Larry caught up with me and passed me, he seemed to have partially recovered from his "camp deer" raid experience. He was still disturbed, however, about his saliva-covered T-shirt.

On my morning walk, I enjoyed an easy, pleasant hike on a well-marked trail. On a ridge, I was treated to a view of snow-capped, 10,457-foot Lassen Peak. By noon, following a short, mild descent, I reached the North Fork of the Feather River. My lunch and rest spot were pleasantly embellished by the river's singing, gushing water music. After lunch, again making a mild ascent, I climbed up out of the river gorge. I was saying goodbye to the last stream crossing of the Feather River.

My next benchmark where I had planned to camp was

Little Willow Lake. I turned off the trail following the path to the lake. Arriving at the lake, I found the shallow lakebed covered with over-my-head-tall tule rushes. I could not see the water. I did not feel like camping there. It was still early afternoon, and I felt fresh and vigorous; I decided to move on. Returning to the trail junction, I noticed a Pacific Crest Trail register. I signed my name and then searched. I wondered if tall Mike, my flute-playing friend, had signed his name. I looked and found his signature. I speculated, "Where is he now?" I wondered if he had reached the Oregon border.

By late afternoon, I heard a loud, gurgling, thumping noise and, in a few minutes, the trail broke out to reveal Lassen's Boiling Springs Lake. What a different sight—seeing this steaming, bubbling, hot-springs lake. Nature trail markers issued a warning: "The water can reach 275 degrees." I could also smell its odor—sulfur dioxide—like rotten eggs. I stopped to take photographs. What an unusual trail scene and what a marvel of nature.

Moving on, I soon reached a viewpoint above the creeklet of Warner Valley situated on the south edge of Mount Lassen National Park. Looking to the left, I could see the cabins at Drakesbad Resort; looking to the right, I could see the Warner Valley campground dotted with parked cars and vans. I decided that I did not want to sleep at the crowded campground. I surveyed the scene and discovered a small space slightly off-trail a little above the creeklet. I was satisfied that this would be my hideaway—away from the crowds and near a little spring, which flowed into the creeklet. I made camp and spent a peaceful night.

In the morning, I soon reached the campground, and I walked slowly around to see if I might find Carol and Marge. They had said that they might camp at Warner Valley or spend a night at Drakesbad. I glanced at the cars at the entrance to

Drakesbad and found no sign of them, so I moved slowly along to the trailhead.

A little past the campground, I crossed Boiling Springs Creek on an attractive wooden bridge. Many day-hikers were enjoying the view of the creek from the bridge and I, like them, stopped to take a photo. The trail then wound up out of the valley on a gentle, easy-to-follow path. By noon, I had reached Corral Meadow and enjoyed lunch sitting beside the gently flowing, refreshing Kings Creek. When I was ready to move on, the sun disappeared and a cloud cover moved in. Soon gentle, off-and-on rain showers followed. When the gentle showers grew into a display of lightning and the growling grumbling of thunder, I said to myself, "The Gods must be angry." After a quiet moment, when I was beginning to think that the storm was letting up, hail balls started to descend. They were big—the size of mothballs. They bounced off logs, they bounced off the trail, and they bounced off me. Then the hail stopped. It had been a short but exciting storm. During the off-and-on rain showers, I kept debating whether or not I needed to put on my poncho. I did have some protection from my nylon windbreaker. I liked the feeling of freedom, of not being enclosed in my poncho. So in the end, I kept on going and ended up being just a little damp.

Upon reaching lower Twin Lake, the guidebook described in favorable terms a four-mile alternate route, which would pass by the Cluster Lakes. In contrast, the Pacific Crest Trail's 5¼-mile route would be waterless. I chose the lake trail. By evening, I reached and found a campsite on the shore of attractive, tree-lined Feather Lake. I had the lake to myself. By bedtime, it grew cold. I ended up sleeping with all of my layers on. I had to admit that I had been unwise in not putting on my poncho during the rain shower, as I discovered that my polo shirt layer was slightly damp and contributed to my feeling cold.

In the morning, the rain had stopped. I took a last fond look at Feather Lake and started on my way. At the next Cluster Lake, Silver Lake, there were ruddy ducks swimming and diving. I was delighted to find them. To me, ruddy ducks are familiar friends, as I see them on ponds at home.

While walking through to the next stretch of woods, I looked up to see—approaching from the other direction—a young man with a clipboard, busily looking around and taking notes. I wondered if he was a bird watcher or a geologist. The mystery was solved when, at the next trail register, I scanned the names and found the signature of "Jeffrey Schaffer." I recognized his name as one of the authors of the California Pacific Crest Guide, published by Wilderness Press. No doubt he was preparing notes for a new edition of the guidebook. I wished that I had said hello to him and told him how helpful I had found the guidebook. Some years later, I was to meet him at a Pacific Crest Trail conference, and then I was able to tell him how much I appreciated the helpful guidebook.

While viewing the next, unnamed, Cluster Lake, I met a solo woman hiker. I was delighted when she told me that she was walking on the Pacific Crest Trail in sections. She had come into the trail at Ebbetts Pass and was going north. I told her that in my several years on the trail, she was the first solo woman hiker I had met. She replied that she also had not met another solo woman hiker. I took her picture. She also told me that she had met Carol and Marge at Warner Valley the day before I arrived there and they had asked her to look for me. We were both so pleased to meet each other and to share our common experience as solo hikers on the trail.

By afternoon, after passing Badger Flat, I turned onto an alternate trail in order to reach Old Station post office, where I had mailed a food package. The trail led across an expansive, level, grassy area and afforded pleasing views looking back at Mount Lassen.

By mid-afternoon, a most unpleasant feeling startled me. My little toe, the one that had forced me to leave the trail the year before, started hurting. I was worried. I stopped frequently to pad it so it would not rub against my boot. I did not succeed. It still hurt. I was distraught. Would I have to go out from the trail at Old Station? That would be such a disappointment. Limping along, I reached Big Pine Campground. I started my search. The campground was near a roadway—the roadway leading to Old Station, and it was fairly heavily used. I continued my search by walking up along the edge of Hat Creek. Finally, I found a secluded spot.

After a night of worrying, I put my boots on the next morning and cautiously walked a few steps. My toe did not hurt. I was hopeful. After breakfast, I tried walking further. My toe still did not hurt badly. It was just a little sore. I was exuberant. I thought it was a miracle. My last padding and taping had worked—I could continue on the trail.

Following my previous year's experience with a sore toe that had become infected, I studied about treatment, i.e., treatment and protection of feet. I purchased a book, "How to Doctor Your Feet Without a Doctor," by Myles J. Schneider and Mark D. Sussman, published by Running Times. The main treatment I adopted was the doughnut pad. Rather than just sticking padding over the sore spot, I learned to build up a little wall around the affected area so that it would be protected from rubbing against the side of the boot. I learned to use a variety of materials—tape, moleskin, and foam. I also discovered and used a new material called "second skin." It contains a thin, gelatin-like layer that helps protect skin from rubbing. Through experimenting and trying different paddings, I gradually achieved success.

I thought to myself, "No foot doctor is going to be available to me on the trail, so I must learn to treat my feet myself."

I walked north toward my destination of the Old Station post office. It was Saturday. I wondered if the post office would be open. I was two days ahead of my planned schedule.

Arriving at the small post office at around 10:30 a.m., I found that it was closed. I wondered if I would have to wait until Monday to collect my food package. I crossed the street and went into Old Station Resort Store. I told the clerk that I was hiking on the Pacific Crest Trail and that I had mailed a food package to the post office. She informed me that the post-mistress came to put up the mail at around 12:30 p.m. and I might be able to catch her. I sat down in front of the post office and occupied myself by writing post cards. Promptly at 12:30 p.m., the pleasant postmistress arrived and cheerfully gave me my package. I rejoiced, I felt so fortunate.

I had heard from a San Francisco friend that Hat Creek was a fisherman's paradise. Shortly after leaving Old Station post office, I turned onto a path leading into the Hat Creek Campground, where I had planned to eat my lunch. I picked a pleasant lunch site with a view overlooking the creek. Soon, I noticed an abundance of fishermen casting into the stream. They were hooking and hauling in lots of trout. When a fisherman passed me, I commented, "It looks like you have caught lots of fish." He replied, "The hatchery has just released a load of trout into the stream. The fishermen know and take advantage of the hatchery's fish-planting schedule."

My next stretch of walking to return to the Pacific Crest Trail, which runs along the Hat Creek Rim, was not very enjoyable—I had seven miles of highway walking. First I walked three miles north on fairly busy Highway 89. Then I turned east along Highway 44, the route to Susanville, which climbed for four miles up to the Rim. It was tedious—walking cautiously at the shoulder of the roadway, watching out for fast-moving cars. I eagerly anticipated reaching the trail. At last, around 5 p.m., I arrived at the trail crossing and, rejoicing, I turned north onto the trail. My rejoicing was soon shattered, however. I was greeted by a huge sign stating, "Warning, no potable water for 17 miles." The sign then advised trail hikers to return to Cave Campground. This campground was adjacent to Highway 89, not far from where I had come from. The Forest Service had even constructed a temporary trail leading down to the campground.

I was baffled. What to do? I had planned on securing water at shallow Grassy Lake, mentioned in the guidebook. Had Grassy Lake dried up? I wondered: What about the water at the Hat Creek fire lookout? I didn't feel like retreating after my long, hot walk up from Hat Creek. I had a little water, enough to reach Grassy Lake or, in a pinch, the fire lookout. I decided after some hesitation to go on.

Moving on, I noticed that gradually the trail became fainter and fainter. When I came to a fence, I stopped and searched. I could not see any signs of trail use. I began to question my decision to go on. I said to myself, "It is not wise to go on." Reluctantly, I turned around and walked back to the warning sign.

It was growing dark. I returned to the highway, hoping to beg a ride. After watching several cars speeding swiftly downhill, ignoring me, I realized this was not a hopeful place to find a ride. Reluctantly, I retreated back to the sign and started walking on the temporary trail leading down to Cave Campground. Down I hurried, watching my footing in the dim lighting, being careful to move around rocks and tree stumps. I didn't want to stumble. Could I make it to the campground before dark? As it grew darker, I lifted my feet higher to avoid unseen obstacles. Then I stopped and took out my flashlight. Finally, I reached the edge of the campground safely in the dark. I made camp by flashlight and candlelight and had a cold supper. I had really had a different and adventurous late-evening walk. Crawling into my bedroll, I vowed to spend a leisurely next day.

In the morning, I packed up slowly and leaned my pack, somewhat hidden, against a tree. Then I walked over to the Subway Cave geological area. I decided to tour the cave. It was pitch dark. Fortunately, a family with a large-sized flashlight arrived, and I followed them through the intriguing underground volcanic tube. I marveled that so much volcanic activity had take place in the Mount Lassen and Hat Creek area.

Returning to my pack, I meandered slowly alongside the gurgling creek on pleasant paths used primarily by fishermen. I was determined to stay off the highway. Around noon, I came to a footbridge across the creek and found a perfect, shady spot for my afternoon siesta, within the sound of the music of the creek. I ate lunch, jotted down happenings and thoughts in my journal, and meditated happily on the beauty of my surroundings. When felt ready to move on, I wondered whether I should cross the creek. Happily, just as I was pondering, a young couple came along and, in answer to my question, said that the trail across the creek led to Rocky Campground, a good place to camp. They lingered, and I found them eager to talk. They were interested in my trail walk. Then they enthusiastically told me that they had recently moved to the Hat Creek area from Fremont, in the San Francisco Bay Area, and they liked the area. They volunteered that they were former motorcycle riders. The young man said with much feeling that he wanted his son, who was 10 years old, to experience living in the country and then added in a lowered voice, "I don't want my son to get into trouble the way I did." I felt for this friendly, earnest couple. I shall always hope that their Hat Creek residence turned out well for them and their son.

Happily rested, I felt ready to walk down the river trail. Moving along, I encountered a ranger and asked him about campgrounds. He recommended Rocky Campground, saying it was very beautiful, situated close to the river. I soon came to Rocky Campground and agreed that it was, indeed, attractive, with hardwoods leaning over the stream. Looking around, however, I felt that it was a little crowded. I decided to move on. I then came to Bridge Campground. It was full of RVs. It did not appeal to me. Searching around, I crossed the highway and found water and a picnic table at the Bridge picnic area. It was quiet and pleasant. All the picnickers had left. Like most picnic grounds, a sign announced: NO OVERNIGHT CAMPING. I knew that rangers do sometimes patrol the picnic areas. I wanted a quiet place, not too far from water but not too full of campers. I explored. I found a little niche just outside the picnic area. It was somewhat hidden. I rolled out my bedroll. Here it was quiet. I was near water, but legally outside the picnic area.

On my walk the next day, I soon discovered that I had come to the end of fishermen's paths by the creek. In order to make any sort of progress, I needed to walk on the edge of the highway. Therefore, for most of the day, I was pounding pavement.

When I reached the Hat Creek Texaco Station with its adjoining store and restaurant, I stopped for a drink and to seek information about water and campgrounds ahead on the route to Burney. When I asked about the Boundary Campground that I had seen on the map, the plain-spoken, abrupt proprietor replied, "Boundary Campground has been closed because of violence and destruction by the Indians." I was surprised. When I replied that I didn't realize there were so many Indians in the Hat Creek area and that I found this interesting, he retorted crossly, "No, it's not interesting because they are violent."

I finished my drink and left the store. I was puzzled. I

thought that perhaps the storekeeper was overreacting. Perhaps he wanted me to stay at his private, fee-required campground rather than going on to a Forest Service free campground. I thought to myself, "I'm not afraid of Indians. I have come a long ways on the trail. I am an experienced camper. I am not fearful. I can manage."

Later in the afternoon, when I arrived at Boundary Campground, I was greeted by a mound of gravel that had been pushed up against the entrance road. I had to admit that it appeared that the campground had really been closed. Since the campground possessed the last sure water supply before arriving at Burney, I decided to camp there or nearby. I explored. The campground picnic tables were still in place. I found a level spot near the creek, which was somewhat secluded, and made camp. After supper, when I was resting and viewing the sky, I heard voices and then saw a flashlight. Some campers had arrived and were occupying a nearby campsite. Now I was scared. I heard sounds. Were they Indians hiding out? I thought about what I would say to them if they came my way and discovered me. I debated. Should I remain half-hidden in the dark, or should I light my candle. In the end, I decided to light my candle to let them know of my presence. They did not come my way. Soon they were quiet. In the morning, they left before I broke camp. I did not see them. I shall always wonder, "Were they Indians?"

On my morning's walk, my coming-out day, I strolled up the highway eagerly looking for Cassel Road, the turnoff road to Burney. Searching carefully, I soon found a sign proclaiming, "Cassel Road," but the road was leading east and I needed to go west to reach Burney. I was puzzled. I decided to go on and, in a short time, I came to a gravel road leading west. It was not signed. I felt uncertain. I decided that I would wait and ask directions from a passing car. Searching around, I soon saw a woman driving out of a nearby roadway. "Yoo-hoo!" I hollered. She looked around briefly, but appeared to ignore me. Perhaps she thought, "There is another backpacker begging for a ride." I decided to holler loudly, saying, "Is this the road to Burney?" Hearing this, she stopped and said, "Yes, this the road to Burney." I was relieved.

Striding along the gravel road as I approached a hilly ascent, I thought I heard some shots. Pacing slower, the shooting sounds grew louder. I was worried. I felt frustrated—I was so near Burney, I did not want to interrupt my walk. After some thought, however, I decided to play it safe. I would wait. I sat down by the side of the road. After awhile, the shooting stopped. Would it be safe for me to move on? I wondered. I could not see ahead because my view was blocked by the crest of the hill. Playing it safe, I resolved to wait another 20 minutes. Then an idea struck me. I would let the sharpshooters know of my approach. I reached into my backpack and pulled out my harmonica. I played vigorously and continuously for the next mile. I made up tunes that I had never played or heard of before. Some of the tunes I created sounded quite good I thought. I rather enjoyed my improvised tunes. When I came to the top of the hill, I searched ahead and down the other side. I did not see or hear any sharpshooters. I felt relatively safe. When I reached the bottom of the hill, I came to a side clearing. I thought that perhaps the shooters had used this space to engage in a little target practice during their lunch hour.

I arrived safely and thankfully in Burney at around 2 p.m. First, I stopped at a service station to use the restroom and to ask for directions. A friendly woman who was interested in hearing about my walk gave me directions for reaching the bus terminal at the Family Liquor Store. Then she asked, "Do you mind if I ask you your age?" I replied, "I am 62." She smiled and congratulated me. At the Family Liquor Store, I encountered another friendly, helpful couple. They told me that I could board the Mountain Bus for Redding at 10:30 in the morning. They then suggested that I might want to spend the night at the nearby Sleepy Hollow Motel. I phoned and secured a room.

This was my first coming-out experience where I had come out to a shower and laundromat, except when I had met Carol and Marge at Sierra City. It was rather nice. I also learned that the motel was next to a church—Saint Francis of Assissi—and that I could attend church in the morning before departing on the bus. What a pleasant coming-out experience, with a chance to clean up, rest up, and pray.

The next morning, I attended the service at the small church. I said lots of prayers of thanksgiving. I had time for breakfast before boarding the Mountain Bus for Redding, There, I transferred to the Greyhound bus to San Francisco.

At home, sharing my trail experience with my friend Carol, I learned that a sizeable Native American group, the Pit River Tribe, lived in the Hat Creek/Burney area.

In 1992, the Forest Service announced that it would be reconstructing the Pacific Crest Trail—moving it from the Hat Creek Rim to the valley. The Hat Creek lookout had closed, and with its closing, had cut off the main source of water. This announcement followed numerous complaints about the water shortage on the Rim trail. Hopefully, by now, Pacific Crest Trail hikers will not have to "pound pavement."

Chapter 18
Burney Falls to Castle Crags State Park
August 1981 • 82 miles

Water
Impetuous and majestic, in all its wild, snowy thundering,
ever making tremendous displays of power and motion...
Think of camping beside it, seeing it white and undefined
like a ghost in the dark, mixing it with our dreams.
— John Muir

In this section the trail turns west, as it had in the San Gabriel Mountains, in order to reach the crest of the Trinity Alps and Siskiyou Mountains.

The altitude ranges from 2100 feet at the crossing of the Sacramento River to 6100 feet around the summit of Mushroom Rock. Although this section does not include many high mountains, it is not lacking in variety and interesting features. It includes ample ups and downs, mountaintop views, deep, rock canyon floors, and running streams and waterfalls. Mount Shasta often comes into view, dominating the surrounding scene with its picturesque, snow-white cone piercing the sky.

Mount Shasta has been revered by many peoples as a sacred mountain. There are accounts of Native American tribes regarding the mountain as possessing supernatural powers. Some Native Americans have held gatherings to perform ceremonial dances around its base. The Rosicrucians regard the mountain as the home of a mystical people called Lemurians. Periodically, reports emerge of people hiding in the recesses of Mount Shasta. A Zen Buddhist monastery has been established in the nearby town of Mount Shasta, and pilgrims from near and far come to attend conferences and to meditate with a view of the mysterious mountain.

Reaching the trailhead near Burney Falls State Park was not difficult. I boarded the Greyhound bus in San Francisco to reach Redding, where I transferred to the small Inter-Mountain stage to travel to the town of Burney. As I arrived in Burney late in the day, I spent the evening at the Green Gable Motel (last year's delightful Sleepy Hollow Motel did not have space.) The following day, I walked on the Black Ranch Road to Burney Falls State Park, where I would meet the Pacific Crest Trail. I was surprised to see sitting adjacent to the road a full-sized railroad boxcar marked "McCloud River Railroad." I was curious. It appeared to be a real moving, working freightliner. Later in the park, I asked the ranger about the boxcar; he told me that, indeed, it was a working railroad with a line running from Burney to the logging town of McCloud and on to the nearby town of Shasta. The ranger added that there was still considerable logging activity in the McCloud area.

Arriving at the park by early afternoon, I went to the store and asked if Lori was in. I had met her at a lunch break when I was skiing at the Donner Ski Ranch, and she had invited me to visit her in Burney. Unfortunately, it was her day off. I ordered a cold drink and then went out to look at Burney Falls. What an attractive sight. I spent a long time gazing at these magnetic, splashing falls. Every waterfall, I thought, has its own design, pattern, and unique characteristics. Burney Falls, I think, has its own very special attraction. From the top ledge, the stream splits into two and falls to the river bottom as twin falls. In the middle, between these two cascading streams hanging on a little jutting rock, clung a small, tenacious evergreen tree. I was enchanted. I had never seen such a design in any other waterfalls. I sat down and spent a long time just looking. Finally, I pulled myself up and found the Pacific Crest Trail on the west side of the creek. But soon I stopped again. I decided to explore a small trail that lead down to the base of the falls. Arriving at the base of the falls and looking up at the misting, splashing stream of water, I was again enchanted. I hardly wanted to leave the scene.

By the time I finally walked up to the top again, I decided I did not want to walk on the trail further that afternoon. This was such an attractive scene. I decided to spend the night nearby. I searched and found a secluded spot on the west side of the stream where I could hear the splashing sound of waterfalls.

After supper, I needed to refill my water bag, so I returned to the campground. Then I decided to attend the ranger-led evening program. The ranger showed slides and told the campers about the park's winter activities. There were scenes of the ranger splitting and stacking wood and of the cabins that were almost buried in the snow. After the slide show, awards were given to junior rangers. These were young volunteers who, under the ranger's direction, had spent a number of hours cleaning the campground. What a good idea, I thought, to recognize these young people for helping in their own way to preserve and restore the wilderness.

In the morning, when I was finally ready to pull myself away from enchanting Burney Falls, I started on the trail from

Burney Falls State Park. The trail leads north, following the creek for quite a ways, and then climbs up and leads across the dam at the end of Lake Britton. Lake Britton is a large reservoir lake that is fed by water flowing from springs that feed into Burney Creek. From the dam, I could see boats floating on the lake and fishermen casting from along the shore. The trail then turns to the west, traverses through a rocky canyon and then switchbacks down to a crossing of Rock Creek. Near the bridge crossing, I looked up to see the splashing water of Rock Creek Falls—a pleasant sight. I stopped near the bridge for lunch. It seemed to me that it had grown quite hot. I took out my thermometer and saw that it registered 92 degrees. I sought refuge under the bridge, where I ate my lunch and had my midday siesta. I studied the trail map. It would be nine miles to the next water. What should I do? Although it was early in the day, I seemed to have become really hot. I was in a rocky, treeless area. I decided to stop for the night.

In the morning, I started early, hoping to beat the heat. Very soon, however, it grew hot again. Fortunately, the trail led through a shade-covered forest a good deal of the time. By midafternoon, I reached water at Peavine Creek. I stopped to study my trail map and learned that it would be 15 ½ miles to the next trailside water. Again, I decided to stop early. I made camp in a nondescript, gravely site near the bank of the river that was frequented by cows. I decided to purify my water. During the night, I was serenaded by coyotes.

In the morning, I measured out my water in anticipation of a long, waterless walk. I planned to stop before reaching Bartle Gap, the next on-trail water 15 ½ miles from Peavine Creek, and to go off-trail to a pond described in the guidebook. I plodded along. By late afternoon, I started my search for the road that would lead to the pond. I did not find it. It was growing

BURNEY FALLS

dark. I had only a little water left. As I drank my next-to-last ration of water, it became warm and did not satisfy my thirst. By now, it was almost dark. Finally I came to a clearing. Two young men were stretched out on a sandy bank near the trail. They announced, "There is water under the willow trees."

Hastily, I started looking for a campsite. I did not see a site that appealed to me in this sandy, brushy area. I plodded on, hoping to find a more scenic and secluded campsite. I did not see one. Finally, I realized that it did not make sense to continue on. My sensible thoughts tuned in, and I knew that I needed to obtain water. I turned around and hurried back to the willows. I pushed my cup underneath the willow branches and found delicious, cold, spring water. I drank and drank—I drank nine cups of water without stopping. Afterwards, I realized that I must have been dehydrated to some degree and had not been thinking sensibly when I pushed on past the young men camping on the sandy bank. After finally drinking my fill, I got around to filling my water bag with 12 cups. I made camp hurriedly in a small, unaesthetic, somewhat level spot. I ate a cold supper by flashlight. It had been a confusing day. As I reviewed the events of the day, I was bothered and unhappy that I had not found the road to the pond and, most of all, that I had not stopped immediately upon hearing that there was water under the willows and had walked on seeking a better campsite. Perhaps I was on automatic pilot, rhythmically placing one foot ahead of the other. Perhaps I was not as alert late in the day when the pressure of darkness descended. I pondered. I was also unsure as to where I was. Had I reached Bartle Gap?

In the morning, I eagerly studied my map, compass, and guidebook. No wonder I was confused. I discovered that I had been following the trail maps in the 1977 edition of the guidebook and the 1980 Wilderness Press supplement. New trail sections had been constructed recently. The confusion was that I had been reading the old trail map and trying to find the road to the pond, only to discover later that was following a new trail section.

As I studied my route for the day, I decided to detour from

the new trail to reach water and a campsite at South Meadow, approximately ten miles distant. If I continued on the new trail, I would have to hike 14 ½ miles to the next trailside water. Fortunately, this time I had no trouble finding the turnoff leading to Stouts Meadow. I was enchanted by the meadow. It was a long, cheerful, grass-covered space complete with delicious, cold spring water, a charming small pond filled with cheerful, bright-yellow water lilies, a tall, interesting-looking snow gauge, and two small, neat, wood-framed cabins for use by the snow surveyors. No one else was camped by the meadow. Exploring around the outside of the cabins, I discovered that one of them was not locked—it had only a wooden stick in the latch holding the door shut. I was curious. I cautiously unlatched the door and peeked in. The neatly arranged interior held a wooden bed, a table and chairs, and a small cast-iron stove. I ponder to myself: if I had happened to arrive at the meadow during a rainstorm, would I have been tempted to stay inside? Then I decided that I probably would have braved the storm and stayed outside, as I would have felt that I was invading the snow surveyors' privacy.

In the morning, I was treated to an orange-pink sunrise. I leisurely broke camp, as I was enjoying the peaceful ambience of the meadow. Later, I wished I had started earlier. It grew very hot as I trudged up the treeless trail to 6252-foot Grizzly Peak. I planned to visit the fire lookout, a suggested short detour recommended by the guidebook.

When I finally arrived and climbed up the ladder to the fire lookout, the fire spotter looked surprised to see me. She immediately offered me a tall glass of ice water. It tasted so good. She then showed me views in all directions. They were spectacular. To the north, the view of Mount Shasta with its conical top mingling with puffs of floating clouds was dramatic. I could see the historic lumber town of McCloud. Looking to the west, I could make out faintly the Castle Crags and much of the route I would be following to reach the Sacramento River, which is just to the east of Castle Crags.

I had a pleasant visit with the friendly fire spotter. She told me that she lived in Hornbrook, north of Yreka. She had been a fire spotter for the past 20 years and had spent the last 18 years at Grizzly Peak Lookout. She did not work in the winter and enjoyed the income from her summer job. "It helps to fight inflation," she added. She was usually called to report in June, depending on the season, and usually stayed until October. All of her groceries were brought by jeep once a week. She pointed out where current fires were burning: one near Ukiah and one near Yreka. Twice during my visit she answered radio calls. When it was time for me to leave, she gave me directions to return to the trail. Hurrying down the hot trail to reach tree cover, I was glad I had made the visit. It was the most interesting description I had had of the daily life of a summer fire spotter.

By afternoon, I had reached good water at Deer Creek. The guidebook noted "…water but camping space is nil." I did not go on to the next water at Ash Camp. I rolled my bedroll out in a wide, level space at the edge of the trail.

In the morning, as I was enjoying a leisurely breakfast, I began to think that I ought to pack my bedroll, as it was stretched out so close to the trail. Then I answered to myself, "Oh well, no one will be coming. I have plenty of time." There had been very few hikers. I had only seen the two backpackers two days before at Bartle Gap. Then it happened when I least expected it—a backpacker appeared. I stood up quickly and apologized for having my bed so near the trail. "That's all right," he replied. "I camped near the trail about a mile back." He told me that he was a through Pacific Crest Trail hiker, having started at the Mexican border on May 1. Then, after a pause, he asked, "Could you do me a favor?" "I'd be glad to try to help," I answered, wondering what he had in mind. "I need someone to remove my stitches," he replied, pointing toward the side of his face. "They should have been removed two days ago." "I will try," I replied without much enthusiasm. He rummaged around in his huge pack and produced tweezers, a razor (from his snakebite kit) and a small vial of iodine. I decided to get out some of my own equipment that I thought might be helpful. I dug out my ten-power magnifier (used for flower identification) and my German steel fingernail scissors. I started my task. I worked slowly. I succeeded in removing all four stitches. I felt relieved. I was thankful for my magnifier, as the early-morning lighting was very poor. I also felt much more confident using my scissors than I would have using his razor blade. We both rejoiced as I finished by rubbing iodine on and placing a Band-Aid over his wound. Then he told me his story. He was walking by the side of the road near Old Station and had moved over when he saw a wide-load truck approaching. He didn't see a smaller potato chip truck, which swept so close to him that he landed in the ditch. The next thing he remembered was being surrounded by a crowd of people. The hustled him off to a nearby clinic, where it was discovered that the side mirror of the truck had gashed his skin near the eye. He had a black eye and a laceration by the side of his eye; fortunately, his eye was not injured. He had been delayed a couple of days while he was recovering and now was anxious to catch up to his hiking companions, Howie and Jim. "Have you seen them, he asked? "I saw two hikers at Bartle Gap," I replied. He said he had hiked with them a good deal of the time all the way from Mexico. He hoped to catch up with them. He went on to tell me that he had recently retired, that he had worked in a government job in Hawaii. He grew tired of the job and just quit. Shortly after his voluntary retirement, he decided to walk the trail.

When I told him that I was walking the trail in sections during my summer vacations, as I was still working, and that I hoped to reach Canada some day, he replied, "You will." His remark made me feel very good. He went on his way, hoping to find Howie and Jim, and I finished breaking camp.

The trail walk for the rest of the day was quite pleasant, running alongside streams and through forested canyons. I reached Ash Camp on the McCloud River around 2:30. I had all afternoon to rest. I felt like I was having a free day or one-half day off. I found a scenic rest spot by the river and enjoyed a relaxing afternoon watching the water rush over the rocks and listening to the water music. How good I felt to be drinking in the sights and sounds of this scene by the riverbank. I made camp an acceptable distance from the river, but still near enough to hear the water music all during the night.

The trail in the morning led alongside the McCloud River. As I drew near to the trail junction leading south to the Ah-Di-Na Camp, I met a young man attired in waist-high boots. He was surrounded by fishing boxes. I asked, "Are you having any luck?" He replied by telling me the story of his interesting project. He explained that he was a student at Humboldt State University in the Department of Fisheries and was completing a research project to determine if the Dolly Varden trout is a distinct species of fish. For years, there have been reports of sightings of Dolly Varden trout, a special species found only in the McCloud River. He reported that some fishermen he had met had told him that they had caught Dolly Varden trout. As they were not allowed by licensing requirements to keep the fish, they had thrown them back and, therefore, could not produce a sample for his survey. "I don't think that they correctly identified the fish," he commented. He speculated that when the McCloud Dam was built, it changed the temperature of the water and that now the stream is warmer than before and that in turn, he believed, affected the fish habitat. He doubted that there were any Dolly Varden trout left in the McCloud River. As part of his survey, he planned to do some snorkeling. He was looking forward to that phase of his study, as he might be able to identify some of the trout swimming in the river and also have a better look at the total environment of the stream. As I moved on, I waved and said, "I wish you well with completing the survey."

By midday, the trail left the McCloud River and climbed up onto a ridge offering views looking down into the surrounding valleys. The trail then descended, and by evening I reached the bridge crossing Squaw Valley Creek. I planned to camp nearby to be sure of water.

Following a small trail a few yards up alongside the creek, I soon found an enchanting campsite—one of the most perfect bedroom campsites of my entire journey. My just-right-sized bedroom was surrounded on three sides by rock walls, with the remaining side opening out toward the creek. My floor was

Bedroom by Squaw Valley Creek

soft, light-colored sand. On closer inspection, I found that one sidewall even had waist-high shelves. Unpacking my gear, I was captivated with planning the placement of my gear. I used one set of shelves for my kitchenware—my water bottles and cooking pans—and a second set of shelves for my bedroom supplies, including my flashlight and my stocking cap. It was really fun to arrange my bedroom. I guess it was a little like playing house.

The night was pleasantly warm. My bed, resting on sand, was soft and comfortable, and all night long I could hear the creek's water music. This campsite was so enchanting that I almost hated to move on in the morning.

I wondered if the naming of this creek may have been related to Joaquin Miller (1840-1913), a poet and miner who spent some time in this area and who had married a Native American woman, who in his time was referred to as a squaw. (My cousin, Margaret Guilford Hardell, a Joaquin Miller historian, confirmed that Joaquin Miller had lived and explored this area.)

The following day, I climbed up and out of the Squaw Creek Canyon and by midday reached the top of 4600-foot Girard Ridge. There, I paused to enjoy an expansive view. To the north arose the snowy pyramid cone of Mount Shasta, with its peak reaching into the clouds. To the south, I could still catch a glimpse of Mount Lassen, with its patch of white snowbank. Closer to me, to the west, a new landmark appeared—the light-colored, jagged granite pinnacles of the Castle Crags. I would be walking through the Castle Crags State Park on my next walk. After drinking in the view, I started my descent. My destination was the Sacramento River. Winding down on a newly constructed trail with its gentle switchbacks, I soon discovered that the walk was taking twice as long as expected. To pass this time, I started counting the switchbacks. At around 28, I gave up. The view of the Sacramento River valley seemed so close. I could hear the noise of the traffic on busy Interstate 5, which runs parallel to the river. Just as I thought that I had almost reached the river, the trail swung around again, taking another seemingly level contour parallel but away from the river. I began to wish that I was still on an old-style trail, which typically would head steeply straight down the mountainside. When the trail crossed a jeep road, after feeling the monotony of the trail's slowness, I moved onto the road. I finally arrived in the valley at dusk. My day's walk had covered approximately 14 miles. I had entered the Castle Crags State Park and arrived at the Soda Creek Campground. I searched around hurriedly and found an unaesthetic level spot beside small Soda Creek, which runs into the nearby Sacramento River.

In the growing dark, in my crowded, awkward campsite, I stirred up some Milkman with water and pulled out some crackers for a cold supper. Tomorrow, I would be coming out and could start feasting, surrounded by a plenitude of food choices.

In the morning, I walked along the border of the railroad bed, an easy four miles to the town of Dunsmuir, then a brief walk up to the main street of the town to the bus depot. Passing by the old hotel and picturesque old-frame buildings, I thought Dunsmuir was charming. I was lucky. I arrived at the bus depot just as the southbound bus was pulling in. I boarded the bus for San Francisco and home.

At home, when I called my friend Carol, she said, "I have been wondering about you—the temperature reached 108 degrees in Redding." No wonder I had felt the heat as I took shelter under the bridge at Rock Creek.

Bernbaum, Edwin. 1992. Sacred Mountains of the World. Sierra Club Books

Chapter 19
Castle Crags State Park to Scott Mountain
August 1981 • 60 miles

Accidents in the mountains are less common than in the lowlands, and these mountain mansions are decent, delightful, even divine, places to die in compared with the doleful chambers of civilization. Few places in this world are more dangerous than home. Fear not, therefore, to try the mountain-passes. They will kill care, save you from deadly apathy, set you free, and call forth every faculty into vigorous, enthusiastic action. Even the sick should try these so-called dangerous passes, because for every unfortunate they kill, they cure a thousand. — *John Muir*

I was able to squeeze out time in the summer of 1981 for a second week's trip. It was good to be able to return to Dunsmuir and the Castle Crags area just ten days after departing from there.

This short section of the trail was highlighted by views of the light-colored, granite peaks and pinnacles of the Castle Crags State Park. To the west and the north of the park, the trail passes by small lakes and through pleasant meadows. For the most part, I found the walk relatively easy and pleasant.

Reaching the trailhead was fairly easy. I boarded the Greyhound bus to Dunsmuir and, arriving late in the day, I decided to spend the night at the historic Victorian-style Travelers Hotel. In the evening and in the morning, I enjoyed observing the local scene. Like many older hotels, the residents were older adults; two ladies near me in the coffee shop were talking about bus tours to the casinos in Reno. They were having an animated discussion about which tours were best and whether they like the one-day or two-day trips best. One lady concluded, "I think one day is best because if you stay for a second day you have spent all your money and have nothing to do."

At the counter in the morning, while I was enjoying a delicious ham-and-egg breakfast, two Southern Pacific employees (Dunsmuir is a railroad town) were challenging the waitress by asking if they could have both a Senior discount and a Southern Pacific discount. She smiled and replied that one discount was all she could accept.

As I started on my way, I stopped for a drink at the town's fountain, which proclaimed "The best water in the world." I asked a man standing by the fountain for directions to the railroad station. He directed me to the street that led down the bluff to the railroad. I started my walk south on the road beside the railroad tracks.

While admiring the small-framed, well-kept homes, built on the hillside adjoining the tracks and adorned with well-kept vegetable and flower gardens, I reached a railroad siding where a freight train sat on the tracks. I wondered to myself if there were still "hobos" who rode the rails. Just then, a man near a boxcar door jumped out from the door, walked toward me, and asked, "What is the name of this town?" I replied, "Dunsmuir." He then turned around, collected his small sack of belongings, and started walking to Dunsmuir. I assumed that he, indeed, had ridden into town in a boxcar like the fabled hobos of the Depression Era.

I ate lunch at the Soda Creek Campground—a familiar sight, as this was where I had camped after my long hike down from Girard Ridge on my last section's walk from Burney Falls.

After crossing busy Interstate 5, I soon reached the trail. Curiosity led me to take a short spur detour to see a small, refreshing waterfall on the Root Creek trail. Returning to the trail, I enjoyed an easy afternoon hike. It was a perfect day weather wise—neither too hot nor too cold. Periodically, where there were window openings between the trees, I enjoyed views to the east of Mount Shasta and to the north of the Castle Crags Pinnacles poking their light, granite-colored peaks into the sky. By evening, I reached water at Indian Creek and made camp.

In the morning after packing up, I followed the trail first through a wooded area; then the trail started a moderately steep climb that led up to a grassy hillside. I was glad to be out in the open again and soon enjoyed pleasing views, looking

CASTLE CRAGS

back toward the granitic gray pinnacles of Castle Crags and to the south looking down toward the Seven Lakes Basin. I was walking on a newly constructed section of the trail. The older trail led along the Seven Lakes Basin valley. Now the new trail traversed along high bluffs above the valley. After traveling west for quite a long way, the hilltop trail turned, making a long loop swinging to the north to circle around a valley between hills.

While hiking along this long loop, two young men traveling north caught up with me. They announced that they were through Pacific Crest Trail hikers. They had both started at the Mexican border in early May. Tom volunteered that he was from Michigan and Rick added that he was from Toronto. They both commented about the long loop route in this new trail. After several minutes, in which they had slowed their pace to walk and talk with me, they sped on. This proved to be a long day's walk. When I finally reached the Meadow Spring area, where I was ready and eager for a drink of refreshing spring water and to find a campsite, Tom and Rick were already there to greet me and offered me some fresh, cold spring water. It tasted so good.

The new high trail had not passed any water for several miles. Rick was complaining that the Forest Service had not taken into consideration accessibility of water in planning this new trail. I heartily agreed with him. I felt fortunate that Tom and Rick had arrived ahead of me and had scouted out the route to the spring, as it was not very easy to find. In order to reach water, a hiker had to walk off-trail, through fairly high brush for around 50 yards. The only sign leading to the spring in the summer of 1981 was some little white-colored stones imbedded in the sandy trail with a hard-to-interpret arrow and "H_2O."

I made camp in a very ordinary, level, grassy spot by a stump. I completed my dinner by candlelight. The friendly hikers invited me to join their campfire. I visited with them for a while. I learned that Tom had hiked in the National Walk-a-thon, starting from San Francisco and ending in Washington D.C. He reported that 67 walkers had started the trek and 34 had completed it. After an enjoyable but short visit, I bid my hiking friends good night. I had had a fairly long day, having started my hike early, and was ready for bed.

I wove my way in the morning through the underbrush down to the spring to fill my water bag. In the morning light, I paused to look at the large, oddly shaped pitcher plants. How intriguing! They had large, trumpet-shaped heads that can catch and kill insects. The insects enter the trumpet head and can't get out because they are caught by descending, downward-pointing hairs. They end up being devoured by the plant, which receives nourishment from the captured insects.

Around mid-morning, I met a southbound hiker. He was clad in khaki, the classical hiker's style of an earlier day. The first question that he asked me was, "Where is the next water?" I described the location of the spring. Then, apparently reassured, he looked at me smiling and said, "One doesn't see many mature hikers, does one?" It was easy for me to agree with him. Actually, Julian from South Carolina, was only the second older hiker I had seen on my walk—the first was Richard, who had come down the trail early in the morning, catching me camped near the trail at Deer Creak and had asked, "Will you do me a favor?" I agreed and ended up removing stitches from his forehead near his eye, which were placed there at Old Station when he had been struck by a truck's mirror.

Julian told me that he had come onto the trail near the Oregon border and had planned to walk south until he was stopped by snow and winter weather. I wished him well. Indeed, it felt good to meet an age-mate. Julian was right about not meeting many mature hikers. The majority of the trail walkers whom I had met were lanky, long-legged, strong-looking young men of high school or college age.

By lunchtime, I arrived at an overlook, affording a glorious view down to the Seven Lakes and the Seven Lakes Basin. I felt exalted. I love views from ridge-tops. They offer such a vast feeling of space. I enjoyed

JULIAN "A MATURE HIKER"

looking from one end of the valley to the other, discovering and picking out small details—where the tree line ends and where the grassy meadows begin. I liked looking down at the little lakes strung out like blue dots and looking like jewels on a necklace. This glorious ridge-top view gave me a "top of the mountain feeling."

After lunch at the Seven Lakes Basin overlook, the trail curved north following a low ridge. Looking toward the west, I could see views of the Mumbo Lakes Basin, which was dotted with small pines and firs. By late afternoon, I proceeded cautiously, as I didn't want to miss the turn-off described in the guidebook as, "a little past a second crest saddle reached by a road," where I planned to cross-country 250 yards down to a campsite on Upper Gunboat Lake. I found what I thought was the "second crest saddle" and scurried down a steep slope. Searching eagerly, I soon saw some open skies through the trees, which signaled to me a sign of hope. Was I approaching the lake? I soon broke out of the trees to view the lakeshore of small, pleasant Upper Gunboat Lake. How pleased I was. I had reached water and a campsite. I was greeted by an already settled camper who shouted, "Hi! There is a good campsite over there." It was Rick from Toronto. He directed me to a grassy space adjacent to his camp. It was indeed a most peaceful and pleasant site. It felt good to be camped by a lake again, as it had been a long time since I enjoyed a lakeside campsite. After dinner and wood gathering, I was looking forward to an evening campfire. Soon, Rick appeared and asked, "Can I join you?" "Yes, of course, you are most welcome." I replied. Rick, I found, was certainly ready to talk and to tell me all about his trail experiences and plans. He had decided that he would leave the trail at the Oregon border, as he would not be able to reach the border before snowfall. "What about next year?" I asked, thinking that he could easily complete Oregon and Washington in another summer. "Next year I'm going on a canoe trip on the Hudson Bay," he replied. Rick then eagerly turned to study the guidebook. He proclaimed enthusiastically that it would be possible to take a shortcut to Bull Lake, following the road leading off the trail to the left, shortly after the crest saddle above the lake. As Rick kept thumbing through the guidebook, he grew more and more eager about following this route. He encouraged me to also try the shortcut route. I agreed that I would consider it.

As the night grew on, I began to wonder when Rick might retire to his camp for the night. He was so wound up and eager to talk. I usually climb into my bedroll around 9:30 p.m., and I was growing sleepy. Finally I said, yawning, that it was getting close to my bedtime. Rick took the hint and finally departed. I thought to myself that he, after many days alone on the trail, felt ready and eager to socialize. It was fun to talk to him, but I was unaccustomed to staying up so late.

In the morning, I climbed back up to the ridge and turned onto the trail. Rick had already departed. Soon I came to the road that Rick had advised me to take as the shortcut to reach Bull Lake. I turned onto the road, plunged down a fairly steep logging road, and arrived in a canyon where the road ended abruptly amidst a lot of fairly recent logging debris. What to do? I decided to play it safe and hike back up to the trail. I had quickly lost my enthusiasm for taking the shortcut. I didn't feel challenged to try to find all the road junctions that Rick had enumerated and that would lead to Bull Lake. Besides, I liked to travel on trails rather than roads whenever possible.

On the trail again, heading north, the route continued along a broad forested path. During the late afternoon, I was greeted by a large sign. Drawing closer, I was surprised to read: BLASTING—DANGER! I stopped and waited. I didn't hear a sound for what seemed like a long time. I decided to creep forward cautiously. Presently, I saw a man wearing a hard hat. I waved. He saw me and yelled back, "Wait under the tree. We will be through in about 20 minutes." I waited—had an unplanned rest on the ridge above Toad Lake—until I heard a shout, "All clear." I walked ahead until I reached the trail crew. "Which way do I go now?" I asked. The trail foreman extended his arm, bowed, and said, "Be my guest. You are the first person to walk on our new trail section." I also asked, "Where is the next water?" Again, the helpful foreman gave me clear directions on how to reach an unmarked spring half hidden in a hard-to-see ravine some 50 yards below the trail. He went on to say that he thought it was exceedingly poor planning on the part of the Forest Service trail map crew to pay so little attention to water resources on or near the new trail. He continued,

"We had to help a hiker out a few weeks ago who was seriously dehydrated." I listened, nodding my head in agreement. I was to hear this complaint frequently from trail walkers regarding new sections of the trail during the next several years. I hope that by now the off-trail springs and other needed water resources are better marked.

I thanked the helpful foreman, as I was ready to move on to the newly constructed trail.

The below-trail spring was a bit hard to reach. I had to plunge down a steep bank and plow through high, dense bushes to reach water. Once located, it was cold and delicious. What a treat!

I carried the precious cold water up to the new trail and walked on until the trail leveled off. By evening, I reached a campsite alongside small, trickling Upper Bear Creek.

While still in my bedroll in the morning, I heard voices. I was surprised. Raising my head, I saw a procession of eight trail-crew members riding on motorbikes. The were probably returning to work on the new trail section that I had passed yesterday. What a contrast, I thought, in the National Forest trail crews' use of machines in comparison to trail-crew work in National Parks and Wilderness areas. The trail crews I had met in Yosemite walk to their work sites, and their supplies are transported by pack animals.

Leaving my Bear Creek campsite, the trail now descended down a slope heading west. Soon the trail grew faint and then became barely visible. I had arrived at a place where the old temporary trail was routed across a cross-country section. The guidebook directions were: "Use Bear Creek as your only guide." There were no Pacific Crest Trail decal markings to sight. I started through the forest, feeling alert and stimulated by the cross-country challenge. I wove my way between trees, glancing to my left to observe that I was staying in sight of the creek. After what seemed like about an hour, I emerged out of the woods onto a visible trail—an old trail being used as a temporary trail, marked with an old sign that read, "Sisson-Callahan Trail. In another hour, I reached the Trinity River crossing. I found a pleasing resting place on the river bank for my lunch stop. Gazing at the river's rocky bottom, I marveled at seeing such a relatively small, gentle stream, which would grow into such a formidable stream as it flowed south toward the Trinity Center's Clair Engle Lake. I was viewing the river near its mountain stream beginnings.

After crossing the Trinity, I climbed up on the trail leading to Bull Lake, where I had planned to camp. I was disappointed. It was windy, and looking out over the treeless lake, it seemed inhospitable to me. I studied my map and guidebook and decided to go on to the next campsite at Robbers Meadow. Moving ahead, I was again soon on a new section of trail; I discovered that the new trail did not go to Robbers Meadow. What to do? I decided to try a cross-country hike to reach the meadow. I climbed up a ridge and happily sighted the meadow below me. I was pleased. It proved to be a relatively easy walk, and it was worth it. The meadow, with its shallow lake, was peaceful, private, and hospitable.

In the morning I leisurely broke camp. I speculated on how this peaceful meadow had been bestowed with the name of Robbers Meadow. Had it been a hiding place for some early stagecoach robbers?

In the morning, I climbed back up the ridge and soon reached the trail. My destination was the Whiskeytown-Callahan Road, Highway 3—my coming-out trailhead. In this section of commingled old and new trail sections, I found myself striding again on a fairly freshly groomed, new trail. It was easy and pleasant walking.

By midday, I reached the ridge above large Masterson Meadow and enjoyed fine views looking to the west toward the Trinity Alps. I then descended on the new trail to grass-covered Masterson Meadow. I stopped for lunch by a small steam, which flowed through green-carpeted Masterson Meadow. I really enjoyed this peaceful spot, as it offered such a feeling of spaciousness.

Returning to the trail, I started to pray for a ride as I drew near to my coming-out destination. When I arrived at the Whiskeytown-Callahan Road near Scott Mountain, I took out my "to bus" sign. I had decided that I could go either way—north to Yreka or south to Redding. Fortunately, in answer to my prayers, the first car going south stopped and offered me a ride to Trinity Center. The friendly driver told me that he had recently moved from the Los Angeles area to Trinity Center. He had moved because he wanted his young son to grow up in a friendly, safe environment. He was very pleased with his new home. He was enjoying living in a small, friendly community and being surrounded by lakes and mountains. His story reminded me of the couple I had met at Hat Creek, who had also fled from a city in hopes of giving their young son a safe, rural environment.

At Trinity Center, I thanked my helpful driver and started my search for a second ride, as I had still not reached a bus stop. Again, I was fortunate—soon a couple with a young son stopped and offered me a ride to Yreka. I really appreciated their generosity, as they were really quite crowded. They were moving, and their son had to give up his seat for me and squeeze into the front seat beside his parents. I learned that the driver was enlisted in the Army and that they were moving to a new base assignment in the state of Washington. They had made a short detour to visit the Trinity Alps.

Arriving in Yreka, I was pleased to find that the next bus to San Francisco would be arriving in half an hour. I was soon on my way home. Safely aboard the Greyhound bus, my thoughts turned back to my experiences in finding rides to and from trailheads. I was always fearful that I would not find a ride but, to date, I was always fortunate in finding rides with interesting and kind people. How generous most people are, I thought. At the same time, I began to wonder if I would again be lucky in finding a ride to the trailhead at Scott Mountain when I returned the next year.

Chapter 20
Highway 3 at Scott Mountain Summit
to Ashland, Oregon
August 1982 • 160 Miles

Never more, however weary, should one faint by the way who gains the blessings of one mountain day; whatever his fate, long life, short life, stormy or calm, he is rich forever.
— *John Muir*

This, one of my longest walks, was marked by a variety of views and topography. With the trail still leading west, my journey started at the north edge of the Trinity Mountains and then reached the Marble Mountain wilderness area, a section unique and of special beauty. At the crossing of the mighty Klamath River, alongside the town of Seiad Valley, the trail ascends into the exceptional wilderness of the Siskiyou Mountains and then begins the turn east toward the Cascade Mountain range.

My entrance into Oregon was unspectacular. I crossed into the state in a viewless area, which had been fairly recently logged. Further along the trail in southern Oregon, I enjoyed pleasant views from the shoulder at Mount Ashland, looking north toward large Emigrant Lake Reservoir near the town of Ashland.

To reach the Scott Mountain trailhead, I needed to maneuver several rides. First I took the Greyhound bus to the northern California town of Yreka. There I boarded a local Scott Valley bus, which I had learned about from a visit to the Caltrans office in San Francisco. On this van bus, I was able to ride south to the town of Etna. This was a friendly bus, and I enjoyed a conversation with a passenger who was returning from San Francisco to her Scott Valley home in Fort Jones. She had been attending a family reunion in North Beach. We discovered that we had mutual friends living in North Beach, and we had an enjoyable time comparing friendships and experiences.

At the highway junction at the edge of Etna, after extending my arm and signaling my need for a ride, a friendly young couple offered me a ride to the next junction where they would turn off to reach their ranch. They had moved to Scott Valley recently, and they were full of enthusiasm for their new home and plans for developing their property. It was fun talking to them.

After disembarking at the road junction, I was again fortunate in finding a ride with a pleasant man who was returning from Yreka to his home in Coffey Creek, south of Scott Mountain. After two bus rides and two car rides, I felt so good upon reaching the trailhead at Scott Mountain.

As it was late in the day, I decided to camp at the nearby Scott Mountain campground. No one else was there. It was quiet and peaceful. I felt so exalted at my return to the wilderness. Sitting around my small campfire after supper, I asked myself, "What is it that upon my return to the wilderness causes me to feel such a glorious, uplifting feeling?" I thought of some of the things and jotted them down in my small pocket notebook. There is the quiet of the evening; the soothing water music of the streams and waterfalls; the gentle sound of the breeze rustling through the pine trees; and the deep blue sky, decorated with puffy cumulus clouds that float sometimes gently and sometimes swiftly and are constantly transforming themselves into myriad shapes of cloud castles. There are silhouettes of mountain peaks and ranges that rise up sharply, piercing the sky. There are the lush, green meadows that color the floor of the earth. At night, there is the moon and the star-filled sky, the fascinating galaxies, and the white-dotted path of the Milky Way.

Finally I thought, "It is all of these qualities and much more that add together to create a total ambiance that surrounds me and exults me and fills me with a great and glorious feeling."

My next day's walk started with a 1000-foot climb, as I entered the Salmon-Trinity Alps Wilderness. Upon reaching a high ridge, another magnificent view lay before me. Looking to the south, I could see the rugged Bear Lake crest. To the east, Mount Shasta loomed upward with a fluffy white cloud floating around its snow-capped cone. I recalled that this was my third summer in which I was viewing Mount Shasta. It was beginning to seem like a familiar friend. Each view, however, was unique. Its cone often wore a different cloud cover and was clothed with different shades of lighting.

My lunch spot was at the side of a beautiful, small meadow. It had its own spring, which furnished me with luscious, cool water and was adorned with cheerful, yellow-blooming flowers.

By evening I turned off the trail, climbing down a steep, rocky trail to reach East Boulder Lake. Arriving at the lake, the smallest of the three Boulder lakes, I found it to be a shallow, uninviting pond. I decided to move on. I made camp at the somewhat larger Middle Boulder Lake. It was quiet and peaceful, although unspectacular. Cows were grazing in the adjoining meadow.

I experienced an annoyingly slow start in the morning. I woke to find my campsite covered with dew. After packing my partially wet bivouac sack, I started my climb back up to the trail. It was slow and laborious. I had forgotten how steep and rocky the climb down had been. I reminded myself that climbing up takes longer than climbing down.

Reaching the trail at last, I soon met a group of young hikers. They told me that they were camped at nearby Mosquito Lake at Camp Au Aoa. Their leader explained that their camp featured backpack trips into the surrounding wilderness areas. They looked fresh and eager.

The trail contoured along high ridges and offered pleasant views to the south of the Trinity Alps. There were also interesting scenes to the east, looking down on the Scott River Valley, where I could see cultivated and irrigated ranchland that offered patches of bright green grasses. Water was not a problem on this stretch of the trail, as the trail passed by several cold, refreshing springs.

By evening, I went off-trail to camp at small Lake Mevis. It was like a small pond. I was delighted to find it full of bright yellow water lilies, one of my favorite flowers.

After leaving Lake Mevis in the morning, I encountered a day of lots of ups and downs. First the trail descended steeply down to the crossing of the South Fork of Scott River. Then the trail climbed up on sharply turning switchbacks to a ridge and following still more rocky switchbacks, the trail climbed up to the 6100-foot Carter Meadow Summit. As I moved along slowly, I thought, "Oh dear, I am behind schedule. Will I reach the post office at the town of Etna and my food package on the weekend and have to wait for the post office to open on Monday?" Then I reminded myself, "I'm here to enjoy the walk and not to worry about time." With this reminder, I relaxed.

When it was time to plan for a campsite, I went off-trail, following a cow path down to a little meadow near the Siphoon

Lake trail. I was pleased with my little meadow site and its creeklet and thought to myself that as a solo hiker I could be creative as to where I could camp—just needing a small space near water. Then I thought about how precious is water. At home when we only have to turn on the faucet, we don't really appreciate its value.

The following day, I enjoyed more glorious ridge views. My friend, Mount Shasta, came into view again. There were more scenes looking down at the Scott River Valley and still more views looking south to the peaks of the Salmon Mountains. Around mid-day, the trail turned north, and a different view and feel presented itself. I had moved into a granitic mountain canyon. The feel of the canyon was a little reminiscent of the feel of Yosemite but, of course, I said to myself, "There is nothing really as magnificent as the Yosemite Valley."

I soon came to "The Statue," a light granite pillar that rose up all by itself. It, indeed, created a picturesque scene standing all by itself. A little further on, the views from the ridge looked down on bright green irrigated fields of ranchlands lining the Scott Valley. These scenes were new and interesting to me, as I had not visited this part of northern California before, and I had no idea that there were these lush, green, irrigated grasslands. Also, views looking down into valleys always held a fascination for me.

By evening, I turned off-trail to camp at attractive Paynes Lake. The lake was framed on one side by a high rock sidewall rising up from the lakeshore. It was somewhat reminiscent of lakes of the Sierras. It was quiet and peaceful. No one was there. I had not passed any hikers since Mosquito Lake.

At twilight, the fish started jumping and making big splashes and creating little circle ripples. There was evidence that campers, perhaps fishermen, had used this site. Some clever camper had constructed a chair of tree branches. I sat in it for a while, eating my supper while watching the evening light slowly fade from the lake's rock hillside before climbing into my bedroll.

I arose early, ate breakfast, and packed up and took a last fond look at quiet, peaceful Paynes Lake. I was soon on my way. I eagerly anticipated coming out for a food package. From the lake, the trail climbed up again to a ridge and afforded me still another glorious view looking down into the bright green Scott River Valley. There again, to the east, was my friend Mount Shasta. The trail then turned west and entered a forest. Upon crossing a lingering, shaded snowbank, I slipped. Fortunately, I regained my balance before falling. I thought to myself, "This late snowbank is deceptive." It looked so simple to cross, but underneath it was slippery. It alerted me to take care upon future snowbank crossings.

I arrived at the Etna Summit, where the Somes Bar-Etna Road crosses the trail, around 2 p.m. I took up my place by the side of the road, hoping and waiting for a ride to the town of Etna, some eight miles distant and the site of my food package. In about 20 minutes, two men in a pickup stopped and offered me a ride. I climbed into the back of their pickup bed. I was so thankful to find a ride so soon.

I had reached Etna on Sunday and planned to spend the night and pick up my food package on Monday morning. The downtown main street was quite deserted. Searching around, I ducked into a small grocery store, where a helpful store clerk gave me directions to reach the forest service campground at the edge of town. Arriving at the campground, I picked out a campsite and was resting quietly, leaning against a tree, when the campground manager—a tall, thin man—approached me. He started complaining about forest service personnel. I listened politely but did not enjoy the conversation. I was still visualizing the glorious scene looking out over Paynes Lake and felt the unpleasant jolt of being back in town. He did tell me one thing, however, that I was glad to hear—that there was an older man in the forest service in his eighties who was still working during the summer months. How good, I thought, that he was not forced to retire at 65 and that he could still offer his talents.

For a change of menu, I walked back to town and ate supper at Archie's Pizza Parlor. I ordered salad and pizza. It tasted so very good.

In the morning, I stopped for coffee and a roll at a small coffee shop near the post office. Sitting around the counter were four older men, deep in conversation with one another. They were talking about their gardens and their fishing trips. They seemed to be enjoying themselves, and I enjoyed observing and listening to them. I wondered if they met every morning to exchange stories about their day's events. How good that they enjoyed socializing together.

After picking up my food package at the post office, I looked around and pondered where to place myself to find a ride to return to the Etna Summit. I observed that most of the traffic turned off the main roadway onto local streets. I decided to walk to the edge of the town.

At the town's edge, I took up my post, took out my "To trail" sign, and hoped. Not many cars passed. Those that did pass did not stop. I was becoming discouraged. Finally, a friendly lumber truck driver stopped and asked me how far I was going. When I said, "Etna Summit," he said, "I will be turning off before the summit." I asked, "Do you think I will find a ride?" He replied, "You will." I started praying. Soon, a considerate rancher in a pickup stopped and offered me a ride. I climbed into his truck bed and joined his two friendly dogs. They were characters. One of them, a birddog type, bounded from one side to the other, appearing to be hunting and pointing at something or other all during the trip. The other, a heavyset bulldog-terrier type, wanted my attention and to be petted constantly. He kept leaning his heavy body against me, seemingly to make sure that I would pet him. I don't think I have ever experienced before such a heavy dog leaning against me. I was beginning to be thankful that the ride to Etna Summit was a relatively short one.

Climbing out of the pickup at the summit and thanking the kind rancher, I eagerly started my trip north on the trail. I planned to reach water and a campsite at Shelley Meadow some 11 miles distant. Striding along, I was soon overtaken by two tall young men. They announced that they had seen me in the grocery store at Etna. They were through-Pacific Crest Trail hikers, having started at the Mexican border. They, too, were planning to camp at Shelley Meadow and said, "We will see you soon." as they strolled on by me.

I reached Shelley Meadow at around 8 p.m. and quickly found water and made camp. I spent a peaceful, comfortable night on the edge of this large, spacious meadow.

In the morning, one of the hikers who had passed me the day before came to my camp and asked, "I wonder if I might interview you. I am writing a story of my Pacific Crest Trail walk for my local paper, and I would like to include an interview with you in my write-up." I agreed. We sat down while he asked me a number of questions: Why was I drawn to the idea of walking on the trail? How many days and what sections would I be walking this year? What were my favorite places or sections of the trail? He ended by saying, "I will send you a copy of my write-up when I return home." Don, I learned, was from Bothell, Washington. As he rose to return to his camp, he said, "We need to move on, as we need to make 17 miles a day to reach the border before we are snowbound. I wish we had more time to enjoy the trail."

His remark was in my thoughts often when I felt that I was moving along the trail too slowly. I remembered his saying, "I wish I had more time to enjoy the trail." Then I resolved all over again to always place a high priority on enjoying the sights and sounds of the trail.

Another question rose up in my thoughts periodically as I met young hikers hurrying along to complete the trail in one or two summers, while I continued to plod along, completing my 10-day, 100-mile summers. I would question myself, "If I had not been committed to an ongoing job, would I have wanted to spend a whole summer or two walking the entire trail?" Although I could never answer this question with absolute certainty, I usually found myself thinking that my slow way of hiking the trail had many advantages Each year, I enjoyed anticipating the next year's walk. My 100-mile summers provided me with many years of joyful memories.

From Shelley Meadow, the trail winds up a ridge. As I was traversing along the side of a slope, I came to a snowbank. It had a curious mark on it. Coming closer, I read, "Hi, Eleanor." My young hiker friends had decided to leave me a greeting. How delightful.

Walking along through the next soft, harmless-looking snowbank, I experienced a sudden surprise. Unexpectedly and without warning, I fell. I sat up slowly, rubbing the knee that I had landed on, hoping and praying I was all right. Happily, I found out that I was perfectly all right. How fortunate. Either instinctively or perhaps by just plain good luck, I had gone down very gently on my knee and then rolled over onto my pack, which is a soft object to land on. I was so happy to discover that I was not hurt.

By lunchtime, I had reached the overview above deep, dark-purple-blue Cliff Lake. What a glorious scene. The lake rested in a basin ringed by stately green pines. With the trail passing so high above the lake, it created a picture-perfect view.

As the trail veered to the west, I came upon another surprising sight. Ahead of me was a long, steep snowbank, and it appeared that the trail would traverse its upper steep edge. Drawing still nearer, it seemed that the upper end of the bank had, through the summer snowmelt, pulled away from its steep, rocky bank. Moving slowly and cautiously over the rocky trail, I arrived at the snowbank's edge and saw that, yes indeed, the icy snow had pulled away from the rock cliff and had left a narrow path through which I could squeeze. It seemed to be safer to try the rocky path rather than traversing the steep, icy snowbank. I entered the tunnel-like path. It was rocky but not difficult. The ice face of the snowbank evolved into interesting colors.

DEEP CLIFF LAKE & SHALLOW CAMPBELL LAKE

In places, it took on a blue-green glacier color and in other places it reflected a snowy white color. At the far end, the crevasse ended, leaving a short distance to walk over the far edge of the snowbank. I placed my feet in the boot marks left by previous hikers. It was not too difficult. Soon I was safely across.

Later, after my snowbank walk, I read reports from other

hikers and learned that this was a scary, dreaded crossing, especially for early season hikers. Still later, upon reading trail update reports, I found that the forest service planned to rebuild this section of the trail.

By late afternoon, I had entered the Marble Mountain Wilderness. I had a glimpse in the distance of the majestic peaks of the white Marble Mountains.

By late evening, I turned off the trail to reach Shadow Lake, a recommended camping place. Arriving at its rocky shores, I thought that it did, indeed, present a dramatic sight. It was like a large tarn surrounded by rock cliffs that cupped the peaceful, rippling waters in its center. It was also crowded with campers. The Shadow Lake trail is easily accessible from a Scott Valley roadhead. I had to search diligently to find a campsite. During my search, I encountered a man standing on the rock attired in clean white pants. He looked me over and said, "Aren't you quite far into the mountains to be carrying such a small pack?" I felt like replying that I had succeeded in completing the 200-mile John Muir Trail and a goodly portion of the Pacific Crest Trail with a small pack, but I refrained. He looked so sure of himself, so I smiled and said quietly, "I think that I have sufficient supplies."

I continued to search for a campsite. I tested possible sites and decided they were too windy. Ultimately, Frisby helped me to find my campsite. Frisby was a small, friendly dog that came leaping out from a small rock crevice. He alerted me to peek into this small valley between the rocks, and I decided that this was the perfect wind shelter that I had been searching for. I was pleased. It was just barely large enough to accommodate my bedroll.

After supper, I was treated to a glorious scene. As the sky darkened, misty rainclouds descended, first reaching the high rocks on the cliff and then moving down and settling onto the lake. I was glad that I had hiked in to this jewel of a lake.

It rained off and on during the night, but I was warm and dry, snuggled into my bivouac sack in my little crevice between the rock cliffs.

In the morning after packing up, I climbed up out of my rock shelter and was ready to start on my journey. Standing on the top of the lakeshore rock as if he were surveying the landscape was the man in the clean white pants. I greeted him by saying, ""Are you planning a hike for the day?" He replied, "I think that I will stay here today and perhaps do some fishing." I replied, "I am heading toward Seiad Valley." I hoped that by now, perhaps, I was being a little smug—that he might realize that I was a long-distance backpacker with my "small pack to be in so far."

As the Shadow Lake trail climbed up to the junction and I turned onto the main trail, I was treated to a spectacular sky view. Rain clouds were rising and falling and swirling around. The sky colors were a mixture of dark blue-gray rain clouds interspersed with light gray-and-white, puffy clouds. When I reached the top of the ridge, I paused to look and to absorb this very special scene. Also, from the ridgetop, a whole new, exciting view opened up to the north—the view into Little Marble Mountain Valley. From here, I could see the light-colored Marble Mountain. It seemed so different from all the other mountains that I had hiked through to date. I felt that it was a miracle of nature. Surrounding the white Marble Mountain were other mountains representing a variety of colors—medium-gray and volcanic reds and blacks. Tall Black Mountain could be seen in the distance and, still further to the north and piercing the skyline were the summits of the Red Buttes. Between the variegated colors of the mountains and the spectacular sky colors, I was uplifted and in awe of such a magnificent scene.

By noon, I reached the Marble Mountain guard station. There stood some old army-style rectangular framed buildings. I walked around them. There were no signs of a ranger or any lived-in look to the buildings. I wondered about their history, but as there was no ranger present, I was not to learn the story of their origins. A merrily shouting and laughing group of teenagers was camped nearby in a cluster of trees.

My afternoon walk was pleasant and easy with some gentle ups and downs. By early afternoon, I arrived at Paradise Lake and found a campsite on a ridge with a fine view overlooking the lake. Since I had made camp early, I had ample time after supper to view my surroundings. To the north, I could see the tall, red-black rock—King's Castle looming up in the horizon. It did, indeed, look like a fortress. I felt good. It had been a day of different scenes and full of inspiring views.

As I hiked north in the morning, the trail led up a ridge and treated me with still more views of King's Castle clothed in morning light. I had read hurriedly in the guidebook that this would be a day for downhill walks, but here I was hiking up a fairly steep grade. During my morning milk-and-honey refreshment break, I reviewed the map. I was not yet ready for the downhill. Onward and upward I climbed until, finally, I reached a 6800-foot saddle below Buckhorn Mountain. I rejoiced. I was ready to start the 13-mile, 4400-foot descent down to the Klamath River.

My lunch break was beside refreshing Buckhorn Springs. By late in the day, around 8 p.m., I reached water and a campsite by Cold Springs Creek. My bedroom was unaesthetic and different. I was treading around slowly to a crunching sound. I was camping on gravel. I had left the Marble Mountains and its exquisite scenery and was now looking at low-level, scrubby bushes.

After leaving Cold Springs Creek in the morning, I soon

reached the Grider Creek trail. The trail clings closely to the bank of north-flowing Grider Creek, which I would be walking beside for many miles as it ran its course downward to empty into the mighty Klamath in the Seiad Valley.

My journey had many pleasant pauses to pick luscious, ripe blackberries. I also found some pale-pink salmonberries. It was good to add a sweet touch to my backpack menu.

Nearing the Grider Creek campground, the peaceful sound of the steam was interrupted by a yapping bark. Looking ahead, I saw a little black dog standing on the trail. He barked ferociously until I drew closer to him, and then he turned tail and ran. Soon a young man appeared and assured me that his barking dog would not bite. When I came up to the dog's family, I learned that they were gold seekers. They were floating a sluice box in the stream. They were talkative and friendly. I learned that they were from Grants Pass and that the family consisted of an uncle and two teenaged boys. They volunteered that they hadn't found any gold yet, but that the stream had been recommended to them by a gold-seeker friend and they were hopeful. I sensed that they were really enjoying themselves.

Upon reaching the campground early in the afternoon, I sat down and was lured into watching the stream. I was torn. Should I continue to lounge by the stream and revel in listening to the water music, or should I hurry on road walking to the village to call for my food package? I decided on a plan. I calculated that it would be hard to reach the post office in Seiad Valley by 5 p.m. It was Friday. I didn't feel like hurrying on. I decided that I would try to beg a ride from any passing car. I anticipated that campers might be going to town for supplies and then returning to the campground for the night. I wanted to continue to enjoy the streamside solitude.

I sat listening. No car approached. Pondering the plan

again, I concluded that the only car campers were the gold seekers, and they were not moving from their panning efforts. I remained, enjoying the peaceful scene beside the creek. Toward dusk, I moved up the stream a little way to find a more secluded, level spot on which to place my bedroll. It had been such an enjoyable, restful afternoon, lounging by the stream.

It was an easy walk the next morning from Grider Creek to the village of Seiad Valley. I soon arrived at the junction with Highway 76, the main road leading to the village. The highway followed on the south side of the river for a short distance and then turned north to bridge the river. I paused in the center of the bridge crossing to look down at the infamous, mighty Klamath. At this time of year, it was relatively gentle and well contained within its banks. I had read so very often of immense flooding along the Klamath during spring runoffs.

On the north side of the river, the highway turned west to reach the village of Seiad Valley. I was full of apprehension. It was Saturday morning. Would I be able to retrieve my food package from the post office, or would I need to wait until Monday morning? Arriving at the store around 10:30, I inquired of the proprietor, "Is the post office open on Saturday? I want to call for a food package." She replied, "The postmistress comes to the post office to put up the mail around noon." I was so relieved and hopeful. I moved to the café, which was at one end of the store. I had time to order a big breakfast—hash browns and scrambled eggs. It tasted good. Near me, sitting on a stool at the café counter, a woman was saying to the café's manager, "It is going to take four loads for the truck to haul it all away." I had seen a huge truck loading some debris as I had passed a campground on my way to the store. Curiously, I asked, "What are they hauling away?" The woman at the counter, whom I later learned was the mobile home manager, replied, "A mobile home was destroyed by fire two days ago, and the couple who were its owners were unable to get out. I lost my best friends." I was shocked and managed only to say, feeling that it was grossly inadequate, "I am sorry." I had heard that mobile homes are often fire hazards. Never before had I been so close to a real-life exhibit of such a tragedy. Still, to this day, when I pass a mobile home park, I have a flashback of this tragic story.

I moved over to the front of the post office and waited hopefully. Happily, the postmistress arrived on time to meet a postal truck, which deposited a bag of mail. She cheerfully opened up, found my food package, and gave it to me. I felt so lucky.

I carried my package to the nearby campground where I leisurely repacked my backpack. It was still early in the day when I finished my packing. I decided to return to the trail and hike on to the next water at Fern Springs.

I walked west of the town for a short distance and started my search for the trailhead. Happily, without too much difficulty, I found it. The trail was signed for the "Lower Devil's Peak Lookout." I started up the ascending grade slowly. I knew from the guidebook that I would be climbing, as it would be a 4600-foot ascent up to Kangaroo Mountain, some 10 miles distant. I rather looked forward to the ascent as I felt that I had been in the dry, hot valley long enough and was looking forward to returning to the cooler, breeze-filled mountains. I also was eager to reach Mount Ashland and the Cascade mountain range if southern Oregon.

When I arrived at Fern Springs, I looked around. I saw a lot of poison oak. I had not climbed high enough (2100 feet) to reach an environment in which poison oak could no longer grow. I decided to move on. I loaded up with enough water for the night and for breakfast.

As I climbed up toward lower Devil's Peak, the trail soon

entered a Douglas fir forest. While hiking along, enjoying the cool shade of the forest, I heard ahead of me a rattle of twigs. I stopped to listen. I thought some creature was leaping across the slope. I guessed that it was probably a deer, as so often when I heard rattling and scuffling in the underbrush, I would soon see a deer. I searched ahead to locate the noise. Then I spotted the animal. This time, it was not a deer—it was a small, light-cinnamon-colored bear. He was loping down the mountain slope and crossed the trail not far ahead of me and then descended slightly and buried his nose in a decaying log just a short distance from the trail. I was delighted. I had time to snap a photo of him before he took off again. I don't think that he ever saw me. I was so pleased because he was the first bear I had encountered on the trail during my 12 years of backpacking. Every summer, when I returned from my walk and shared my trail experience with friends, the first thing they would ask me was, "Did you see any bears?" I replied, "No, I did not." Thus, I was beginning to feel that something was lacking in my hiking experience. Now at last, I had seen my bear. I was so glad that my first sighting was of a bear in a natural wilderness setting. My colorful little cinnamon bear was foraging in the woods—grubbing in a fallen log for insects—eating natural foods rather than foraging in a campsite garbage bin. I was so happy that I had seen my bear at last.

I moved on and found a campsite on a pleasant saddle crest just below lower Devil's Peak It proved to be a good campsite, as after dark I was treated to a light show. I looked down at the Seiad Valley village and saw the valley dotted with lights.

In the morning, I reached lower Devil's Peak. I briefly explored the site of the abandoned lookout tower, marked by concrete blocks. It offered another pleasant view looking down toward Seiad Valley.

Climbing up the trail, I heard a sound—a tapping sound coming from someplace hidden from my view. I was puzzled. The tapping noise grew louder. Rounding a bend in the trail, I was surprised to see a tall man with a pickaxe. He announced, "I'm studying rocks of this area. I'm a geology student at Stanford, and I'm working on my Ph.D. This is the location of my summer research project." After a pleasant conversation with the geology student, I moved on again, climbing up to Middle Devil's Peak and, finally, to upper Devil's Peak. Again, I enjoyed views of Mount Shasta. Each time Mount Shasta came into view, I felt like I was greeting an old friend.

After upper Devil's Peak, the trail contours around Kangaroo Mountain and from a crest saddle along the side of Kangaroo Mountain, I looked down on small, picturesque, Lily Pad Lake. It was time to look for a campsite. I decided to make camp at the small Lily Pad Lake, even though the guidebook described it as having poor campsites with hundreds of frogs. From the trail, it looked pleasant. I turned off the trail and strolled down to the lakeshore. Later, I had to admit that small Lily Pad Lake did have some deficiencies. The campsite had been visited by cows and was dotted with cowpies. Collecting water presented a challenge, as I had to push through thickly growing alder branches to reach the lakeshore. I decided to play it safe by sterilizing the water. I pulled out my iodine tablets. After supper, a strong wind arose and whipped up the canyon. I went to bed early to keep warm. Although my campsite was far from ideal, I was compensated by seeing a rock wren in a side canyon. I was excited, as the rock wren is a reclusive bird that hides in rock crevices and is rarely seen.

In the morning, after climbing up to the saddle crest above Lily Pad Lake and turning onto the trail, I coasted down easily to the Cook and Green Pass (4770 feet). Approaching the pass, I was met by a loud barking dog that came racing toward me. Just before he came close enough to threaten to attack me, a curly-headed young girl, thankfully, appeared and quieted him. The engaging, talkative youngster told me that her father had "gold fever." He was working a mine that summer. She said he was looking for rocks with veins and that a certain type of rock could contain chromium. As she chattered on, we caught up with her mother, who was standing near her car that was parked on a road near the pass. She was also friendly and talkative and told me that they were living in their trailer, which was parked on a nearby spur road. Her husband, she added, had a big contract to work the Chrome King Mine. "Where are you from?" she asked. "Santa Rosa," I replied. She was excited and said that she had grown up near Santa Rosa on Fulton Road and that she had fond memories of the Fulton Road neighbors. Moving toward their car, she said that they were on their way to Seiad Valley to buy groceries. When I told her that I was sorry to hear about the tragic fire in the mobile home in Seiad Valley, she said that she had known the couple that perished in the fire. Frowning and shaking her head, she said that she could not understand why they were not able to get out through the bedroom door.

After filling my water bottle at the spring by the pass, I waved goodbye to the friendly family as they got into their pickup, and I shouldered my pack and started up the trail.

From the Cook and Green Pass, the eastbound trail climbs gently through low-growing shrubs and forest and reaches up to a ridge, which skirts around the side of reddish-colored Copper Butte. When I reached the trail junction to Lowden's Cabin site, where I had planned to camp, I felt energetic and decided to go on to the next water site. Nearing the site of a spring described in the guidebook, I searched and searched but could not find the elusive spring. While I was searching, a horseman came along. He said that he didn't know of any spring in the area. Fortunately, I had a reserve of water, so at dusk, I pulled off the path and camped on a level spot.

My next morning's primary quest was for water. Would the Reeves Ranch spring be fruitful and easy to find? I moved on eagerly. It was, thankfully, not very far and it was easy to find.

Back on the trail refreshed, I strolled on until lunchtime, when I again chose to go off-trail to the inviting-sounding Alex Hole Campground. The guidebook description proclaims, "A delightful campsite with a willow-lined spring and Swiss chalet-styled outhouse, with a far-reaching view to the north." First, I enjoyed the refreshing cold water from the spring. Unfortunately, the campsite, which could be reached by road, was strewn with beer cans. "How inappropriate and unnecessary," I thought.

After lunch, I searched for the Swiss chalet-styled outhouse. I could not find it. I gave up, but did enjoy the far-reaching view looking over a valley to the north, as seen from the edge of the steeply dropping cliff.

On the trail again after lunch, I met a horseman. When he learned that had come from Alex Hole, he said, "The guide-book author has a sense of humor." He went on to explain that the lip of the cliff, which drops down so steeply, creates "the Swiss chalet outhouse." I was surprised. Now, at last, the out-house mystery was solved.

My afternoon walk was pleasant and easy with moderate ups and downs. I decided to pass up Bearground Spring as a possible campsite, as I did not feel ready to retire for the night. I continued on for another two hours and arrived at large, green, grass-covered Donomore Meadow. There I had ample space for my campsite and plenty of water from gently flowing Donomore Creek.

On my morning's walk, I crossed Donomore Creek and circled around the large meadow. Upon reaching the far end of the meadow, I encountered some cows wearing jingling cowbells. They looked up and stared at me. Would they stomp their feet or run toward me if I tried to pass? I moved forward slowly. Happily, they slowly moved over and I walked on ahead. I reached two old cabins standing near the meadow's edge, creating a picturesque, pastoral scene.

Shortly after leaving the meadow, the trail entered a clear-cut area. Looking up, I saw a small sign announcing, "You are entering Oregon." I was disappointed. I felt that the border crossing should be an important landmark. I also regretted that the trail's entry into Oregon was in a clear-cut logging area rather than offering a scenic view.

Now striding ahead in Oregon, I climbed up the trail that traversed around Observation Peak and on to Jackson Gap, which offered pleasant views of mixed green-grass-covered hills and small trees. There were, however, patches that showed evidence of logging.

While I was sitting at the edge of the trail eating a snack, a tall, slender young hiker traveling from the north approached me. "Where is the next water?" he asked. As I gave him information about water and the trail ahead, I noticed his accent and asked, "Where are you from?" "Switzerland," he replied. He reported that he had started at the Canadian border and hoped to complete the entire trail before October. He was glad to hear about water and campsites ahead. I refrained from telling him about the "Swiss-chalet-styled outhouse at Alex Hole."

In moving along from Gap to Gap that marked this area of the trail, I reached Wrangle Gap by late afternoon and descended west on a spur road that lead down to Wrangle Campground. I inspected the camp's impressive rock shelter. This was the first of a number of shelters that had been constructed in campgrounds along the trail in Oregon. After looking inside, I decided that I did not want to sleep in a shelter. I felt that I would feel cooped in and would miss looking up at the starlit sky. I hiked on until I reached a small spring in a grass-covered valley with a view looking toward Siskkiyou Peak and Mount Ashland. The spring water trickled down a grass-covered slope. To fill my water bag, I had to place my cup in a small-moss-covered space to catch the drip. I had to slowly fill several cups to obtain enough water to fill my water bag for the night. The water, however, was fresh and cold. It tasted so good. Returning to a level space in the valley, I experimented by moving my bedroll around until I found the desired angle to enjoy the view looking toward the mountain from my bedsite.

In the morning, I refilled my water bag from the enchanting spring with its trickling waterfall and bid farewell to this tranquil, enjoyable campsite. I was eagerly anticipating my day's walk as I planned to reach Mount Ashland that would bring me close to my coming-out trailhead at the town of Ashland.

In the morning, I followed the trail leading east as it made a moderate ascent up to a shoulder perched by the side of Siskiyou Peak and then descended to Grouse Gap, where I turned off the trail. I was ready for a rest and a snack and was curious to catch a glimpse of the Grouse Gap shelter. It was an impressive sturdy structure built with light-colored stone sidewalls. Nevertheless, I preferred my starlit campsite.

By mid-afternoon, I reached the Mount Ashland campground. I explored the campsites and was disappointed. The campground was situated on a high, unprotected slope, and it was buffeted by strong winds. I decided to move on. I was now walking on a blacktop road, following the alternate route from Mount Ashland to the town of Ashland. I passed by the

Mount Ashland Ski Area. It was quiet and deserted, except for one man who was hammering on some machinery. I walked quite a ways on the blacktop while searching for the alternate trail turnoff. Finally, I spotted Pacific Crest Trail decals—a welcome sight—and turned off onto a gravel road. Strolling along, I felt good at having found the trail marker. Soon, I arrived at a junction with roads turning to the right and to the left. Where were the trail decals? I searched and searched, pacing up and down in both directions. I could not find a Pacific Crest Trail marker. I was puzzled. I hoped that a car would come so I could ask for directions. I waited. It was quiet. No car appeared. I had to guess; I decided to turn right. It appeared to be the general direction indicated in the guidebook's map. Soon it began to grow dark. It was time to look for a campsite. I had no idea where I might find water; finally I reached a spring-fed creeklet. I searched around for a place to camp. There were not a lot of choices. I debated whether to choose a level spot on the shoulder of the road or an unlevel brush-covered spot in the trees. Would there be any cars traveling on this road during the night? I had no idea. I decided to play it safe and I opted for the unlevel spot in the trees where I would be hidden from traffic. I spent an uncomfortable night sliding down the bumpy brush-covered slope. What does it matter? I thought. I will be in a real bed tomorrow night.

In the morning, I picked my way out of my unlevel bed site and discovered that my bed had moved downhill about two feet during the night—gravity takes over when you sleep on a slant. I filled my water bag and started on my way to Ashland. It was an easy walk on the gravel road through the shaded forest. No cars came along. By early afternoon, I expected to see signs of Ashland, as the guidebook described the alternate route as an eight-and-a-half-mile walk. I was disappointed. I was still walking in the forest. I was growing impatient for signs of Ashland. Finally around 3:30 p.m., some outlying houses came into view. A little later, I finally arrived at the outskirts of Ashland and turned onto a main road. At the small store, I stopped to ask directions for reaching the post office. I still had two miles to go. I had mailed a package of clean clothing to the post office. I needed to reach the post office before the 5:00 closing. I picked up my pace. It was hot and I was tired. Would I make it on time? I hurried, and I finally arrived at the general delivery window at three minutes before the 5:00 closing time. Thankfully, I clutched my package containing a clean change of clothes to attend the Ashland Shakespearean Theater.

After my hot, long, hurried walk, I did have some good breaks. First, a kind man in the post office, after hearing the story of my final push to reach the post office before closing time, offered me a ride to the hostel. Then, after I paid my $6.00 hostel fee, the manager looked for me and gave me a dollar back, saying, "The hostel offers a reduced rate for Pacific Crest Trail hikers." How nice. Then I discovered that the hostel had a bathtub. Oh, how glorious it was to soak in the large tub. The hostel was conveniently located very near the Shakespearean Theater. Walking to the theater ticket office, I was again lucky in obtaining a good seat. Someone had turned in a ticket at the last minute. I enjoyed seeing a performance of "The Comedy of Errors." It was superbly performed, with very fine actors.

I really liked Ashland and decided that I would plan to see another play the following year.

Early the next morning, I boarded the Greyhound bus for home. I expected to sit back and relax and watch the landscape role by. However, I became enchanted by a charming lady who took the seat across the aisle from me. I had noticed her waiting at the bus stop, as she was wearing a charming and somewhat quaint French voile jumper. I smiled at her, and when she sat down near me, she entertained me all the way to Sacramento with her stories. She told me that she had grown up in Montana and that her family was Norwegian pioneers. She remembered that she and her brothers and sisters did not have store-bought toys, so they made toys from clay. Her family lived near an Indian reservation. She recalled that as a young adult, she earned money by pulling tumbleweeds from the alfalfa. She commented that although her family had very few conveniences, she had happy memories of growing up in Montana. Now she lives in Ashland and is very proud of her city and of the accomplishments of its Shakespeare Festival. I felt good at having experienced this brief friendship and hearing the stories told by this interesting and cheerful woman.

On the way home and for many years after, I puzzled over the long route taken to reach Ashland. According to the guidebook, I should have reached Ashland in about 8 ½ miles. I estimated that I had walked approximately 16 miles. Should I have taken the left turn instead of turning to the right at the junction where I could not find a Pacific Crest Trail decal? I studied the map; I could not find a junction. I shall always wonder about "the road not taken."

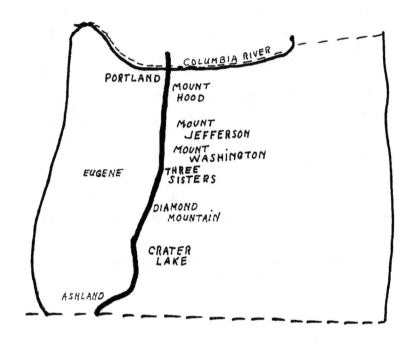

PACIFIC CREST
TRAIL

OREGON

INTRODUCTION TO OREGON
526 Miles

For me, hiking through Oregon seemed like walking from one volcano to another. The list includes—from south to north—Mt. McLoughlin, Mt. Thielsen, Diamond Peak, the Three Sisters, Mt. Washington, Three Fingered Jack, Mount Jefferson, and finally, majestic, snow-capped Mt. Hood.

In addition to the volcanic peaks, an interesting and beautiful landmark of volcanic origin is seen upon passing Crater Lake, designated as Crater Lake National Park. It bears the distinction of being the deepest lake in the United States. The lake was formed on the site of a large volcano, which erupted years ago leaving a deep depression—a caldera, which slowly filled with water. Wizard Island, resting toward the center of the island, represents a piece of the former volcanic peak.

Oregon also included walking through forests and sections dotted by numerous lakes. The Sky Lakes Basin in southern Oregon is lush with lakes. It is also lush with mosquitoes. Although I waited to enter the Sky Lake Basin until August, when reportedly the mosquitoes no longer present a threat, the loud buzzing and bothersome biting still surrounded me.

I found the up-and-down climbs much less frequent than in California. Many trails led through woods and through relatively level areas. To me, Oregon seemed like the easiest of the trail sections to hike.

The Oregon-Washington border crossing at the Columbia River is the lowest elevation on the entire Pacific Crest Trail. Walking across the river on the long, high Bridge of the Gods, the elevation is near sea level.

Chapter 21
Ashland to Crater Lake
August 1983
130 Miles

All the wilderness seems to be full of tricks and plans to drive and draw us up into God's light.
—John Muir, My First Summer in the Sierra

My first year of a full-time walk in Oregon held some surprises. In contrast to expectations of typical Oregon weather of rain and moisture, my first days of traversing east were over dry, grassy, sometimes treeless ridges. This section is sometimes described as Oregon desert. The trail continued to lead east to reach the Cascades until it reached Fish Lake, about halfway through my walk. The circle loop, which started around Burney Falls, led west to the Siskiyou Mountains near Seiad Valley, then circled back east and around Mt. Shasta and the dry plains surrounding it to reach the crest of the Cascade Mountains. Upon reaching the Fish Lake area, the landscape changed. I was again walking north, wending my way from lake to lake through the Sky Lakes Area. Approaching Crater Lake, I was greeted by still another unexpected view—that of fairly deep snowbanks, which in places covered the trail even into mid-August. The view of deep-purple-blue Crater Lake at the end of my section's journey was enchanting. It held my gaze for a long time.

Getting to Trailhead was delightfully easy. My good friends, Kareen and Madeline, decided to take in a play at the Shakespearean Theatre in Ashland, so I had a ride all the way to Trailhead. We saw Richard III, and I listened for the remembered line "In Kent my liege, the Guilfords are in arms."

The next morning, after a good breakfast, my friends drove me the nine miles south, and we began our search for the trail marker near Callahan's Restaurant. Where, oh where, was the trail marker? We went down one small gravel road, but found no marker. We went up another small road and, again, found no marker. We went back to Callahan's to ask, but found the restaurant was closed Sunday mornings. Finally, a man rattling around near the restaurant gave us directions. We again went down the first road and found a little road turning left—there, at last, was the trail marker. I waved goodbye to my friends and started my journey.

The trail leading east traversed grassy ridges. From a high ridgetop, I was once again greeted by a familiar view—that of Mt. Shasta. As this dry area was lacking abundant water, I was aiming for a fenced-in spring. I reached the spring by early evening and made camp. My campsite was unaesthetic. There was an unused, boarded-up hut near the piped spring. The unaesthetic setting was redeemed by its very refreshing cold, piped water.

On my next morning's walk, I enjoyed an easy, pleasant walking trail and some very nice views. The trail moved along alternately through forests and up to ridgetops. My friend, Mt. Shasta, was still viewed towards the south, and there were expansive views to the west of Mt. Ashland. During the late morning, I stopped at a seeping spring to load up with water for the next eight-mile stretch.

Reaching the next water at Keene Creek in the early evening, I stopped for the night. My campsite was just a little south of Little Hyatt Reservoir. I enjoyed a most pleasant campsite on the edge of a spacious meadow bordering Keene Creek. My night music was provided by cowbells jingling from somewhere across the meadow. This was indeed cow country; I had walked beside and passed three groups of cows during my day's walk.

After bidding farewell to tranquil Keene Creek Meadow, it was a short walk to Little Hyatt Reservoir, where I enjoyed my mid-morning snack with a view looking across the lake. It was my day for lake views, as moving on I arrived at large Hyatt Lake Reservoir for lunch. There, near the picnic grounds, I found a place with a view of the lake. I enjoyed a leisurely lunch followed by a siesta. Lingering by the lake, I drank in the expansive feeling of space offered by the water view and listened to the lap, lap, lap of the waves. Feeling leisurely and relaxed, I even took time out for some bathing. I was not brave enough to plunge into the cold lake water, but I splashed around in the picnic washroom. I felt so good.

Slowly moving on, I met a friendly couple that gave me trail suggestions. They told me how to detour around a recent logging area. They also, in their enthusiasm, alerted me to watch for a great view from the top of a ridge, where I could again see Mt. Shasta and Mt. Ashland.

Their suggested detour proved to be a good route to follow. I did see evidence of past logging, but avoided current logging activity. I walked through a messy area strewn with downed branches. It did not look nice. I was glad when the trail moved on and climbed up for still another glorious view of Mt. Shasta and Mt. Ashland. I wondered if this would be my last view of Shasta.

I camped just a little off-trail by a seeping creek that ran through Wildcat Glades Meadow. I wondered who might have spotted a wildcat and bestowed the name on the meadow. I would have loved to have a peek at a wildcat, but had no such luck.

On my next morning's walk, I met three southbound Pacific Crest Trail hikers. Kurt from Danville told me he had started at the Canadian border but soon encountered so much snow that he skipped most of Washington and had been hiking through Oregon. He planned to come out from the trail at Seiad Valley. Then, just as I was getting settled for lunch at Grizzly Creek near the Howard Prairie Lake Reservoir, two young men came along who told me they had started at Fish Lake and had been hiking for three days. They planned to continue on to Mexico. They asked me, "Have you had any troubles with blisters?" "No," I replied, "I do not have any blisters; my feet are fine." I added that I did not even have to use any tape and that my boots were very comfortable. They looked at me and at each other and seemed perplexed and puzzled that I was not having foot troubles. As I left them and wished them well, I could not help but wonder if they would make it to the Mexican border. I had some doubts.

On my afternoon climb from Grizzly Peak toward Griffin Pass, I was watchful. I was anxiously looking for an off-trail pond that was described in the guidebook as the "last reliable water until reaching the highway near Fish Lake some 70 miles distant." I planned to camp there. As it turned out, although the directions on how to reach the pond sounded rather complex, I had no trouble spotting it from the trail. Confidently, I pulled off the trail and walked straight to the pond.

After a leisurely water break at the pond's edge and before selecting a campsite, I noticed that the wind was starting to blow up the canyon. The prospect of spending a windy night with no protection from trees or rocks made me uncomfortable. I waited. It was growing colder and windier. I decided not to stay in this windswept place. I was uncertain about how much water I would need to carry, but I made a rough estimate, loaded up my three canteens and my blue water carrier, and hurried back onto the trail. I walked on for about two hours in an exciting windstorm. I circled around the side of Old Baldy Mountain. I knew that after Old Baldy, the trail would start descending. I was walking under gray, dark-looking clouds. Rain was threatening. It grew colder. When I had descended far enough to evade the worst of the sweeping, cold, gusty wind, I spotted a small dip and pulled off the trail. It was still cold. I went to bed almost immediately to keep warm. My supper consisted of a few cold snacks. It had been an exciting walk hurrying away from the storm. I snuggled into my bedroll feeling safe and warm and good about having evaded the worst of the storm.

After the storm, I awoke to see fog intermingled amongst the pine trees. It was cold. I hurried to break camp, then continued on the trail down the mountain. The path wove through a beautiful pine forest carpeted by a floor of green strewn with glorious wildflowers. By midday, the fog had lifted. I came out of the forest onto black-topped Indian Road where I planned to take the alternate route, which led to the Lake of the Woods Resort. There, I would pick up a food package.

I turned onto the roadway and started to walk by the side of the road. Soon, a camper van passed me, turned around, and pulled up beside me. The driver leaned out the window and asked, "Where are you hiking to?" "To Crater Lake," I answered," with a stop tonight at Lake of the Woods to pick up a food package." The woman driver said, "I admire you as a woman walking alone. I could not do this—I would be afraid." She added, "I am from Texas." I waved goodbye to the friendly Texas woman and said, "Perhaps I shall see you at Lake of the Woods."

By mid-afternoon, I reached the south end of Lake of the Woods and turned onto the west shore road. I walked past some pleasant-looking summer homes. Two women walking two black dogs accompanied me part of the way and assured me I was following the right route to Sunset Campground.

Arriving at the campground, my first destination was the water faucet. I had been rationing my water and had just a little left. It felt good to drink as much as I wanted. I then surveyed the campground. It was pleasant—not too crowded or noisy. I parked my pack by a picnic table that I planned to use for my cooking area. Then I picked out a private little bed space just outside the campground boundary and very near the lake. With this small space, I felt very happy.

After dinner, I enjoyed sitting by the shore of this beautiful, deep-blue lake. I gazed out over the water until the last of the boats returned to the docks before retiring to my bedsite.

My morning at Lake of the Woods was pleasant and filled with meeting friendly, helpful people. When I called for my food package, the woman in the store was very cordial and invited me to sign the Pacific Crest Trail register. It was fun to look through the register to see names and read the comments of other hikers. I read the names of the two young men from Oregon, whom I had met last year at Grizzly Meadow, as well as the couple I had met this year at Keene Creek. I then moved to the lunch counter and was enjoying a cold drink while writing postcards when a very friendly, helpful ranger asked me about my walk. He then gave me good, up-to-date advice on how to reach the alternate route to Badger Lake and the Sky Lakes Basin. He added that there were mosquitoes around the lake areas. I was forewarned. As I started walking up the roadway to meet the trailhead, a pleasant young man in a pick-up with a motorbike perched on the back stopped and asked, " Would you like a ride to the trailhead?" I gave my usual response: "I am walking from Mexico to Canada on the Pacific Crest Trail, so I do not want to accept the ride." He then announced proudly that he had just purchased a new motorbike and was on his way to a bike race. I wished him well.

I located the trailhead and happily turned onto the trail. I had decided to take the recommended alternate route through the Sky Lakes wilderness, as it sounded so attractive with its lushly dotted lakes. When I arrived at pleasant Four Mile Lake and stopped for a snack, I met a delightful older couple that had driven up to the lake. They asked me lots of questions about my hike; then the woman asked, "Do you mind if I ask you your age?" "I'm 66," I replied. She responded proudly, "I'm 72." Then she asked, "Aren't you worried about bear?" "No," I replied. "I have not had any encounters with bears. " She told me that her son had hiked in Alaska's Brooks Range and had come very close to a grizzly bear. He did not have a gun; he just stood quietly in the doorway of his tent and took a picture of the grizzly bear. She said, "I was so thankful when he arrived home safely."

As we ended our pleasant conversation, she gave me her address and asked if I would write her a postcard assuring her that I had come out from the trail safely. I responded to her friendly concern by promising that I would. She also invited me to stop by their home near Klamath Falls. She was so pleasant, I felt that I had grown to know her and that I would really like to visit them.

Upon my return home, I sent them a postcard and a photo I had taken at Four Mile Lake. In response, I received the following welcome letter:

Dear Eleanor Guilford,

It was nice of you to send us the picture taken at Four Mile Lake. I'm glad we met you there. We thought of you the other night when we saw some very beautiful pictures of Crater Lake. Everything was covered with snow. The snowfall in December set a record.

If you take another trip this summer, please let us know about it. If you are up this way again, please stop by.

Sincerely,
Miriam Crosslin

I hiked through the pleasant woods to Badger Lake, where I made camp. As I approached the lake, I encountered the familiar buzz of mosquitoes. I found a high, level platform for my bedsite where there was a gentle breeze—hopefully, enough breeze to blow the mosquitoes away. From my bedsite platform, I enjoyed a view of the lake during dusk and sunset.

From my Badger Lake campsite the alternate trail through the Sky Lakes wilderness led on to a treasure-trove of lakes. I was passing more lakes than I would have believed possible. On my morning's walk, I passed Long Lake, Center Lake, Island Lake, and Red Lake. I had to admit, however, that this remarkable string of lakes did harbor an abundance of mosquitoes. The guidebook had warned that mosquitoes would be a problem until mid-July. Surprise! They were still there in abundance on August 13th. To manage in their midst, I covered up with long sleeves and my turtleneck T-shirt and then painted my face and hands with Cutter's Bug Repellant. It worked quite well; however, the mosquitoes were thick and I never got used to their noisy, high-pitched hum as they swarmed around my

head, then backed off when they came close to the bug repellant. I found it difficult to stop for a leisurely lunch amidst
their noisy humming. I ate hurriedly, standing up.

On my afternoon's walk, I passed Deep Lake, Lake Nota-
sha, Heavenly Twin Lakes, Lake Land, and large Horse Shoe
Lake before making camp at beautiful Margurette Lake. Arriving at the lake around 5 pm, I had plenty of time to select
a campsite. I found a site with an open-window view looking
across the lake at a high, granite-colored rock cliff.

I took time to wash socks and study my map. I was enjoying my leisurely, relaxing evening time propped up against a
tree near my kitchen, when suddenly, swiftly and unexpectedly,
a storm moved in. First, I saw a streak of lightning followed by
a thunder blast. Then came the rain, a heavy rain—a virtual
cloudburst. It happened so suddenly, I was unprepared. I wondered if I had closed my bivouac sack and plastic bag containing my flashlight and other night articles? My bedroom was
about 50 feet away from my kitchen. Standing under a large fir
tree, I was somewhat sheltered. I looked toward my bedroom,
but decided not to run over to it for an inspection because
the cloudburst was so heavy I did not want to move from the
shelter of the tree. I waited until the heavy rain had subsided,
then hurried over to my bedroom. To my dismay, my bivouac
sack opening had not been closed, and water had entered my
sleeping area. Anxiously, I proceeded to make an inspection. I
discovered a puddle in a low spot between my bivouac sack and
my bedroll. Thankfully, the damage was not great. There was
just a small, damp spot. Then I inspected my plastic bag, which
had not been shut. It, too, had a puddle. By then, the rain had
stopped, so I went to work repairing the damage by cleaning
and wiping out the two puddle areas. Then, feeling cautious, I
made preparations for the possibility of further rain. I got out

rope and strung a tarp above my bed. Now, I felt prepared for more rain. I had learned a lesson: I would never again leave my bivouac sack without first closing the top.

Now that I was well prepared for rain, the sky cleared. The setting sun poked through the cloud cover, and patches of blue sky appeared. I sat watching the light fade into the lake.

I arose early in the morning and did not take time to dry my somewhat damp bedding. I wanted to start early. I was going to climb 7500-foot Devil's Peak.

By midday, I had reached the trail junction where the alternate Sky Lake Trail joined the Pacific Crest Trail, and I turned onto the Pacific Crest Trail. By early afternoon, I reached Devil's Peak saddle and took the recommended climb up Devil's Peak. The ascent went well. I soon gained enough altitude to leave the mosquitoes behind. From the peak, a splendid view opened up. I could see Mt. McLoughlin, Mt. Thielsen, the upper Klamath Lake basin, and the mountains surrounding the southern rim of Crater Lake. It was well worth the climb.

Returning to the trail at a saddle, I soon approached a steep snowbank. There, a young couple was standing upright and balancing with their boots on, joyously sliding down the soft snow. It looked like fun. I was slightly tempted to try it, but caution took over and I decided that it would be hard to balance with my pack on. I proceeded down the snowbanks slowly, and finally arrived at the bottom safely. I then detoured off-trail half a mile. After a stop for a refreshing snowcone, I arrived at scenic Cliff Lake. I stopped to look. Here was still another beautiful lake, embellished with two cliffs reflecting into the water. Selecting a pleasant campsite, I strung up a line to dry my damp groundcloth, wiping rags, and other items. With a little breeze, they were quickly dry.

As I was washing my feet, a backcountry ranger came along

and stopped to talk. He told me about the trail up ahead. He was interested in my Gore Tex bivouac sack and remarked that he liked to travel light.

As I was viewing the lake after supper, the breeze died down, and suddenly, the mosquitoes moved in. I hurried for cover, getting into my bed and zipping up my no-see-them insect screen that is attached to my bivouac sack.

From Cliff Lake, the next morning I walked an easy, pleasant trail and reached water at Honeymoon Creek. I had decided to take the Bunchgrass Trail to McKie Meadow, which the ranger at Cliff Lake had recommended. He told me that I would have more water taking this route than if I stayed on the Pacific Crest Trail. It was a little-used trail, and I found it interesting and enjoyable. The first part of the trail seemed almost like hiking cross-country. Later, I came to the better-used Meadow Trail. I stopped for a late lunch at Solace Camp Meadow. This peaceful meadow offered a spacious view, and I enjoyed a leisurely lunch stop. I then walked on to McKie Meadow where I planned to camp. There, I met a ranger standing beside his horse near a broken-down cabin. When I commented that I had planned to camp at McKie Meadow, he replied rather sternly, "A trail crew will be camping here. You better move on. You can find water three-fourths of a mile down the trail, and you can camp there." I was puzzled by his insistence that I move on and by the seriousness of his request. Dutifully, I agreed and proceeded on my way. In three-fourths of a mile, I came to a stagnant pool. One glance at it and I quickly decided that I did not want to stop at this place. I kept walking on. Next, I came to a series of dried-up ravines in a dense, bushy area, and I was back into mosquito habitat. Out came my remaining Cutter's Bug Repellant. Although it was getting late, I still felt good and kept walking until I arrived at Stuart Falls Camp around 8 pm. This was a very picturesque location, with a small trickling waterfall. Hurriedly, I located a camping spot within view of the waterfalls. I collected my water, made my supper in the dimming light, and climbed into my bedroll.

After quickly studying my map in the morning, I concluded that this would be my coming-out day. I would be a day ahead of schedule, thanks to hurrying through the mosquito area and to the ranger at McKie Meadow who insisted I move on. (Later, still puzzled by his insistence that I move on, I mentioned this experience to a ranger friend at home. He explained to me that the trail crew may have been made up of prisoners who are used for trail work in the summer. I hadn't thought of that possibility.) Walking ahead on a pleasant, easy trail, I soon arrived at the Pacific Crest Trail junction and turned onto the trail. The trail route first lead through a dry area where small, stunted trees grew, then ascended to 6500 feet. Looking ahead, I was facing a sizeable snowbank, which blocked the trail. I stopped and surveyed the scene. Finally, I saw a trail marker sticking out through the top of the snow and carefully proceeded on my way. In all, I passed nearly a dozen sizeable snowbanks before arriving at the highway crossing—Highway 62, which would lead to Crater Lake.

In 1983, the Pacific Crest Trail did not go to Crater Lake. At that time, the guidebook recommended an alternate route, stating that no hiker would want to miss this special, spectacular deep-blue lake. More recently, the trail has been re-routed to take hikers to the lake view.

Arriving at the highway in the early afternoon, I turned onto the blacktop. It was an easy but hot and tedious road walk to reach the south rim of Crater Lake. At the large lakeside store, I stopped for a cold drink and an ice cream cone, which I enjoyed while viewing the spectacular, appealing, deep-blue lake. Refreshed, I decided it was time to seek a ride to the nearest bus stop. I could go either south to Klamath Falls or north to Medford.

Looking around the large parking lot, I decided not to put up my "To Bus" sign, but decided instead to directly ask a driver of a departing car. I approached a young couple climbing into a pick-up truck, and they were happy to give me a ride to Klamath Falls. I arrived at the Greyhound depot around 8 pm. I had planned to return to the Ashland Shakespearean Theater to see Cymbeline. As there were no buses departing for Ashland until around midnight, I decided to head for the nearby Winema Hotel, a big, old-style, interesting-looking structure with a 24-hour coffee shop. I enjoyed a good meal and an even more enjoyable shower at the hotel.

In the morning, after a satisfying breakfast in the hotel's coffee shop, I phoned my friend, Carol to let her know that I'd come out safely. Then, I phoned my brother, but the line was busy. Calling a second time, my brother replied, "I am glad you called. Mother died Tuesday night. The funeral will be held on Friday." I was stunned. I went into action. I found a helpful travel agent near the hotel who quickly arranged plane reservations for me to fly to Minneapolis on Thursday. I would arrive in time for the funeral. I boarded the next bus for San Francisco.

On the bus trip, there was time to reflect. Where was I on Tuesday night when my mother passed away? I was camped at tranquil Stuart's Falls. I remembered that some time during the night, I had awakened with a jolt, as if I'd had some kind of fearful dream. Was this the moment of my mother's passing?

On the way to the funeral, I reflected. I was thankful that I had come out from the trail in time to join my family in bidding my mother goodbye. At 97, approaching her 98th birthday, it was time for her to go. She had been slowly fading away. Nevertheless, I knew I would miss her.

CRATER LAKE

Chapter 22
Crater Lake to Santiam Pass
August 1984 • 168 Miles

Nature is always lovely, invincible, glad, whatever is done and suffered by her creatures. All scars she heals, whether in rocks or water or sky or hearts. — *John Muir*

The highlights that remain etched in my memory of this central Oregon section include enchanting, deep-blue-purple Crater Lake, the sky-piercing, high, jagged peaks of volcanic Mt. Thielsen, the tranquil silhouette of Diamond Peak as viewed across the Diamond View Lake, and the attractive charm of the volcanic figures dotting the Three Sisters Wilderness.

This year's summer walk had a special leisurely feeling for me. It was my first summer without a set date to return to work. I retired, after 40 years as a professional social worker, on August 1st. A special sense of freedom surrounded my walk

Getting to Trailhead was a trip adventure in itself. In early August, the Guilford family reunion was held at the home of Leon and Alice Guilford on Orcas Island, one of the San Juan Islands north of Seattle. This event was most enjoyable and attended by some 70 Guilford cousins. It was my first trip to the attractive San Juan Islands. My indirect route to Trailhead was by way of Amtrak from San Francisco to Seattle, by car and ferry to Orcas Island, and a return trip on Amtrak from Seattle to Chemult, the town nearest to Crater Lake on the Amtrak line.

Boarding Amtrak in Oakland after riding on a connecting bus from San Francisco offered a challenge. The platform was crowded with noisy, shoving people. The Amtrak Starlight Train, which originates in Los Angeles, was late—as often was the case. Upon arrival, the conductor announced, "Pick a seat, but I don't think any are left. You have to ride in the lounge car until a seat opens up." As I entered the coach car, a door opened on the lower level, and I saw some empty seats. Exploring, I walked in and sat in front of a well dressed, white-haired woman. Inquiring about the vacant seat, I learned that this small section of 12 seats was reserved for "elderly and handicapped." Then I thought to myself, "I'm riding on a Senior-rate ticket. I'm eligible at age 66, and I have an I.D. I should be eligible to ride in this section." When the conductor arrived and I showed him my ticket, I repeated that I was a Senior. He hurriedly punched my ticket and replied, "You may have to move if we board some handicapped passengers. They have priority." In the end, I rode all the way to Seattle in this quiet, small section. I experienced many enjoyable conversations with other Senior passengers. They were interested in my walking trip. Admittedly, wearing my khaki outfit and backpacking boots, I looked a little different from my fellow passengers. I had discovered a new Amtrak accommodation. On subsequent trips, I sought out the elderly and handicapped section whenever possible.

On my return trip from Seattle on Amtrak, I enjoyed gazing out the window at interesting landscapes in Washington and northern Oregon. The train first wanders along Puget Sound on its journey to Portland. I again rode in the elderly and handicapped section. A very pleasant woman from Corvallis pointed out some of the sights. From the train window, I saw the outline of sawed-off looking Mt. St. Helens, which had erupted four years before. Nearing Portland, I caught a glimpse of snow-capped Mt. Hood. Shortly after the train stopped at Eugene, Oregon, the route turned east and climbed up to the Cascade Pass before descending toward Klamath Falls.

It was dark before our arrival at Chemult. Before reaching the Chemult station, a serious-faced conductor asked me, "Are you planning to get off at Chemult?" "Yes," I replied. "Is anybody going to meet you?" he asked. "No." I replied. Then he said, "Then you had better stay on the train to Klamath Falls." I was puzzled. I asked him if there were motels in Chemult and he affirmed that there were. He insisted it would be hard to get to Crater Lake from Chemult. I asked if there were any Greyhound buses running from Klamath Falls to Crater Lake. He replied that, as far as he knew, there were none—only charter tour buses. I thought about it and decided to stick with my plan to get off at Chemult. When he came back, I tried to explain that it was usually easier to find a ride from a small town than from a big city. He scowled a look of disapproval. I stuck to my original plan and disembarked at Chemult.

After the train stopped, a nice-looking, young, female train attendant put down a step for me to get off. It was a long step to the ground. When my foot touched the ground, I was standing on wiggly, loose, large gravel pebbles. At 9:30 pm, it was dark. No one else had gotten off the train. I was beginning to sense some of the conductor's reluctance to have me get off in Chemult.

Should I have stayed on? I didn't want to go all the way to Klamath Falls. I found my way on the dark path to the nearest Texaco gas station, where a very helpful young woman called the City Motel and asked them to give me a room with a good rate. At the nearby motel, the friendly manager told me I could have a room for $15.00. She then suggested that I watch a movie on TV and turned on a big TV set. Although I seldom watch TV movies, I was grateful for her courtesy. I watched a Japanese movie, which kept me up very late, past my usual bedtime.

After a filling, satisfying breakfast of scrambled eggs, potatoes, and toast, I took up my post by the gas station to seek a ride to Crater Lake. Soon, I learned that most of the cars weren't headed for Crater Lake. My ride begging was not producing results. At the gas station, I approached a sympathetic woman forest ranger who listened but told me she was going only to a nearby junction. That gave me an idea. Why not ask for a ride at the forest station office? I trudged down the road about a half-mile to the office and stated my plans. "We don't go to Crater Lake. It's a National Park and we are Forest Service." Of course, why hadn't I thought of that? Back to the gas station. Again, my progress was exceedingly slow. I was starting to hear the voice of the concerned trained conductor, "You had better go to Klamath Falls." Then, I turned on my positive thoughts and said to myself, "I have all day. I will find a ride." Shortly thereafter, around 11:30 am, my pleas were successful. I found a ride with a young service couple who were moving to a new base. They waited while I ran back to the Texaco station where I had left my pack. At last, I was headed for Crater Lake.

Arriving at the lake, I paused to gaze at the attractive lake again. It was as magnetic as ever with its deep-purple sheen. I then sought out the park's ranger station and obtained my wilderness permit. As I was eating a little lunch near the hotel, uniformed members of the National Guard arrived and started setting up musical instruments by a small grandstand. They were preparing to give a concert. Although I was somewhat tempted to stay to hear their band, the urge to hit the trail was still stronger. I started walking on along the west side of the lake. After a long, last look at the peaceful, dark-purple-blue lake, I turned west onto the Lightning Trail, which would take me to the Pacific Crest Trail junction.

My afternoon walk led into a forest. Late in the day, I met a day hiker who recommended a campsite near Bybee Creek. I arrived there around 6:30 pm and set up camp in a comfortable spot within the sound of gurgling Bybee Creek.

During the night, I awoke to hear a new and different sound—a stomping of feet. When I clapped my hands, the creature responded with a distinctive snort and then a bugle-like sound. This sound was different from a deer's, and I wondered what animal was making this sound. In the morning, as I started north on the trail, I caught a glimpse of a huge animal with a shiny, light-brown rear about the size of a horse. Now I knew that the mysterious animal I had heard stomping and buggling in the night was an elk. I had read about elk in Oregon, and now I knew I had entered elk country.

I was now walking on the Pacific Crest Trail, which I had met near the Bybee Springs Campground. My walk north was mostly through forest. I was watchful, as I planned to take the recommended alternate trail, which would offer more water and scenery and would lead to the Diamond Lake Lodge where I would pick up a food package.

By midday, I found the turn-off and headed northwest. By evening, I reached an idyllic campsite, which I assumed was Gushing Springs, as described in the 1983 Guide Book Supplement. Looking around, I saw a sign reading "Boundary Springs." Boundary or Gushing, it proved to be a veritable gushing stream of water surrounded by a small, pleasant meadow full of brightly colored wildflowers. I enjoyed my evening's campsite, complete with water music from the gushing stream.

On my morning's walk on the alternate trail, I reached a small stream. My map showed that this was the Rogue River—a well-known river for rafting, which reaches the sea at Gold Beach. How exciting to be walking along the bank of the Rogue River near its beginning. By midday, the trail left the riverbank and crossed a busy highway. I reached the south side of Large Diamond Lake and stopped for lunch by the side of the lake at Broken Arrow Campground.

My afternoon's walk skirted the eastern edge of the lake, passing noisy, camper-filled campgrounds. I reached the Diamond Lake Lodge at the north end of the lake a little too late to retrieve my food package from the post office. I spent the remainder of the afternoon writing postcards and watching the boats moving about on the lake. I ordered a B.L.T. sandwich in the small resort restaurant. When it was time to find a place to spend the night, I searched up and down, but could find no good hiding places with a view looking across the lake. I then searched around the back of the lodge and finally succeeded in finding a somewhat secluded corner. My secluded corner was not at all scenic, and I spent a noisy night. People kept coming and going in and out of the lodge until very late. I was eager to hit the trail again in the morning and leave the noisy crowd.

After collecting my food package in the morning and re-packing my backpack, I threaded my way carefully through a confusing route that led through the resort's corral with its dusty labyrinth of horse-trampled trails. I eventually found the sought-after Tipsoo Trail. My destination was Tipsoo Peak and the junction with the Pacific Crest Trail.

On the climb up, I reached water and an enjoyable lunch site by the swiftly splashing water of Theilsen Creek around midday. After lunch, the climb grew steeper. I experienced the phenomenon of the "receding peak." I would periodically peek upwards and think I was looking at the peak's top. Then, when I arrived at the perceived top, I would look up and see another, higher top. I tried to play games with myself. I would say, "I'm not going to peek again until I reach the top." But of course, it was hard not to peek, and I would look up periodically. By late afternoon, I finally reached the high point—the real top. I had ascended around 2400 feet from the Diamond Lake Shore. The views were splendid. Dominating the skyscape to the south was the needle-like, volcanic Mt. Theilsen.

After catching my breath and feeling fulfilled by the view, I started my descent. I reached the junction of the Tipsoo and Pacific Crest Trails and turned north. In about an hour, I reached a spring and made camp. For my pre-dinner drinks, I mixed snow with powdered fruit juice. It tasted good. I spent a pleasant night.

From my camp on the small saddle beyond Tipsoo Peak, I drifted down switchbacks to descend to Lake Maidu. I arrived there in time for a late lunch. Originally, I had planned to camp at Lake Maidu, which was on the old Oregon Skyline Trail, about a mile off the newer Pacific Crest Trail. I inspected the old eight-person camp shelter. It was no longer inviting. The guidebook featured a picture of a hiker sitting out a storm in the doorway of the shelter. By the time of my visit, the roof had fallen in on one side, and inside the floor was covered with debris. I turned away and walked down to the lakefront where I enjoyed a pleasant view looking across the blue, rippling water of the small lake. There were two groups of campers with tents near the lake. I met two hikers from Kansas, whom I had encountered at the Diamond Lake Resort. We compared notes. They had walked through a rainstorm around Tipsoo Peak. I had not. I felt so lucky that I had missed it. After my leisurely lunch, I looked around. I was growing restless, and the camp area was a little noisy. I felt like moving on but did not want to walk to the next water at Tolo Camp, some six-and-a-half miles further. I pondered what to do then decided I would pack water for supper and breakfast and walk on. After filling my water bag, I climbed up the nearby ridge and soon met the Pacific Crest Trail. I then descended to a small saddle where I found a little, level place and happily spent the night.

In the morning, I had an easy descent to reach water at the springs near Tolo Camp. It was then an easy traverse along the slopes of Tolo Mountain to Windigo Pass. A group of hikers approached from a trailhead parking lot on the Cascade Road near the pass. "I forgot and left my permit in the car," announced one of the women as we were about to meet. As we drew closer, she looked at me and said, "I thought that you were a ranger." I was surprised and amused, as it never occurred to me that my traditional khaki hiking gear looked that much like that of a ranger. We both had a good laugh. They were walking in to camp at Tolo Camp.

By evening, I reached Nip and Tuck Lakes. These charming lakes are special and different. In high water, they become one lake. In the summer, as the water recedes, a grassy peninsula rises up and separates the water into two lakes. I explored the lakeshore and found an attractive campsite near the peninsula. This campsite offered such an enjoyable, scenic view and ambience.

During the night, the wind came up and it grew cold. I went to bed early to keep warm. In the morning, I awoke to find frozen water in my little plastic water basin.

After sun-drying my frost-covered bivouac sac, I took a last look at the peaceful lakes and started my day's journey. The trail climbed up to a ridge, where I found a refreshing view looking south toward Mt. Theilsen. For the rest of the day, my walk led onto an easy descent. The trail passed several lakes. First, I passed Oldenberg Lake and then the two Bingham Lakes. I then arrived at the small Pinewan Lake where, in a forest clearing, I found a sign that read, "Pinewan Immigrant Trail 1853." I read that the trail in this section follows an immigrant road that was built and used by the Elliot wagon train in October 1853. I tried to visualize how slow moving it would have been to travel by wagon train.

Next, I arrived at large Crescent Lake, which can be reached by road and was busy with campers and fishermen. I decided to walk further, in hopes of avoiding the crowds. I threaded my way through the busy Whitefish Horse Camp. When I asked a large lady in the horse camp for directions for reaching the Whitefish Creek Trail, she asked, "Are you going to hike this late in the day?" I smiled and said I would just be going a little further. I was glad to move on and walked until I found a quiet campsite near Whitefish Creek.

I was eager to start on my walk in the morning, as it was a food package pick-up day for me. I moved along easily on a trail that led mostly through forest. I stopped to take a photo at the edge of Diamond View Lake, which offers a splendid view looking across the lake at volcanic Diamond Peak. I had entered the Diamond Peak Wilderness. After climbing up a small ridge, I started watching diligently for a crossroad that would lead me to the Shelter Cover store and post office. I did not want to miss it. I was eager to reach my food package.

Happily, I found the crossroad. After a short walk, I reached the railroad tracks—the route of Amtrak. I paused to make a mental note of the railroad markers—a switchbox and an overhead signal. I wanted to be able to gaze out the window on my many subsequent Amtrak rides. I would say to myself and to anyone else who was interested, "This is where I crossed the railroad tracks when I was walking the Pacific Crest Trail on my way to Lake Odell."

I followed the road to the lake and to the Shelter Cove Resort. Happily, my food package had arrived safely. The resort store was a busy place, with lots of boat people coming in and out from the nearby dock. I enjoyed a leisurely stop at the store—having a cold drink, repacking my backpack, writing postcards, and phoning home.

Refreshed and rested by late afternoon, I hiked around the west end of the lake and climbed up onto a bluff above the lake, where I found a delightful, small campsite. From this bluffsight, I spent an evening watching the boats going in and out across the lake. When the moon rose in a clear sky, I watched the moon's reflection on the water.

All through the night, I heard trains with their wheels rhythmically clanging while spinning along the tracks. I wondered why I could not see the trains in the morning light from my high lookout. I was puzzled. I studied the map and finally discovered that there was a long tunnel near the bluff's end of the lake.

In the morning, I soon reached the junction of the Pacific Crest Trail and turned onto it. The trail switched back down to the crossing of wide Highway 58, which runs from Eugene to Chemult. The crossing was just east of Willamette Pass. A new section of the Pacific Crest Trail starts here. I carefully wove my way through the large trailhead parking lot and finally found the trail's resumption at the north end of the lot.

By late morning, I came to the first of three attractive Rosary Lakes—South Rosary, Middle Rosary, and North Rosary. At South Rosary Lake, I stopped for a view and a snack. How appropriate, I thought, that I should arrive at the Rosary Lakes on

August 15th, a day honoring Mary—the Feast of the Assumption. By noon, I arrived at deep-blue Middle Rosary Lake. A group of enthusiastic, young campers had pitched their tents nearby. I met their leader and learned they were from St. Peter's Youth Group in Eugene, Oregon. He told me this was the first camping experience for many of the young people and that they were learning a lot and having a lot of fun.

Moving along on an easy, pleasant trail, I went off-trail a fourth of a mile to camp at scenic Bobby Lake. There, I met another Pacific Crest Trail hiker—Mark June from Alaska. After supper, he invited me join his campfire, and we enjoyed comparing notes about our hiking experiences. He had started at the Mexican border in April, was averaging around 20 miles a day, and planned to finish at the Canadian border in late September. He told me how his summer's hiking experience and his respite from work allowed him time to think about a decision he was facing. As a recent law-school graduate, he had spent a year in a small law office in Alaska. He was facing a decision: "Should I join a large, well-known firm in one of the Eastern cities, as many of my colleagues had done, or should I remain in the small, interesting office in Alaska?" At this time, he was favoring Alaska.

On awakening, I was greeted by a glorious, intriguing scene. The lake was shrouded in a misty fog that was steaming upwards. Slowly, the sun started creeping through the mist, creating an ethereal, mystical mood. I contemplated the immense variety of nature's displays. Some scenes are still and peaceful, other scenes are constantly evolving like this scene of the changing, rising mist. These splendid displays of nature are the experiences that bring me back to the wilderness again and again.

I moved onwards slowly, climbing up a ridge from which I could see snow-topped Diamond Peak and the large, long Waldo

Lake. I reached Charlton Lake by lunchtime and enjoyed the view looking across the water towards Gerdine Butte. I pondered my plans for the afternoon. I didn't want to count on walking to the next lake —Taylor Lake about 6 miles distant—but I wasn't ready to stop for the night at Charlton Lake. I decided to carry water for the night. During my afternoon walk, I encountered some annoying mosquitoes. I took out my Sierra Club songbook and started singing. It helped me to forget my tiredness and lifted my spirits. By evening camp time, I reached a clearing, a dry gulch, and made camp. I was surrounded by corn lilies. Although not an inspiring spot, I spent a comfortable night.

My walk the following day was through forests and beside lakes. It seemed to me that the trail in Central Oregon will be remembered by an abundance of forests and lakes. In the morning, I skirted along the shores of Taylor Lake, Irish Lake, Riffle Lake, and two large, unnamed lily ponds. Near Riffle Lake, I entered the well-known Three Sisters Wilderness. Next came Brahma Lake, Jezebel Lake, Stormy Lake, and Blaze Lake, followed by a string of unnamed pools, before reaching Lake 5678. This was not the end of my walk from lake to lake. Soon, I was drifting down a ridge to Tadpole Lake. A little later, as I entered Willamette National Forest, I came to Desane Lake, followed by Mink Lake.

The next group of lakes are seen as making a necklace for the South Sister Volcano: S Lake, Mac Lake, Merril Lake, and Horseshoe Lake. How they all acquired their names would make an interesting story in itself.

My plan was to camp at Cliff Lake, which was noted for its cliff view and many pleasant campsites. Drifting along, I felt that it was time to stop and read my map. Could it be that I had passed the Cliff Lake turn-off? I was dismayed. I must have been daydreaming—drifting along on the easy, forest-lined trail. Thus, instead of camping at scenic Cliff Lake, I ended up camping by a stagnant pond. I didn't feel like backtracking to the Cliff Lake trail. Instead of a campsite with a lake view, here I was camped by a shallow, stagnant pond. It was, however, quiet and peaceful. Perhaps Cliff Lake would have been noisy, as it did have the potential for attracting crowds with its numerous campsites and a shelter.

During my morning's walk from my quiet space on the stagnant pond, I soon met a southbound lone hiker. As he approached, I noticed that his head was covered with a mosquito net, and on the net by his forehead was perched a big mosquito. I began to prepare psychologically for an upcoming mosquito invasion. Pausing to exchange trail notes, the hiker told me he had come into the trail at McKenzie Pass and was planning to complete the 75-mile stretch between McKenzie Pass and Willamette Pass. He assured me that I would enjoy the Three Sisters Wilderness scenery.

Near Dumbbell Lake, as I was having a snack, I met a Boy Scout group that was camped by the lake. I began to realize that, after not passing any hikers the previous day, I was drawing near to a popular area—the Three Sisters Wilderness.

Towards midday, I climbed up steep switchbacks to the top of the slope near Koosah Mountain. It was slow going toward the top, as there had been a blowdown and fallen trees covered the trail. Soon I heard the humming sound of a saw and came to where two trail workers were laboring with handsaws. I said to them, "I'm glad you're cleaning the path for me." One of the trail workers looked up and replied, "This is hard, slow work. The Forest Service won't let us use power saws." He was obviously unhappy with this policy. I had read that it is the policy not to use mechanical machinery in wilderness areas. I rather like this policy.

Reaching the top of the slope, I had a glorious view. It was my first clear view of the fabled Three Sisters—the South Sister came into view.

Drifting down the slope, I met still another group. I learned that they were from Outward Bound and that they were camped a little to the north of Koosah Mountain.

That evening, I camped at enchanting Sisters Mirror Lake. The lake is known as a photographer's delight, as it offers a reflection, when the water is calm, of the volcanic South Sister peak. As it was a little hazy, I did not see the reflection during my evening's camp. However, I enjoyed the pleasant view looking across the lake. Reviewing my trail notes, I was excited at the prospect of viewing more of the fabled Sister Volcanos on my next day's hike. My map showed that I would be viewing, from south to north, The Wife, South Sister, The Husband, Middle Sister, North Sister, and finally Little Brother. I wondered who had the idea of naming this intriguing small group of volcanoes.

After a leisurely breakfast, I paused to absorb a last view of the tranquil Sisters Mirror Lake before starting up the trail. Soon I was greeted by a friendly couple that caught up with me—Sonny and Cathy. They had also camped at Sisters Mirror Lake. They proved to be two of the most delightful trail companions I had ever met. Walking together all during the morning, they let me know that they were on their honeymoon. They were so enthusiastic and interested in the walk and in their total surroundings. The morning's walk led across grassy meadows, which opened up countless views and silhouettes of the many Three Sisters Volcanos. Suddenly, Sonny stopped and spoke quietly. He had spotted a herd of elk moving along the trail ahead of us. He guessed that the elk had started to rut and that a bull was gathering his harem and fighting off younger, challenging bulls. The rich brown color of the elk made a splendid foreground against the distant views of the Sisters Volcanos.

As we walked along, we shared lots of ideas about wilderness hiking. Sonny was interested in learning more and acquiring new backpacking equipment. Before we parted, I promised to send him some of my most-used backpacking catalogs. We parted at midday, as Sonny and Cathy were taking a trail that would lead them toward South Sister, where they planned to do some climbing.

I stopped for lunch near Separation Creek where I enjoyed a splendid view looking up toward the gently sloping Little Sister. Soon I encountered an energetic woman ranger wearing a backpack who came striding down the trail. I explained that I couldn't find a permit form in the last registration box. She smiled and, much to my relief, replied that some of the boxes were for registration only and did not issue permits. She assured me that my last permit was still valid. Oregon, at the time of my hike, relied primarily on self-issuing permits, which made me feel a little uncertain as to whether I had a valid permit for the area in which I was hiking.

By evening, I made camp in an ideal view spot near Linton Creek. Looking around, I discovered a tree-lined bedroom. Looking out from my bedroom and kitchen I could see the Middle Sister, South Sister, and Husband. After dinner, I was treated to an orange-red sunset and caught some of the afterglow on the South Sister. What a glorious day of views.

Shortly after leaving my pleasant, scenic campsite near Linton Creek, I spied a group of llamas a few yards in from the trail. I stopped to watch. The llamas, with their quizzical faces and colorful harnesses, presented an interesting scene. I took a photo. It appeared that the campers using the llamas had completed packing their gear on the animals and were ready to

396   One Hundred Mile Summers –

THREE SISTERS ROCK MESA

start moving down the trail. Their leader was patting and coaxing the llamas. They hissed and stomped but were not moving forward. I didn't wait to learn the outcome. I had read about llamas being used for trail pack animals, and from the train window I had seen very large llama farms. This was the first time, however, that I had met a llama party on the trail.

My morning's walk, in contrast to the smooth and easy trail of the previous day, presented some rocky ascents and descents. It was also a busy trail. I passed more hikers who were coming in from a nearby trailhead on the McKenzie Pass Highway than I had encountered during any day of my walk. "Where are you headed?" asked a group of three older men. "To Santiam Pass," I replied. When I mentioned that I planned to stop at the Santiam Lodge before boarding the bus for home, they replied, "You'll like the lodge—the people are very friendly and hospitable to hikers."

I wanted to reach to 50-foot-high Obsidian Falls for lunch.

Upon reaching this destination, I picked out a level spot with a view looking toward the falls. I was so pleased with my view point. Soon, however, my peaceful lunch spot grew crowded with hikers. Most of them were clad in t-shirts and shorts and were kept very busy slapping mosquitoes. After lunch, I climbed to the top of the falls. There I met two young, slender men who were also clad in t-shirts and shorts. They had stopped to smoke cigarettes. "We are hiking to Tahoe," they announced. I wondered whether these smokers, with lots of climbs and mileage ahead of them, would make it to Tahoe. I had my doubts.

My afternoon walk led across crackling glass obsidian and then across lava flows as the trail skirted the side of Collier Cone. The wavy, black lava rock looked as if it had flowed out of its cone very recently. I thought to myself that this was an example of how the earth is still constantly evolving.

By evening, I reached a pleasant meadow near Mini Scott Spring and camped. My view stretched across more lava flows.

By early evening it had grown cold. To add warmth, I made a vapor barrier from a large black garbage bag by cutting holes for my head and arms. It helped. While hiking in the Sierras, I had used a heavier, Eddie Bauer sleeping bag. When it grew warm when I was travelling in northern California, I sewed a lighter bag from Holubar sleeping bag kit. It was a fun project. Now I was writing in my notebook to remind myself that I needed to add more feathers to my bag for next year's trip.

From my grassy bedroom near Mini Scott Spring, I started to climb as the trail switched back up and curved around the Yapoah Crater. Views opened up looking north toward Mt. Washington and volcanic Three Fingered Jack. Descending, the trail soon led across black cinder cones. The sound of my boot step was crunch, crunch, crunch. As I navigated across the uneven, black, sharp rocks, I kept saying to myself, "Take care."

I could easily turn an ankle on this uneven path. It was slow going. I also thought that this trail was hard on boots. It could cut into boot leather quickly. At the same time, I felt thankful a trail had been made across the lava bed, rough as it was. How hard it would have been to walk on these cinder rocks if they had not been somewhat smoothed into a trail bed.

Around noon, I had a brief respite from the crunch, crunch, crunch as I went off-trail to reach Lava Lake Campground. This was a lunch and water stop. I measured out my portion of water for the remainder of the afternoon, supper, and breakfast in preparation for a long, waterless stretch ahead. While adding water, I was thankful that my pack was growing lighter as I neared the end of my journey.

Returning to the trail, I again returned to crunch, crunch, crunch as I crossed on Lava Flow Trail. Finally, I reached the McKenzie Highway—Highway 20. At the highway crossing, I took a recommended detour to visit the Dee Wright Observatory. I climbed the rock-constructed steps of the lookout tower and, from the top, enjoyed still another clear view of Mt. Washington and jagged Three Fingered Jack.

Returning to the trail leading north of the highway, I soon encountered more cinder-cone walking as the trail led up and across the slopes of the Belknap Crater. Again, I reminded myself to take care. In addition to the uneven, rocky path, I was buffeted by gusty winds. I felt so good when the trail finally descended and led into a forested area. I found a level, sheltered spot for my campsite.

I awoke in my quiet forest bedroom with anticipation. Would I reach Santiam Pass, my coming out-destination, by nightfall? I estimated that it was about 13 miles. My next benchmark was to obtain water at Coldwater Spring. The trail continued through forests as it skirted around, but well below, the brown tooth-like top of Mt. Washington. Occasionally, I had a peek at its top through the trees.

Nearing Coldwater Spring, a lone hiker came down the trail and announced, "Coldwater Spring has run dry, but you can gather water from the snowbanks." I thanked him. I truly appreciated this helpful advice. On arrival at Coldwater Spring, I spotted a dry pipe protruding from the spring area. I did not worry, as I found an ample snowbank on a slope above the spring. For my mid-morning break, I mixed Wyler's lemon powder with snow slush. It tasted so good—cold and flavorful. I gathered additional snow slush in a plastic bag for my lunch and my afternoon's water supply.

My afternoon's walk, in contrast to yesterday's, continued on an easy path through the forest. In the afternoon, I stopped for a snack leaning against a tree and looking across a shallow lily pond. I was excited about coming out. I felt good but oh, so very dirty. It would feel nice to have a bath and get into clean clothes. At the same time, I felt my usual reluctance to leave the peace and quiet of the wilderness. I would miss the music of the wind in the trees and the sparkle of the starlit sky.

Not long after my rest stop at the quiet lily pond, I started hearing a familiar non-wilderness sound —that of highway traffic. Slowly, it grew louder and louder, and finally I emerged from the forest onto the highway's edge. I turned west and in half a mile reached the welcome sign, "Santiam Lodge."

Thanks to the easy trail, I arrived at the lodge earlier than I had expected and entered the large, wood-framed, rambling lodge. I did not see or hear anyone. Looking around, I spotted an open book. Upon closer examination, it appeared to be a register. I signed my name. Finally, I heard a voice from a room down the hall. A friendly woman approached me, and I met Alice Patterson who managed the Lodge with her husband, the

Reverend Edward Patterson. She asked me if I would like dinner and breakfast, and I happily responded that I would. I then found my way down some stairs to the dormitory rooms, which were lined with bunk beds. Searching around, I found one occupant, who assured me that I could pick any bed I wished. I was glad to have time to at least wash my face and hands before dinner. I then returned to the upstairs living room/dining room, where I enjoyed a delicious, fresh salad and a hearty pasta dish. I met the Rev. Edward Patterson, whom I learned was a Presbyterian minister who served his church by managing the lodge as a summer conference and retreat center. I also met the couple's friendly assistant, Amy Sutton, whom I discovered was from Petaluma, a town that is north of San Francisco and south of Santa Rosa. This was a summer job for Amy, which she had learned about through her church. We enthusiastically exchanged information about happenings in Sonoma County. I told her about upcoming Sierra Club events in Sonoma County and promised to send her Sierra Club hike announcements.

After dinner, I spent a short time in the living room, looking through old Pacific Crest Trail Club newsletters. Although old, they were interesting to me because I had not seen them before.

By the time I was ready to explore the showers, I found that the temperature had dropped and it had grown cold. The shower cubicle was drafty. I longed for a hot bath, but no such offering was available. I contemplated whether or not I should brave the cold shower and recalled a time when I had caught a cold after a cold, drafty shower. I lost my courage. I settled for a washcloth bath, consoling myself by saying that I could have a good soak when I arrived home. In the meantime, I loaded the coin-operated washing machine with my dirty hiking clothes. It was good to fall into my warm goosedown sleeping bag feeling at least halfway clean.

In the morning, after a hearty breakfast, I double-checked the westbound bus schedule. As a precaution, I phoned the bus station in Bend, Oregon—requesting that the driver pick me up at the flag stop in Santiam. I didn't want to take any chance of being passed up. I walked out of the lodge to the highway and took up my post. I watched and waited, and when I finally saw the bus coming, I waved my red bandana vigorously. Thankfully, the driver stopped. When I requested a one-way ticket to Eugene and added, "Senior rate," the driver responded, "No kidding." It was a pleasant ride to Eugene, first drifting downhill through forests and then gliding along through prosperous-looking farmland.

In Eugene, I had a three-and-a-half hour wait for the 5:30 pm Amtrak train. I found an attractive vegetarian restaurant, where I ate lunch. Then, roaming around the attractive pedestrian mall, I wandered into a bookstore and became all excited about finding a book entitled Hiking Light. I bought it. Later, aboard the train, I plunged into my new book. I was very disappointed. I had expected to find some new suggestions to add to my store of tips on hiking light. However, I did not find any new ideas; I found that the book repeated old ideas and was full of lots of dos and don'ts. To me, the emphasis was on the don'ts. I felt let down.

On the train, I found a seat in the elderly and handicapped section and spent the remainder of the day glued to the window as the train climbed up to the Cascade Divide. It was dusk by the time the train reached the Lake Odell crossing, so I could not see the place where I had crossed the train tracks. I had to be content with the memory of the trail in the Lake Odell area.

Arriving home with my dirty pack, I felt so good as I kept reminding myself, "I have lots of time to clean up. I don't have to return to work any more. I am retired."

At home, I was pleasantly surprised to receive a card postmarked, "Tower City, Pa." It was from the friendly couple I had met on the trip north on Amtrak. Enclosed with the card was a photo of me sitting in an Amtrak lounge seat. The card read, "We've been wondering how your hike turned out. Perhaps you can tell us that you came out okay after walking the trail in Oregon through bear country! Not to mention the two-legged wolves you might encounter. We showed your picture all around and told friends of your adventure hiking at your age." I was so happy to receive their card. I wrote them a thank-you note and added their card to my growing collection of cards from people I had met along the trail.

Chapter 23
Santiam Pass to the Columbia River at the Bridge of the Gods
August 1985 • 152 Miles

As long as I live, I'll hear waterfalls and birds and winds sing. I'll interpret the rocks, learn the language of flood, storm, and the avalanche. I'll acquaint myself with the glaciers and wild gardens, and get as near the heart of the world as I can. — *John Muir*

For me, this section of the trail through Northern Oregon will be remembered for its comfortable, earth-covered paths through forests, its small lake basins, and its forever-present picturesque volcanoes. I remember so much of my walk through Oregon as hiking from one volcano to another. The highlights of this section were two scenic giants—Mt. Jefferson and Mt. Hood.

Getting to trailhead at Santiam Pass was accomplished totally by bus. I had two interesting layovers en route—Ashland and Eugene, Oregon. At my first stop in Ashland, I had decided to attend another performance at the famed Ashland Shakespearean theatre. I arrived in Ashland around 3:30 pm, too early for the 5:00 pm check-in time at the hostel. Leaving my pack parked on the hostel's front porch—Ashland seemed to me to be the kind of place in which I could trust leaving a backpack on a porch—I the walked two blocks back to the main street to shop and purchase my theatre ticket. Sometime during the bus ride, I discovered I had left my cotton shirt behind. I had ironed it, a habitual but probably unnecessary task, then left it neatly draped on a hanger where it was overlooked when I left for the bus in the dim, early-morning light. I decided to purchase a substitute in Ashland for warm days on the trail.

I first entered a small men's-clothing store, where I had seen some shirts in the window. Actually, most of my hiking shirts were men's or unisex shirts, which offered the desirable feature of pockets. A tall, well-dressed, young clerk approached me. First, he showed me what seemed to me to be a dress shirt. I protested, "Don't you have any blue-cotton workshirts?" He turned to another rack, only to find another semi-dressy-looking shirt. It was then that I sensed his uneasiness. He looked troubled. Then it dawned on me—he wasn't used to waiting on women, much less an older woman in backpacking clothes. I thanked him, knowing I needed to do some more looking, and departed.

Down the street two doors, I found a specialty shop with a rack of shirt blouses. I examined a little blue shirt with lots of pockets—even little pockets on a sleeve. I was thankful that it fit and was happy to purchase it. I wore the shirt on this trip and for several succeeding years. It always reminded me of my shirt shopping in Ashland.

At the Elizabethan theatre, tickets for the Merchant of Venice were scarce. I purchased a standing-room ticket.

I returned to the hostel's porch and my pack a few minutes before the 5:00 pm opening. It felt so good to return to the comfortable Ashland Hostel. It was clean and neat and so conveniently close to the theatre.

Before the 8:00 pm performance, I returned to town in search of a little cafe for supper. I found a small restaurant and ordered cheese soup and a vegetarian sandwich. The cheese soup, which I thought sounded good, turned out to be way too salty. Outside again after supper, I noticed the weather was surprisingly cool. Although I had planned to go directly to the theatre, I decided that I had enough time to return to the hostel for my sweater. I had already brought my windbreaker with me. Returning to the theatre, I took up my post in the front row of standing room, where I had an excellent view of the stage.

The night air grew colder and colder. I shifted from one foot to the other and patted my sweater and windbreaker close to myself, but I still could not keep warm. At intermission I considered leaving, but the cadence of the poetic lines, delivered so eloquently, held me entranced. By the final curtain, I was miserably cold. I had started to shiver. I limped back to my bunk bed at the hostel and hurried into my feathered bedroll for warmth. It took longer than usual for me to warm up. Then I became feverish. I felt sick. I wondered as I tossed and turned if it was the cold or the too-salty soup, or both that had made me sick. How ironic! I was well schooled in the dangers of hypothermia. On the trail, I had been extremely careful to keep warm and dry. Did I experience hypothermia in Ashland at the Elizabethan Theatre on a cold night, but never on the trail?

Fortunately, by the next morning, I had basically recuperated and was able to leave the hostel to catch the 6:30 am bus to Eugene. On a reclining bus seat, I found myself drifting in and out of catnaps.

In Eugene, with two hours to spare between buses, I had time to eat lunch and do a little shopping. I hunted for a vegetarian restaurant I had enjoyed the previous year and found that it had closed. How disappointing. I settled for an ordinary sandwich in an ordinary cafe. Still having time, I decided to buy a small flashlight to supplement my pinchlight, which was showing signs of dimming.

The afternoon bus ride to Santiam Pass was interesting and pleasant. I had recovered from the previous night's illness and was awake. I looked out the window at the scenery as the bus climbed toward the east, starting from low-lying grasslands dotted with prosperous-looking farms, then ascending to the mountain's pine forest. The forest cover grew more dense as the bus reached the Santiam Pass at 5000 feet. I arrived at the pass around 5:00 pm and decided to spend the night at Santiam Lodge. I wanted to stay at the lodge again to visit with the managers, Ed and Alice Patterson.

At the lodge, Alice had prepared a great dinner, with heaping helpings of fresh salad and filling pasta. In addition to a young summer volunteer, there was a mother and her 6-year-old who were vacationing at the lodge. Adjourning to the large, rustic living room after dinner, the young guest and volunteer were indignant upon receiving the news that the Presbyterian Church Board had decided to close the lodge at the end of the season. The Patterson's had managed the lodge for 23 years and had acquired a loyal band of supporters who were expressing their anger at the Church Board for their decision to close the lodge. I listened sympathetically.

By bedtime, it was cold and rainy, and I was glad to be inside. I hoped I would not be greeted by a storm in the morning.

At breakfast, Alice was cheerful and helpful. She gave me directions for reaching the nearby northbound trailhead. Then she described some of her favorite camping places, which included the Breitenbush Lake campground. I decided I would try to plan my trip so I would reach the lake for my evening campsite. Alice then enthusiastically announced, "We plan to backpack on the Pacific Crest Trail next summer when we will be free." I responded, "I think that's a good idea. I hope your plan to hike the trail works out well for you." I felt that after all of their years of serving conference groups, hikers, and backpackers, they certainly deserved some time off to enjoy themselves.

I was so happy to start my first day's walk in northern Oregon in sunshine and thankful that the rain had stopped. It was still cold and damp, but pleasant. At the large trailhead parking lot, an obliging couple took my photo.

I moved north on a good and easy trail. Periodically, through open spaces in the forest, I could see the outline of Three Fingered Jack. Each volcanic mountain has its own shape and character. Three Fingered Jack appeared especially different to me. Like all mountains, it presented a different face and shape as I moved along the trail and viewed it from different angles. First, viewing it from the south, I was struck by its steep, tooth-like, dark-brown finger. As I moved north on an ascending trail and walked along its western side, it was like walking along a very steep, dark-brown cliff. The guidebook states that the easiest route to climb the highest summit is a plus-three ascent. I was not tempted to climb it. Later in the afternoon, I could look back from a more northerly view and see that the jagged, tooth-like pinnacles really did form three fingers.

Water was not plentiful along the trail, so when I spotted a snowbank, I climbed up a few feet and scooped up some refreshing snow. As I was enjoying my cold drink, a southbound hiker came along and announced, "There is water up ahead at a pond in about two miles." "That's good to hear," I replied. "Thank you so much." He told me he had been camping by Mt. Jefferson and was on his way out. He complained a bit because it had been raining.

By evening, I turned off on a side-trail, planning to camp at Wasco Lake. I soon found a pleasing campsite on a little peninsula above the lake. Studying the map, I realized I not reached large Wasco Lake. I pondered and wondered if I was camping at Catlin Lake or at one of the small blue spots on the map designating unnamed lakes. I shall never be sure whether my pleasing campsite was Catlin Lake or not, but I enjoyed its pleasant view.

After sundown, it quickly grew cold. I went to bed early to stay warm. It grew colder and colder. I zipped up by bedroll higher and pulled my hood tightly around my head to keep out any cold night drafts. When I have to pull my hood closely around my face to shut off almost all the cold drafts, I know it is a cold night.

It was still cold in the morning. I crawled out of my sleeping bag and quickly moved my kitchen utensils and breakfast bag and water next to my bedroll. I hurried back to the warmth of my feathers to eat breakfast in bed. After breakfast, I hurriedly broke camp. I started hiking wearing my ski underwear and all of my layers, including my vapor-barrier nylon suit, which I usually wear only at night. It is designed to keep body heat in and does not breathe. Ordinarily, a hiker wearing it while walking would become drenched with perspiration, but not today. With a cold, gusty west wind blowing, it was one of the coldest mornings that I have spent on the trail.

The trail north was in good condition, lending itself to easy hiking. It climbed moderately as it skirted around the side of 6500-foot Rockpile Mountain. I stopped at small, beautiful Rockpile Lake for lunch. The cold west wind swept across the little lake. I found a small, sheltered valley between two grassy hammocks, where I hid from the wind during my lunch break.

As I was settling down in my little sheltered valley, two older women accompanied by three young people came down the trail. I greeted them, "Hello, where are you headed?" They stopped and proved to be very friendly. They told me they had come in from a trailhead near Jefferson Park for a week's campout with their grandchildren. I was impressed. They were strong, healthy-looking women. I believe they were the oldest, unaccompanied women backpackers I had met on the trail. As they moved on, one of them said to me, "I have backpacked alone and enjoyed it." This was music to my soul.

From Rockpile Lake the trail skirts around the side of South Cinder Peak. From a clearing, I had my first view of majestic, conical, snow-capped Mt. Jefferson. I stopped for afternoon tea in a somewhat sheltered place near a trail junction. Soon my tea break was interrupted by the arrival of a tall young man, seemingly struggling and limping along, and carrying a heavy-looking, slightly lopsided backpack. He complained, "I took the wrong trail. I went to Carl Lake and the trail ended at the lake. Someone gave me the wrong directions. I had planned to walk to Jefferson Park." This was my initial meeting with Dan, who was to accompany me for most of the afternoon and evening. Dan was full of questions. He let me know he had learned about the Pacific Crest Trail from a workshop offered by his college in Eugene. The workshop was given by Warren Rogers, Executive Director of the Pacific Crest Trail Conference. Using strip maps obtained from Warren Rogers, Dan was having a great deal of trouble finding the route. I managed to answer some of Dan's questions and gave him a few suggestions on how to bandage troublesome, painful blisters and where to look for water on the trail ahead. I went ahead, leaving him slowly limping along.

As I moved along the trail, I was alert and observant, as I wanted to find a side trail that led to the meadow. According to the guidebook, a hidden, rock-lined pond could be found on the meadow's border. Happily I found it and set up camp. I thought I was alone beside this hidden, rock-lined pond. A little later, however, I heard a voice, "Hi, can I camp near you?" "Surely," I replied. It was Dan. Dan volunteered to help with wood gathering and we shared an evening fire. Dan went over a litany of questions about backpacking equipment and backpacking "how-tos." I described my equipment in some detail and expressed my strong belief in travelling light. Smiling, Dan asked me politely if I minded if he asked me my age. Obligingly, I replied that I was 63. "You are the same age as my mother," he exclaimed. "I wish that she would get outside and exercise more," Dan added. I replied that I thought it was good for people of all ages, and especially for older people, to keep exercising and to stay active. I added that I thought walking was one of the best exercises. Before we parted for the night, Dan smiled and said, "I had hoped to meet a knowledgeable mountain man; instead have met a mountain woman."

In the morning before I started on the trail, Dan came over and asked me to inspect his blister wrappings. He had piled on so many layers of bandaging that it would have been hard to get his foot in his boot. I recommended a smaller, donut dressing that would exert less pressure between his heel and boot. He seemed pleased, then told me that he had decided to hike out to Trailhead and head for home that day. He did not want to continue hiking with his painful feet. Before I shouldered my pack, he lifted it up and exclaimed, "My goodness, your pack is so light!"

Before waving goodbye, Dan asked if he could take a photo of me to show his mother. I obligingly smiled. In parting, I promised to send him some backpacking equipment catalogs when I returned home. After waving goodbye to Dan, I thought to myself that I had met so many delightful and different people while walking the Trail. It is one of the fun things about trail walking. No one, I thought, could quite match Dan. He was obviously a neophyte when it came to backpacking, but he was so open to asking questions and delighted at receiving answers.

Back on the trail heading north, I soon reached a clearing through which a glorious, panoramic view of Mt. Jefferson unfolded. It presented such an intriguing pattern of the various shapes of snowbanks resting in the deep crevices of Mt. Jefferson's folds. Moving along, I arrived at a junction where I had the choice of three trails leading north: the old trail, the 1972 Pacific Crest Trail, and the newest Crest Trail. I chose the high trail, the newest. All three trails would come together again that afternoon near Milk Creek. The high trail contoured along the slopes of grayish, Cathedral Rocks. After walking through miles of black volcanic rocks, I was glad to come to a small section of glaciated gray rocks. It unearthed for me in a small way a remembrance of glaciated gray canyons in the Sierras. It was an agreeable scene. I stopped for lunch at rocky, pleasant, glacier-colored Shale Lake. During my afternoon walk, the trail climbed down into rock-strewn Milk Creek Canyon. Here in the canyon, I enjoyed viewing some delightful, lusciously colored wildflowers. I then crossed the well-named, chalky-white Milk Creek. By late afternoon, I reached a small pond, where I made camp. I had planned to camp before reaching the gorge crossing Russell Creek. The guidebook recommended that hikers, in order to make a safe crossing, cross Russell Creek before 11:00 am to avoid the danger of being swept down the gorge.

I was eager to start on the trail early in the morning in order to cross Russell Creek before 11:00. Like many glacier bedstreams that I would encounter as I hiked north, the streams grow wider and swifter as the daytime rising sun warms and melts the snow

MT. JEFFERSON WITH LAKE

and ice. As I approached the stream with excitement, I debated which pair of socks I would wear to get wet while wading across the stream. Soon after arriving at the stream at 10:00 am, I found to my delight that someone had placed a log across the stream. It was an easy crossing and my feet remained dry.

Safely on the other side, I found a little space to sit and

enjoy my mid-morning snack of milk and honey, all within the sound and sight of rushing water. Moving along, I arrived at the Jefferson Park trail junction. This trail offers easy access for day hikers to reach Jefferson Park. I continued on past Scout Lake, a popular campsite lake, as from its north shore it offers views of majestic Mt. Jefferson. I moved on to be still closer to the mountain and picked out a level view space near shallow Russell Lake. I enjoyed my lunch and a leisurely after-lunch viewing of Mt. Jefferson. Although there were campers and picnickers in the vicinity, I was fortunately alone.

Feeling rested and fulfilled after drinking in the Mt. Jefferson view, I started slowly up the steep trail from Jefferson Park on my journey to Breitenbush Lake. I stopped often at the ends of switchbacks to look back at the mountain. A sizeable group of day hikers ahead of me was talking loudly. I slowed my pace to place some distance between us. Toward the top of the climb, I walked off the trail a short distance to a viewpoint where I could look back at Mt. Jefferson as well as to the north, where I could see the tall, looming top of snow-capped Mt. Hood. The trail's descent to the north was slow and somewhat difficult. I climbed over three large snowbanks and plodded through a rocky area. I was glad when the trail leveled off and led through a forest of hemlocks.

My campsite near large Breitenbush Lake was comfortable but a little disappointing. The shore was lined with tall grasses, so my campsite did not have a view of the lake. I compensated by viewing the lake and then returning to my viewless campsite.

My morning's walk was pleasant and easy with some gentle ups and downs. Striding along, I thought about taking a couple of hours off to rest and wash socks at Olallie Lake, where I had mailed a food package to the Forest Service Guard Station. Just as I was contemplating this plan, two rangers with a friendly

Labrador-looking dog appeared. They greeted me and said, "Are you planning on picking up a food package?" "Yes," I replied. "We will be returning around 5:00 pm." "I'll see you then," I answered. My plan to wash socks and rest was confirmed. I would have a half-day rest at the Olallie Lake Resort picnic area. I ate lunch at a nearby picnic table. After lunch, I strung up my clothesline, washed my socks, and hung them up to dry in the wind. Just as I was feeling good about having an afternoon rest with such an ideal view spot, a very noisy family moved in to occupy the next picnic table. They yelled at their children constantly and left their yapping dog in the car. The high-pitched, yapping dog kept up his barking for two full hours. Again I thought, campgrounds are so often not peaceful, quiet places.

Around 4:30, the ranger's dog appeared, followed soon by the two rangers. They found my package and, as usual, I was relieved that it had arrived safely. I repacked and, although it was late afternoon, I was eager and ready to move on. I would seek a quieter campsite.

I returned to the trail and climbed a ridge. In about an hour, I arrived at my planned destination at small, shallow Jude Lake. I found a small bedroom campsite on a ridge above the lake. It was not an ideal campsite in some respects, as I could not find an outlet to obtain running water. I decided to play it safe and purified my water. After dinner, one of my favorite quiet times of the day, I walked a few feet to the shoreline and enjoyed a glorious sunset.

My walk the following day was almost entirely through viewless forest. It was easy walking and the kind of trail on which hikers can make good time. After a long stretch of viewless forest, I began wanting to see out—to see views of valleys and mountains. When this feeling came upon me, I took out my Sierra Club Songbook and strode along humming and singing familiar songs: "Oh Give Me a Home Where the Buffalo Roam," "It's a long way to Tipperary," and "Amazing Grace." I found that the songs lifted my spirit and helped time to pass swiftly.

At noon at Lemiti Meadow, while I was enjoying cold, refreshing water from nearby Trooper Springs, two young men caught up with me and stopped for lunch. They were through Pacific Crest Trail hikers, the first I had met on this summer's walk. One was from Fresno and one from the state of Washington. They told me they had started at the Mexican border on April 15th. They reported that of the 35 hikers who had started at the border, only 6 of them were still on the trail. They hoped to reach Canada by mid-September. I wished them well.

During my afternoon walk, I met two other hiking groups who were travelling south. First, I met two young women who told me they had started at Barlow Pass to the north and planned to go out at McKenzie Pass to the south—a 112-mile section. Later I met two young men who had started at the Canadian border and were "going as far as they could."

In the evening I reached water at a seeping spring south of the Warm Springs River basin and made camp.

In the morning, after leaving my comfortable campsite by the seeping spring, I drifted down the trail on switchbacks that led to a bridge crossing Warm Springs River. I stopped and found a resting place on the riverbank for my mid-morning repast of milk and honey. The river's flow was wide and swift enough to create ample water music, which held me entranced and made me reluctant to hurry on.

My afternoon walk was mostly through forest. By mid-afternoon, I had reached Clackamas Lake Campground, which had road access and appeared to be a fairly busy place. I did not want to set up camp amongst the noisy car campers, so I filled my water bag and moved on up the trail.

I found a delightful, small campsite on a bluff above large Timothy Lake. I could look out onto the lake and see sailboats and fishing boats. I was not far from the Timothy Lake Campground, yet I had my own small piece of privacy. After supper, I was treated to a glorious view. I watched the setting sun drop down across the lake, then send back a glorious red reflection that lit all the western sky.

The path for my morning's walk led along the north side of Timothy Lake. I looked out and watched the hopeful fishermen launching their boats. At the north end of the lake, I stopped for a snack by pleasant Crater Creek. After passing through the adjoining Crater Creek Meadow, the trail entered and remained in forest for the rest of the day.

By mid-afternoon, I started my search for water. I was looking for a seeping springs that was located shortly beyond Linney Creek Road. It was hard to find, and I was about to give up. Then, following a little-used path, I finally found a dirty, leaf-covered puddle of water surrounded by brush and sticks. It looked as if it had not been used for a long, long time. My first reaction was, "I'm not going to drink this brackish-looking water." My second reaction was, "I'll fill one container for emergency use." After removing needles and leaves and scooping up my drink, I discovered the water was cold and delicious. I changed my attitude toward this water and started drinking and enjoying its cold spring flavor. I said to myself, "Looks can be deceptive."

By late afternoon, I turned off at Wapinitia Pass at the trail crossing Highway 26 to take the recommended alternate route leading to Frog Lake Campground—a water supply route. Like many road-accessible campgrounds, it was busy and noisy. I decided to take advantage of the campground facilities—the water and picnic table—to cook my supper and then move on.

Operating the old-style green water pump proved to be a little tricky. To obtain a water flow, I needed to press down on a long handle with two hands and all my weight. Then when I hurried to the spout, using my hands to place the water bag under the stream of water, it would stop. I waited until a young camper came along and said, "Could you hold my water bag?" He was eager to help. For him, I think, operating the old-style pump was probably a new experience.

After supper, I started up the trail. I was again in the forest. It was growing dark. I searched for quite a while for a level spot. They were very scarce. I finally settled for a wide bulge in the trail and placed my bedroll alongside the trail. Just as I was hoping that no hikers would come along, a couple came up the trail at dusk. I attempted to make a clumsy apology about being camped so near the trail, but they were not concerned. They were concerned about meeting a couple of friends at Twin Lakes, which was a 45-minute hike up the trail. "Have you seen a couple pass?" they asked. "No," I replied. I settled into my bedroll for the night, feeling unsure about future trail traffic. Fortunately, no one else came.

I arose early and packed my bedroll before breakfast. I didn't want any early-morning hikers to catch me camped so near the trail. Fortunately, no one appeared. After packing my bedroll, I hurried through my breakfast, as I was eager to reach Mt. Hood and the famous Timberline Lodge.

My walk continued through the forest. I arrived at the crossing of Highway 35 near Barlow Pass. Soon after the crossing, I caught a glimpse through a break in the trees of towering, snow-capped Mt. Hood. I was amazed. It rose so high in the sky that I could hardly believe it was real. For the next hour, I was treated intermittently to glimpses of the mountain. Finally, the trail emerged from the trees, offering a complete, uninterrupted view of the giant. I stopped for a snack. From my rocky resting spot, I enjoyed an unobstructed view of Mt. Hood's volcanic peak, adorned with huge, white patches of glaciers that were cradled in the rocky valleys below the side of the peak. What a spectacular sight!

The trail leading north to well-named Timberline Lodge was a considerable distance through gravel-covered debris deposits. The rocky debris is also deposited by frequent avalanches and carried down by glacial streams.

My remaining afternoon's walk to the Lodge was slow and noisy as my boots crunched along over the uneven rocks. By late afternoon, I arrived at the large, historic Lodge and hurried inside to claim my food package. Two handsome, friendly, St. Bernards were ranged on the front entrance porch, looking as if they belonged in this snowy, mountain setting.

Inside, I found the registration desk and approached the clerk to ask for my package. "Are you a Pacific Crest Trail hiker?" she asked. "Yes," I replied. "You need to go to the gift shop to collect your package," she stated. "It is located across the street." I was puzzled but dutifully walked out and found the gift shop. When I told the gift shop clerk that I had come to call for my food package, she searched in a back room, returned, and reported that they did not have my package. I was beginning to worry. I really needed my food for the next four or five days, as well as the extra fuel tablets to heat my water. I hurried back to the registration desk to tell them the story. There was a new clerk on duty who seemed willing to make a helpful search. He went behind the counter to search in the storeroom, then returned with my food package. What a relief. I retreated outside to find a quiet, "out-of-the-crowd" corner to repack my pack. A quiet space, however, was not easy to find. It was Saturday evening, and the lodge was bustling with activities. Across from the front of the lodge in a space reserved for recreational activities, there was a noisy, festive celebration taking place. I was curious. I asked a passing participant, "What are you celebrating?" "We are having a Chili Hoedown," he replied. Their festivities included some loud music. I moved to the other side of the lodge, the east side towards the mountain, and walked up to the trail junction. There I found a small, relatively quiet, level space among a cluster of trees. I staked out my bedroom and accomplished my repacking with my pack leaned against a nearby tree.

I had decided that for a change of pace I would have dinner in the lodge restaurant. In addition, I wanted to explore further the interesting art and architecture of the lodge. The large, log structure was a product of the WPA—Works Progress Administration—completed in the 1930s. The program offered employment to architects, artists, and others during the depression. Not only is the lodge magnificent architecturally, but there's quite a lot of art displayed inside, including beautiful wrought-iron railings, stone mosaics decorating the entrance floors, and hangings featuring beautiful hand-woven rugs. It is one of the most impressive wilderness lodges I have visited.

After an enjoyable dinner and a tour of the Lodge, I returned to my bedroom amongst the trees. Even though I was quite close to the lodge, this eastern area was relatively quiet. I was treated to a red-rose sunset followed by a red-rose reflection in the clouds and an afterglow on the mountain. I felt inspired and spent a restful night on my mountain-view campsite.

In the morning, I awoke to see a rosy sunrise lighting up the eastern slope of the mountain and reflecting its pinkish glow onto the snow glaciers. What a glorious sight. I was thankful that I had camped on the mountainside of the lodge where I was treated to a great view and was away from the crowds.

In my excitement to capture the scene on film, I over-wound my camera and lost the film end, making it impossible to rewind my film. Therefore, before I started my day's walk, I visited the lodge's camera shop, which, fortunately, was open early. They retrieved my film, I purchased new film, and I was on my way around 9:00 am.

Striding northwest on the trail, I soon found myself looking skyward, feeling that there was some activity going on high above me. From an opening in the trees, I was able to look up and see a busy, well-used ski chair lift cranking its way up the mountain to a groomed ski run on a glacier! There I was, looking up at active skiers on a North-American mountain in August. Later, I heard from a trail walker that this glacier ski run is heavily used by championship skiers who are practicing for the Olympics and other special events. With my binoculars, I was able to watch them weaving their way down the glacier ski run.

I encountered a lot of trail traffic, mostly made up of day hikers. I also met two groups of backpackers who were happily celebrating their completion of the Circle Tour, which, I learned, loops around the base of the mountain for approximately 26 miles. They were so pleased with their accomplishment. One kindly gentleman recommended I take the Paradise Park Trail, which was listed in the guidebook as a recommended alternate. This proved to be very valuable advice. By lunchtime, I had reached the Paradise Park Shelter and enjoyed my lunch, not in but near the shelter. It offered a glorious view across a sweeping field of wildflowers, with the mountain framing the background.

Finally pulling myself away from this engaging view, I started my walk as the trail wound down into the Rushing Creek Canyon. Again, I was treated to magnificent views of the canyon, and I passed lots of bright-colored wildflowers. These included

Indian paintbrush and Mariposa Lilly. I saw a small, white flower that was new to me. I was puzzled—what could it be? Soon I passed a gentleman who told me that these flowers were Western Bistorts. I was glad to find the name of a new flower.

Toward evening, it started to rain. I hurriedly found a campsite on level ground near Rushing Creek and strung up my poncho. Now I felt prepared for rain. Soon, the rain stopped and I ate my supper outside my little lean-to shelter. I was glad that it wasn't raining but, at the same time, I felt good that I was ready and prepared for rain.

After supper in the quiet of the evening, I had time to reflect on my day's walk. What extraordinary scenes I had viewed—majestic Mt. Hood, Paradise Park with its carpet of wildflowers, and, finally, the descent into spectacular Rushing Creek Canyon.

I awoke to a fog-shrouded landscape. It was not raining, but I needed my rain gear for protection from the fog dew. After breakfast and breaking camp, I walked a short distance and then was ready to tackle my first stream crossing of the day—Sandy River, labeled in the Forest Service map as "hazardous stream crossing." It was a formidable-looking stream, with swiftly moving grayish-white glacier run-off. As I moved closer, I could see that two logs had been placed across the stream. How good to see them! I wondered if they had been placed by Forest Service rangers or by volunteer hikers. I loosened my pack's hip belt. One of the logs that almost rested in the water looked slippery. I concentrated on maintaining my balance and was relieved when I reached the other side safely.

After the river crossing, the trail climbed up and arrived at beautiful Ramona Falls. I stopped to have a snack and drink in this attractive scene. Ramona Falls cascades over a rocky cliff made up of numerous stone ledges. One of these ledges held one of my favorite wildflowers, the lovely, yellow-faced mimulus.

The trail continued to climb, winding in and out of gullies before dropping down to my second "hazardous crossing" of the day—Muddy Fork. Happily, I found that it was also bridged by a log. I found it to be a fairly easy crossing.

After the Muddy Fork crossing, the trail ascended and contoured the slope of Bald Mountain. Here along the mountain slopes, the fog clouds were rolling in. It reminded me of the fog clouds that sweep in around the Golden Gate Bridge. In reading the guidebook, I learned that I was missing some good views of Bald Mountain and Mt. Hood. How fortunate I had been, I thought, that I had had two clear days of spectacular views.

As I was walking along, a group of hikers emerged through the fog. They were day hikers carrying food baskets. They announced, "We are part of a wedding party attending a friend's wedding on Bald Mountain." I was surprised. I replied, " I hope that the fog will lift." Later, I met two of the wedding party's returning members who reported happily that the fog had lifted for five minutes during the wedding.

I also met a party of eight happy and excited, young-adult hikers who were returning from having completed the circle walk around Mt. Hood. When I let them know I was walking to complete the Pacific Crest Trail in sections, they congratulated me.

By evening, I reached water at Lola Pass. It was still misty and drippy, and a cold wind blew across the pass. I spent considerable time walking back and forth, seeking a campsite that would be somewhat sheltered from the wind. Finally, I found a small bedroom nestled in a slight depression. The wind blew fiercely and noisily all night. I was glad to have found my small, protected bedroom.

I awoke to see continuing misty fog. My thermometer registered 40 degrees. After breakfast, as I started on the trail, the cloud cover momentarily lifted. Turning around to look, I was happy to have another glimpse of Mt. Hood. I looked forward to a clear, sunny day. Soon, I was disappointed. At Lola Pass, the fog poured in again.

Shortly after crossing the Lola Pass road, I caught up with a couple—a man with his young daughter, Julie. They reported that they had camped near Lola Pass and had spent a very windy, noisy night. Their tent had rattled and swayed all night long. They asked me if I had been troubled by the wind. When I explained that I had found a sheltered dip south of the pass, they were very puzzled. Julie's father complained that he could not find a protected camping space. I did not try to explain to him that with a bivouac sack, I could squeeze into small spaces, whereas campers with tents needed to look for more spacious camping sites.

After Lola Pass, the trail lead mostly through a bushy area, and I saw some tempting blue berries on the bushes. As I was not sure whether or not they were edible, I said to myself that I had better play it safe and not eat any. When I caught up with Julie and her father at a snack break, I asked, "Are these berries edible?" "Yes," they replied, "These are huckleberries." Now that I knew they were huckleberries, I started nibbling and enjoyed them all the rest of the day.

At lunchtime, I sat down near the junction of the Huckleberry Mountain Trail, which led to Lost Lake. While I was chewing on my cracker and peanut butter, I hole broke through the fog cover, and I could suddenly see the water and two boats on the lake. To me, this opening of the fog clouds seemed so very mysterious and like a miracle.

Back on the trail, the fog continued for most of the day. Periodically, I caught up with Julie and her father. We seemed to leapfrog all day long. In the afternoon, they told me they were going to camp at Indian Springs campground. I replied that I also planned to camp at Indian Springs.

I slowed my pace as the trail led over a rough, rocky ridge. Julie and her father arrived at the campground before I did. They had found the only sheltered place in the entire campground to pitch their tent. I searched and searched, but could not find a good, level, sheltered place. I finally settled for a small space by a little tree. As the evening wore on, the wind grew stronger. I became so cold that before I finished my supper I crawled into my bedroll to warm up. When I finally warmed up, I poked my head out of my bedroll hood and ate my dessert, retreating again to stay warm. Later, I hurried out to clean up my dishes and pack them away. I did not want to leave food out with aromas that could attract roving animals.

During the night when I peeked up at the sky, I saw stars. I rejoiced in anticipation of a clear day. As I broke camp in the morning, the sun broke through the clouds. I eagerly anticipated starting my descent to the mighty Columbia River, which I planned to reach in a day and a half. I would be descending a big drop of around 4000 feet. At the Columbia River, I would reach the lowest point on the entire Pacific Crest Trail at 150 feet.

The trail leading to Wahtum Lake was an easy one. At the Wahtum Lake junction, I bid farewell to the father-and-daughter hikers, as they were going to take the Pacific Crest Trail down to the river. I had decided to take the scenic trail—the slightly longer but highly recommended alternate, Eagle Falls Trail. Looking forward to a beautiful descent, I crossed several trickling creeklets before arriving at the first impressive, cascading, waterfalls of Eagle Creek. The trail became steeper as it descended the gorge. The scenery that unfolded was spectacular, as I viewed one majestic waterfall after another—all of them exciting to behold. Soon, I came to one of the most spectacular of them all—the 150-foot

Tunnel Falls, which drops straight down over the lip of a cliff. To me, it looked like a giant, white, lacy ribbon, spectacular in sight and sound. Part of the way down, the trail led underneath the falls through a tunnel that was carefully constructed and supported by handrails and cables. It was exciting to walk on a rocky, wet trail underneath a cascading waterfall.

When I reached the entrance of one of the Eagle Creek campgrounds, I paused to celebrate. It had warmed up and I shed my windbreaker, my wool sweater, and finally my ski underwear for the first time in three days. It felt good.

Foot traffic increased. Day hikers came up the trail from an easily accessible parking lot. A helpful forest ranger who I met coming up the trail advised me to pick a campsite early, as they soon become full. Heeding her good advice, I stopped early and found a campsite at the Four Mile Camp. I spent a leisurely evening. After supper, I walked down to view the waterfalls and, to my delight, spotted John Muir's favorite bird, two Water Ouzles, which were feeding beneath the falls. What a glorious end to a wonder-filled day.

During my morning's walk, the path alongside Eagle Creek gradually leveled off, and I soon arrived at the parking lot of Eagle Creek Campground. The trail leading to the town of Cascade Locks, where I would catch a bus, was unspectacular. Arriving in the town, my first objective was to find bus information. Walking down the main street, I found a Greyhound bus schedule posted outside a small store. The next bus would be departing for Portland in three hours. I had time to explore. I walked down to a park, which was adjacent to the riverbank. On my way, I came to train tracks. Looking down the tracks, I saw a shelter-like structure. Could it be a train station? I walked over to the shelter and, to my delight, found that the Portland-bound train would stop here.

Before the train arrived, a sizeable group of men and women met at the shelter station. I learned that they were members of the Senior Center. They had come to Cascade Locks on the morning train, had enjoyed a ride on a riverboat, and were returning home.

The train ride following alongside the mighty Columbia River offered scenery and a pleasant end to my northern Oregon walk.

In Portland, I found my way to a comfortable Youth Hostel and had ample time in the evening to shower and wash clothes. In the morning, I boarded an Amtrak train for home and had time to reflect. It had been a good trip and I felt spiritually uplifted.

INTRODUCTION TO WASHINGTON
505 Miles

Upon entering Washington, the hiker can still sight striking, high, volcanic mountains as the trail passes close to Mt. Adams and Mt. Rainier. Moving north, the volcanoes give way to a return of some granitic peaks, including Granite Mountain. There is a touch of resemblance to scenes in the High Sierra. Of course, nothing can really resemble John Muir's "Range of Light."

Unlike the High Sierra, the Washington mountains receive an abundance of rain. The trail often leads through a floor covering thick with green grasses and shrubs. For the hiker, it is a challenge to stay dry and warm. For my walk through Washington, I packed a tent and raingear.

Landmarks of special interest and beauty for me were the Goat Rock Wilderness, followed by the Packwood Glacier and Lakeview Ridge.

The Goat Rock Wilderness is highlighted by two tall, statue-like split rocks that sit on a ridge with a spectacular backdrop, which, on a clear day, reveals the snowy head of Mt. Rainier rising in the far distance. Shortly after viewing the Goat Rocks and Mt. Rainier, the trail leads across the upper side of the perpetual-snow slope of the Packwood Glacier. It presents a challenge to the hiker to step securely to avoid sliding down the icy slope. I crossed by digging my boots into previously made foot holes.

Near the Canadian border, the trail leads across the Lakeview Ridge, which presents the hiker with a spectacular view. High rocky peaks and ridges come into view, together with steep, slanting sidewalls carpeted with varying shades of green grasses and reddish rocks. This view provided me with a long-lasting and inspiring memory of my approach to Canada and the completion of my journey.

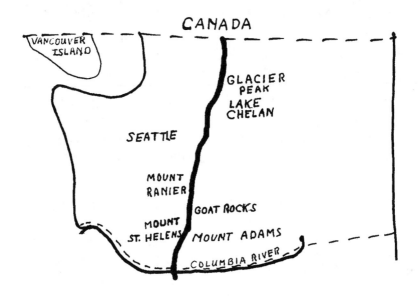

PACIFIC CREST
TRAIL

WASHINGTON

Chapter 24
Bridge of the Gods to Snoqualmie Pass
August 1987 • 225 Miles

Few are altogether deaf to the preaching of pine trees.
Their sermons on the mountains go to our hearts; and if
people in general could be got into the woods, even for once,
to hear the trees speak for themselves, all difficulties in the
way of forest preservation would vanish. — *John Muir*

For me, this was a long section. As my summer's planned
trail sections became further and further from home, resulting
in a longer trip to reach Trailhead, it seemed good to spend
more time on the trail. When I was planning to walk this long
section, I left open an option: I could exit from the trail at
White Pass if I felt the need, as the trail crosses a major east-
west highway at the pass.

As I contemplated my approach to Washington, it was
with mixed feelings. I looked forward to immersing myself in
its scenic beauty, but felt unsure about traversing a terrain that
was well known for its abundant rain. The Sierras were different—rain showers seldom lasted long during the summer
months. If a hiker got a little damp, there was little to worry
about. The sun would soon come out and the hiker would be
dry again. In Washington, however, I had heard stories of trail-
walkers trudging along for 16 straight days of rain.

To prepare for my Washington Crest Trail walk, I planned to purchase a light-weight tent and to add an additional layer of clothing. My winter and spring preparation activities included visiting backpacking equipment stores, studying catalogs, and comparing the weights and sizes of prospective tents. Some of the lightweight tents that I looked at in sporting goods stores seemed awfully small; I could barely sit up in them. I was discouraged. Finally, a helpful young clerk suggested I consider a Stephenson Warmlite tent, available through catalog order. I found a catalog and ordered their lightest model, which weighed two pounds including poles. When I set it up in my living room, I was pleased. It was made of very lightweight, waterproof materials. This two-man tent was amazingly roomy and proved to be a good choice. I wasn't quite ready, however, to abandon my beloved bivouac sack. I had become so enamored of viewing the night sky, I packed the sack with the idea of only using the tent when needed. For an extra layer of warmth, I added a fleece vest.

The first 125-mile section of this trail, starting at the Columbia River Gorge and ending at White Pass, offers the hiker a great variety of terrain. Starting at the lowest point on the entire trail at 125 feet, the route climbs to 7000 feet at White Pass. A trail walker first strolls through lush green ferns, flowers, and bushes and then reaches the first southern Washington volcano as the trail circles around the base of snow-capped Mt. Adams. The trail then leads through the Goat Rocks Wilderness area, which offers exciting and dramatic views, highlighted by one of the first views of Mt. Rainier. The 98-mile section between White Pass and Snoqualmie is dominated by frequent views of Mt. Rainier. The trail leads along the east side of the Mt. Rainier National Park.

For my approach to the southern border of the trail in Washington, I boarded the evening Amtrak train to Portland. Again, I rode in the senior and handicapped section and enjoyed the company of a delightful woman pianist from Tucson. In the morning, I excitedly looked out the train window to see the trail crossing near Lake Odell.

Arriving in Portland in the late afternoon, I boarded the city bus and checked into the Youth Hostel. I had arranged to have dinner with a college friend who lives in Portland. We spent the evening in animated conversation, catching up on lots of happenings since our last get-together.

In the morning, I boarded the eastbound Chicago train to reach the trailhead near the town of Cascade Locks. Again, I enjoyed this short ride as the train moved slowly along the banks of the Columbia River. Arriving at Cascade Locks, I walked eagerly through the town to reach the river crossing at the Bridge of the Gods.

The walk across the mighty Columbia was anything but a wilderness experience. The mile-long bridge is used primarily by large trucks and seldom by pedestrians. I strode along, carefully watching my balance as the passing trucks emitted gusts of wind and rattled and shook the bridge. I was relieved to reach stable land on the other side and to enter the State of Washington.

I turned right at the end of the bridge for a short walk to reach the town of Stevenson, a recommended post office for package pick-ups on the 1987 temporary trail route. I was happy to find that my food package had arrived safely. As I was repacking my backpack in a corner of the post office, a neatly dressed, pleasant-looking woman approached and asked me where I would be backpacking. After I told her I was walking on the Pacific Crest Trail, she commented, "I think it's wonder-

ful what you are doing." This made me feel really good. My
pack felt heavy. I was carrying 12 days of food; my next post-
office stop would be at White Pass, 118 miles distant.

Toward evening, I found a small campsite beside gently
flowing Rock Creek. It felt so good to again hear the water
music of the creek. Just as I was enjoying the feeling that it was
good to be back on the trail again, my thoughts were interrupted by a blast of rock music. I was still near a road, and a car
had driven in and parked. How annoying!

The next morning, I anticipated unenthusiastically more
road walking on the temporary trail before reaching the completed trail. Strolling along the gravel road, I noticed a side trail.
Studying the map, it appeared that the side trail would climb
over a ridge and reach the temporary trail near Trout Creek,
eliminating a longer loop of road walking. I debated. Should
I try it? It presented some uncertainty, as there was no mention of this trail in the guidebook. My curiosity was piqued.
I decided to take a chance and try this trail. I was excited as I
climbed toward a ridge. I was exploring. The trail was heavily
wooded and lush with ferns and wildflowers. Like many little-
used trails, it became more obscure the further I traveled. I
wondered, do trail walkers start on trails, then give up so that
the first part is more traveled than the further reaches? When
it was time for me to look for a lunch spot to sit down, I had
to search for a resting place amidst the heavy undergrowth. I
finally found a decaying fallen log to sit on.

By late afternoon, I happily came down the ridge and out
onto the road used by the temporary trail. I had enjoyed the
shortcut. Time-wise, however, I hadn't gained much, as the
rough, brush-lined trail had been slow going. The road walk
would have been faster. By evening, I made camp at the edge of
the Sunset Hemlock Road.

I was happy to reach trail in the morning. The trail led through a beautiful forest of tall, stately pines before descending to gurgling Trout Creek, where I enjoyed my morning snack.

After crossing Trout Creek on a new-looking bridge, I stopped to study the map and guidebook. I was confronted with some confusing directions, such as, "The trail parallels an unseen road." and then "Our trail heads northwest along one edge of a tree farm." I moved slowly. The tree farm was evident—busy and loud, with large, noisy green trucks moving back and forth near me. Two young men in one of the trucks shouted at me, but I was not sure what they were saying. I was relieved when the trail left the fence and switchbacked up and around Bunker Hill before descending to the wide Wind River. The Wind River Crossing was bridged by a substantial, unaesthetic-looking bridge. My lunch spot beside the river was also uninspiring. After crossing the Wind River bridge, the trail crossed a busy road, then lead east and descended to Panther Creek. I headed for the Panther Creek campground, my planned destination for the night.

At the Panther Creek campground, I rested my pack against a tree to survey the camping sites and was soon greeted by Margaret and Bruce, who were resting near their tent. They announced that they were also Pacific Crest Trail hikers and that there were three other solo hikers camping at Panther Creek. We compared trail notes. Bruce and Margaret were from Illinois and had hiked most of the trail. They told me they liked the Oregon and the Washington trail very much, but had not enjoyed Southern California. They hoped to go as far north as possible with the remaining days of summer. I did not have much time to talk to the other young men, as they were busy setting up their tents. As I left Margaret to look for my own campsite, she said enthusiastically, "This is the largest number of Pacific Crest Trail hikers that we have met at one campsite." I agreed: six trail campers.

As rain was threatening, I sought out a campsite at the edge of the campground and hurried to prepare my bedsite and eat supper. Just a few minutes after I crawled into my bivouac sack, it started to rain. What great timing, I thought.

In the morning, as I was packing up, one of the solo hikers stopped by to announce that Bruce and Margaret had left at 5:00 am—planning to reach Crest Camp 15 ½ miles distant. The other hikers were also eagerly packing up and talking about reaching Crest Camp. In response to their questions about where I planned to camp, I replied that I would probably stop by the spring this side of Crest Camp. Actually, I was reluctant to make a commitment to reach a certain point and really didn't want to plan on hiking the 15 miles to Crest Camp.

Packing up leisurely, I was thankful that the rain had only been a light shower. I was able to pack up my bivouac sack without a lot of sponging to sweep off the water.

My walk from Panther Creek seemed like a succession of ups and downs. First the trail led up and around 4000-foot Big Huckleberry Mountain. On the way down to the big lava beds, the trail moved in and out of gullies and up and down saddles— too many for me to count. Toward late afternoon, I started looking for a spring described in the guidebook. I could not find it. What to do? I did not want to hike to Crest Camp, some five miles distant. I decided to ration my water. I relaxed and strode on slowly. Then, when least expected, I spotted a nicely flowing spring. Rejoicing, I made camp near the spring and enjoyed its fresh, cool water. I was alone and it was quiet and peaceful.

In the morning, after measuring out my water in preparation for a long, waterless walk, I rounded a crest bordering the edge of Big Lava Bed and arrived at Crest Campground. The campground was near a road and was equipped with a horse corral but no water. One of the Pacific crest hikers whom I had met at Panther Creek was still breaking camp. He announced that all of the hikers whom I had met at Panther Creek had camped at Crest Campground that night. He asked me where I had camped and if I had found water. I replied that I found good, fresh, cold water at a spring about two miles away and that I had camped there. He was puzzled and said that the spring described in the guidebook had dried up. Then I realized how fortunate I was to have found the little spring for my water and campsite. I also realized that through my years of solo backpacking, I had become experienced at finding and using little water resources and small campsites.

I looked around to survey the Crest Campground with its picnic table and corral. I thought to myself, "This is not my style of wilderness camping." In addition, I was glad that I had not been part of the hiking group. I perceived from their conversations at Panther Creek that they were focused on "making miles." Their conversation was directed toward, "How far are you going tomorrow?" I felt relieved that I had dropped behind them. I did not want to hurry—my goal was not to make miles. Observing their style of trail walking challenged me to review my goals. I wanted, as much as possible, to enjoy my walk and to pause and drink in the views and enjoy the beauties and wonders of nature.

Moving along on a pleasant trail through lush trailside greenery, the trail climbed up and around Berry Mountain. It was aptly named. I kept stopping to pick mouth-watering huckleberries. I even found a small, deliciously sweet wild strawberry.

Rounding a curve, I looked up and noticed two men and a woman crouched in the bushes. On looking closer, I saw that they were fully equipped for serious berry picking, with pails and a center container pouch belted around their waists. I stopped and asked, "How is your berry picking going?" They looked up and stopped their picking momentarily. I learned that they were year-round pickers and that they had come to this site after picking cherries in eastern Washington. During the spring, they had picked oranges in Florida. They went on to complain that pickers from Mexico had taken over the orange picking in Southern California. One of the older men commented that he stays in Washington in the winter and prunes apple and cherry trees. He asked me if I was a Sierra Club member. I replied that I was. He went on to comment that President Reagan was hard on environmentalists. I agreed. Before I stood up from my enjoyable rest and huckleberry snack, he said, "You won't like the trail between White Pass and Snoqualomie Pass. It was full of clear-cut logging." I replied, "I am sorry to hear this." As I stood up to move on down the trail, I thought to myself that these were the first real year-round pickers who are wholly dependent on picking for their livelihood that I have ever had the opportunity to meet. I had had a small glimpse of what life must be like for them.

From near the summit of the crest, I was treated to a glorious view of two snow-topped volcanoes—Mt. Adams to the north and Mt. Hood to the south. Was I also catching a glimpse in the far distant horizon of Mt. Jefferson? I thought I was, but could not be sure. Also from this crest, the 1979 edition of the guidebook states that conical Mt. St. Helens can be seen to the northwest! Since it blew its top in 1980, it no longer wore its conical top. I searched to the northwest with uncertainty, wondering if I could see any remnants of its blown-out top. I thought I spotted a piece of its jagged silhouette, but I could never be sure.

By evening, I reached water and made camp beside clear, pleasant Blue Lake. I felt good. On my fifth day of hiking, I was feeling my stride.

Leaving attractive Blue Lake in the morning, I enjoyed a most enjoyable walk along an easy trail that passed by a string of lakes. After beautiful Blue Lake, I came to peaceful Junction Lake, where I paused for an after-breakfast snack. Then, I went on to deep-blue, beautiful Bear Lake, where I stopped for my mid-morning milk and honey. Still further on, I was treated to a view looking down onto an attractive unnamed lakelet. I found a view site where I ate my lunch. After passing the string of lakes, the trail started switchbacking up to the side of Sawtooth Mt. Near the top of the crest, another glorious view opened up, profiling jagged Sawtooth Mountain and offering still another distant view of majestic Mt. Adams. Upon winding down the north side of Sawtooth Mountain, the trail crossed road 123. Near the road, there was a sign "Huckleberry Field = Indians Only." I learned that the "Indians Only" applied to the berry bushes on the east side of the road only. If I had wanted to stop to pick berries, it would have been legal for me to pick them on the west side of the road. Walking ahead, I came to three men with pails who I presumed were Indians. I felt prompted to say hello. "Are you finding some good berries?" I asked. One responded, "Yes, we have a few." Then he asked, "How do you like backpacking?" I replied, "I really like backpacking on this trail, as I see so much beautiful country." "I'd like to try it one day," he responded. "I hope you do," I replied.

By evening, I reached water at Mosquito Lake. I was eager to make camp, as it was around 7:00 pm. As I was drinking water at the outlet of the Lake, a hiker appeared and said, "Didn't I meet you two years ago at Three Fingered Jack?" I was amazed and replied, "Yes, I was hiking there two years ago. You have a very good memory." Ken, then offered to show me a bigger and better campsite than the one I had hurriedly selected. I joined him. Upon my return to the creek for additional water for supper, I looked up and there, to my amazement, stood Tony, a trail hiker whom I had met at Panther Creek. He explained that he had taken a day off and left the trail near Trout Creek to go out and visit a friend. Now, as it was growing late, he was eager to find water and a campsite. I told him where I was camped, near Ken. He was eager to join us and placed his tent near us. After supper, I joined Ken and Tony around a small campfire where we had a good time talking about our trail experiences. Ken had been attracted to Bear Lake and had stopped and caught a trout, which he joyfully ate for lunch. Later he told us about his adventures on last summer's canoe trip on Vancouver Island, which included being caught in a frightening wind storm and reaching shore just as his canoe filled with water. When Tony returned from fetching water at the creek, he announced that he had seen a bear. I looked quickly but could see no creature moving in the direction to which he pointed. It was quite dark. Had I been missing bear sightings by not seeing them in the dark? I wondered. When it was time to crawl into my bedroll, I thought to myself that I had enjoyed the conversation but, at the same time, I missed my evening's solitude and time for reflection. No doubt, I would be back to camping alone most nights.

My walk the following day led through forests, dipped down and across gullies, and led up to a number of ridges. On one of these green-grass ridge descents, Tony caught up with me. He was striding along swiftly and called out, "I'll meet you again at Snoqualmie Pass."

I continued to marvel at the lush, green foliage, so abundant in the state of Washington. Graceful ferns bordered the trail. Periodically, I stopped to pick huckleberries and an occasional strawberry. Surrounded by such beauty, I felt truly inspired. By evening, I made camp on White Salmon Creek. Nearby was a cold, freshwater spring. I was camped at the edge of the Mt. Adams Wilderness.

On the trail the next morning, I climbed to the junction of Round the Mountain Trail. Here, I was treated to yet another glorious view of the four volcanoes. To the south, I could still make out the snowy peak of Mt. Hood. To the west, I thought I was seeing the jagged silhouette of Mt. St. Helens. In the hazy distance to the far north loomed the tall, majestic peak of Mt. Rainier. Closer by, to the northeast, views of Mt. Adams with its prominent snowy glaciers appeared. What a spectacular view to store in my memory.

Round the Mountain Trail traverses the base of Mt. Adams. From it, hikers can connect to trails that climb to the peak of Mt. Adams. After enjoying my mid-morning snack, I descended on the trail to Sheep Lake and by its shore found a pleasant lunch spot. After lunch, while walking along the trail near the lake shore, a party of horseback riders caught up with me. There were two men mounted on their horses and a loud, complaining woman walking beside her horse. Passing me, she complained loudly that her horse was lame, so she had to walk. She told me that they were returning to Dean's Horse Camp, after riding on the Round-the-Mountain Trail. I thought to myself that solo backpacking was much more peaceful than horse pack trips.

On my afternoon's walk, I started seeing fields of alpine flowers. I was exalted as I walked slowly beside these colorful wildflower gardens. I remember seeing lupine, Indian warriors, daisies, heather, phlox, white lilies, intermingled with other delicate, brightly colored flowers. At the same time that I was exalted at viewing the alpine flower gardens I was glimpsing views of Mt. Adams bedecked with its snowy glaciers. Upon reaching the next gurgling, snow-melt creek—Mutton Creek—I turned off the trail and searched out a campsite with a view. I was so pleased when I found just the right campsite, with a view from my bed looking up at snow-topped Mt. Adams.

After supper, I enjoyed another special treat—a beautiful sunset that lit up the western sky. I was kept busy turning my head to watch the rose-red western sky and then turning to the east to see the setting sun's reflection lighting up the snowy glaciers of Mt. Adams and painting them in reddish colors. When I finally climbed into my bedroll, feeling inspired by the beauty of my surroundings, I decided that this was the best campsite that I had to date on my walk in the State of Washington.

My next morning's walk treated me to continuing magnificent scenes of Mt. Adams and its snowy glaciers. Frequently, the trail dipped down to cross chalk-colored glacier-melt streams. First, I crossed the Lewis River, then the west fork of Adams Creek, the middle fork of Adams Creek, and then the scenic, gurgling flow of Killen Creek. For my morning snack, I chose a small rise beside Killen Creek that looked over an alpine wildflower garden decorating these lower slopes of Mt. Adams. This was a prize scene, one which I thought could adorn a wilderness prize photo such as those chosen for Sierra Club calendars.

Soon I was joined by a couple who were also was attracted to this peaceful scene. "Would you care to have some dried apples?" they offered. "Thank you," I answered, as I reached into a plastic bag filled with moist apple slices. "Are the apple slices from Washington?" I asked. "No," they replied, "they are from Sebastopol, California." "What a coincidence," I replied. "I live next to Sebastopol, in Santa Rosa." Then the man who had offered me the apples explained that he had grown up in

Sebastopol, but now lives in Seattle. His father, who is in his '80s, still lives in Sebastopol and maintains his own orchard. He visits him frequently and returns to Washington with apples, apple juice, and dried apples. With the change in the market for Gravenstein apples, for which Sebastopol is well known, most of his father's crop now goes into producing apple juice.

As we sat enjoying our snacks with the glorious view of Mt. Adams as a backdrop, I commented on how I liked to store such memorable scenes in my memory bank and enjoy them when I have returned home. The woman responded enthusiastically, saying that she also had made it a practice to store favorite memories and that she liked to bring them back and visualize the beautiful scenes during rainy days. We both enthusiastically affirmed that we liked this idea.

By midday, the trail led toward a forested area of small trees. Soon afterward, I left the views of Mt. Adams and its snowy glaciers. I had been treated to these spectacular, sweeping views for most of the past day-and-a-half. I regretted leaving Mt. Adams behind, but told myself that this could not go on forever. I consoled myself with the thought that it was time to move north, toward the next snowy glacier—Mt. Rainier.

Later, as the trail advanced to a forest of taller trees, I was startled to see ahead, by the side of the trail, some large, bright-orange, plastic-covered objects. I was really puzzled. What were these man-made objects doing in the forest? Moving closer, I discovered some blackened tree branches. Now I knew that there had been a fire. Walking along gingerly, I soon saw a firefighter approaching. He told me the story. There had been a fire a month ago and they had now come back to collect the equipment. Fortunately, it had not been a big fire and had been contained fairly easily. I felt lucky that my walk did not take place during the days of the fire.

By late afternoon, I came to a junction and turned off the trail a short distance to reach the former Midway Guard Station, where I planned to camp. The Guard Station, where hikers formerly had been able to pick up mailed food packages, had burned down in 1976 and had not been replaced. There remained an open grassy clearing that was suitable for camping and which was equipped with restrooms and clean, potable water. Searching around, I saw that the center of the clearing was already occupied by a large tent. A found a small, level place for my bedroom in a corner of the clearing. Upon returning for water, I met the tent's occupants—a family consisting of a father, and a young son and daughter. They volunteered that they were traveling south, having entered the trail at White Pass. They were eager to tell me about the challenging trail traversing the north end of Goat Rocks Wilderness, which I expected to reach in two to three days. The young boy said excitedly that the trail runs along the peak of a ridge that is very narrow and rocky. He described it as a knife-edge and said, "You will have to walk carefully across the ridge. If you step too near the edge, you could slide down to the bottom of the valley." I listened and was intrigued. I wondered how difficult it would really be and wondered if the young boy might be exaggerating a little. Nevertheless, I was concerned enough to hope that I would arrive at the ridge in good weather, rather than in a snow or rainstorm.

While listening to the family's trail stories, I could not help but notice that both the father and son were smoking. I did not expect to see many trail hikers who were smokers. In the morning as I was breaking camp, I heard loud coughing as I passed the large tent. How unfortunate, I thought.

Returning to the trail the next morning, I walked through woods for most of the day. Two hikers traveling from the north approached me and surprised me by asking, "Are you Eleanor?"

GOAT ROCKS WILDERNESS, SPLIT ROCK, WITH MT. RANIER IN DISTANCE

"Yes," I replied. "Tony told us to look for you on the trail. He's up ahead." What a friendly gesture on Tony's part, I thought. A little further on, I met two women backpackers. We stopped to compare notes. I was pleased to meet women who were backpacking as, at that time (1987), it was a pretty rare encounter. We all agreed that there was no reason why healthy and knowledgeable women could not backpack. They said that they also hiked alone sometimes and enjoyed the sense of freedom it gave them. I agreed. We felt commonness.

In the afternoon, I came to a sign announcing the entry to the Goat Rocks Wilderness. This was an exciting trail mark for me, as I had seen photographs and read about this unique and beautiful Wilderness. Soon the trail climbed up to a ridgecrest that offered a tremendous view looking toward the gigantic free-standing Goat Rocks and the summit of tall, Old Snowy Mountain. By evening, I reached the junction of the Walupt Lake Trail. I turned onto the trail and walked a short distance until I reached water and a campsite beside a clear-flowing creeklet.

The trail north the next morning from my campsite near the Walupt Trail junction climbed up for most of the day. Striding along, I came to a sign announcing, "You are passing through the Yakima Indian Reservation—no trespassing." I had no intention or desire to trespass, but as I walked on, I began to wonder what I would do about rest stops and my lunch stop. Continuing on and seeing no hoped-for sign announcing the end of the reservation land, I became a little weary and felt that it was time for a rest stop. I decided to sit down, cautiously, and to have my customary snack by the side of the trail. I did not feel relaxed, however, and after a short break, I decided that I had better move on. Finally, after ascending Cispus Pass, a sign announced, "Leaving the Yakima reservation." Now I could relax.

As I approached the heart of the Goat Rocks Wilderness, trail traffic increased. I passed two groups of day hikers, followed by three southbound backpackers who asked, "Are you Eleanor?" "Yes," I replied. "Tony says 'hello.' We passed him at White Pass." Again, I was delighted and amazed. The three hikers were completing a section of the Pacific Crest Trail between White Pass and the Oregon border.

I decided to make camp early to avoid the crowds that were likely to be camping around the Goat Rocks and the popular Dana May Yelverton Shelter. I started my search. Shortly after crossing a stream—a tributary of the Cispus River, I spotted a potential sight near a small waterfall. Removing my pack, I climbed up for a closer inspection. I found a small shelf, just large enough for my bedroom. I was delighted by the attractive ambience of the little waterfall and had gained enough elevation to afford an exciting view of the protruding, glaciated Goat Rocks near the Dana May Yelverton Shelter. Faintly and mysteriously in the background, I could see the snowy peak of Mt. Rainier. I felt so good. I was thankful for good weather and good views. I did notice, however, some cloud formation to the northwest. I hoped that it did not present an immediate threat of stormy weather.

In the morning, I thought I had only a short distance to go until I would reach the glaciated Goat Rocks and the Dana May Yelverton Shelter, but I encountered an unanticipated

**MT. RAINIER WITH PACKWOOD
GLACIER IN FOREGROUND**

steep, hard climb. It was slow going. Near the shelter, the trail reaches its highest elevation in the state of Washington at 7080 ft. Upon finally reaching the rocks, I found it surrounded by crowds of hikers. It was Sunday, and I was near a roadhead. I was glad I had stopped early and camped by the beautiful, picturesque waterfalls.

I lingered for awhile to drink in the views and take some photographs. It was indeed a special place. The two giant upright rocks, rising high with trees growing in between them, stood alone—like sentinels guarding the high grassland. I presumed they were dropped to their resting place by a huge glacier. A little further on, I reached the rock-walled Dana May Yelverton Shelter. Erected in memory of a sixteen-year-old girl who had died of hypothermia, it is graphic reminder of the hazards of this high-mountain land of wind, cold, and snow.

The scene upon looking out from near the shelter is most appealing. The ledge upon which the shelter rests borders the Upper Lake Creek canyon, and around the edges of the canyon stand numerous white-topped snowy peaks. In the far distance, the snowy summit of Mt. Rainier rises in all its majesty.

Fulfilled with the views and ready to move on, I approached a slanting, snow-filled crossing—the upper Packwood Glacier. I moved cautiously, digging my feet into steps made by other hikers, and concentrated on maintaining my balance. I was thankful when I reached solid ground at the far end of the glacier. Beyond the snow-filled glacier walk, trail hikers encounter still another challenge—a walk across a narrow, knife-edged rocky ridge. I remember hearing about this challenge from the family camped near Midway Creek. Actually, I enjoyed this walk, both because of its challenge and uniqueness and because it afforded still more glorious views of snowy peaks and canyons, with majestic Mt. Rainier looming in the distance. Midway across, I wanted to sit down to eat my lunch. I searched for a small space. It was not easy to find a place wide enough to sit down without completely blocking the narrow trail. Sitting down among some rocks at the edge of a trail, I created a miniature rockslide, causing a rock or two to tumble noisily down the slope. I felt guilty having disturbed the delicate balance of the knife-edged trail. The walk led down to Elk Pass and followed up still more difficult, steep descents. Again, I stepped cautiously. By late afternoon, I reached the forest and the trail leveled off. By evening, I came to shallow Lutz Lake and made camp. Looking at the shallow, still water, I decided to purify my water. This was the first time during my walk in wet Washington that I had felt the need to purify water. I went to bed accompanied by the sound of a squeaking tree. A tree leaning against another tree bowed and bent in response to gentle gusts of the wind.

Breaking camp in the morning, I was eager but doubtful that I would reach White Pass by the end of the day. I still had some 13 miles to go.

From Lutz Lake, the trail descended through forests. It was easy going until the trail switchbacked up to a ridge, where I enjoyed a view of Mt. Rainier. The trail then contoured around the side of Hogback Mountain, offering still more scenes of distant Mt. Rainier. Descending again into a forest, I came to a beautifully brushed trail and soon caught up with a trail crew. I greeted them and said, "This is a beautiful trail to walk on. Thank you for your fine work." They smiled appreciatively. I was really grateful for their trail-brushing. All too soon, the new trail ended and I found myself walking on old, unimproved trail, which was full of protruding roots. I had to slow down and watch my step. This last trail section before reaching the highway seemed eternally long. I kept telling myself, "Don't expect to reach the highway until it appears." I reminded myself to relax and enjoy the walk. Finally, I heard cars passing on the highway. I reached the roadway around 5:30 pm and turned to the west to walk to White Pass Village, which I reached about 6:00 pm.

It was too late to collect my food package. I pondered over where to spend the night. I usually liked to sleep out until my final destination, as I felt that I did not want to break the spell of being surrounded by the ambience of the wilderness and the magic of looking at the night sky. At White Pass, however, I was torn. I was eager for a shower and clean clothes. It was growing cold and windy. The campground was about a mile away from the village, which housed the post office, as well as a laundromat, store, and resort. I was ready to stop. I decided to sleep in, and I registered for a room at the White Pass Ski Lodge. Snug inside my Ski Lodge room as the night grew colder, I took advantage of the room's small fireplace. I watched and warmed myself by the fire while eating my supper, which had been supplemented by a sandwich and potato chips purchased at the village store. I spent a warm and comfortable night.

Since my walk from the Columbia River Gorge to White Pass had been a rather long stretch, I had planned to spend a leisurely, rest-filled day at White Pass. My first special treat was to have a sit-down breakfast at the Ski Lodge. I ordered scrambled eggs, bacon, potatoes, toast, and coffee. From there, I strolled down to the store—the everything-in-one store: groceries, post office, and laundromat. I lined up for the laundromat. There were two couples ahead of me. One of the couples recognized me. They had been camped at Panther Creek when I was there. They announced that Byron and Margaret had hurried on ahead to collect a food package at Crystal Mountain Ski Resort. The two brothers from Kansas City, they reported, had dropped out. Before departing, they gave me a plastic bag containing assorted spices and herbs. For the rest of my journey, I sprinkled the herbs on my stew. I really enjoyed their pungent taste, smell and fragrance. From then on, I have added an herb bag to my food supply. Finally, my turn to use the laundromat came up. I had another long wait while I watched my hiking gear go through the wash and dry cycles.

I carried my food package, which had arrived safely at the post office, to my lodge room, where I enjoyed the luxury of space to sort out my packages while repacking my bag. This resulted in a well-organized pack. Afterward, I returned to the store for my lunch snack and was greeted by Ken McTeague, whom I had last seen at Mosquito Lake outlet. He had just arrived and seemed excited. He told me the story of how he had camped near the Yelverton Shelter and crossed the snowfield of the precarious Packwood Glacier in the morning when it was frozen and icy. He had crawled across on his hands and knees. Admitting that it was scary, he was thankful when he finally arrived safely on the other side. He added that he felt good that he had been able to accomplish this backpack trip, following bypass surgery last winter.

By mid-afternoon, I felt eager to move on. Although I had planned for a rest stop, I felt I had rested long enough. The familiar attraction of the trail was calling me. I shouldered my pack and started my walk to rejoin the trail. Soon, I arrived at the White Pass Campground. Looking over the campground, I saw it was crowded and decided to move on. I walked about three miles further and found a quiet, secluded campsite on the shores of shallow, peaceful Sand Lake.

My next day's walk was an easy one—mostly on level trail through forests. The trail passed by numerous ponds and small tarns, and periodically colorful gardens of wildflowers appeared. I was reminded again that I was hiking through wet, green Washington. Traffic was light. I met only a trail crew. By late afternoon, it had become cloudy. It looked like there was the possibility of rain some time in the future. I stopped for the night, camping in a grassy area near Fish Lake.

I awoke early in the morning—a rude awakening. It was raining. My head, which had been protruding outside of my bivouac sack was wet. Feeling around, I discovered, unhappily, that a lot more things were wet: my pillow, the hood of my sleeping bag, and, I suspected, a lot more. I had placed my bedroll in a little gully-like depression, so actually I had been sleeping in a little puddle. What poor planning! I had been sleeping so soundly that the rain had not awakened me.

As soon as there was some morning light, I pulled myself out of bed and put up my tent. Crawling into the tent with my wet gear, I began to survey the extent of the wetness. My air mattress cover was soaked. A good deal of my bivouac sack was wet and, worst of all, half of my down bedroll was damp.

I lay in my damp surroundings for a long time before I was ready to make a move. Finally, I was aroused by voices outside. Some hikers were searching for the side trail to Fish Lake. I finally poked my head out of the tent. It was still raining, but not too hard, and it was not too cold. Slowly, I faced my planning for the day. In my tent, after I surveyed my wet equipment, I kept telling myself that I must be careful to guard against the threat of hypothermia, which could be brought on by wet and cold. My predominant thought was to play it safe and return to White Pass. Something, however, kept me from carrying out this plan. I really wanted to move on and not lose trail mileage. I weighed the prospects. It was 15 miles to Chinook Pass. The guidebook described the trail ahead as being "dangerous" when there are lingering snow patches. While still debating my plan, a hiker came down the trail from the north looking for water. Eagerly, I asked him about the trail ahead. "No it is not dangerous," he said, "just a lot of ups and downs." Slowly, I developed my plan. I would need to spend one more night camping out before reaching Chinook Pass. It was too late in the day for me to hike 15 miles of ups and downs on a wet trail. I devised a plan to protect myself from hypothermia during the night that I would spend with my wet gear. First, I would clothe myself with dry layers. Fortunately, my clothing, including my first layer of polyurethane ski underwear, had not gotten wet. I would add an additional layer—a vapor-barrier suit. I had a lot of faith in the vapor-barrier, non-breathable material protecting me by not letting my body heat escape. My next idea was inspired by reading John Muir's account of a time he was out at night with little gear. He kept a fire going. I also remembered hearing a story told by a Sierra Club member who had participated in a group hike in which the pack animals had stumbled and dumped the gear, including bedrolls, into a creek. The group spent much of the night around a fire, holding up their down bedrolls to dry. Armed with these thoughts, I grew quite confident that I could make it safely through the night.

I packed up my wet equipment, while wiping off what excess water I could with absorbent towels. It was an unpleasant task. It was not until around 11:00 am that I started north on the trail. This trail was slow with its ups and downs, but it was not difficult. Toward evening, a mist descended. In the distance, I could see a hiker approaching. His silhouette, with his poncho extended broadly, reminded me of a giant bat. When he drew near, I asked him about the trail to Two Lakes—a possible campsite with water. "Yes," he assured me. I passed the trail junction, and it was not far ahead. Soon I found it and pulled off the trail to camp at the first of the Two Lakes.

After erecting my tent and surveying the campsite, I rejected the idea of spending the night by a fire. In the misty rain, it seemed too laborious to spend my energy finding firewood. I devised another plan. I would eat and drink something every hour during the night to safeguard against hypothermia.

I gathered water for the night and breakfast. After eating a good supper, I carefully donned my clothing for the night, including my vapor-barrier suit. I crawled into my half-wet bedroll and tried to snuggle toward the dry side. I was reasonably comfortable. I carried out my plan of eating and drinking every hour. My flashlight had a real workout. It seemed cold around 4:00 am. It was a long night. Finally, I was glad to see the first rays of daylight. I had made it through the night safely. I was thankful.

When morning arrived, I was eager to be up and on my way. I kept saying "Oh, Lord, I'm thankful to have come through the night safely." It was still foggy, with an off-and-on light rain falling. I ate my breakfast, packed my damp gear, climbed up the path, and turned onto the main trail. I sloshed on. Soon my damp boots became saturated. Looking down, I could see little water spouts rising out of my boots. I had developed cracks toward the front of the boots. I reminded myself to write a note for next year's list that I must buy new boots for walking wet Washington.

Fortunately, the trail from Two Lakes to Chinook Pass was not difficult, although marked by gentle ups and downs, it was a little slow. Midday, I passed Dewey Lake, which was near the edge of Mt. Rainier National Park. In clear weather, I would have been searching for a view of the snowy top of majestic Mt. Rainier. Today, with such low visibility, this was not to be.

When I arrived at Highway 410 at Chinook Pass, I was greeted by a lineup of waiting cars. The pass area was busy with a road-construction crew, and big, noisy machines were swinging back and forth. I ventured out onto the edge of the roadway and asked a man wearing a red jacket, "Which direction can I go to find lodging?" "You can go either way—west to Paradise, or east to Naches," he replied hurriedly. I pondered for a moment, but not for long; looking up, I saw two men in a pickup truck pulling a horse trailer who were waiting for the pilot car to signal them forward. I remembered that they had passed me on the trail near Dewey Lake and we had had a brief, friendly conversation. Quickly, I approached them and asked for a ride. Happily, they invited me into their cab. They were friendly and pleasant and suggested that they would let me off at the Whistling Rock Resort, where I would find lodging. I felt fortunate to find a ride so easily. The friendly horsemen delivered me right to the door of the Whistling Rock office, where I thanked them and bailed out. Inside the office, a cordial resort manager upon hearing my story replied, "We are full—it is Friday night." I felt a bit of a let-down. She was, however, sympathetic and helpful and offered to phone Squaw Rock Resort. Happily I was able to reserve their last vacant cabin.

Squaw Rock was a short distance down the highway, but too far to walk. I went outside and begged for a ride from two friendly men who were on their way to join their families at a campground. They let me off at the Squaw Rock Resort office. In a short time, I was happily ensconced in a small, rustic, framed cabin, equipped with a gas heater, which I immediately turned on. I spent the next hour strewing my wet articles all around the room. Some of them I hung from the cabin's rafters and others I spread out on the floor. I had created a mosaic of my gear so I could hardly move from one end of the room to the other. I rejoiced, feeling fortunate to be inside a warm, dry space. Satisfied that I had started the drying process, I moved over to the resort's restaurant. The dining room was surprisingly full, resounding with a multitude of conversations. I ordered catfish and sat back to listen and observe. There were a goodly number of tall, sun-burned-looking men. As I listened to their conversations about rigs and saws, I deduced that they were lumber workers. I felt that I was observing a group of workers whom I had heard much about but had never been close to before—the loggers of the northwest. Listening more intensively, I thought I was hearing a distinct northwestern drawl. They appeared to be enjoying a good deal of camaraderie. After looking at a menu, one of them drawled, "Rice pilaf? What in the world is pilaf?"

In the morning, I surveyed my equipment. Most things were dry. I decided that my tent could use some attention, as it had been too big to spread out completely in the cabin. I moved outside and hung my tent over a clothesline to dry out the remaining damp corners. I then took my bedroll and wool socks to the lodge's laundromat and put them in the dryer. I was so happy when my goosedown bedroll came out of the dryer all dry and puffy. The wool socks took a little longer but soon were nearly dry.

By late morning, I was packed with dry gear and felt re-freshed and eager to return to the trail. It was time to seek a ride to Chinook Pass. I stationed myself by the side of the small, old-style gas station in front of the resort store and of-fice. Soon, I discovered that the majority of traffic was going in the other direction—east toward Naches. I felt hopeful, however, when a car pulled into the gas station that was headed west towards Mt. Rainier. There were two middle-aged men in the car, and they had what seemed to me at first glance to be a vacant back seat. I approached one of the men as he was pump-ing gas. I told him that I was backpacking on the Pacific Crest Trail and that I needed a ride to return to the trail at Chinook Pass. He hesitated, then said crossly, "I guess I could give you a ride, but I don't want to." His reply has puzzled and haunted me ever since. I felt rejected. Feeling rejected, I felt sad. "Why did he not want to?" I kept asking myself.

Finally, after a long wait, a young couple in a new car pulled in for gas. I approached them. They did not hesitate and happily offered me a ride. What a relief. There was a good deal of enjoyable excitement, as the young woman exclaimed that she had won her new car in a drawing at a car dealership. She and her friend were out to test the car on its first run. I rejoiced with her at her good fortune all the way to the pass. She was, understandably, still happily excited. She became apprehensive when, approaching the pass, we arrived at the road-repair section, where there was a detour consisting of a road surface of rocky gravel. She cautioned her friend to drive slowly, as she did not want rocks to dent her new car. As I disembarked at Chinook Pass, I again thanked them profusely and wished her great happiness in driving her new car.

At the pass, I really had to search for the trail amidst the piles of rubble pushed up by the highway construction. I followed a trail for a few yards with uncertainty. It did not seem to be going in the right direction—to the northeast. A couple appeared. "Is this the trail to Sheep Lake?" I asked. "No," they replied. "this is the Tipsoo Trail." I retreated to the highway shoulder and asked a highway worker for directions to the trail to Sheep Lake. "Go along the side of the highway until you find a trail sign," he directed. I trudged along the excavated highway rubble and finally spotted the trail.

As I climbed up the trail to Sheep Lake, the fog descended and it grew colder. Arriving at the lake, I hurried to put up my tent so I would have shelter from the wind and cold. With my tent erected, I eagerly crawled into my sleeping bag to warm up. When I was comfortable and warm, I crawled out of my bed to make supper. I noticed some busy, enthusiastic campers next to me and became curious about the group because it appeared to be mostly men and young girls. My curiosity compelled me to walk over to their campsite. I asked, "Where are you from?" A man replied, "From Seattle. We are members of our men's church club, and we decided to take our daughters camping." They asked me to join their large, inviting campfire, which I did. They were interested in my walk and asked me lots of questions. A wide-eyed young girl asked, "Did you see any wild animals?" "I have only seen deer," I replied.

It was still somewhat cold and foggy when I packed up my gear in the morning. The lake was steaming with rising and falling mist that gave it an intriguing, mystical look.

The trail north from Sheep Lake was marked by moderate ups and downs. By late morning, I reached Bear Gap, where I could look across a canyon and see the Crystal Mountain Ski Area. This was a possible supply point for Pacific Crest Trail walkers and could be reached by turning off onto the Silver Creek Trail.

In the afternoon, the air cleared and the trail climbed up to Crown Point. Looking back, I could finally see clearly the glorious view of snow-capped Mt. Rainier. I took its picture. This was the first clear view I had had of the mountain since Goat Rocks.

By late afternoon, I turned off-trail to camp at the Big Crow Shelter, a recommended resource for water. I surveyed the campsite and decided to use the three-sided shelter for my bedroom, as it offered protection from a brisk wind that was sweeping down the Big Crow Basin. I rolled out my bedroll in the shelter, gathered wood and water, and was preparing my supper by the fire ring adjacent to the open end of the shelter when I heard voices and hoof beats approaching. Two horse-men arrived and announced that they were planning to use the shelter for the night. Mike and Craig, who lived not too far away in the state of Washington, explained that they were on a short trail outing.

After unloading their gear, collecting water, and staking their horses, the two horsemen pulled out dinner utensils and opened cans of Dinty Moore Stew. I was intrigued when I saw Mike's blue-granite-style plate and large, old-style tin cup. He explained enthusiastically that he was active in the Civil War reenactment group. He proudly showed me other historic replica equipment that he had acquired, including a poncho made of real rubber and blue, 100% wool pants. As we sat around a huge, roaring campfire, in contrast to my usual twig-branch fire, I heard a good deal more about Mike's Civil War reenactment adventures. He and Charlotte, his horse, had traveled all the way to Tennessee to take part in a reenactment of the Battle of Shiloh. He planned to go to another battlefield enactment the following year. Periodically, his storytelling was interrupted by a visit to Charlotte, who was roped to a tree. He would check on Charlotte's position to see that she had enough grass and water. Quite often during the evening's conversation, he would interject, "How are you doing Char?"

It was, indeed, an interesting evening, and I carried away from my experience with Mike and Craig a high respect for the devotion between horsemen and their horses. They were most caring, making sure that their horses were well fed and comfortable.

In the morning, I bid farewell to Mike and Craig as they were preparing what looked like a substantial, good-sized horserider's breakfast.

Back on the trail, I soon reached an open, level ridge and turning around, I beheld, to my delight, another gloriously clear view of Mt. Rainier's snowy head.

Moving along on a moderately easy trail, I heard hoof beats approaching. Mike and Craig had caught up with me. They greeted me by saying, "You are hiking along at a pretty fast clip. You have a good stride." Of course, I was pleased with their remark. They were returning to Government Meadow, where their horse trailers were parked.

Rounding another rise in the trail, I was startled. Trotting along ahead of me were two tall, red-brown elk. They glanced at me and slowly ambled to one side. I was discovering that animals, elk and deer in particular, like to travel on man-made trails. There was much evidence of this, as I often saw their footprints while walking along the trail.

I found the trail stretch between Crow Basin and Government Meadow to be wonderfully pleasant. There were frequent views in all directions, and there were sections in which I delighted in gazing at abundant beds of brightly colored wildflowers.

By mid-afternoon, I went off-trail a short distance to view the Arch Rock Shelter. The shelter offered a pleasant campsite possibility, but I wasn't ready to camp, so I enjoyed an afternoon snack and rest before moving on.

A southbound hiker whom I passed recognized me. He reminded me that we met each other on the trail at Goat Rocks Wilderness. He had gone out at White Pass and then hitchhiked to Government Meadow. He was now walking south, returning to White Pass.

By evening, I reached the south edge of large, Government Meadow. The meadow is accessible by road, offering hikers and horsemen a convenient trailhead. My campsite was unaesthetic. In my effort to stay away from the road area, I ended up pitching my bivouac sack in a grassy, viewless area.

In the morning after packing my gear, I explored Government Meadow. No one was there. A pickup however, was parked at trailhead. I peeked into the rustic, weather-beaten cabin at the edge of the meadow and paused to read a tribute etched on a wooden sign that read:

Camp Mike Urich—Dedicated to Memory of Mike Ulrich
1888-1957
The mountain Gods from seats on high
Rejoiced to see Mike Urich die
And at his death gave this decree
"To all who pass here know that we
Entrust to Big Mike Urich's hands
These camps, these trails, these forest lands
To rule, protect, to love and scan
Well as he did while mortal man;
And deal out sentence stern and just
To those who violate this trust.'
Stranger, beware, leave not a fire—
Foul not Mike's camp, rouse not his ire."

Mike Urich was a Forest Service trail-maintenance worker. I was tremendously pleased to see this tribute to a dedicated worker who had committed years to improving the trails.

Before saying goodbye to the Meadow, I filled my water bag, counting out my water needs for the next seven miles.

The trail walk in the morning was easy, I felt good, and it was a sunny pleasant day. I slowed my pace in the afternoon as the trail climbed up and contoured around Pyramid Peak. After another descent, I became alert that it was time to start my search for water. The description in the guidebook presented some uncertainties as to the location of water near Green Pass. In addition, a more-recent guidebook supplement announced that the trail in the Green Pass area had been rerouted and that a new trail section would pass a spring. I searched and, happily, I spotted a spring not far from the trail. Reassured to have located water for the night, I found a level spot for my bedroom and made camp near the spring.

In the morning, I climbed up the slopes of barren, grass-covered Blowout Mountain. Nearing the top, I paused and turned around; here again, I could still see in the far distance, the snowy peak of Mt. Rainier. The view to the north was not so pleasant. I was about to enter the area in which forests had been stripped of their trees and left covered by desolate stumps—areas of clear-cutting!

Walking ahead, the trail led through a recently clear-cut area. I was mad and sad. If they must log, I thought, at least they should leave a corridor of trees along the sides of the trail. I was beginning to understand why so many wilderness lovers were advocating for changes in the forest service principles and practices. Congress had placed the Pacific Crest Trail in the care of the National Forest Service—for planning of the route and for maintenance. Yet the very trail they were asked to develop and maintain was being completely devastated by permits that the Forest Service granted to logging companies. I was very angry.

I was also walking in a scarce-water area. I planned to camp at a creek beyond Sheets Pass, which was described as "possibly carrying water through September." I wondered if I would find water for the night. Before arriving at Sheets Pass, I reached a well-maintained logging road crossing at Tacoma Pass. I hesitated. With the uncertainty of water ahead, I decided to try to beg for water from a passing car. I sat down, by the side of the road, chewed on my trail mix, and waited. Fortunately, I did not have long to wait. A pickup with two men in the cab came bouncing along. I hailed them and asked, "Do you have any extra water?" The driver, looking a little puzzled, slowly got out of the car, went around to the pickup bed, and reached for a pinkish-colored plastic bottle. I was pleased. I got out my water bag and held it upright, ready to receive water. Much to my surprise, the liquid flowing out of the plastic bottle was bright red. I had received about a quart of Kool-Aid. I thanked the man profusely. I felt greatly relieved that I was sure of liquid for the night—pink or white. He seemed pleased also, as we both went our respective ways. Walking along and laughing to myself, I could not help but be amused at my Kool-Aid gift. I wondered what my supper stew would taste like rehydrated with Kool-Aid.

After climbing up to Sheets Pass through more devastated clear-cut forest area, I arrived at the creek. I was delighted—it still had a moderately good flow of water. I made camp and I had fresh, white water for my stew. I could not convince myself, however, to let go completely of the Kool-Aid that the two men had so generously given me. It was an appreciated gift, and I was reluctant to throw it away. For the next two days I just added fresh water, as needed, to my Kool-Aid gift so that my water became gradually less pink.

My next day's walk from the creek campsite near Sheets Pass to a campsite near Lizard Lake was slow and tedious. The trail climbed up and down, and some of the ups were rather steep. Additionally, some sections of the trail itself were rough and poorly graded. Worst of all, the trail continued to lead in and out of clear-cut patches. I felt sad and enervated. I was still thinking that this trail, designated as a National Scenic Trail, should not be devastated by clear-cutting.

As I was pacing along around midday, I became aware that three young, fast, sturdy hikers were approaching. I had not met any trail walkers for the past two days "Hi, how are you?" one called out as he approached. It was cheerful Tony, hiking with two friends who lived in the town of Yakima. He was full of questions about how I was doing and how I was feeling. I assured him that I was fine and then I voiced my sadness about the clear-cutting. He was more inclined to accept this phenomenon as inevitable: "Loggers make money." But he did like my idea of advocating for a tree corridor surrounding the trail.

In the afternoon, I went off-trail a short distance to beg for water at the Stampede Weather Station. I walked up the steps of the neat wood-frame house, rang the bell, and prepared to give my speech about my need and appreciation for water. I waited for quite a long time, but there was no answer. There was a car in the driveway, but apparently no one was home. I felt that it was time to help myself—I had attempted to ask. I found the outside water faucet and filled my water bag with fresh, good-tasting water.

I plodded on. Originally, I had tentatively planned to camp at Stirrup Lake, some three-miles distant, but I was tired. I stopped and made camp in a cluster of trees near Lizard Lake. Usually, I was not tired while walking on the trail. Was my tiredness due to seeing the sad sites of the clear-cutting?

My walk the following day from Lizard Lake to Mirror Lake was far more pleasant than the preceding day's walk. I walked through forest-lined trails most of the day, with clear-cut areas becoming less numerous. I walked through huckleberry patches and stopped frequently to sample the berries. They were so good—just at the right stage of ripeness.

After passing Stampede Pass, I paused among a group of huckleberry bushes, where I met an older couple who were busily filling their cans with berries. I stopped for a brief chat. They explained to me the difference between the high-bushed berry and the low-bushed berry. The low-bushed berries, they pointed out, were generally sweeter. They said that they liked to freeze the berries and they enjoyed them all winter. They particularly like to have them on their cereal.

I was pleased to find fresh water at Stirrup Creek and then again at Meadow Creek. Near Yakima Pass, I met a young man clad in a white t-shirt and khaki shorts slowly walking south along the trail. He stopped and asked me, "How far is it to the next water?" I pulled out my map and showed him that he would reach water at Meadow Creek and Stirrup Creek. In a relaxed and laid-back manner, he volunteered, "I don't like to walk, but I like to camp." When I told him that I was coming out at Snoqualmie Pass he said, "I guess one has to return to civilization some time." He volunteered that he'd been out for four months and then said, "I guess I will have to go back to work in the winter."

I arrived at Mirror Lake around 4:30 pm. What a delightful, view-filled lake. Its calm, deep-blue waters seemed to be set in a rock-sided bowl. Trees often perched on rocks hugged the shoreline, adding splashes of green between the deep-blue water and the gray-granite stone walls. On the lake's west side, tall Pinkham Peak rose steeply. I searched for quite a while, pausing to test for views before choosing a campsite that offered a view looking across the lake toward Pinkham Peak. After supper, I sat on a bank near my campsite and watched the reflections cast by the rock walls and trees on the water grow longer and dimmer until they faded into darkness and it was time for me to climb into my bedroll.

In the morning upon my return to the trail, I stopped to talk to a young man who had come in from Snoqualmie Pass the day before. He warned me that the route to Snoqualmie Pass was scarred with logging roads and was difficult to follow. He directed me to be sure to turn right when the trail crossed the first dirt road. I thanked him and kept repeating to myself, "Turn right at the first road crossing."

The first segment of my morning's walk climbing up toward Silver Peak was pleasant. Dropping down, I was pleased to locate the junction at which I was to make my first right-hand turn. Actually, it was easy, as there was a couple standing there. They were day hikers who had come in from Snoqualmie Pass and were on their way to Mirror Lake. Shortly after passing the junction, I arrived at a rocky, excavated area, bedecked with orange plastic tapes and blue-painted rocks indicating a detour around a newly and dreadfully scarred clear-cut area. The next hour or so, I had to carefully search to find my way, which alternated between the forest-lined trail and the detour section of blue-painted rocks. In one short section, I started ahead on a usable-looking piece of trail, only to be stopped by a fresh rockslide avalanche. From the blocked trail, I climbed up a steep rockslide area to reach the unaesthetic, blue-painted-rock logging detour. Traversing through this torn-up, messy section, I was really angry. How wrong it seemed to me to plow up a designated National Scenic Trail. My final hiking stretch led through the Snoqualmie Pass Summit Ski Area. Ski slopes in the summer, with their gravel beds, offered another scarred, messy scene.

I arrived at the general store around 3:30 pm. The woman in the store was newly hired and could not find the forms to issue a Greyhound Bus ticket. She was frantically searching for the forms when I looked out the store door and saw a Greyhound bus pull away. How disappointing. The next bus would be arriving at 6:00 pm. I had two hours to wait. I retreated outside and found a shady place to chew on snacks and drink the last of my pink, diluted Kool-Aid water. It had served me well, lasting me three-and-a-half days.

Aboard the bus to Seattle, I felt good. I had completed one of my longest stretches—225 miles.

In Seattle, I found my way to the large Y.M.C.A. As usual, it was a great feeling to be able to bathe and wash clothes.

In the morning, I walked up a hill and in three blocks arrived at the St. James Cathedral, where I attended a Sunday Morning Mass, complete with a full choir and organ. I was inspired. I was also overflowing with prayers of thanksgiving for having completed another safe and satisfying journey.

In the afternoon, my cousin, Cathy called for me and drove me to her lovely home, located in a neighborhood south of downtown Seattle. From her front yard, I enjoyed a view looking out over the water and islands of Seattle's Puget Sound. I could see boats—both good-sized passenger ferries and pleasure boats—moving back and forth. What a glorious sight!

After another night of comfort at the Y.M.C.A., but still missing looking up at the star-filled sky, I boarded the morning Coast Starlight Amtrak for my ride home. I have found train travel to be a good way to meet interesting people, and this train trip was no exception. I was pleased to meet Mary Otway, who had, like myself, graduated from the University of Chicago's School of Social Service Administration. We had a good time comparing notes and finding fellow students whom we both knew. I also met Alfred Lum, who was interested in hearing about my trail travels and encouraged me to read William O. Douglas' "Of Men and Mountains." At home, I checked it out of the library and enjoyed it immensely.

Chapter 25
Snoqualmie Pass to Agnes Creek Trailhead
August 1988 • 169 Miles

Reading these grand mountain manuscripts displayed through every vicissitude of heat and cold, calm and storm, upheaving volcanoes and down-grinding glaciers, we see that everything in Nature called destruction must be creation—a change from beauty to beauty. —*John Muir*

I felt a special excitement on approaching my trailhead at Snoqualmie Pass this summer. This section should be, God-willing, my next-to-last walk before reaching the Canadian border. Intermingled with my excitement, however, was a small corner of apprehension. Would I make it? I felt optimistic, yet worried that something might happen to disrupt the completion of my trail walk. I resolved to be extra careful. I wanted so very much to arrive safely at the trail's end at the Canadian border.

I also realized that, with a little extra time and push, it would be possible to reach the border this summer. I really did not want to. I wanted to finish the Southern California sections before touching the trail marker at the Canadian border. The northern border trail marker should be my final celebration.

This 169-mile trail section is marked by rugged, rock ascents and descents. North of Snoqualmie Pass, the trail traverses along rocky cliffs, many of which have been blasted to construct the trail. The trail then leads across the Alpine Lakes Wilderness, offering, in clear weather, some soul-stirring lake views. As the trail continues north, it traverses into rugged, rocky areas of the north Cascades wilderness, including the rocky peaks and valleys in the Glacier Peak area. This section offered much in challenge, spectacular views, and a feeling of being surrounded by pristine wilderness.

I boarded the Amtrak train in San Francisco and again found a seat in the senior and handicapped section. As usual, I enjoyed talking with some pleasant, older woman. My good fortune in meeting interesting passengers on the train happened again. While walking through the dining car, I met my good friend from San Jose, Betty Jane Rank. She and a friend were on their way to Alaska. We had a joyful time anticipating our upcoming adventures.

Arriving in Seattle, I headed for the newly remodeled American Youth Hostel. It was ideally located. From the hostel's front door, I walked down some steep steps to the water's edge of Puget Sound. In the evening, I watched the ferryboats coming and going, depositing many passengers at the large passenger mall. I wondered where they were all going. Toward the back of the hostel, I could walk a short distance to the attractive Pike Place Market. I retreated to the Market to view the colorful flower stands and lush displays of fruits and vegetables and to admire the stands displaying many varieties of fish. Also at Pike Place Market, tucked in between fruit and fish stalls, were a few small restaurants. In the morning, I had time for a delicious oatmeal and muffin breakfast at Lowett's Café, while sitting at a window seat and viewing the busy scene of ferryboats and ocean liners plying their courses across Puget Sound.

Before leaving for the bus depot, I had a special shopping errand—to pick up my new sleeping bag at Seattle's North Face store. In preparation for my walk in the rainy north Cascades, I had decided to "play it safe." I was going to purchase a water-resistant sleeping bag. After reviewing outfitters catalogues, I selected a lightweight, synthetic-filled bag with a water-resistant cover from the North Face catalogue. Upon visiting the North Face store in Berkeley, I found that they did not have the bag in my size in stock. When I proposed that I might pick up the bag in Seattle, the Berkeley store's clerk called and reserved a bag in my size at the Seattle store. How convenient! The North Face store in Seattle was only a three-block walk from the Hostel. I had the added adventure of visiting Seattle's North Face store, where I happily picked up my new water-resistant sleeping bag.

Now I was finally ready for my trek to the bus depot, where I soon boarded the 11:30 Greyhound bus for Snoqualmie Pass. Arriving at the Pass, I headed for the general store and post office and picked up my food package, which, happily, had arrived safely. I had time left in the late afternoon to start my trail walk. By evening, I had reached a comfortable but unaesthetic campsite near Commonwealth Creek. As I was fixing supper, the fog rolled in, prompting me to crawl into my tent and the warm comfort of my sleeping bag.

In the morning, from my foggy resting place at Commonwealth Creek, I peeked out of my small tent window vent and saw that the fog was still thick. I snuggled back into my bedroll, not feeling like venturing out. I was thankful for the protection of my tent. Finally, the sound of loud, laughing voices coming down the trail jolted me out of my warm cocoon. I decided it was time to get up.

After packing up, I moved ahead steadily on a good trail that kept climbing up. Happily, the fog lifted. By late afternoon, the trail emerged onto an open crest that afforded some splendid views of the surrounding peaks. Moving along, the trail led over a razor-sharp pass, followed by a narrow, rocky path. I moved cautiously.

Rounding a bend on the rocky path, I heard shouting. I wondered what was going on. The shouting grew louder and, to me, more annoying. Don't trail hikers appreciate that quietness is one of the reasons for coming into the wilderness? Drawing closer to the shouting man, I learned that he was a Boy Scout leader and that one of his young charges, a small boy with a too-big, lop-sided pack, had fallen behind. I concluded and reluctantly accepted that weekend Scout leaders are not necessarily drawn to the wilderness for its peace and quiet.

The trail finally wound down to a ridge above Ridge and Gravel Lakes. It was time to seek out a campsite. The guidebook indicated that Ridge Lake was closed to campers because of overuse. I had passed a goodly number of hikers. I discovered that in addition to day hikers, this 72-mile section between Snoqualmie Pass and Stevens Pass afforded backpackers convenient trailheads at each end. Therefore, it was quite a busy stretch. I finally found a small, grassy shelf, where I pitched my tent.

During the night, the wind howled, and thick fog rolled in. Again, I was thankful for my protective tent, which remained essentially dry. I thought of the young man whom I had met on the trail who explained regretfully, "I'm going out, as my tent is getting wetter and wetter."

After slowly breaking camp in the cheerless morning fog, I wondered, while reminding myself that I was hiking in wet northern Washington, if it would be like this all day. I was trying to convince myself to accept the fog, when around 10 am, the curtain of fog lifted and the sun burst through. I could see spectacular views of mountain peaks. How wonderful, I rejoiced. I continued to move slowly, however, as in addition to ups and downs, the trail was still rocky and uneven. I stepped along cautiously and kept saying, "Watch your balance."

During my morning's rocky ridge walk, I enjoyed some glorious views looking down onto lakes and valleys. By mid-day, I circled around Huckleberry Mountain. I approached the Park Lakes basin, my planned campsite, which offered accessible water for the first time since leaving my camp near Gravel Lake. Here, the trail traversed some grassy slopes, bedecked with bright, colorful wildflowers. What a delightful scene. As I drew near to the Park Lakes, I started my search for a campsite above the lakes. I wanted to stay away from the lower-level, grassy, lake shores, which mosquitoes love. Looking around, I found a small shelf near a pleasant mountain stream and made camp. As I was filling my water bag, a lone woman hiker came down the trail and stopped by the stream. "Where are you hiking to?" I asked her. She replied, "I'm hiking in on the Trail in Oregon and Washington." "Are you hiking alone?" I asked. "Yes," she replied. I told her that she was only the second lone woman hiker I had met beside myself walking on the Pacific Crest Trail. I said that I was glad to meet another woman who was ready to hike the trail alone.

After leaving my campsite at Park Lakes basin, I climbed up on the trail to a ridge that offered glorious views looking down on large, blue Spectacle Lake. The scene changed as the trail switched back down some 36 turns and led into a wooded area. I then arrived at Delate Creek, which I crossed on a bridge, and stopped at the creek's bank for a snack. After my snack stop, I strolled through a pleasant wooded area with small ups and downs. The trail continued to drop down to still another creek, the Lemah Creek. I was eager to move on in order to be poised and ready for a good start the next morning, when I planned to push up the 2200-foot ascent to Escondido Ridge. I walked on to the next creek—the North Fork of Lemah Creek, where I made camp. As there was no fog and no wind, I returned to my familiar style of sleeping out in the open in my bivouac sack, gazing up at my beloved sky ceiling. For this trip, I had brought both my tent and my bivouac sack so that I could choose between the two. It was good to be viewing the sky again.

I started early in the morning—around 7 am, in anticipation of a day of ascending and descending. I shifted into my uphill climbing mode—short steps, steady pace, sometimes chanting "step two-three-four…" I kept reminding myself not to anticipate the top too soon. I rejoiced, however, when I reached the cirque near the top of Escondido Ridge. The trail levels off as it crosses small streams. I did not stop for long, as I planned to reach Waptus River for my campsite. I knew that I would have a long descent. Plodding on, I reached the river and a campsite around 6 pm. I felt exhilarated. I had walked approximately 13 miles—5 miles up, 3 miles along the ridge, and 5 miles down.

In the morning, my walk was pleasant. The trail led through woods and grassy areas where I was treated to some lovely patches of familiar wildflowers—penstemon, honeysuckle, mimulus, and fireweed.

During my lunch break, while I was sitting comfortably under some trees by the side of the trail, three groups of hikers passed by. I continued to be amazed at the number of hikers walking on this section between Snoqualmie and Stevens Pass. During the afternoon, the trail climbed up a ridge above Spinola Creek. I started looking for a steam crossing, which would alert me to seek out and turn onto a side trail that would lead me to a campsite on Deep Lake. After crossing a little stream, I saw a faint path and turned onto it. As I moved on, it seemed to me that the little path grew more obscure. "Oh, well," I thought, "spur trails often fade away as people make their own paths along lake shores." Coming out to an open meadow and then sighting a small lake, I saw two hikers surveying the lakeshore. "Is this Deep Lake?" I asked. "No," they replied, "this is Deer Lake. We plan to camp here tonight." I was surprised. They cheerfully showed me on my map that I had reached Deer Lake and then gave me directions for reaching Deep Lake. I then realized that, in my eagerness, I had turned off the trail too soon. I had turned off after the first stream crossing and I should have waited to turn off after the second steam crossing.

One of the tall, smiling hikers commented, "I bet you got you hiking pants at a surplus store." He added, "I bought mine for nine dollars and they are just fine." "Yes," I agreed. "I really do like my khaki six-pocket pants." I felt a kinship with these two older hikers. Khaki was the predominant color of choice for hikers in earlier years. Now, on the trail, I pass hikers in purple shorts and all sorts of styles and colors. I still like the idea of wearing colors that blend with nature, such as the older styles of greens, browns, or khaki. As I said goodbye and started on my way, I thought to myself, "I really like those two hikers. We have much in common in our choice of khaki trail wear and in our loyalty to a style of an earlier generation of hikers."

I retraced my steps and enjoyed some cross-country hiking, armed with suggestions offered by the two khaki-clad hikers, and soon reached the trail. I walked to the second stream crossing, then turned left to reach Deep Lake, where I found a campsite. Actually, the Deep Lake campsite was rather ordinary. The little-used, quiet Deer Lake chosen by my khaki-clad hiking friends was much more rustic and charming. I had chosen to camp at Deep Lake to position myself for another climb up to the next pass on the following day.

I again moved into my climbing mode in the morning to ascend the numerous switchbacks and reach 5610-foot Cathedral Pass. As I broke out of the trees and small bushes into open space, glorious views opened up, revealing glimpses of cone-shaped, towering Cathedral Rock and other peaks and ridges. When I finally reached the top, I found, somewhat to my surprise, a little crowd of day hikers. They had climbed up from the Cle Elum River Valley, where there are roadheads to reach campsites.

Soon, I was approached by a tall, lanky man wearing clean white pants. He asked, "Do you know which trail I should take to reach Squaw Lake?" I replied, "I will be glad to check it out on my map." I took off my pack, unfolded my map, and resting it on a flat-topped rock, I oriented the map with my compass. I started to give him directions to the trail leading south when he interrupted, "The map is upside down." I was surprised and replied, "I turned the map to the north, in line with the compass reading." "Oh," he responded. Then I pointed to the trail on the map that would lead to Squaw Lake. He started off, but soon returned, looking puzzled, and said, "This trail ended in a short way." I looked around and saw that he had taken a short, unofficial, hiker-made view trail. I then pointed to the other trail. Off he went again, but soon returned, saying, "This is the trail I came up on." Again, I pointed to the map, explaining that he needed to reach a junction before he turned onto the trail. He replied, "I don't remember any junction when I came up." There seemed to be nothing more that I could say. Finally, he started down again, and in a few minutes called up, "I found the junction." He seemed finally convinced of the trail directions. He left me laughing to myself about his comment, "The map is upside-down." I believe I had met a true neophyte.

After hearing that my neophyte hiker friend had finally located the junction and, hopefully, was on his way, a group of five people came up the trail, including an older woman. They asked about my backpacking walk and, hearing that I was walking on the Pacific Crest Trail from Mexico to Canada, they became interested and asked me lots of questions. Smiling and looking up hesitantly, the older woman asked, "Do you mind if I ask you how old you are?" adding, "I am 67." "I am 70, I replied." Smiling, she responded, "I am happy to know that there are older women walking the trail." They all expressed their admiration for my walking project and wished me well.

I did let them know that I faced an important decision regarding my next trail section. A new trail section going north would save me many miles but it presented a warning of a hazardous glacial-stream crossing. I had encountered two Forest Service signs cautioning, in big red letters, "Danger! Swift Water Crossing." I was full of excitement. I decided on a plan. I would proceed down the new trail and inspect the hazardous stream crossing. If I felt that it was dangerous, I would return to Cathedral Pass and take the old trail. When I shared my plan with the older woman, she responded, "Use your good judgment and don't take any chances. If it looks dangerous, come back." I heartily agreed with her. Proceeding excitedly and carefully down the trail, I finally reached the "hazardous stream crossing." Drawing closer, I studied it. I saw that there was a small log balanced across the swiftly moving stream. I felt assured that I could carefully make the log crossing. Looking up, I saw a couple of hikers coming up the trail from the other direction. They watched me cross the stream balancing on the log. Safely on the other side, they said, "It looks easy." I replied, "Easy as

pie." Admittedly, I was pleased with myself and, at the same
time, pleased that they had arrived to witness my safe crossing.

I continued my descent and reached Deception Pass, a
lower-elevation pass at 4450 feet. A little beyond the pass, I
found a pleasant campsite beside a small stream.

I awoke the following morning to look out onto a heavy,
dense fog. I was not in a hurry to get up and stayed snuggled
in my bedroll until around 8 am. After breakfast and packing
up, I moved on slowly through the fog. I regretted not being able to view towering Cathedral Peak, as described in the
guidebook. As the trail climbed up to Pieper Pass, I saw a small
side trail leading to a viewpoint near the pass. My first thought
was, "It is not worthwhile to follow the viewpoint trail in this
heavy fog." But something beckoned me to turn onto the path.
Besides, it was time for my morning snack. I followed the little
path and found a comfortable resting place. While I was enjoying my milk and honey, quite suddenly and unexpectedly, a
hole broke through the fog. I looked ahead through the window and saw that I was looking at a rugged, rocky, mountain
range. I rejoiced. I was experiencing another of the miracles
of nature. I continued to look ahead, searching the mountain
peaks and valleys as the fog floated in and out, alternately hiding the mountains and then lifting to reveal a whole, beautiful
mountain scene. I found it enchanting.

After reluctantly leaving the fog scene, I followed the trail
as it switched back down to a pleasant alpine meadow. During the walk down, the sun broke through, and finally the fog
completely disappeared. In the afternoon, just as I was thinking
that I had not passed any hikers since Deception Pass, a young
man caught up with me. He announced that he had planned to
camp at the Glacier Lake shelter, but he had heard that it had
been torn down. He was disappointed. He said he might camp

at Glacier Lake. After awhile, he announced that he was going to hike on ahead. I think he was ready to move on at a faster pace.

By late afternoon, I found a comfortable campsite beside a small stream on a ridge that looked down at pleasant, blue, Surprise Lake. I had had another good day. I especially had enjoyed witnessing the fog scene, which still seemed to me like one of Mother Nature's miracles.

In the morning after moving on from my campsite, I climbed up the trail as it switchbacked to 5800-foot Trap Pass. Near the top, I was startled when I heard a rustling in a bush; turning my head, I was surprised and delighted to see a white-coated, majestic-looking mountain goat staring at me. He continued to stare at me for several seconds before he decided to move. He slowly stepped down on a side path and disappeared. What a magnificent sight. The erect, graceful creature blended so perfectly with the rocky mountain summit.

The trail continued along the ridge for several yards before descending to a meadow and on to pleasant Hope Lake, where I stopped for lunch. At the lake, I met two hikers who sat near me and soon started telling me of their mountain-hiking recollections. One of them recalled that he had been in a Civilian Conservation Corps in the thirties and had worked on construction of the Cascade Trail. Much of the Cascade Trail has been used by the Pacific Crest Trail. He said that Ernie Pyle was the first person to ride a horse over the Cascade Trail. After service in the CCC, he stayed on with the Forest Service and built many trails. Most of the forest trails, he said, were built as fire trails and had steeper grades than the present Pacific Crest Trail.

A second hiker, an interesting-looking man with long, bleached hair, said he had walked from Washington to Mexico—not on the Pacific Crest Trail, but by taking various routes, some of which were along the coast. He especially liked his walk and his stops around the Big Sur area, south of Monterey. When I finally stood up to leave, he jumped up to help me with my pack. How unaccustomed I was, after taking my pack on and off for days, to have someone offer me assistance.

During my afternoon snack, a couple came toward me and asked, "Are you Eleanor?" I was surprised. They said they had heard about me from the young man I had met and walked with the day before. They asked me lots of questions and were most interested in hearing more about my trail walk. They said that they would like to complete more trail sections.

I made camp at Susan Jane Lake, a small, pretty lake with a steep cliff rising up on one side. Here, I met two robust-looking women who had just hiked in from Stevens Pass and were planning to hike to Snoqualmie Pass. They were planning to be on the trail for two weeks. They were pleased to meet another woman who had made the trip successfully. We enthusiastically exchanged information about sleeping bags and other backpacking equipment.

I was eager to break camp in the morning, as I would be coming out for a food package. As I approached Stevens Pass and climbed up the hilly trail dotted with ski lifts, I started to pass a number of enthusiastic Boy Scouts. They kept asking me, "Have you seen two adults?" They were searching for their troop leader. Upon seeing this sizeable group of young Scouts, I had an idea. They, too, would be going out. Perhaps I could arrange a ride with them to Skykomish, some 16 miles to the west, where my food package would be waiting. When I reached the Stevens Pass parking lot, I looked around and saw two pleasant-looking adults greeting their young hikers. I approached one of them and said, "I am looking for a ride to Skykomish to collect my food package." My plan worked. A very nice parent who was driving west offered to give me a ride.

Upon reaching Skykomish, I thanked the Scout-leader driver and walked down the main street of this small town. It was Sunday, so I would be staying overnight. I walked by a fairly modern-looking motel and went on to the old, two-story frame hotel that was situated near the railroad. Upon entering the hotel, I had to search for the clerk, who finally appeared from the dining room. I asked for a room. "The railroad crew is staying with us this summer, he replied. "The only room I can give you is the bridal suite, with a bath down the hall." I eagerly accepted. My room was delightfully decked with antiques. I learned that the hotel had been built in 1904. I also was blessed with a balcony, where I spread my tent and groundcloth out to dry. The bath down the hall proved to be somewhat of a surprise. I learned that two of the railroad crew members were women and that they had strung their laundry all over the bathroom. I ducked under their clotheslines. Although the hotel's upstairs hallways were bedecked with cracked plaster that needed repair, the dining room was in good shape and busy with diners. I enjoyed a good dinner, surrounded by the old-fashioned ambiance of the 1904 hotel.

For the last two days, I had been mulling over a possible change of plans, which would add one more layover day. At Susan Jane Lake, while attempting to take a picture of the attractive rock cliff, I noticed that my camera film was not advancing. It was stuck. I felt distressed. I had always taken slides of my trail walk and did not want to miss taking photos of my walk between Stevens Pass and Agnes Creek gorge. I decided to take the bus to Everett, Washington, a sizeable town, and see if I could have my camera repaired.

In the morning, after a good breakfast at the vintage hotel, I picked up my food package at the post office, repacked my pack, and walked to the store, where there was a Greyhound

Bus sign. I was informed by a store clerk that the bus stop had moved out onto the highway. So, I walked out to the highway. After waiting some time, I saw a bus coming. It wasn't slowing down, so I waved frantically. The driver finally stopped. I boarded the bus, and the driver insisted that the bus stop was a block ahead. How confusing.

From the Everett bus station, it was a short walk to the Travel Lodge, where I checked in and then hurried on to visit the National Camera Shop. A friendly, interested man checked my camera and announced, "It will take three weeks to repair and will cost around $58.00." I was really disappointed. I decided to purchase a second-hand camera or an inexpensive new one. The man suggested I go to Crown Photo and gave me directions. Unfortunately, a good second-hand camera was not available, and I reluctantly purchased a fixed-focus Eastman Kodak camera. Later at home, where the slides were developed, they were inferior to those taken with my 35-mm camera. At least I preserved some memories of the walk.

The next day, I boarded an early-morning bus leaving Everett at 8:15. Another backpacker on the bus was planning to get off at Stevens Pass. We were both watching for the Stevens Pass bus stop; it was a good thing we were, because the bus driver did not show any inclination of stopping at Stevens Pass until we reminded him that we wanted to get off. For him, this was probably a flag stop that was not used much.

After I disembarked from the tardily stopping bus and claimed by backpack from the luggage compartment, my fellow bus rider-backpacker said, "Your pack looks heavy." "Not particularly." I replied. "But since I added a tent and one additional layer of clothing for wet Washington, my pack has grown taller." He test-lifted my pack and exclaimed with astonishment, "Oh, your pack is light—so much lighter than mine."

We bid each other goodbye. He was hiking south. I looked around. The big question for me was, "what was the weather going to be like?" It was hard to tell if it was misting, or if a light shower was falling. I was hopeful, as there was a little bright sky toward the east.

I found the trail going north from Stevens Pass without difficulty. As I moved up the trail, still wondering about the weather, a few light showers fell, and then the sun peeked through. It was an off-and-on weather day. I arrived at a possible campsite along Lake Valhalla around 3:30 pm. (had someone who named the lake had visions of Wagner's Home of the Gods?). I debated: should I go on or should I camp by this pretty but mist-cloaked lake? While debating, my question was answered. It started to rain. First, light sprinkles fell and then heavier raindrops descended. Hurriedly, I picked a campsite. I put up my tent and crawled inside, pulling my pack in as the rain descended in heavy bursts. Inside, I inspected my clothing for rain damage. I was thankful that I was still quite dry, except for a damp area around my waist, which is ordinarily covered by my rain skirt. I hadn't taken time to get it out of my pack. Snug inside, I had plenty of time for resting and daydreaming. I was thankful that I had chosen to purchase the Stephenson's Warmlite Tent. It was not only the lightest tent I had tested—two pounds with poles—it was also the roomiest. Now I was enjoying having ample space to wiggle around inside. It would be a long night.

I was not eager to get up in the morning. It was raining off and on. Slowly, I sat up; reached for my breakfast foods, utensils, and stove; and ate my breakfast of juice, cereal, and coffee in a leisurely manner, still ensconced in my sleeping bag.

When it was time to roll up my tent, it started to rain again. How annoying. I kept attempting to wipe off my tent as I rolled it up. It was not possible to keep it dry, however. I was not comfortable with packing wet equipment. This was a different experience for me than in the Sierras, where rainstorms usually did not last long, and I could almost always dry off my equipment before rolling it up. I felt that I was being hard on my tent by packing it wet. Furthermore, wet equipment is heavier to carry than dry equipment. As I slowly packed up, I tried to convince myself that this was one of the realities of hiking in Washington.

It was foggy most of the day. As I slushed on through the wet grass, my feet became wet. Fortunately, they stayed warm as long as I kept moving.

I did not pass any hikers. I did meet a trail maintenance crew. On passing, one of the trail crew members called out, "We heard a weather report announcing that it would be clearing by Friday." I felt mildly hopeful, but thought, "This is only Wednesday." At lunchtime, I stopped at shallow Janus Lake near the somewhat large, dilapidated Janus Shelter. There, I met a second trail crew. They told me that the shelter was scheduled to be demolished, as it was now in a newly designated Wilderness Area—the Henry Jackson Wilderness. This plan is in accordance with keeping Wilderness Areas as natural as possible.

Peering up at threatening skies, I decided to stop early. I wanted to set my tent up before it started raining again. I found a campsite in a meadow above Glasses Lake. This proved to be a good plan, as it soon started raining. It rained off and on all through the night. Again, I was thankful to be snug inside my Stephenson's tent.

The heavy rain had stopped by morning. Peeking from my tent, I looked out upon thick fog. I was disappointed. I was not eager to start my day's journey. Slowly, I stirred, prepared my breakfast, and started packing. Again, I attempted to wipe the surplus water off my wet tent, not too successfully.

The fog had one compensation. As I walked along the trail, the fog danced and skirted through valleys and floated in and out around mountain peaks. It made some intriguing and mystical scenes. I thought that I was beholding one of the many wonders of nature.

The only people I saw on the trail were workers from another trail crew. They told me, happily, that I would be walking a newly constructed section of the trail between Pear Lake and Saddle Gap. They assured me that this new section was much improved over the old section and that it was shorter. I replied, "I am happy to hear this. I shall enjoy my walk." They seemed pleased that I appreciated their trail work.

I stopped for an afternoon snack at Pear Lake, but as I was not ready to make camp, I moved on. I found a comfortable campsite by a little creek that was adjacent to a pleasant meadow.

When I peeked out of my tent in the morning, it was not raining. I rejoiced. There was a little misty fog, which I hoped would lift by midday.

There were more people on the trail this day. They had come in from side trails. At Pass Creek, while I was enjoying a snack, two women came down the trail and stopped to talk to me. They told me that they knew Ed and Alice Patterson, the former proprietors of Santian Lodge. They reported that Ed and Alice were now retired and were walking the Pacific Crest Trail and that they had finished the southern section of the Trail, bused to Burney Falls, and were walking south to reach the Sierras. We all enthusiastically agreed that it was good to hear that the Pattersons were enjoying their free time and having the opportunity to walk on the Pacific Crest Trail.

A little further along, I met a man wearing two packs—one on his back and one on his front. I stopped to ask him about his two packs and learned that he was a photographer and that one of the packs was full of cameras.

By late afternoon, I reached Lake Sally Ann, but I didn't feel ready to camp, so I filled my water bag and moved on. I found a campsite on a crest, which afforded an expansive view of mountain tops and valleys. After supper, I watched a fog flow in and out of the surrounding passes. It was awesome, but it began to grow cold. I retreated to my tent.

During the night, the wind howled and shook my tent. Once again, I was thankful to be snug inside with the protection of my trusty, sturdy, Stephenson's tent.

In the morning as I peeked out, there was a low cloud cover. It was still cold, but it was not raining. I was hopeful of a clear, dry day. My trail walk today was mostly uphill. I shifted into my climbing mode, and my steady pace felt good. It was a gradual uphill walk. First, the trail climbed up to 5904-foot White Pass. Then it climbed up still higher to 6500-foot Red Pass, which is the highest point in this trail section—Stevens Pass to Rainy Pass. The views along this high-mountain-ridge trail were truly spectacular. From Red Pass, I could see to the northeast the towering, snow-covered Glacier Peak at 10, 541 feet. All along this high-ridge walk, I watched the clouds drift in and out of the mountain passes and valleys and float in and around the mountain peaks. At times, the swiftly moving fog clouds reminded me of fog pouring through the dips between hills just north of the Golden Gate Bridge.

After descending from Red Pass, I came to wide, swift-flowing, White Chuck River. I found a good campsite along the riverbank. I felt good. I had had a good walk, some splendid views, and no rain.

During my morning walk, the cloud cover lifted. Was it going to clear, I wondered? I kept looking at the sky. Soon the sun broke out. I rejoiced. It was clear for the rest of the day, with no rain or fog. It was glorious. By afternoon, as I was switchbacking up to Kennedy Ridge, I even needed to stop to take off my ski underwear. This was an event—I had not taken them off for days.

By evening, I reached a small campsite beside narrow but swiftly flowing Pumice Creek. As I was setting up camp, a friendly hiker named Ken, who was hiking south from the Canadian border, came by. He stopped and sat down beside my camp. He volunteered to tell me all about the trail ahead and possible campsites. He commented that I could expect some rugged trail ahead. I listened, wondering if tomorrow morning's uphill walk would prove to be more difficult than described in the guidebook. Often, hikers have told me about difficult trail sections that have not seemed that difficult when I reached them. Perhaps, if I am prepared for a hard walk, it actually seems easier upon completing it. When Ken stood up to hike on, he explained that he was going off-trail to visit the nearby Kennedy Hot Springs—a small, natural hot springs.

After dinner, it was actually warm enough to enjoy sitting outside and to watch the sunset. This was the first day during my walk on this section that I was warm and comfortable enough to watch the evening sky.

In the morning, I took time to wipe off my dew-laden tent. I had had to place the tent close to the creek, as the creek bank rose steeply from a narrow shoreline. There was no other choice.

The 1000-foot climb up to Fire Pass in the cool of the morning did not seem difficult. Approaching the summit, a glorious view opened up. I was gazing at layers of snow-capped peaks of the rugged North Cascades. How wonderful, I thought, to be walking up to this pass on a clear, sunny day. I stopped to drink in the view.

Switchbacking down over a rocky trailbed dotted with loose scree, proved to be much more difficult than the uphill climb to Fire Pass. I stopped by Mica Creek to have a snack and was joined by a young man who wanted to know all about my trail walk. He seemed intrigued that I was hiking from Mexico to Canada. He concluded, "I admire your courage and persistence in walking from border to border."

Later on in the afternoon, I passed a young man who had heard about my walk. He seemed worried and commented that my pack looked heavy. He said, with a most serious face, "Take care." What a contrast, I thought, between the people who supported my idea of walking the trail from Mexico to Canada and those who did not think it was a great idea at all.

By evening, I reached Milk Creek, which was well named. It was another glacier-melt, milk-colored creek. By evening, the creek was running swiftly, but fortunately it could be crossed on a sturdy bridge on the far side of the creek. I found a dry camp on a level spot. It proved to be a good choice. My tent was dry all night.

My walk from Milk Creek to my next campsite on Vista Creek was marked by a long climb up, followed by a long switchback down. I plodded along, thankful for beautiful, clear, sunny weather with beautiful views. On a ridge above Milk Creek, I was treated to another spectacular view of 10,000-foot Glacier Peak. This volcanic peak was surrounded by numerous patches of glaciers interspersed with rocky formations. It was a fine sight.

Near the top of the ridge, I met a thorough Pacific Crest Trail hiker who had started in Mexico on April 1st and was on his way to the Canadian border. He had already completed the Appalachian Trail (and had a patch to prove it). I congratulated him. After switchbacking down to 3600-foot Vista Creek, I found a comfortable campsite.

From my Vista Creek campsite the next morning, I once again enjoyed a clear, sunny day. The trail presented some ups and downs, but it was a relatively easy walk. I reached Miners Creek, where I had tentatively planned to stop for the day at around 3:30 pm. I felt like going on. I studied the map and decided to try to reach a meadow located on a spur trail near Suiattle Pass. I watched carefully for the spur trail. After reaching the turnoff, I turned off and found a delightful, broad, grassy, green meadow. The meadow sight offered fine views toward the pass and of an intriguingly shaped mountaintop called "the Fortress." I liked the feeling of spaciousness offered by this meadow. I decided that it was one of my favorite campsites in this section.

Two men, father and son, were already camped in the meadow. As I was putting up my tent, they came over and offered to help me. They told me that they were from New Jersey and this was their first trip into the Cascade Mountains. They had hiked in from Holden, a Lutheran Retreat Center, where the son, a college student, had spent two weeks as a volunteer. He had heard about Holden from a college classmate. When I asked what college he was attending, his father replied that he attended a small college in Minnesota, which I probably never heard of—Carleton College. I replied, "I have heard of it. My brother and sister both graduated from Carleton College." They were pleased and surprised.

I had heard about Holden from a San Francisco friend who had visited there several years ago. Holden was a successful copper-mining town. When the copper ore had all been mined and the mine closed, a dedicated Lutheran layman spearheaded a successful drive to acquire the town for a Lutheran retreat center. Near this meadow, there was a trail that led into Holden.

After supper, I climbed up to a nearby ridge and watched a

full moon rise from behind "the Fortress." I felt good.

In the morning, after packing up, I waved goodbye to my pleasant New Jersey friends. After reaching the trail junction, I turned north onto the trail to start the long descent down to the South Fork of Agnes Creek. This should be an easy walk, I thought. I soon learned, however, that the trail route did not always drift straight down the canyon. Periodically, there were uphill climbs over rocky ridges. I also encountered some late-lasting snow patches that caused me to pause. At one point, the trail disappeared into a snow patch, and I had to walk back and forth two or three times before I found the place where the trail emerged out of the snowdrift. It was tricky.

As the trail continued its up-and-down, but ultimately downhill, journey, I passed two trail camps. First, there was Big Spruce Camp, which was complete with tables and benches. Next I came to Hemlock Camp, which, again, was complete with tables and benches. I thought to myself, "This is a sign that I am approaching a trailhead. It is adapted to hikers who go in to camp for a day or a day-and-a-half."

By evening, I reached Spruce Creek Camp, which was more to my style. It did not have tables and benches, but did have a fire pit. Looking around, I met a couple who were camped for the night. They recognized me. They said that they had seen me at Granite Creek. In comparing trail notes, I learned that they also were planning to leave the trail at Agnes Creek and go out at Stehekin.

The town of Stehekin is park headquarters for the Lake Chelan National Recreation Area. It is located at the eastern end of long, fjord-like Lake Chelan and is reached by a ferry that runs between Stehekin and the town of Chelan. One of the reasons that I had picked Agnes Creek as a trailhead was that I was attracted to the prospect of riding the ferry on Lake Chelan.

The nine-mile walk from Spruce Creek Camp to trailhead at Agnes Creek was an easy one. The trail leads mostly downhill. I felt good. I was feeling a sense of accomplishment. I was completing my next-to-last Washington section of the trail.

At Agnes Creek Gorge, the trail crosses over the swiftly flowing stream on a high bridge. I paused in the middle of the bridge to look, listen, and absorb the exciting scene created by the roaring, rushing, splashing, powerful water.

The National Park Service runs a shuttlebus from Stehekin to the nearby High Bridge Ranger Station. I found the sign for the shuttle bus stop and sat down to wait for the bus. I hoped that it would not be too long a wait. Soon, the hikers I had met at Glacier Peak and Spruce Creek Camp arrived. We sat on a log, waiting impatiently for the shuttlebus. Soon, we heard the rattle and roar of an approaching car. When it came into view, we saw that it was not the shuttlebus, but rather a large touring car with a couple of well-dressed, middle-aged couples occupying the front seat. They stopped. When we told them that we had been backpacking on the Pacific Crest Trail, they were impressed. They offered us a ride to Stehekin, which we happily accepted.

They told us that they were from Athens, Georgia. This was their first trip to Washington, and they were enjoying seeing the Cascade Mountains, Lake Chelan, and many other sights.

My backpacking friends, Donna and Dale, talked eagerly about celebrating their coming-out from the trail by partaking of a full-course meal at the Stehekin Lodge. As usual, I was torn between eating my first non-trail food and finding a shower. Which did I want first? Upon arrival at Stehekin, I ended up indulging in an ice-cream cone, then I searched for a space at the crowded campground. I finally located a space near the campground's edge, which appeared to be in the quietest area. Then I lined up a shower. After showering, I did not feel ready for a full-course dinner. I bought some snacks and enjoyed supper at my campsite.

After dark, I joined the ranger-led campfire program and listened to interesting stories about the history of the area. I learned that Stehekin was an Indian word relating to pass, and that Indians had come to Stehekin looking for a pass across the cascades. Frontier people came into the area in 1890-1900 when gold was discovered. After the gold disappeared, the area became a resort area and later a National Park Recreation Area. Although there are a few cars in Stehekin, which run up and down on the 12-mile road to Agnes Gorge, there is no main road leading out to other towns. The few cars located in Stehekin were brought in by barge. The few that I saw looked like vintage cars. The campfire program ended with inspiring quotations from Robert Service and Robert Frost.

Back at my campsite, I snuggled into my sleeping bag. I was ready for sleep, but hoped that I would wake up around 4 am, as the rangers said that there would be an eclipse of the moon. I slept soundly, but finally, as my resolve to wake up for the eclipse turned on, I awoke around 4:15 am. I looked up and saw only a small sliver of the moon before it faded completely. What an exciting sky event.

In the morning, I enjoyed a leisurely, full breakfast at the lodge. Then I sought out a resting space with a view looking across the lake to await the arrival of Our Lady of the Lake. I was exciting to see the white, two-decked ferryboat sailing up the lake to dock at Stehekin. The boat was crowded with passengers who had come for a day tour— disembarking for lunch and a quick look at Stehekin, and then reboarding for the return trip.

On board Our Lady of the Lake, I enjoyed the ride and spent most of the time drinking in the views. Lake Chelan is a long, narrow lake, bordered by steep side walls and distant mountain views. It seemed to me to resemble the Norwegian fjords.

Our Lady of the Lake pulled into a large landing dock named Lucern. Here, a sizeable crowd boarded the ferry. I learned that this enthusiastic crowd had all been attending classes and conferences at the Holden Retreat Center.

Upon arrival in Chelan, I had a bit of a surprise. I phoned several motels, to find that they were fully booked. I looked around and found a woman sitting in the office of the Ferry Boat Company. I walked in and asked, "Is there a campground where I can spend the night?" "No," she replied, "we do not have an overnight campground." Looking up at me, the only backpacker to disembark, she explained, "We are a resort city, and this is our busy season." The pleasant woman then volunteered to call a motel some distance from the town center. Happily, she found a room for me at Mom's Motel. I had a promise that the Mom's Motel would provide me with a ride to the bus station in the morning.

At the bus station in the morning, I met two young men who were returning after having spent two weeks at the Holden Retreat Center. They were so enthusiastic about their experience, they could hardly say enough good things.

On the bus trip from Chelan to Seattle, I had my first view of central Washington's fruit-growing area. Surrounding the town of Wenatchee, I was truly amazed when I saw the abundance of orchards. In this area, the fruit trees receive water from irrigation ditches. I passed by acres of trees, which were so loaded with big, red apples that the branches were propped up by supporting stakes to keep their heavy-laden boughs from breaking.

Arriving in Seattle around 3 pm, I hurried to the waterfront Youth Hostel and eagerly waited on the porch of the hostel for the 5 pm opening. Again, I enjoyed viewing Puget Sound, which was busy with ferryboats arriving and leaving from the large ferryboat terminal. At the Hostel, I decided to dine on some of my leftover trail food. I joined a busy crowd of Hostel residents, including a group from Australia. They were talking about feeling a yearning for yeast spread for their bread. "I don't care what people from other countries feel about our yeast spread," she commented. "Some say it's bitter, but I like it and miss it."

In the morning, I partook of my favorite oatmeal and home-made wheat bread breakfast at Pike Place Market. I then board-ed the city bus and joined a long line of passengers waiting to board the Amtrak Coast Starlight train to return home. Aboard the train, thoughts of happenings on the trail returned to me. I recalled a woman on a horse saying, "Aren't you adventurous!"

Chapter 26
Final Section—
Agnes Creek to the Canadian Border
August 1989 • 89 Miles

Thousands of tired, nerve-shaken, over-civilized people are beginning to find out that going to the mountains is going home; that wildness is a necessity; and that mountain parks and reservations are useful not only as fountains of timber and irrigating rivers, but as fountains of life.
—John Muir

I was excited in preparing for my 1989 August walk. Each summer, I became excited in anticipation of my summer's journey, but this was a journey of special anticipation—my last trail walk. At its completion, I would cross into Canada and would celebrate the completion of my Pacific Crest Trail journey.

Adding to my special anticipation, the guidebook described this last section as marked by some spectacular mountain scenery—rocky spires near Rainy Pass and rugged mountain ridges north of Harts Pass. The views of this spectacular mountain wilderness would be glorious "in good weather," and I reminded myself that I would be walking in northern Washington, where the potential for rain is high. What would the weather be like? For me, that was the big question.

My journey to the trailhead was a relatively long one. I boarded Amtrak in Oakland for my now familiar one night and one day train ride to Seattle. Upon arrival in Seattle in the late afternoon, I boarded a city bus to reach the now-familiar Waterfront Youth Hostel. In the morning, I had time to enjoy a leisurely breakfast at Lowett's Café in Pike's Place Market. I hurried to pick a place in the café with a view of the waterfront where I could watch the ferries glide in and out of the harbor. What a glorious sight.

Before boarding the 2:15 bus for Wenatchee, the transfer point to the small bus to Chelan, I had time to phone my cousin, Cathy, who would share my special anticipation of the final section of my journey.

Upon arrival in Chelan, I was happy to be met at the depot by Kevin from the Parkway Motel. After last year's experience of phoning and finding "no vacancy," I had phoned for a reservation. How reassuring to be met at the depot. In the evening, I had a pleasant walk around the town and ended my walk at the lakeshore, where I was treated to a glorious sunset.

Again, the ferry ride to Stehekin was delightful. From the deck of "Our Lady of the Lake," I enjoyed looking across the water toward the steep, green hillsides rising up from the lakeshore. I talked to a young man from Minnesota who was on his way to Holden. He was overflowing with enthusiasm for his volunteer participation. I thought this must be a very special place. Perhaps this would be a place I would like to come to on some future visit and to enroll in an Elder Hostel program.

Upon arrival in Stehekin, I had a two-hour wait for the shuttle bus that would take me to trailhead. When the waiting passengers gathered to board the bus, there was quite a crowd. The ranger counted and then arranged for a second shuttle bus. I noticed that the woman ranger wore a different style of blouse than the usual ranger's uniform. Looking more closely, I noticed that she was pregnant. How good, I thought, that the Park Service, with its growing number of women rangers, had designed a maternity blouse.

I was so happy to be on my way at last. Seated on the bus, I let some of my fellow passengers know that I was on my way to complete my last section of the Pacific Crest Trail. They clapped. What a great send-off.

At the end of the shuttle run, I alighted, grabbed my pack, then happily waved goodbye to the passengers and ranger. I searched around for the Pacific Crest Trail marker. The 1983 edition of the guidebook indicated that a new section of trail was (or should be) completed, which would lead to Coon Lake. I searched. I could find no sign of either a new trail or a marker. I gave up and decided to walk on the temporary trail. This trail was clearly marked on my trail map. After crossing the High Bridge, the limited-use dirt road lead past three campgrounds. I could see and hear campers moving about at the first campground—the High Bridge Campground. At the Tumwater Campground, I did not see any campers. The campground prominently displayed rope pulleys to store food for bear proofing. Had the bears scared campers away? Upon arrival at the next campground, Dolly Varden Campground, I was ready to start my search for a campsite. From the guidebook, I was aware that the trail from the starting point near this campground coincided with an "Old Wagon Trail." Happily, I moved off the dirt road onto the nearby Old Wagon Trail. Soon, I was attracted to a campsite near a weathered and needle-covered picnic table. It looked, indeed, like it belonged to "old wagon trail days." Although it was pleasantly warm, I decided reluctantly to put up my tent—saying to myself, "I'm in Washington, and it might rain at any time." Nearby, I located a charming, almost–hidden spring beneath lush greenery, where I drew fresh, cold water from under some big fern fronds. I was so pleased to be on the trail again and to be camped beside the peaceful, picturesque, old wagon trail site.

I awoke in the morning to see a faint beam of light peeking through the tree branches. I wondered if I would have another sunny day. Soon, the morning light grew brighter. I felt hopeful. I was building up a tantalizing refrain: how many sunny days without rain would I have before reaching the Canadian border?

Before starting on my way, I gazed fondly at the moss-covered picnic table—a reminder of the wagon trail days. I filled my water bag with fresh, cold water from the hidden, fern-covered spring.

Near the Bridge Creek Ranger Station, I saw a ranger's car parked beside the limited-use dirt road. I looked around, but did not see a live ranger. Just beyond the Ranger Station, the trail leaves the road—the temporary trail—and moves onto the permanent trail section. I was glad to be back on a foot-trail again.

Walking alongside lush, green foliage, I stopped beside a huckleberry bush. I searched but could not find any berries. How disappointing. Had a bear eaten them? Or could it have been trail hikers? Later, I was pleased to find some delicious, ripe berries.

I met a southbound hiker who told me that he had started in Canada and was going out at Stehekin. He reported that he had been in a bad, cold, rainstorm four days before, and that at times he had walked through snow patches. I felt all the more thankful that I had enjoyed two days of sunshine.

For my lunch stop, I sat on the edge of a horse bridge above roaring Bridge Creek and said to myself, "What exciting, loud, water music." The trail in this area near the junction of the

North Fork Bridge Creek trail climbs up and affords a glorious view looking down at the river gorge. The trail then descends and crosses Maple Creek on a charming, small, hanging suspension bridge. I stopped on the other side for my afternoon snack.

By evening, I reached Hide-Away Camp—a charming, small campsite for backpackers only, beside Bridge Creek. It was well named. As I happily climbed into my bedroll, I thought to myself that the creek's melodious sounds sometimes seemed like they were singing me a lullaby.

From my Hide-Away camping site, I enjoyed another morning of glorious views. The trail continued to follow alongside splashing Bridge Creek, all the way to Rainy Pass at the crossing of Highway 20, the most northern east-west highway in the United States. There were some moderate ups and downs, which were easy to navigate as the trail was well graded and well maintained. Views from higher elevations looked down on the river gorge and up at high mountain peaks. On some of the down grades, the trail passed through forests and meadows. While I was walking through a grassy meadow, I was delighted to sight some beautiful wildflowers. Ones that I knew seemed to me, by now, like familiar friends: purple larkspur, bleeding hearts, elephant trunks, and some beautiful and unusually colored purple-blue mimulus. These all added to a beautiful walking day.

As it was Saturday, I met several weekend hikers. They were walking from the Rainy Pass trailhead on Highway 20 to Stehekin. I also met a hiker traveling north who had come onto the trail at the Columbia Gorge on the Oregon-Washington border and was planning to walk to the Canadian border. He surprised me by asking, "Are you Eleanor?" Indeed, he piqued my curiosity. He said that he had heard about me from Donna, whom I had met the previous year. "Oh," I replied, "I should have written to her, and I certainly will upon my return home."

When I arrived at the Highway 20 crossing at Rainy Pass, I stopped to take a photo with a large sign in the foreground announcing "Rainy Pass." I had enjoyed another sunny day, but now I noticed that the clouds had moved in. As I turned around to shoulder my pack, I felt a drop of water on my arm. Yes, it had started to sprinkle. How prophetic: rain starting at Rainy Pass. I wondered if an early explorer had experienced rain on this pass and bestowed its name. I wasn't ready to predict with this light sprinkle that I would be walking in rainy weather all the way from Rainy Pass to the Canadian border.

Crossing the highway, I explored the large trailhead and the adjacent rest area. Originally, I had planned to camp near Rainy Pass. I searched. The trailhead was equipped with a large, wooden horse-loading dock. The surrounding area showed signs of heavy usage. I did not like the trailhead area. I decided to move on, although I felt some uncertainty, as I did not have any information about nearby campsites. The trail leading north from the pass climbs up a moderately steady grade. In about an hour, I came to a bridge that crossed small Porcupine Creek. It was growing dark. I found a very small, level niche beside the trail. I decided that I could just barely fit my tent into this space. I made camp amidst light rain sprinkles. As I snuggled inside my tent, I started to worry that I might be too close to the trail for horse traffic to move past me. There was much evidence that horses used this trail. Would a horse be startled and shy and buck at the sight of my shining, aluminum-colored tent? I decided that I must get up early in the morning.

Still anxious in the morning about horses coming up the trail, I arose early and packed up my still-damp tent before breakfast. Luckily, no horses appeared. It was foggy. From Porcupine Creek, the trail switched back up to 6820-foot Cutthroat Pass. Upon reaching the Pass, I searched and found a perch on a level ridge. There I stayed for quite awhile, drinking in the glorious, spacious, fog-touched scene. I was surrounded by ridges and peaks on both sides. I watched the fog clouds advance and retreat as they came swirling up from the valleys. Periodically, a new peak poked its head up from out of the fog clouds. It was an awesome sight to behold.

While I was absorbed in watching the view, a couple of hikers came up from the trail and joined me. They announced that they had heard a weather prediction that called for clearing weather the next day. This was good news. The fog continued to dance around peaks as the trail led along a steep, narrow ridge and then descended to 6290-foot Granite Pass. Again, spectacular views emerged, looking down on Swamp Creek Valley. In the afternoon, I walked on to reach a campsite near the junction of the Snowy Lake Trail. Here, I found a large, level, grassy plateau with a fresh, coldwater stream trickling through it. I pitched my tent, ate a leisurely supper, and crawled into my tent, anticipating a pleasant, quiet evening. Soon, I was startled by the now-familiar pitter-patter of rain striking my tent. How disappointing! I had hoped for clearing weather.

I awoke feeling discouraged. It had rained off and on during the night—quite hard at times. When I peeked out of my tent window, I was viewing a dense, heavy fog. I was not in a hurry to get up. After lots of peeking out in the hope of signs of clearing, I gave up. I decided that it was time to get started. I reminded myself that this was not the Sierras but the Washington Cascades. I moved around slowly. I was still reluctant to pack up my wet tent. Wet material is so much heavier and messier than dry. I attempted to wipe off my tent twice between intermittent sprinkles. It was still damp. I finally plodded down the trail around 8:45 am.

I climbed up on a good trail to Methow Pass. Although

visibility was limited, I saw a spot of light breaking through the clouds, and soon I saw a piece of rainbow. How hopeful, I thought. As the trail led down to follow alongside the West Fork of the Methow River, I passed some charming, small, feathery Tamarack trees. As these trees are not frequently seen, they are special—a treat to behold. After walking through a pleasant wooded area on a good trail, I came to a clearing and, looking around, saw that I was about to cross an avalanche area. What a sight! Trees had been uprooted and knocked down and were lying in scattered heaps on a wide path across the slope. What awesome power Mother Nature can produce!

During my afternoon walk, I hoped and prayed for clearing weather. I wanted to dry out my wet rags. It was overcast but not raining when I stopped early, around 4:30 pm, at a pleasant campsite beside Brush Creek. Eagerly, I hurried to string up my line to dry my wet rags.

By 5:30 pm, my wet items were almost dry and my tent was set up for the night. I was ready for dinner and was looking forward to having my supper by the campsite fireplace, replete with a bench. Then suddenly, at 6 pm, it started to rain. I hurried and pushed everything into the tent. Reluctantly, I resigned myself to eating supper inside my tent. At 7 pm, when I peeked out to check on the weather, the sun broke through the clouds and there was blue sky. What exotic and changeable weather. Again I said to myself, "Washington is a rainy state, and I must be prepared for anything."

In the morning, when I crawled out of my tent for breakfast and gazed above my tent roof, I was startled. Leaning over my tent at a 40-degree angle was a small pine tree. It looked, indeed, as if it were about to fall. Here on this little shelf, I had felt so comfortable and secure. Did the little tree lean down during the night, or had I not seen it while setting up my tent in the gray light of dusk? Fortunately, it had not crashed down on me during the night.

What strange and changeable weather! During breakfast, the sun peeked out and I rejoiced. When I stopped for my mid-morning snack, suddenly it started to shower again. Hurriedly, I reached for my rain jacket and hustled to retrieve my wet rags, which were hanging outside on my pack to dry. The on-and-off weather was hard to predict.

The trail led alongside Brush Creek for quite a ways and then started to climb up to the 5520-foot Glacier Pass. I stopped at the pass to survey the view. The sky was mixed with both storm clouds and patches of blue. While I was enjoying the sky-filled view, suddenly I was startled by a loud, piercing sound. I turned around just in time to see a peregrine falcon take off, carrying some small creature it had captured. What a sight! This was my first sighting of this majestic, swiftly flying bird.

By mid-afternoon, I started my search. I wanted to find the grassy ridge that harbored a trailside campsite with water—the only reliable water until Harts Pass. After rounding a bend, I spotted a grassy, sloping ridge. I concentrated my focus to search out a campsite and water. Drawing closer and looking down the slope, I could just see two tents. I turned off-trail on a small path. Descending from the grassy ridge, I found smaller ridges sloping down from the ridge trail. Almost hidden amidst some tall grass, I found water in a narrow, flowing stream. I searched for a level camping space.

After supper, two friendly campers from the nearby tents walked over to my campsite to exchange trail notes. Here, I met Kathy and Chris from Seattle. They were also hiking north to the Canadian border.

After spending a comfortable but somewhat foggy night at my ridgetop campsite, I packed up and climbed back onto the

ELEANOR WITH DONNA, CHRIS,
AND KATHY AT HEART'S PASS

trail. The trail leading down to Harts Pass was an easy one. It offered some pleasant ridgetop views as the trail circled around 7386-foot Tatie Peak.

I was striding along making good time on this nicely graded trail when I looked up to see a ranger coming toward me. He greeted me with, "Are you Eleanor?" "Yes," I replied. I was amazed and puzzled as to how he knew my name. Then he explained that Donna was waiting for me at the Forest Service Guard Station. Soon the trail broke out into an open space and I was facing the small, wooden-frame Guard Station. There by the front steps, Donna was waving at me. What a glorious surprise! I thought it was a miracle that she had found me.

Kathy and Chris had also arrived at the Guard Station, and we were all spilling over with joyful excitement. Donna told me her story. She had decided to help me celebrate my completion of the trail by accompanying me to the Canadian border. Somehow, after our meeting on the trail the year before, she had lost my address. She telephone the National Office of the Sierra Club in San Francisco and asked if they had the address and phone number of Eleanor, the older hiker who was completing the Pacific Crest Trail. They were of no help. I chuckled as I imagined a busy, puzzled switchboard operator at the national office of the Sierra Club. With over 500,000 members, the operator surely gave up quickly on answering that question. Then Donna remembered that I was planning to come into the trail during the second week in August. (Actually, I had left for Seattle around the 14th of August and started on the trail on the 17th.) She decided to try to intercept me at Harts Pass.

At the road leading into Harts Pass, she had parked her car and sent out flyers with passing hikers to look for Eleanor. Ted, whom I had met briefly near Six-mile Camp, had relayed word to her that I was on the trail and on my way to Harts Pass. What a wonderful surprise! To this day, it still seems to me to have been a miracle.

After a joyful celebration posing and smiling for picture taking, we were finally ready to start on our journey to the Canadian border. To cap off my joy—the proverbial "icing on the cake"—the trail leaving Harts Pass offered spectacular views. The trail contoured along a ridge, and stretching out below us was the Slate Creek Valley. This valley had been a popular mining site in the 1890s, producing gold, silver, lead, copper, and zinc. This was one of the reasons a road had been built to the Harts Pass Guard Station. In the distance, we viewed 10,000-foot Mount Baker. Everywhere we looked, there were majestic peaks and enchanting valleys. It was one of those views at which I stopped and exclaimed to myself, "Oh, what beauty!"

By late afternoon, the trial led into the Pasayten Wilderness. Periodically, we began to see clusters of feathery-branched Tamaracks. Toward late afternoon, we reached a campsite and water near 7290-foot Tamarack Peak. Kathy and Chris were already there. I staked out my place and started threading my tent poles when, much to my dismay, the sky opened up and a cloudburst descended upon us. Kathy and Chris helped me to finish setting up my tent. I hurriedly crawled inside. What a sudden downpour! I stayed in my tent all night, listening to the rain pound on my tent roof. At times, strong gusts of wind shook my tent. By morning, the downpour had ceased and I awoke and peered out my tent window onto a foggy scene. Again I reminded myself that this was northern Washington.

Thankfully, it wasn't pouring when I packed up my damp tent. Reluctantly I again had to pack my wet wiping rags on top of my damp ground cloth and tent.

The trail leading north to Holman Pass was an easy one. Donna and I did not plan to walk together. We each cherished our own walking pace. Frequently, we met at snack stops and enjoyed comparing notes. It was a day of off-and-on rain. Once, the sun broke through, and I rejoiced and peeled off my rain gear. In a very short time, it started to sprinkle again. I sighed and decided to keep my rain gear on for the rest of the day. As we approached 5000-foot Holman Pass, the trail passed through a wooded area. At the pass, our trail met a cross trail. The campsite was crowded. There were five other campers, in addition to Donna and myself. I paced up and down in search of a level campsite. I could not find what I was hoping for. Finally, I settled for a damp, grassy niche surrounded by bushes so that I had to maneuver carefully going in and out so as not to get hit in the face by a branch. Before retiring into my tent, Donna and I had a chance to exchange notes with the other campers. Three of the men had arrived at the pass from the cross trail. The other three had hiked on the Pacific Crest Trail from the Canadian border. They announced that they had experienced light snow the day before. The two women also added that the hike from here to the border offered spectacular views. One of the proclaimed, "It's like paradise."

During the night, it rained off and on. When I peeked out of my tent in the early morning light, I saw a soft layer of slush. I wondered if we would be walking in snow before we reached the border.

Again, I packed up my damp belongings. I started on my way, slushing through wet grass. I met a group of hikers traveling south from the Canadian border. They reported they had heard that clearing weather was predicted. I replied that this was good to hear. Then, I recalled that I had heard a report

LAKEVIEW RIDGE NEAR HOPKINS LAKE

predicting clearing weather the previous Sunday at Cutthroat Pass and that it had not been accurate.

By midday, however, the sky cleared and a glorious panorama of views opened up before me. I sat down for a snack and took in the view. I was looking out toward a many-colored mountain slope. Toward the top, there were patches of rusty red rocks and in the middle, patches of bright, light-green brushes and grass. The scene created such a rich harmony of colors—nature's beautiful paintbrush.

Before reaching our meadow campsite below Woody Pass, we came to an avalanche-washed scree path. It offered a puzzling choice of trails. There was what appeared to be the original trail, with a mid-section washed out, and a new, temporary, longer trail. After studying the scene, I opted to take the new, temporary trail. I thought that I would play it safe. Donna soon followed, choosing the original trail and happily slid down the washed-out mid-section. We both enjoyed our choices. We made camp happily, before the fog rolled in. Later, Pat and Chris joined us. It was good to see them and to compare notes. As they were planning to go on ahead of us, it was our last night of camping together.

I awoke to gaze out of my tent onto another day of uncertain skies of mixed rain clouds and weak sunshine. At least I was able to pack up in dry weather, for which I was most thankful.

The trail climbed up to Lakeview Ridge and views started to open up. By my mid-morning break, I stopped at an irresistible viewpoint scene. I remembered that the ranger at Harts Pass had said that the Lakeview Ridge offered a spectacular view and was one of his favorite sites. He was right.

Continuing along the Ridge Trail, I reached a 71,000 unnamed summit. Views opened in all directions. Looking toward the west, among dark clouds in a blue sky, I could see layer after layer of peaks, as far as the eye could see. This splendid panorama view also opened up glorious combinations of colors. The highest peaks were snow-covered pinnacles and cones. Looking down to a middle view, dark green evergreen trees decorated the scene; still lower down, the scene was dotted with grassy slopes intermingled with the browns and grays of rocky patches. As I drank in this glorious scene, I decided that it would be entered into my bank of memories as one of my most beautiful trail scenes. To this day, in recalling this scene, I have a vision of the rugged and remote, many-colored mountain peaks of the North Cascades.

While I was enjoying my mid-morning snack, Donna arrived and joined me in drinking in this beautiful view. We had developed a very compatible pace, with each one following her own schedule preferences. I usually woke up early and started down the trail earlier than Donna. We each hiked along at our comfortable space, but we met often enough just by natural breaks to talk about where we were going to camp in the evening. With this comfortable arrangement, we each enjoyed a combination of happily comparing notes on views and locations and, at the same time, enjoying our own pace and solitude.

The Lakeview Ridge continued to offer views for some distance. As the trail gradually started down, we caught a glimpse to the right of large Hopkins Lake. The lake offered campsites, but, as we were not ready to stop, we traveled on down to Hopkins Pass, then to Castle Pass. Shortly after Castle Pass, we selected a campsite in a grassy meadow beside a small creek.

The sun had peeked through when we made camp at 4:00 pm, so I strung up my clothesline and hung up my wet rags and ground cloth. I was so eager to dry all of my wet things. Alas, shortly after I had everything spread out to dry, it started to rain again. What a let down! Quickly, I gathered my still-damp rags and ground cloth, laid my damp ground cloth on the wet grass, erected my tent, and crawled inside.

After awhile, the rain stopped. I crawled out of my tent to fill my water bag and prepare supper. As soon as I started to enjoy my supper, it started to rain again—this time, the rain poured down with a vengeance. I crawled inside again, thinking to myself that these on-and-off storms are so typical for this country that by now I should be used to them. Still, it was hard to believe.

I awoke in the morning to discover frozen tent zippers; a frozen water bucket; and stiff, partially frozen, boots and laces. Oh, well, I thought, it hardly matters, for this was my last day. We were only four miles from the Canadian border, and then I would have seven miles to walk to reach the highway at Manning Provincial Park, where I would catch the bus for Vancouver and home.

I warmed the frozen tent zippers with my hands and then warmed the water bag enough to squeeze out enough water for breakfast. Thankfully, by the time I was ready to pack up, the tent had melted enough to fold up. Again I thought that packing wet doesn't really matter, as I would have plenty of time to dry out that evening.

Donna and I were so excited and eager. We made good time, wading through damp bushes on a downhill trail, and arrived on the border—Monument 78—at 11:15 am. We rejoiced. I had made it! I had completed the 2638-mile trail from Mexico to Canada. Out came the cameras. I had saved just enough film for the completion photos at the border.

There are two monuments marking the border. Monument 78 is a miniature, 4.5-foot-high bronze "Washington Monument." A new wooden-beam monument topped with a large trail emblem had been erected by the Pacific Crest Trail Association.

In a few minutes, another trail hiker arrived—Peter from Maine. He had started his journey at the Oregon border and was completing the Oregon-Washington section. He greeted me by announcing, "Sue says hello to Eleanor." We had met Sue at Holman Pass campsite. She was enthusiastic and excited about my completing the trail.

It was good to have Peter with us at the border monument, as we had another photo taken so that Donna and I could pose together. Donna showed me that the top of the "Washington Monument" lifted off and revealed a depository of notes written by trail walkers. Donna encouraged me to enter my note. Before gathering my thoughts together, I read the note on top. The note had been entered by Ted, the hiker I had met at Six-mile Camp who had relayed the message to Donna at Harts Pass that I was on my way. In Ted's note, he very thoughtfully described the trail experience as a microcosm of life. Yes, I thought, this is true. There are hard days, difficult trails, rainy days, and good days, easy trails, and glorious views. Yes, I agreed with Ted's idea of the trail walk experience expressing a microcosm of life. At the same time, another thought came forth to me, expressing my predominant feeling. Above all else, I was thankful—thankful for the opportunity to walk the entire trail and to complete the walk in good health and good spirits. A pinnacle in my experience was that of being surrounded by the sounds and sights and exquisite beauty of the natural world.

It was time to say goodbye to Donna. She needed to return to her car at Harts Pass, and I needed to walk on to Manning Provincial Park, where I would catch the bus to Vancouver. We hugged and, with mixed feelings, said goodbye. Donna described it as a bittersweet feeling. I agreed. I was still feeling how fantastic it was that she had found me on the trail and accompanied me to celebrate my Pacific Crest Trail completion. Donna said, "I knew I would find you." So finally, we waved goodbye.

It was hard to fully express my feelings upon completing the trail. I had been so excited the last few days, and now at the trail's end, I felt rather sober. It seemed somewhat unreal. Perhaps I felt sober because it was all so overwhelming and so beyond expression of feeling. I did, with certainty, feel thankful at having actually completed the trail. I had heard so many stories about trail drop-outs: of those affected by physical ailments—knees, ankles, and backs—and with psychological afflictions—fear and loneliness. As I walked along pondering it all, one feeling emerged with considerable surety and predominated. I felt very good about my accomplishment. In one aspect, I felt like I had conquered a beast in myself—my fear of walking and camping in rainy weather. I had stayed warm and dry in my inner layers and at night in my bedroll. I had halfway, but never completely, accepted packing up a damp tent and ground cloth and the hardest of all to accept—the dirty, wet rags.

The next seven miles leading to Manning Park and Highway 3 seemed a bit anticlimactic. I had finished at the border, but still had seven miles to walk. The border crossing is deep in the wilderness, which, in some ways, seemed appropriate. I just drifted down, walking on an easy but unspectacular trail, still dreaming about my happy trail ending. At a trail junction, Peter announced that he would be taking a trail that wound up Windy Joe Mountain. I opted for the river trail, as it had been strongly recommended by Sue at Holman Pass. It was easy, but a little muddy. Nearing the highway, I missed a junction turn-off and started momentarily on the wrong trail. How ironic, I thought, to miss a trail on the last stretch of my last day. I backtracked and soon reached the highway leading to the Manning Park Lodge. At the lodge, Peter met me. We reviewed the bus schedule. He decided to take a night bus, and I opted for a morning bus. I was eager to clean up and dry out before boarding the bus. We agreed to meet for dinner. Upon checking into a room at the lodge, I was happy to learn that there was a washer and dryer. My first desire was to wash my hiking pants and shirt. Then, I took time for a real tub bath. How wonderful it felt to soak in the warm water. This was like

ELEANOR AND DONNA AT MONUMENT #78

ELEANOR AND PETER AT MONUMENT #78 AT
CANADIAN BORDER

paradise. I then spread out my damp ground cloth and wet rags to dry. What a great relief. By suppertime, I felt superb.

Before supper, I called my brother, who exclaimed, "You've done it all now." "Congratulations!" was my good friend Carol's response.

I met Peter in the lodge restaurant. I chose to have soup, spaghetti, and wine, topped off with ice cream. It tasted good. Peter asked lots of questions about my ideas on trail walking. He planned to complete the California trail section the next year. I let him know that I thought it was good to proceed at a moderate pace so as to truly enjoy the beauty of wilderness. I added that I had met a number of trail walkers who had planned an ambitious walk of 20 or more miles per day who had to give up because they sprained an ankle or became sick and tired. He thanked me for the ideas. I felt again that I was being called upon to give advice as an older hiker-mentor.

All in all, it was a pleasant way to spend my final evening upon finishing the trail—an evening to celebrate. I climbed into bed feeling dry and clean and still feeling very good. I was tired, but I had trouble falling asleep. I was still too excited.

The next morning, I had time to walk a short distance to the Manning Park Ranger Office to sign the Pacific Crest Trail Register. I then walked back to the lodge, where I boarded the 11:00 am bus for Vancouver. It was still raining off and on.

Arriving in Vancouver at 4:30 pm, I checked the bus schedule. The next bus to Seattle would leave at 8:30 pm and arrive in Seattle at 12:30 am. I chose to remain in Vancouver overnight and registered at a small nearby hotel—Hotel Regis. When I walked out of the hotel to eat in a downtown restaurant—Michael's—I happily walked past a church, the Holy Rosary Cathedral. I went inside and lit a candle in thanksgiving. It added another touch to my trail completion celebration.

In the morning, I boarded the 9:15 am Greyhound bus for Seattle. Happily, the border crossing was easy. I sailed through the Immigration Office, presenting my letter obtained from the Canadian Consul in San Francisco.

Upon arrival in Seattle, I called my cousin, Cathy Corser Hollis. She came to meet me and to take me to her lovely home in the Three Pines district of south Seattle. For me, it was still another celebration. Cathy invited two hiking friends for supper—Betty and Pat. They asked me lots of questions about my hiking gear—food, stove, backpack. They were especially interested in my lightweight equipment. They gave me an opportunity to tell about my journey, which was enjoyable for me.

Cathy drove me to the Downtown Youth Hostel, where I registered at 7:30 pm. On a chance, I called my cousin, Jack Griswold. He had just returned from a camping trip on Vancouver Island. He and his wife, Lois, picked me up and took me on a most enjoyable night tour of downtown Seattle. We visited the Civic Center. It was a clear evening, and we enjoyed a spectacular view of the lights of the harbor. For me, it was like still another celebration, and I still felt good.

In the morning, I indulged in my favorite oatmeal breakfast at Pike Place Market before boarding Amtrak for my now-familiar ride home. As the train rolled along through the flatlands of central Oregon, I thought I would miss the mountains. I had more celebrations to look forward to at home, and the thought came to me: "I can enjoy a lifetime of memories of my walk on the Pacific Crest Trail."

Acknowledgements

My first thoughts of acknowledgement flow toward the spirit of John Muir, the inspiration that I forever feel upon reading his stories, and the seeds which he planted —the members of the Sierra Club—the organization he founded.

It was at a Sierra Club meeting of the Redwood Chapter that I first heard about the John Muir Trail. This precious fragment of news grabbed hold of me. I was impelled to sign up to explore the Muir Trail with Wampler Tours. My Sierra Club hiking companions on that trip were: Madeline Coles, Evelyn Dodge, the late Maguerite Ross, and the late Koreen Osborn. After completing the first small section from Tuolumne Meadows to Reds Meadow, I was hooked; I had to complete the Muir Trail.

As I became more deeply committed to completing the Muir Trail, I needed to learn how to backpack. I asked the late Carl Sharsmith, longtime Ranger at Tuolumne Meadows, "Do you think I can learn to backpack?" "Try it on a long trip," he replied. I tried it in the summer of 1969. I was hooked, thanks to Carl Sharsmith's wise advise.

Upon completion of the Muir Trail, another Redwood Chapter member, John Dooley said, "There is a Tahoe-Yosemite Trail," I completed it next. At this point, I was beginning to hear about the Pacific Crest Trail. I started on it at Lake Tahoe and just kept going—a section at a time, not necessarily in order. I eventually stepped across the Mexico/U.S. border on my way north in 1985, and reached Canada in August, 1989.

I am indepted to so many helpers and supporters. The late Marge Chance; my good friend, the late Carol MacMillan, who often drove me to the trailheads in California. Her friend, the late Marjorie Richart, often accompanied her.

I couldn't have done it without the many unnamed helpers who responded to my raised hand and gave me a ride from the trailhead to the nearest bus stop.

There was also my family at home, and especially my brother, the late Richard Guilford, who accepted a copy of the itinerary, supposedly to start a search if I did not come out on time. Fortunately, that was never necessary. He once surprised and delighted me with a birthday greeting at a postal pickup stop in Agua Dulce.

To those who challenged me to write: the late Sister Mary Frances RSM; my high school English teacher who asked our class to write our own version of "The Canterbury Tales," an experience that challenged and helped me to want to write more; and Father George Twigg-Porter SJ, a gifted writer and communicator whose straightforward, simple style gave me a boost with writing.

To those who helped me put this book together: Margaret Guilford Kardell, Ellen Davenport, Mark A. Hetts, and Nancy Merrill. My former neighbor and good friend Ella Hogan, who shepherded me throughout he journey of publishing. Mark Weiman and Roz Abraham who guided me throughout the process of design and publishing.

During my walk I was very much dependant on *The Pacific Crest Guide, Volume I and II*, as I am sure most trail walkers are

(Wilderness Press, Berkeley, CA). The Pacific Crest Association was and continues to be most helpful in keeping me up to date on PCTrail changes and activities through annual meetings and their newsletter, *The Communicator*.

For quotations from John Muir I am indebted to: *Quotations from John Muir*, Selected by Harold Wood; also, *John Muir in His Own Words: A Book of Quotations*, compiled and edited by Peter Browning (Great West Brooks, 1998, Lafayette, CA).

To many Sonoma Group friends who have cheered me on: especially, Len Swenson, Marge Change, Barrett Lewis. And to many others whose names have passed through my memory, I express my sincere thanks.